The Legacy

of

W. A. Criswell

Dr. Jim Towns

STEPHEN F. AUSTIN STATE UNIVERSITY PRESS, 2017

STEPHEN F. AUSTIN STATE UNIVERSITY PRESS

Copyright 2017 by Jim Towns
Book Design: Jonathan Grant

Library of Congress Cataloging-in-Publication Data

Towns, Jim
    The Legacy of W. A. Criswell
    Jim Towns—1st Ed.

ISBN: 978-1-62288-170-3

CONTENTS

FOREWORD ～ 9

INTRODUCTION ～ 11

THE SOUTHERN BAPTIST CONVENTION ～ 17

WALLIE AMOS CRISWELL: THE PERSON, THE SPEAKER, THE LEADER ～ 37

DR. W. A. CRISWELL SERMONS AND COMMENTARY

"The Fifth Sparrow" ～ 49

"The Downtown Church" ～ 55

"Segregation in Society" ～ 64

"The Church of the Open Door" ～ 70

"Religious Freedom, the Church, the State, and Senator Kennedy" ～ 77

"The Counterfeit Church" ～ 83

"My Favorite Sermon: God's Last Invitation" ～ 93

"Drugs is Spelled D-E-A-T-H" ～ 103

"The Ministry of Reconciliation" ～ 113

"Why I Preach the Bible is Literally True" ～ 122

"The Baptism of the Holy Spirit" ～ 133

"Why I Became a Premillennialist" ～ 143

"Whether We Live or Die" ～ 149

"The Old Time Religion" ～ 159

"Christ is Coming Back" ～ 166

RETROSPECTIVE: SUMMARY AND INSIGHTS ～ 171

REFERENCES AND APPENDIX ～ 188

Praise for *THE LEGACY OF W.A. CRISWELL*

"The remarkable book that you hold in your hand, *THE LEGACY OF W.A. CRISWELL*, penned by Professor Dr. Jim Towns captures the observations of a man who watched the colorful career of one of the most storied preachers in America for more than five decades. Towns knows that people impact positions, but that positions also alter the course of a man. Choosing famous sermons delivered both before and after Criswell's two terms as president of the Southern Baptist Convention, Towns weaves a scintillating analysis that demonstrates the truth of this contention. Reading most of these messages alone will be a verbal safari. The assessment of Towns adds the adventure of the countryside to the experience itself."
> —Dr. Paige Patterson, President, Southwestern Baptist Theological Seminary,
> Fort Worth, Texas

" I am big fan of the late Southern Baptist pastor, W.A. Criswell (1909–2002). In fact, I believe Dr. Criswell was the greatest American pastor of the 20th Century. He was a pastor, author and a president of the Southern Baptist Convention. He was regarded by many as a major figure behind the right-wing fundamentalist takeover of the Southern Baptist Convention, beginning in the 1960s."
> —Rick Warren, Pastor of Saddleback Church, Lake Forrest, California.

"The preaching skills of W. A. Criswell as a speaker-leader established a heritage during his tenure as pastor of the historic First Baptist Church, Dallas and President of the Southern Baptist Convention in 1968. I am part of the Criswell Legacy."
> —J. Denny Autrey, Dean and Professor of Pastoral Ministries,
> Havard School for Theological Studies, Southwestern Baptist Theological Seminary,
> Houston, Texas

"Throughout his lifetime, Dr. Criswell touched the lives of many—not only in Texas, not only Baptists, but millions around the world. He will be sincerely missed."
> —Rick Perry, Governor of Texas

"My friend, Dr. Criswell, gave leadership, voice, and inspiration to the restoration of the Southern Baptist Convention to its biblical roots. I am so glad he was able to see the victories for which he so earnestly prayed."
> —Judge Paul Pressler

"Tragically, most Americans have lost interest in history. We do not know our political or religious legacies. Yet history, when clearly seen is, "yesterday's current events." But we need good research to tell the story from source materials, not with a revisionist's lens. What did the person write? When did he say it? What was the setting? Dr. Jim Towns looks through the lens of the legendary W.A. Criswell's messages to tell a larger-than-life story. Not that long ago, Criswell's voice was loud and clear. Dr. Towns argues that he is worth listening to again."

—Dr. Michael Easley, President Emeritus, Moody Bible Institute, Current Pastor, Fellowship Nashville, Tennessee

"Dr. Jim Towns offers a captivating analysis of Reverend Dr. W. A. Criswell's most personal and pivital sermons. Criswell is one of the most fascinating preachers in 20th Century American History. In an era where social change, technological achievements, and theological shifts were unpredicatble, Criswell's beliefs, positions, changes, and even omissions, offered striking insights as we contend with the oscillating moments of stability and instability in American thought and culture, both secular and evangelical."

—Dr. Paul R. Shockley, Professor of Bible, Philosophy, and Theology at the college of Biblical Studies-Houston.
Co-Editor of *Evangelical America: An Encyclopedia of Contemporary American Religious Culture.*

"I happen to think that Dr. Criswell is the greatest preacher who ever lived. From the time he was a little boy of 9 years of age until he died at 92 years of age he spiritually influenced people all over the world. Jack Pogue, Longtime friend and caregiver for W. A. Criswell."

— Jack Pogue and Company, Real Estate Broker, Dallas, Texas.

Acknowledgments

No one ever writes a book alone, regardless of what the title page may assert. The writing of acknowledgements and thanks to valued friends and trusted colleagues is a difficult part of preparing a book. It is not possible in syllable and sentence to adequately express my appreciation for the influence and contributions of the many individuals who have encouraged me in this work. I am grateful and indebted to all people who have assisted me in this process.

FOREWORD

"LEGACY" What is it? It has been defined as "something transmitted by or received from an ancestor or predecessor from the past." Is it possible to adequately measure the 'legacy' that has been bequeathed by an individual to coming generations? Or the 'legacy' generated by an individual through the impact of his preaching and personality through one church to his entire denomination?

To understand the influence of the historic First Baptist Church of Dallas, Texas, one has to look back to one of its most colorful and controversial leaders; the Reverend Dr. W. A. (Wallie Amos) Criswell, my legendary predecessor at First Baptist church for over fifty years. When he was 5 years old, little Robert became a Christian. He remembers it started with a conversation he had with his dad at the dinner table. Then he walked down the aisle that Sunday at church, to tell Dr. Criswell he had accepted Jesus into his heart. Criswell had the boy and his father come by his office. He asked Robert a few questions, to see if he knew what he was talking about. Then, Jeffress remembers, Criswell kneeled beside him to pray. Afterward, Criswell warned the boy: "Now, Robert, don't let me see you walking down that aisle again one day because you slipped up." Little Robert nodded. He never slipped. Today he is Pastor of the 12,000 member First Baptist Church Dallas, Texas.

The legacy of W. A. Criswell has been of monumental proportion with regard to my life and ministry. For those of us who proudly embrace the mantle of Southern Baptist life, the heritage of this renowned Bible expositor has cast a long and lasting shadow over the whole of our denomination. From the inception of the Southern Baptist Convention in 1845, the greatest influence exerted on this "people of the Book (Bible)," has been through the sermons of those who were recognized for their unwavering commitment to and their profound preaching of the Bible as the inspired Word of God. Without question, W. A. Criswell falls into the category as one of the most influential pastors in Southern Baptist history with regard to the extraordinary ability to relate to all manner of men and women through his unique style of preaching. Through the elegance and candor of his rhetorical skills as a communicator, he exhibited an uncanny ability to speak to every level of person and move them to action.

Is that not the mark of an effective communicator? In his most recent work, *The Legacy of W. A. Criswell*, Jim E. Towns, PhD, Professor of Communication at Stephen F. Austin State University, has brilliantly captured the essence of this man's footprint on Southern Baptist life through an in depth analysis of fifteen of Criswell's most notable sermons. From his first sermon preached as pastor of First Dallas, November 19, 1944, "The Fifth Sparrow," to his last, preached April 1, 2001, "Christ is Coming Back," Towns evaluated the rhetorical propositions employed by Criswell before and after his election as President of the Southern Baptist Convention. In his comparison, he chronicled six major issues that consistently surfaced in his preaching, they were: 1) The Bible as the inspired word of God; 2) Evangelism; 3) Dissension-unity in the Convention; 4) Racial issues; 5) Social Concern and Responsibility; and 6) Methods and approaches in Convention life. Towns research reveals Criswell's sermons remained consistent on the first three issues but that for the sake of the Convention his preaching concerning the last three issues adjusted his former positions to bring change within the thinking and policies of the Southern Baptist Convention.

Thus, W. A. Criswell's 1968 election to the Presidency of the Southern Baptist Convention was not designed to continue the status quo but was for the purpose of producing progressive change. Change did come and as Jim Towns has so masterfully expressed, "W. A. Criswell's legacy has been burnt deeply into the brand of Texas and Baptist churches around the nation and the world. It is a legacy that will not ride quietly into the sunset."

Robert Jeffress, Senior Pastor
First Baptist Church
Dallas, Texas
May 2017

INTRODUCTION

BRIEF HISTORY OF DALLAS, TEXAS

The city of Dallas is on the Trinity River in the center of Dallas County in North Central Texas. It is crossed by Interstate highways 20, 30, 35, and 45. The city was founded by John Neely Bryan, who settled on the east bank of the Trinity near a natural ford in November 1841. Bryan had picked the best spot for a trading post to serve the population migrating into the region. In 1844, J. P. Dumas surveyed and laid out a townsite comprising a half mile square of blocks and streets. The origin of the name Dallas is unknown. Candidates include George Mifflin Dallas, vice president of the United States, 1845–49; his brother, Commodore Alexander J. Dallas, United States Navy; and Joseph Dallas, who settled near the new town in 1843. When Dallas County was formed in 1846, Dallas was designated as the temporary county seat; in 1850, voters selected it as the permanent county seat over Oak Cliff and Cedar Springs, both of which eventually came within its corporate limits. The Texas legislature granted Dallas a town charter on February 2, 1856. Dr. Samuel Pryor, elected the first mayor, headed a town government consisting of six aldermen, a treasurer-recorder, and a constable.

Dallas quickly became a service center for the rural area surrounding it. By the 1850's it had dry-goods stores, groceries, a drugstore, an insurance agency, a boot, and shoe shop, brickyards, and saddle shops, as well as a weekly newspaper, the *Dallas Herald*, founded in 1849. In 1852, French immigrant Maxime Guillot established the first factory, manufacturing carriages, and wagons. Alexander and Sarah Horton Cockrell, who purchased Bryan's remaining interest in the town site for $7,000 in 1852, built a three-story brick hotel, a steam sawmill, and a flour mill. On July 8, 1860, a fire originating in the W. W. Peak Brothers Drugstore spread to the other buildings on the square and destroyed most of the businesses.

The key to economic expansion had always been better transportation in and out of the region. Early attempts to navigate the Trinity River had proved impractical. Dallas businessmen turned their attention to securing rail service and succeeded in attracting the Houston and Texas Central in 1872 and the Texas and Pacific in 1873, making Dallas one of the first rail crossroads in Texas region. Dallas became the world center for the leather and buffalo-hide trade. Merchants who opened general stores along the railroad route as rail construction crept north settled in Dallas and founded their flagship stores there. By 1880 the population had more than tripled, to 10,385.

The Great Depression put 15,000 Dallas sites on the relief rolls by 1933, and retail sales and bank deposits plummeted. The population, which had soared to 260,475 by 1930, climbed only to 294,734 in 1940. The pain of the depression was eased somewhat for Dallas by the discovery of oil in East Texas in 1930. Dallas bankers such as Nathan Adams of the First National Bank in Dallas were the first in the nation to conceive of the idea of lending money to oil companies using oil reserves in the ground for collateral. Dallas soon became a center for petroleum financing.

Until World War II, Dallas ranked as a minor manufacturing center in the nation. Its three leading industries were food processing, apparel manufacturing, and printing and publishing. The opening of Dallas-Fort Worth International Airport in 1974 attracted numerous corporate headquarters to Dallas and consolidating the city's reputation as a national financial and business center.

Dallas suffered its most traumatic experience on November 22, 1963, when President John F. Kennedy was assassinated while riding in a motorcade through Dealey Plaza, only yards from the site where John Neely Bryan had settled in 1841. Two days later, his alleged assassin, Lee Harvey Oswald, was killed before television cameras by a Dallas nightclub owner, Jack Ruby. In 1989, after twenty-five years of debate about how the city should commemorate the event, the Sixth Floor, a museum, opened in the former Texas School Book Depository. In 1993 Dealey Plaza was declared a National Historic Landmark District, the city's second after Fair Park.

The religious composition of the city has changed considerably over the years. Early Protestant settlers looked to traveling missionaries for religious services. The first Episcopal parish was organized in 1856. Catholics celebrated the first Mass in Dallas in 1859. Permanent places of worship were built as the city began to grow: Lamar Street Methodist (later First Methodist), City Temple Presbyterian, and First Baptist, all in 1868. Congregationalists organized in 1875, Seventh-day Adventists in 1876, Lutherans in 1878, Unitarians in 1889, Christian Scientists in 1894, and Mormons in 1897. The variety of communions helped to make Dallas a spiritual stronghold by the turn of the century, and the continued growth of churches marked Dallas as a city of churchgoers. In the early 1980s, Dallas had six churches among the nation's 100 largest: First Baptist, Lovers Lane United Methodist, Cliff Temple Baptist, Beverly Hills Baptist, First United Methodist, and East Grand Baptist. Three more on the list were in the suburbs: Highland Park United Methodist, Highland Park Presbyterian, and Park Cities Baptist. Subsequently, as the population has diversified, so have the religious faiths.

Educational institutions have been present in Dallas since its earliest years. Private schools and academies preceded the founding of the public school system in 1884. Institutions of higher learning include Southern Methodist University, founded in 1911; Paul Quinn College, a formerly black private institution that moved from Waco in 1990; Bishop College, another historically black institution founded in Marshall in 1881; and the University of Texas Southwestern Medical School, established in 1943. Several campuses of Dallas County Community College, established in 1965, are located within the city.

Sporting events and teams in Dallas had their roots in the nineteenth century when horse racing was popular enough to support a Dallas Jockey Club, founded in 1869. Horse racing was a major attraction at the State Fair of Texas from 1886 until 1909. The national bicycling craze inspired the formation of the Dallas Wheel Club in 1886, and races were held at Cycle Park from its construction in 1896 until its conversion to an open-air theater. Baseball was played in Dallas as early as 1877, when a touring team played a local team. By 1882 Dallas had its first semi-professional team, the Brown Stockings, which won the league championship in 1883 and 1884. The Dallas Hams, a professional team, won the Texas League pennant in 1888; Dallas continued to field minor league teams until 1970. Football made its first appearance in Dallas with the organization of a Dallas Football Club in 1891. A group formed at Dallas High School in 1900 was the first high school team in Texas. SMU sent a team to the 1935 Rose Bowl, and Doak Walker drew crowds to the Cotton Bowl in the late 1940s. Two professional teams, the Dallas Cowboys, and the Dallas Texans, competed for fans in the early 1960s, until owner Lamar Hunt moved the Texans to Kansas City in 1963. The Dallas Cowboys won many Super Bowl titles. Dallas's first professional basketball team, the Chaparrals, was transferred to San Antonio, but the new franchise, the Dallas Mavericks, was organized in 1980. Dallas also hosts a professional soccer team, the Sidekicks, and an NHL hockey team, the Dallas Stars.

The building boom of the 1970s and 1980s produced a distinctive contemporary profile for the downtown area, influenced by nationally prominent architects. At the same time, the establishment of the West End Historic District in the 1980s preserved a group of late-nineteenth-century brick warehouses that have been adapted for use as restaurants and shops.

The twenty-first-century predictions are that Dallas will continue to be one of the crossroads of the world. Anyway one views Dallas; they will proudly call it "Big D."

The First Baptist Church of Dallas

The First Baptist Church of Dallas was organized on July 30, 1868. Its founding marked the fourth attempt at organized Baptist work in the city. The first two churches had disbanded by 1860, while the third moved out of Dallas and changed its name to Pleasant View Baptist Church. First Baptist was organized with eleven charter members on the first floor of the Masonic Hall, on Lamar Street near the intersection of Ross Avenue. Some believe that it was a split from the Pleasant View church; however, there is no evidence to support this belief. W. W. Harris was called as pastor in 1868 and served until 1870. The most famous pastors have included George W. Truett and W. A. Criswell.

Under Truett, the church increased its membership from 797 to 7,804. The growth continued under Criswell, and in 1991, with a membership of more than 30,000, First Baptist was the largest church in the United States. Many well-known figures of American Christianity have been members of First Baptist, including Billy Graham.

In 1897, under the leadership of Truett, First Baptist established the first known training class for Sunday school teachers. Throughout its history, First Baptist has pioneered ministries in Dallas. The services of First Baptist were broadcast on radio in 1921, and by 1926 three radio stations were broadcasting its programs. Its first televised service occurred on January 7, 1951.

In 1970, First Baptist established a biblical institute named for Criswell, which in 1985 became Criswell College. During the controversy that occurred in the Southern Baptist Convention in the 1980s, many saw First Baptist as a leader in the conservative resurgence because of Criswell's commitment to the inerrancy of scripture and conservative theology.

During Criswell's tenure, the church expanded to multiple buildings covering five blocks in downtown Dallas, eventually becoming the largest Southern Baptist church in the world. Dr. Criswell became Pastor Emeritus from 1995 until his death in 2002. Since 1990, four pastors have held the pulpit: Joel Gregory, O.S. Hawkins, Mac Brunson, and, currently, Robert Jeffress.

In society organizations emerge, and leaders rise. It is through communication that organizations and leaders become a moving force. In viewing society, is to be seen as consisting of acting people, and the life of society is to be regarded as composed of their actions. The acting units may be separate individuals, collectivities whose members are acting together on a common quest, or organizations acting on behalf of a constituency. A general observation is that society is the product of man and that man is the result of society is not contradictory. It is from these constructs of society that a cue is taken affirming the concept of similar perspectives causing organizations to emerge in society. An organization is a group of people whose outlook is used as a frame of reference in formulating their perceptual field. As a collectivity forms structure, leaders rise to direct the purpose and courses of action of the group.

In American society, the Southern Baptist Convention has emerged, and W.A. Criswell became its President. The performance of the President was guided by his perception of specified duties of the office. His perspective of the office and his role in that office became significant sources of data by which to assess his performance and that of the convention. The President, like any other official within an organization, has carried with him into office a complexity of personal habits, memories, attitudes, inclinations and predispositions. These elements shape his responses to the pressures stemming from the institutional features of the office.

Some components of perspectives are elusive, while other variables in presidential perspectives and propositions lend themselves to a more exact statement. Perspectives and propositions of a leader are revealed through rhetoric and public address. Rhetoric and public address are relevant only where men are free to speak and act. Free rhetoric is not sufficient; there must be thoughtful and responsible speech. The battle for free speech is perhaps a battle that never ends. The end of rhetoric is persuasion toward goals and purposes. The speaker or leader is attempting to influence the decision-making process. Rhetoric is amoral or non-moral and functions in a setting. Speaking and leadership must be assessed in the backdrop of occurrence. Speaking and leadership attempt to modify ethics and politics of society. It is in this framework of public address that organizations emerge and leaders rise. Leadership is about the situation in which it arises. Common aspirations must unite leader and follower.

It is through the public address that the relationship of leader to an organization is apparent. W.A. Criswell was pastor of the First Baptist Church of Dallas, Texas, where he succeeded the late famous Dr. George W. Truett. Dr. Criswell was elected president of the Southern Baptist Convention in May, 1968.

A brief analysis of Criswell's rhetoric affirmed that the top issues in the convention and policy when Dr. Criswell was elected president were:

1. Social Concern.
2. Evangelism.
3. The Racial Issue.
4. Inspiration of Scripture.
5. Dissension—Unity in the Convention.

It was evident that the leader of the Convention realized the magnitude of the issues and policies. The focus of this book was to discover Dr. Criswell's perspective on issues and policy as revealed by an empirical analysis of propositions in his speaking. This helped to become aware of the reason Criswell was elected—to perpetuate the system or to institute change.

It is significant to focus on the perspective and public address of a man because he is the dynamic center. The leader has to keep the convention going. The convention is the system. That which the speaker-leader of the Southern Baptist Convention advocates will penetrate outside the organizational scene. The task at hand was to discover whether W.A. Criswell was elected president of the Southern Baptist Convention to perpetuate the status quo of the system or to institute changes as shown by an examination of the perspective. Propositions advanced in selected speeches from 1956-2002 compared against statements of Convention policy and Articles of Faith, a pre and post-election descriptive analysis method of rhetorical criticism was employed.

A large number of speeches after Criswell's election as president of the convention were considered. Those which were deemed most representative of his perspective and propositions were selected:

1. "The Fifth Sparrow," the first sermon preached at First Baptist Church, Dallas, Texas, 1944.

2. "The Downtown Church," a sermon delivered to First Baptist Church, Dallas, Texas. January 3, 1954.

3. "Segregation in Society," an address delivered to a joint session of the South Carolina Legislature. February 22, 1956.

4. "Church of the Open Door," an address to First Baptist Church, Dallas, Texas. June 9, 1968.

5. "Religious Freedom, the Church, the State, and Senator Kennedy," an address to First Baptist Church, Dallas, Texas. July 3, 1960

6. "Counterfeit Religion" a sermon delivered at the First Baptist Church, Dallas, Texas, December 9, 1962.

7. "My Favorite Sermon," a sermon delivered at the First Baptist Church, Dallas, Texas on October 4, 1964.

8. "Drugs is spelled D-E-A-T-H," a sermon delivered at the First Baptist Church, Dallas, Texas on and an address given to the 92nd Congress of the United States of Americas on May 3, 1971.

9. "Ministry of Reconciliation," an address to the Southern Baptist Convention. May 31, 1967, Miami Beach, Florida.

10. "Why I Preach the Bible is Literally True," an address to Criswell Bible Institute, October, 14, 1980.

11. "The Baptism of the Holy Spirit," an address delivered at the First Baptist Church, Dallas, Texas, June 26, 1983.

12. "Why I am a Pre-millennialist," an address delivered to Dallas Theological Seminary Chapel, March 16, 1984.

13. "Whether We Live or Die," an address delivered to the Pastors Conference, Dallas, Texas, June, 10, 1985.

14. "Old Time Religion," a sermon given to the First Baptist Church, Dallas, Texas on July 30, 1967.

15. "Christ is Coming Back," April 1, 2001. the last sermon Criswell preached at the First Baptist Church, Dallas, Texas.

CRISWELL'S BEGINNINGS

When W. A. Criswell was a small boy, he slugged another child who tried to insult him by calling him a "Little Bible Reader." All his life he was a Bible reader and fighter of evil. The success story of Criswell at First Baptist Church of Dallas could sound like a chapter out of a Texas Brag Book. He was outspoken on controversial issues in politics, theology, and social issues. Whether from friend or foe, Dr. W.A. Criswell has been described as a cross between Billy Sunday and King Kong. He had a distinct colloquial style in an affluent society. He had "folksy anecdotes" which communicated in the Southland of America.

The speaking of leaders has always moved people. Teachers instruct, but speakers send people into action! Criswell's style of speaking made him a legend in his own time. The rise and fall of events and ideas in history were clearly reflected in the speaking of W. A. Criswell. Perhaps his paradigm of preaching, speaking and writing can best be entailed in the subsequent encapsulation of his life, "Be anchored to the book and geared to the times." The leadership of W.A. Criswell in the Southern Baptist Convention was dynamic in the direction of polarization and unity. He involved the Convention in issues of evangelism and social responsibility. Criswell gave an emphasis on doctrinal integrity. Contemporary society is in an age of theological confusion. People do not know what they believe, not to speak of knowing why they believe. The "new generation" wants to know what is behind a particular belief. Dr. Criswell helped countless numbers of people around the world find spiritual answers.

THE SOUTHERN BAPTIST CONVENTION

Impetus of Christianity

The Christian faith has been a controversial topic since the creation of man. Before the time of Christ, men looked foreward to Christ to find meaning in the faith. Christianity was not a product of a class struggle of any kind. Jesus addressed Himself to the human family as He directed thoughts toward the spiritual aspects of life. Throughout the centuries, there has been the controversy between a secular state and free church application of the faith.

Christianity was narrowed down to the local church. Social and political lives were accepted by the church. At times the early idea of the Gospel, the anarchy of the faith which was responsible to God alone. The ideal of the Faith lived on in monasticism. In its original status, monasticism was a very complex phenomenon, but in its practical effect, it was simply a sanctuary where the early Christian idea had fled for refuge. The doctrines of the ancient Church went through transitional stages during the Middle Ages, but the germ of the ideas has existed until the modern period.

Medieval Christianity produced two great classic types of doctrine. First, the relative type of idea of Christianity and second, the radical idea of Christianity which was evolved by the sects. Protestant movements are of significance since their various ramifications produced results which led to and fostered religious subjectivism, a separation between church and state, the independence of a local congregation, and rights of the individual. All these characteristics of religious motives evolved into the subjectivism of Enlightenment.

Baptists in Europe

Protestantism

The organization called Baptists trace their concepts concerning faith to religious groups which emerged before and during the Renaissance and Reformation. These religious groups have been referred to as the left-wing of Protestantism. To better comprehend the left-wing of Protestantism, the right-wing of Protestantism should be described. National churches were characteristic of the right-wing of Protestantism. The Presbyterian Church of Scotland, the Church of England, the Reformed Churches of the Continent and Lutheranism in Germany all became legal religions.

Nonconformists called Waldensians broke step with the Roman Catholic Church. They took their name from Peter Waldo of Lyons who was financially successful. Waldo gave all his money to help the poor and became a preacher. Some Waldensians retained much Catholic doctrine while others became congregational in polity and highly evangelical. These evangelists rejected transubstantiation and all sacramental grace and infant baptism. This wing of Waldenses filtered into Switzerland and Germany where they profoundly influenced the Anabaptists.

Anabaptists

The Anabaptists were descendants of the Waldens and the direct ancestors of present day Baptists. Anabaptists first became prominent in Zurich as left-wing disciples of Zwingli's Reformation. Anabaptist was a name given to this group to denote "those who baptize again" or "re-baptize." They objected to infant baptism; therefore, they re-baptized the adults who were once baptized as children.

Advocating a mild form of pacifism and the abolition of capital punishment, the Anabaptists asserted the freedom of conscience and soul. This enhanced the movement of separation of church and state and individual liberty. The Anabaptists knew no discouragement. They filtered from Switzerland to Germany, Moravia, and Italy. In the Netherlands, they found renewed strength. In a catastrophic war and bloodshed, a small ultra-radical group of Anabaptists gave the entire organization a bad name for fanaticism. From this war, a remnant was reorganized by Menno Simons. Simons was a priest who deserted the Catholic Church for the Anabaptists in 1536. The men of Simons were a gentle, peaceful, law abiding, virtuous, determined people. They plowed through the snows of Russia, pleaded their cause in Leipzig and on the dikes of Amsterdam. It was somewhere around those dikes that Simons" followers met several English refugees called Separatists. Among the refugees were Thomas Helwys, John Murton, and John Smyth. This group had an influence on John Smyth who became the leader of English Baptists.

English Baptists

John Smyth was a Cambridge graduate and minister of the Church of England. As pastor of a Separatists group at Gainsborough, he studied the scriptures. When James I ran the nonconformists out of England, Smyth took his followers to Amsterdam in 1606. In Amsterdam, John Smyth changed some of his Calvinistic predestination theology to free will theology. He began preaching that the magistrate should not meddle with religion in matters of personal conscience.

One of the Smyth's first followers arose to oppose some ideas Smyth advocated. This follower, Thomas Helwys, led in Smyth's expulsion from the church he had founded. Helwys thought that the congregation should return to England and endure any persecution that might await them. Helwys was assisted by John Murton as the congregation went back to London where they formed the first Baptist Church on English soil about 1611. One of Helwys' publications addressed to James I led to his imprisonment. Therefore, John Murton became pastor of the first English Baptist Church. At the time of the death of James I in 1625, six or seven Baptist churches existed in England. By 1648 fifty churches with an estimated membership of 15,000 existed. These congregations were called Anabaptists at first, but by 1644 they were known as Baptists.

Baptist Churches of three kinds arose in England. The first were General Baptist Churches believing in a general atonement. Particular Baptists followed the limited atonement ideas of John Calvin. The Immersion Baptists broke from Particular Baptists and wrote their Confession of Faith in 1644. This confession was known as the *London Confession of 1644*. It was adopted by seven Baptist churches in that city and was the first comprehensive statement of faith and policy ever made by a group of Baptist churches.

The work of several religious leaders brought new life to the Baptists. John Wesley and William Carey had an influence on the work of all sects. Carey formed a missionary society and went to India as a Baptist missionary in 1793. In the early part of the seventeenth-century religious leaders became interested in escaping persecution and going to the New World.

Baptists in America

New England Baptists

Though many came from England to the colonies as Baptists, others like Roger Williams became Baptist only after they migrated to the colonies. Williams was a Cambridge University man and a Separatist. Roger Williams was one of the many who left England during the reign of Charles I to escape the persecution of the intolerant Archbishop Laud. Williams had been influenced by Thomas Helwys and John Murton. When Williams was offered the pastorate of the Boston Church, he refused to minister to an unseparated people.

Williams was "a young minister, godly and zealous, having precious gifts. But he also had a mind of his own and a loose tongue with which to speak his mind." He clashed with other clergy and state officials in Boston and Salem. The establishment was so riled up that the churches were unable to protect Williams. He fled from Massachusetts to a wilderness south in a relatively safe place with the Indians to escape deportation to England. Here Williams established a new colony at Providence, Rhode Island in 1638. It was there that he organized what is considered to be the first American Baptist Church.

In Rhode Island, Williams' purpose was to achieve complete religious liberty. The doors of Providence were open to all who were victims of religious persecution. This contributed to the advancement of Baptists. Because Williams was not able to attain his ideal, he left the Baptists and became a Seeker.

John Clarke and William Screven became the outstanding Baptists leaders after Williams. John Clarke was a physician who founded the Baptist Church at Newport, Rhode Island in 1644. Clarke was identified with the Puritan movement by proposing that the liberal elements settle in some new jurisdiction. Clarke continued to advance the cause of religious liberty started by Williams.

Clarke returned to England in 1652 to promote the interests of Rhode Island and religious freedom. He wrote a book concerning persecution in the colonies. He obtained a charter from Charles II which provided for religious liberty. After returning from England in 1664, Clarke served as a member of the General Assembly and was elected deputy governor. Some historians believed that Clarke deserved the title of "Father of American Baptists."

Another substantial root in Baptist history can be traced to Maine. It was there that William Screven tried to carry on the work of the church against state control. His preaching caused his jailing because authorities strongly disapproved. Screven was released when he promised to leave Maine. So he and other Baptists began moving southward.

Baptists had organized churches throughout New England, the middle states, and in the South before 1700. The Philadelphia Baptist Association was organized in 1707. After one hundred years in the colonies by 1739, there were fifty Baptist churches in America. The Philadelphia Baptist Association adopted the London Confession with two additional articles known as the *Philadelphia Confession of Faith* in 1742.

Between 1725 and 1750, and continuing for many years, the Great Awakening swept America. This movement in history was characterized by significant and prolonged religious revivals. Baptists were not as intimately involved at first in the Great Awakening as some other groups but shared in the results. Jonathan Edwards set the first flame with famous sermons such as "Sinners in the Hands of an Angry God." This movement emphasized the individual conversion and new birth.

The religious revivalists were persuasive with their ideas. In the 1720's Theodore J. Frelinghuysen of the Dutch Reform Church conducted revivals in New Jersey. At the same time in Pennsylvania, William Tennent directed the Presbyterians. John Wesley arrived in Georgia in 1735 to address the Methodists. The most prominent revivalist came to America in 1739 about the time the others reached their peak. He was George Whitefield. Whitefield preached to enormous crowds in every place he visited from New England to Georgia.

The Baptists profited greatly from the movement in a rather unusual way. Congregational churches were shaken and divided in sympathies. The Old Lights were against the revivals, and the New Lights favored the movement. The New Lights formed the strict Congregational church and were called Separatists. Restrictions caused many Separatists who believed in personal regeneration and believer's baptism to join the Baptists. The Great Awakening produced a remarkable increase for the Baptists. They continued to grow in the North, and the South as the impact of the Great Awakening was felt.

Baptists in Middle and Southern Colonies

The Baptist movement throughout Virginia, the Carolinas, and Georgia were led by men such as Daniel Marshall, William Screven, Shubal Stearns, Elijah and Lewis Craig. Two historical factors transformed Baptists from a tiny persecuted minority to a dominant religious force in the South. They were the Great Awakening and westward migration.

Before the Great Awakening, there were only seven Baptist churches in the South. At the close of the movement, there were 151 Baptist churches in Virginia. There were forty-two in North Carolina and six in Georgia. The South profited from the change almost as much as the North.

The first Baptist church established in the South was in Charleston, South Carolina in 1683. Its founder was William Screven. This church adopted the *London Confession of 1644* as its policy and Articles of Faith. The Charleston Baptist Association, October 21, 751, was the first association in the South and the second in the country.

Pre-Revolutionary War persecution caused Baptists to move in two directions. It scattered them into newly opening areas of the frontier at a faster rate than might have occurred otherwise. It also pushed the Baptists into closer cooperation in the fight for religious liberty. Almost all of the Baptists supported the Revolution against England. It was their strongest hope that out of the Revolution would come religious, as well as political, freedom. By working with all groups who wanted freedom, the Baptists became involved in political history.

In colonial times Baptists applied political pressure by forming a "Grievance Committee" in Rhode Island in 1769. This committee was probably the earliest religious lobby in American history.

In 1775 a disciple of Isaac Backus, John Leland of Massachusetts went to Virginia to combat persecution and speak for the principles of religious freedom. He spoke before the Virginia Assembly and became a promoter of Jefferson's efforts for religious liberty. John Leland contacted George Washington after a clearly defined guarantee of religious freedom was not present in the draft of the Constitution of the United States. James Madison convinced Leland that the best policy was to adopt the Constitution and then draw up a Bill of Rights.

The Constitution was adopted, and George Washington asked Madison to prepare the amendments which seemed necessary. Madison presented the proposed amendments to the Constitution on September 25, 1789. The Legislature approved these amendments. The First Amendment to the Constitution stated:

Congress shall make no law respecting an establishment of religion, or prohibiting the free exercise thereof; or abridging the freedom of speech, or of the press; or the right of the people peaceably to assemble, and to petition the Government for a redress of grievances.

The passing of the First Amendment fulfilled Madison's promise to John Leland and the Baptists. The Baptists were an active group of people who sought to help develop America. By the end of the Revolution, Baptists had changed from a small persecuted lower socio-economic group. They gained many influential people, yet still appealed to the common people.

Baptists on Frontier of America and Education

Toward the end of the eighteenth century, Baptists migrated across the Alleghenies into territories of Tennessee and Kentucky. The greatest factor behind the Baptist increase in the West, however, was not immigration but periodic revivals and frontier preaching. Growth was therefore essentially due to the genius for making Baptists out of the people they found on the frontier. Baptists were adaptable to frontier life.

After the adoption of the Constitution and Bill of Rights, religious liberty on the frontier was not met with the opposition as in early Colonial days. Soon the Baptists had moved throughout Ohio, Indiana, Illinois, Missouri, Mississippi, Louisiana, Texas, Oklahoma, and on westward. As Baptists moved, they were deeply involved in the frontier college movement. As they shared in its weaknesses and strengths, they played a major role in the democratizing of American education. During colonial times, a college education in America was restricted to the aristocracy.

Westerners felt estranged from Atlantic settlements and had no desire to send their children east for education. This resulted in many newly formed colleges. One cannot camp on the prairie but that a college will spring up beside his wagon. These colleges were academically weak but advocated a powerful idea. The idea was that higher education could be available to every young person.

The Baptists also participated in the Latin Grammar School movement. This change prepared for the later rapid development of the free public school. They made their most significant contribution to education in America with the college movement. In 1764 Rhode Island College (now Brown University) was the first Baptist college in America, located in Providence. In 1825 the South Carolina Baptist Convention organized a college that eventually evolved into Furman University. North Carolina Baptists started a school that is now Wake Forest College.

All churches, including Baptists, were sponsoring schools at every level and advocating the importance of an education long before civil government at any level showed any degree of real interest in public education.

Separation of Northern and Southern Baptists

Perhaps the separation of Northern and Southern Baptists would have become inevitable with the outbreak of the Civil War, but it preceded that conflict. In the early 1800's, Baptists left foreign missions largely up to other churches. The Congregational, Presbyterian, and Dutch Reform Churches formed the American Board of Commissioners for Foreign Missions. Among those whom this Board sent were Luther Rice and Adoniram Judson.

Rice and Judson diligently studied the scriptures as they traveled on separate vessels to India. In private study, both men were converted to Baptists beliefs, and both were baptized in the Baptist Church at Calcutta. Judson stayed in India to establish a Baptists mission in Burma. Rice returned to America to challenge Baptists to missionary opportunity.

American Baptists responded immediately to Luther Rice's plea for missions. On May 18, 1814, the General Convention of the Baptist Denomination was organized. At that meeting in Philadelphia, eleven states were represented by thirty-three delegates at this first instance of denominational consciousness of American Baptists. This meeting became known as the Triennial Convention since it met every three years. Richard Furman of Charleston, South Carolina was elected president.

The General Convention dealt only with foreign missions. The North wanted to spend energies on foreign missions, and the South was concerned with missions at home. In April, 1832 the American Baptists Home Mission Society was formed. The Board of the Baptist State Convention of New Hampshire adopted the *New Hampshire Declaration of Faith 2*. This was the most famous statement of faith and policy for nearly one hundred years among Baptists both North and South. By the year 1844 advocates of the abolition of slavery strongly influenced the Triennial Convention. At once the organization of the Southern Baptist Convention followed, and the breach between the Baptists of North and South was complete. That breach has been narrowed in recent years, but it has never been closed.

The Southern Baptist Convention

In response to the call of the Virginia Foreign Mission Society, the Southern Baptist Convention met for organization May 8-12, 1845 in Augusta, Georgia. According to historical tables, there were two hundred and thirty-six "messengers" registered from one hundred and sixty-five churches attending the meeting. The states represented were Maryland, Virginia, North Carolina, South Carolina, Georgia, Alabama, Louisiana, Kentucky and the District of Columbia.

It was evident that within thirty years of the organization of the general convention, at least three major divisive issues emerged causing the separation between Northern and Southern Baptists:

1. The Northern Baptists wanted separate organized conventions for each phase of work. The Baptists in the South desired to have only one organized convention with agencies to accomplish the goals.

2. Baptists in the South charged that the Home Mission Society was neglecting the mission fields in the Southland.

3. The explosion that produced separation came when the Foreign Mission Society refused to appoint a slave-holder as a missionary.

Baptists in the North seemed pleased with the separation and organization of the Southern Convention. They all agreed that further cooperation was impossible. They reached such a crisis, deplore it as it was, they decided there is no prospect for peace or comfort in the continuance, and weakness rather than wisdom would yield to efforts to effect it. They asked why is it not best that our Southern brethren take their position on one side of the line and we take ours on the other and engage in the various departments of benevolent effort with renewed zeal and increased liberality.

As the need has arisen, Southern Baptists have carried on their work through agencies in promoting denominational interests. Boards, committees, institutions, and commissions have served as agencies of the Convention. The Cooperative Program was a method whereby the Convention-wide receipts were augmented in a united and cooperative effort. Finances were distributed to all the boards and agencies on an agreed percentage. These rates arrived through cooperation between the agency and Executive Committee.

On Friday morning, May 9, 1845, the following resolution was submitted and adopted that stated: Resolved, that for peace and harmony, and in order to accomplish the greatest amount of good, and for the maintenance of those scriptural principles on which the General Missionary Convention of the Baptists denomination of the United States, was initially formed, it is proper that this convention at once proceed to organize a Society for the Propagation of the Gospel.

The Constitution adopted on May 10, 1845, created the Southern Baptist Convention. A Charter was enacted by the State of Georgia. As the Convention was formed, *The New Hampshire Declaration of Faith* as adopted as articles of faith and policy. This Confession was drawn up by the Rev. John Newton Brown, D. D., of New Hampshire about 1833, and was adopted by the New Hampshire Convention, and widely accepted by Baptists, especially in the Northern and Western States, as a clear and concise statement of their faith, in harmony with the doctrines of older confessions, but expressed in milder form. The text is taken from the Baptist Church Manual, published by the American Baptist Publication Society, Philadelphia.

Written in 1833 with minor revisions in 1853, the *New Hampshire Declaration of Faith* ranks highly among historical Baptist confessions of faith. While its language and content fall short of the more definitive and eloquent *Second London Confession of Faith 1689*, the NHDF nonetheless is an important historical document that provides great insight to historic Baptist theology. The NHDF is of particular significance to contemporary Southern Baptists who identify themselves as conservative and evangelical, as it is the foundation upon which modern Southern Baptists set forth "those things most surely believed among us" in the *Baptist Faith and Message*. Incumbent upon modern Southern Baptists is the responsibility to contemplate and evaluate both their claims of faith and the integrity of their doctrine in light of this document:

I. Of the Scriptures, we believe that the Holy Bible, written by divinely inspired men, is the perfect treasure of heavenly instruction; that God is the Bible's author; salvation the Bible's end; and, without any mixture of error, truth the Bible's substance; that the Holy Bible reveals the principles by which God will judge humanity; therefore, the Bible is, and shall remain to the world's end as the actual center of Christian unity, and the supreme standard by which all human conduct, creeds, and opinions should be tried.

II. Of the True God, we believe that there is one, and only one, living and true God; that God is an infinite and intelligent Spirit; that God's name is JEHOVAH; and, that JEHOVAH is the Creator and Supreme Ruler of heaven and earth; inexpressibly glorious in holiness; worthy of all possible honor, confidence, and love; revealed under the personal and relative distinctions of the Father, the Son, and the Holy Spirit who are equal in every divine perfection, and who execute distinct but harmonious offices as Father, Son, and Holy Spirit in the great work of redemption.

III. Of the Fall of Humanity, we believe that mankind was created in a state of holiness under the Law of his Maker; that, by voluntary transgression, mankind fell from that holy and happy state, the result of which is that all humanity are now sinners, not by compulsion but by choice; that humanity's nature is completely devoid of that holiness required by God's Law; completely given over to worldly pleasures, Satan, and sinful passions; and, without defense or excuse, humanity is under just condemnation to all humanity's eternal ruin.

IV. Of The way of Salvation, we believe that the salvation of sinners is wholly of grace; that, by the Father's decree, the Son of God freely but sinless took our nature upon Himself; honored the Divine Law by His personal obedience; atoned for our sins by His death; rose from the dead; now reigns in heaven; unites in His wonderful Person the sympathies (as Son of Man) with the Divine perfections (as Son of God); and, is in all ways qualified to be a suitable, compassionate, and all-sufficient Savior.

V. Of Justification, we believe that Justification is the great Gospel blessing that, from His fulness, Jesus Christ bestows upon those who believe in Him; that, based upon principles of righteousness, Justification consists in the pardon of sin and the promise of eternal life; is not bestowed upon us in any consideration of any works of righteousness which we have done, but solely through Christ's own redemption and righteousness; is freely imputed to us by God through faith; brings us into a state of most blessed peace and favor with God; and, secures every other blessing needful for time and eternity.

VI. Of the Freeness of Salvation, we believe that the Gospel freely declares the blessings of Salvation to all humanity; that the gospel demands of all humanity an immediate heartfelt repentance and obedient faith; and, that nothing prevents the Salvation of the greatest sinner on earth except his own total, inherent depravity and voluntary refusal to submit to the Lord Jesus Christ that will result in his awful condemnation.

VII. Of grace in Regeneration, we believe that, in order to be saved, we must be regenerated or born again; that Regeneration consists in giving a holy disposition to the mind; that Regeneration occurs by the Holy Spirit's power through Divine truth in a way that is above our comprehension or calculation; that Regeneration secures our voluntary obedience to the Gospel; and, that Regeneration evidences itself in the holy fruit that we bring forth to God's glory.

VIII. Of Repentance and Faith, we believe that Repentance and Faith are both sacred duties and inseparable graces, produced in our souls by the regenerating work of the Holy Spirit; that Repentance and Faith deeply convince us of our guilt, danger, and helplessness, and the way of salvation by Christ, through whom we turn to God with authentic (genuine and sincere) contrition, confession, and supplication for mercy and, at the same time, heartily receive the Lord Jesus Christ as our Prophet, Priest and King, relying on Him alone as the only and all sufficient Savior.

IX. Of God's Purpose of Grace, we believe that Election is the gracious purpose of God, according to which He freely regenerates, sanctifies, and saves sinners; that, being perfectly consistent with the free agency of human volition, Election includes all the means in connection with (and necessary for) the salvation of sinners; that Election is a most glorious display of God's sovereign goodness, being infinitely free, wise, holy and unchangeable; that Election utterly excludes boasting, and promotes humility, love, prayer, praise, trust in God, and active imitation of His free mercy; that Election encourages the use of means in the highest degree; that Election is demonstrated and proven by its effects in all who truly believe the gospel; that Election is the foundation of Christian assurance; and, that we must exercise utmost diligence to "make our calling and election sure."

X. Of Sanctification, we believe that Sanctification is the process by which, according to the will of God, we are made partakers of His holiness; that Sanctification is a progressive work; that Sanctification begins in regeneration; that the presence and power of the Holy Spirit, our Sealer and Comforter, carries out Sanctification in believers' hearts by the continual use of appointed means, especially the Word of God, self-examination, self-denial, watchfulness, and prayer.

XI. Of the Perseverance of Saints, we believe that only true believers endure to the end; that true believers persevere in their faithfulness to Christ, which is the grand mark that distinguishes them from false professors; that a special Providence watches over the true believers' welfare; and, that true believers are "kept by the power of God through faith unto salvation."

XII. Of the Harmony of the Law and the Gospel, we believe that God's Law is the eternal and unchangeable rule of His moral government; that God's Law is holy, just, and good; that the inability, which the Scriptures ascribe to fallen humans to fulfill the precepts of God's Law, arises entirely from their love of sin; and, that one great end of the Gospel, and one great end of the means of grace connected with the visible Church, is to deliver fallen humanity from their love of sin, and to restore them through a Mediator to authentic (genuine and sincere) obedience to the God's Law.

XIII. Of a Gospel Church, we believe that a visible Church of Christ is a congregation of baptized believers who are associated by covenant in the faith and fellowship of the Gospel; who observe the ordinances of Christ; who are governed by His laws; and, who exercise the gifts, rights, and privileges invested in them by His word; and, that the visible Church's only proper officers are Bishops or Pastors, and Deacons, whose qualifications, claims, and duties are defined in the Epistles to Timothy and Titus.

XIV. Of Baptism and the Lord's Supper, we believe that Christian Baptism is the immersion of a believer in water, in the name of the Father, and the Son, and the Holy Spirit, to show forth in a solemn and beautiful emblem, our faith in a crucified, buried, and risen Savior, with its purifying power; that Christian Baptism is prerequisite to the privileges of a church relation; and, prerequisite to the Lord's Supper, in which the members of the church, by the sacred use of bread and wine, are to commemorate together the dying love of Christ; and, always precede with solemn self-examination.

XV. Of the Christian Sabbath, we believe that the first day of the week is the Lord's-Day, or Christian Sabbath; that the first day of the week is to be kept sacred to religious purposes by abstaining from all secular labor and sinful recreations; by the devout observance of all means of grace, both private and public; and, by preparation for the "rest that remains" for the people of God.

XVI. Of Civil Government, we believe that God establishes civil government for the interests and good order of human society; and, that we should pray for, conscientiously honor, and obey civil magistrates except in things opposed to the will of our Lord Jesus Christ, who is the only Lord of the conscience, and the Prince of the kings of the earth.

XVII. Of the Righteous and the Wicked, we believe that there is a radical and essential difference between the Righteous and the Wicked; that only those who through faith are justified in the name of the Lord Jesus, and sanctified by the Spirit of our God, are truly Righteous in His esteem; that all those who continue in unrepentance and unbelief are Wicked in His sight and under the curse; and, that this distinction between the Righteous and the Wicked remains both in death and after death.

XVIII. Of the World to Come, we believe that the end of this World is approaching; that, at the last day, Christ will descend from heaven, and raise the dead from the grave to final retribution; that a solemn separation of the righteous from wicked will then take place; that the wicked will be condemned to endless punishment, and the righteous to endless joy; and, that, based upon principles of righteousness, the judgement will fix forever the final state of humankind in heaven and hell.

CHARTER OF THE SOUTHERN BAPTIST CONVENTION

An Act to Incorporate ... the Southern Baptist Convention. Be it enacted by the Senate and House of Representatives of the State of Georgia in General Assembly met, and it is hereby enacted by the authority of the same, that from and after the passing of this act ... that William B. Johnson, Wilson Lumpkin, James B. Taylor, A. Docrey, R. B. C. Howell and others their associates and successors be and they are hereby Incorporated and made a body politic by the name and style of the Southern Baptist Convention with authority to receive hold possess retain and dispose of property either real or personal to sue and be sued and to make all bylaws, rules and regulations necessary to the transaction of their business not inconsistent with the laws of this state or of the United States, said corporation being created for the purpose of eliciting combining and directing the energies of the Baptist denomination of Christians for the propagation of the gospel, any law, usage or custom to the contrary notwithstanding.

As the need has arisen, Southern Baptists have carried on their work through agencies in promoting denominational interests. Boards, committees, institutions, and commissions have served as agencies of the Convention. The Cooperative Program was a method whereby the Convention-wide receipts were augmented in a united and cooperative effort. Finances were distributed to all the boards and agencies on an agreed percentage. These percentages arrived through cooperation between the agency and Executive Committee.

Having looked at the reasons for the formation of the Southern Baptist Convention, and having sketched the functioning agencies, a question arises. What authority does the Convention have over churches or individuals? The answer is an indirect pressure: The Convention may pressure through suggestion, but it does not directly issue a single command. It cannot directly compel any church or individual to carry out its proposals.

Contemporary Southern Baptists

Contemporary Southern Baptists have perpetuated the faith of their ancestors. Differences, as well as unity, have characterized the Convention in areas of Biblical interpretation, Ordinances of the church, worship, social involvement and social practices.

The Bible has been accepted as authentic and authoritative Word of God for the Baptist. That fact has created bonds of unity and set them apart from those who have accepted the Bible as the word of man. There has been no more crucial question for religious faith than the question of authority. Southern Baptists have believed God Himself the ultimate authority, but that He has mediated part of His authority to man through the Bible.

Some Southern Baptists mistakenly thought that professing in the truth of the Bible relieves them from the responsibility of reading it intelligently and interpreting it correctly. The reason that every person has the right to read and interpret the Bible for himself was that every individual has equal access to the Holy Spirit. The same spirit who inspired its writing must inspire its interpretation. Therefore, man was not free to interpret the Bible as he pleased, but only as the Holy Spirit pleased. The Bible means what it means. But it may not always mean what man thinks.

Sermons in Southern Baptist churches from coast to coast, classrooms in convention institutions, and their publications have revealed unanimous unity among Southern Baptists on a fundamental belief of Salvation by grace, through the believer's voluntary faith, and not by works of righteousness, church membership, baptism, or secular responsibility. This was more than a casual point of agreement. Southern Baptists have regarded salvation by grace as one of the bedrock realities of the Christian faith. It has been a staple of their rhetoric.

In recent years, perhaps Southern Baptists' most controversial difference has been centered around how the Bible was to be interpreted. Southern Baptists have agreed that the Bible was the inspired, authoritative work of God. The difference has not been about the truth of the Bible, but about how the Bible was to be read and interpreted. Some have felt that the Bible should be understood literally and that its very words were "verbally inspired." Others have felt that the true meaning of the Bible was sometimes symbolic rather than literal and that while the core contents of the Bible were inspired by God, the writers were free to use their vocabulary. This group has also felt that the Bible was to be read in light of its original language and historical setting. This method of interpretation has been called the "historical-grammatical-critical" as opposed to the "literalist" approach.

In the twentieth century controversy among Southern Baptists concerning Biblical interpretation has risen to the surface at least three significant times. In 1925 the Southern Baptist Convention revised the *New Hampshire Declaration of Faith* with some deletions, changes in wording and ten additional articles with a separate section on science and religion. This was prompted by the evolutionary controversy which was raging at the time. The revision became known as *A Statement of the Baptist Faith and Message*. It was updated in 2000. The following represents the update:

The Baptist Faith and Message Study Committee issued the following statement on May 26, 2000, in response to questions and feedback they received from Southern Baptists shortly after the release of their report:

Preamble

The 1999 session of the Southern Baptist Convention, meeting in Atlanta, Georgia, adopted the following motion addressed to the President of the Convention.

Baptist Faith & Message
The 2000 Baptist Faith & Message

Commentary on Article XVIII – The Family

This commentary expands and provides a strong foundation for Article XVIII. While the family statement stands firmly on its own, the commentary enhances understanding. The commentary will be a useful tool for those who seek to comprehend Southern Baptist beliefs regarding family.

Multilingual Baptist Faith & Message

The *Baptist Faith and Message* is also available in different language translations. Comparing text of the 1925, 1963 and 2000 *Baptist Faith & Message* revealed the following:

I. The Scriptures

The *Holy Bible* was written by men divinely inspired and is God's revelation of Himself to man. It is a perfect treasure of divine instruction. It has God for its author, salvation for its end, and truth, without any mixture of error, for its matter. Therefore, all Scripture is totally true and trustworthy. It reveals the principles by which God judges us, and therefore is, and will remain to the end of the world, the true center of Christian union, and the supreme standard by which all human conduct, creeds, and religious opinions should be tried. All Scripture is a testimony to Christ, who is Himself the focus of divine revelation.

Exodus 24:4; Deuteronomy 4:1-2; 17:19; Joshua 8:34; Psalms 19:7-10; 119:11,89,105,140; Isaiah 34:16; 40:8; Jeremiah 15:16; 36:1-32; Matthew 5:17-18; 22:29; Luke 21:33; 24:44-46; John 5:39; 16:13-15; 17:17; Acts 2:16ff.; 17:11; Romans 15:4; 16:25-26; 2 Timothy 3:15-17; Hebrews 1:1-2; 4:12; 1 Peter 1:25; 2 Peter 1:19-21.

II. God

There is one and only one living and true God. He is an intelligent, spiritual, and personal Being, the Creator, Redeemer, Preserver, and Ruler of the universe. God is infinite in holiness and all other perfections. God is all powerful and all knowing; and His perfect knowledge extends to all things, past, present, and future, including the future decisions of His free creatures. To Him we owe the highest love, reverence, and obedience. The eternal triune God reveals Himself to us as Father, Son, and Holy Spirit, with distinct personal attributes, but without division of nature, essence, or being.

A. God the Father

God as Father reigns with providential care over His universe, His creatures, and the flow of the stream of human history according to the purposes of His grace. He is all powerful, all knowing, all loving, and all wise. God is Father in truth to those who become children of God through faith in Jesus Christ. He is fatherly in His attitude toward all men.

Genesis 1:1; 2:7; Exodus 3:14; 6:2-3; 15:11ff.; 20:1ff.; Leviticus 22:2; Deuteronomy 6:4; 32:6; 1 Chronicles 29:10; Psalm 19:1-3; Isaiah 43:3,15; 64:8; Jeremiah 10:10; 17:13; Matthew 6:9ff.; 7:11; 23:9; 28:19; Mark 1:9-11; John 4:24; 5:26; 14:6-13; 17:1-8; Acts 1:7; Romans 8:14-15; 1 Corinthians 8:6; Galatians 4:6; Ephesians 4:6; Colossians 1:15; 1 Timothy 1:17; Hebrews 11:6; 12:9; 1 Peter 1:17; 1 John 5:7.

B. God the Son

Christ is the eternal Son of God. In His incarnation as Jesus Christ He was conceived of the Holy Spirit and born of the virgin Mary. Jesus perfectly revealed and did the will of God, taking upon Himself human nature with its demands and necessities and identifying Himself completely with mankind yet without sin. He honored the divine law by His personal obedience, and in His substitutionary death on the cross He made provision for the redemption of men from sin. He was raised from the dead with a glorified body and appeared to His disciples as the person who was with them before His crucifixion. He ascended into heaven and is now exalted at the right hand of God where He is the One Mediator, fully God, fully man, in whose Person is effected the reconciliation between God and man. He will return in power and glory to judge the world and to consummate His redemptive mission. He now dwells in all believers as the living and ever present Lord.

Genesis 18:1ff.; Psalms 2:7ff.; 110:1ff.; Isaiah 7:14; Isaiah 53:1-12; Matthew 1:18-23; 3:17; 8:29; 11:27; 14:33; 16:16,27; 17:5; 27; 28:1-6,19; Mark 1:1; 3:11; Luke 1:35; 4:41; 22:70; 24:46; John 1:1-18,29; 10:30,38; 11:25-27; 12:44-50; 14:7-11; 16:15-16,28; 17:1-5, 21-22; 20:1-20,28; Acts 1:9; 2:22-24; 7:55-56; 9:4-5,20; Romans 1:3-4; 3:23-26; 5:6-21; 8:1-3,34; 10:4; 1 Corinthians 1:30; 2:2; 8:6; 15:1-8,24-28; 2 Corinthians 5:19-21; 8:9; Galatians 4:4-5; Ephesians 1:20; 3:11; 4:7-10; Philippians 2:5-11; Colossians 1:13-22; 2:9; 1 Thessalonians 4:14-18; 1 Timothy 2:5-6; 3:16; Titus 2:13-

14; *Hebrews 1:1-3; 4:14-15; 7:14-28; 9:12-15,24-28; 12:2; 13:8; 1 Peter 2:21-25; 3:22; 1 John 1:7-9; 3:2; 4:14-15; 5:9; 2 John 7-9; Revelation 1:13-16; 5:9-14; 12:10-11; 13:8; 19:16.*

C. God the Holy Spirit

The Holy Spirit is the Spirit of God, fully divine. He inspired holy men of old to write the Scriptures. Through illumination He enables men to understand truth. He exalts Christ. He convicts men of sin, of righteousness, and of judgment. He calls men to the Savior, and effects regeneration. At the moment of regeneration, He baptizes every believer into the Body of Christ. He cultivates Christian character, comforts believers, and bestows the spiritual gifts by which they serve God through His church. He seals the believer unto the day of final redemption. His presence in the Christian is the guarantee that God will bring the believer into the fullness of the stature of Christ. He enlightens and empowers the believer and the church in worship, evangelism, and service.

Genesis 1:2; Judges 14:6; Job 26:13; Psalms 51:11; 139:7ff.; Isaiah 61:1-3; Joel 2:28-32; Matthew 1:18; 3:16; 4:1; 12:28-32; 28:19; Mark 1:10,12; Luke 1:35; 4:1,18-19; 11:13; 12:12; 24:49; John 4:24; 14:16-17,26; 15:26; 16:7-14; Acts 1:8; 2:1-4,38; 4:31; 5:3; 6:3; 7:55; 8:17,39; 10:44; 13:2; 15:28; 16:6; 19:1-6; Romans 8:9-11,14-16,26-27; 1 Corinthians 2:10-14; 3:16; 12:3-11,13; Galatians 4:6; Ephesians 1:13-14; 4:30; 5:18; 1 Thessalonians 5:19; 1 Timothy 3:16; 4:1; 2 Timothy 1:14; 3:16; Hebrews 9:8,14; 2 Peter 1:21; 1 John 4:13; 5:6-7; Revelation 1:10; 22:17.

III. Man

Man is the special creation of God, made in His own image. He created them male and female as the crowning work of His creation. The gift of gender is thus part of the goodness of God's creation. In the beginning man was innocent of sin and was endowed by his Creator with freedom of choice. By his free choice man sinned against God and brought sin into the human race. Through the temptation of Satan man transgressed the command of God, and fell from his original innocence whereby his posterity inherit a nature and an environment inclined toward sin. Therefore, as soon as they are capable of moral action, they become transgressors and are under condemnation. Only the grace of God can bring man into His holy fellowship and enable man to fulfill the creative purpose of God. The sacredness of human personality is evident in that God created man in His own image, and in that Christ died for man; therefore, every person of every race possesses full dignity and is worthy of respect and Christian love.

Genesis 1:26-30; 2:5,7,18-22; 3; 9:6; Psalms 1; 8:3-6; 32:1-5; 51:5; Isaiah 6:5; Jeremiah 17:5; Matthew 16:26; Acts 17:26-31; Romans 1:19-32; 3:10-18,23; 5:6,12,19; 6:6; 7:14-25; 8:14-18,29; 1 Corinthians 1:21-31; 15:19,21-22; Ephesians 2:1-22; Colossians 1:21-22; 3:9-11.

IV. Salvation

Salvation involves the redemption of the whole man, and is offered freely to all who accept Jesus Christ as Lord and Savior, who by His own blood obtained eternal redemption for the believer. In its broadest sense salvation includes regeneration, justification, sanctification, and glorification. There is no salvation apart from personal faith in Jesus Christ as Lord.

A. Regeneration.

Regeneration, or the new birth, is a work of God's grace whereby believers become new creatures in Christ Jesus. It is a change of heart wrought by the Holy Spirit through conviction of sin, to which the sinner responds in repentance toward God and faith in the Lord Jesus

Christ. Repentance and faith are inseparable experiences of grace. Repentance is a genuine turning from sin toward God. Faith is the acceptance of Jesus Christ and commitment of the entire personality to Him as Lord and Savior.

B. Justification.

Justification is God's gracious and full acquittal upon principles of His righteousness of all sinners who repent and believe in Christ. Justification brings the believer unto a relationship of peace and favor with God.

C. Sanctification.

Sanctification is the experience, beginning in regeneration, by which the believer is set apart to God's purposes, and is enabled to progress toward moral and spiritual maturity through the presence and power of the Holy Spirit dwelling in him. Growth in grace should continue throughout the regenerate person's life.

D. Glorification.

Glorification is the culmination of salvation and is the final blessed and abiding state of the redeemed.

Genesis 3:15; Exodus 3:14-17; 6:2-8; Matthew 1:21; 4:17; 16:21-26; 27:22-28:6; Luke 1:68-69; 2:28-32; John 1:11-14,29; 3:3-21,36; 5:24; 10:9,28-29; 15:1-16; 17:17; Acts 2:21; 4:12; 15:11; 16:30-31; 17:30-31; 20:32; Romans 1:16-18; 2:4; 3:23-25; 4:3ff.; 5:8-10; 6:1-23; 8:1-18,29-39; 10:9-10,13; 13:11-14; 1 Corinthians 1:18,30; 6:19-20; 15:10; 2 Corinthians 5:17-20; Galatians 2:20; 3:13; 5:22-25; 6:15; Ephesians 1:7; 2:8-22; 4:11-16; Philippians 2:12-13; Colossians 1:9-22; 3:1ff.; 1 Thessalonians 5:23-24; 2 Timothy 1:12; Titus 2:11-14; Hebrews 2:1-3; 5:8-9; 9:24-28; 11:1-12:8,14; James 2:14-26; 1 Peter 1:2-23; 1 John 1:6-2:11; Revelation 3:20; 21:1-22:5.

V. God's Purpose of Grace

Election is the gracious purpose of God, according to which He regenerates, justifies, sanctifies, and glorifies sinners. It is consistent with the free agency of man, and comprehends all the means in connection with the end. It is the glorious display of God's sovereign goodness, and is infinitely wise, holy, and unchangeable. It excludes boasting and promotes humility.

All true believers endure to the end. Those whom God has accepted in Christ, and sanctified by His Spirit, will never fall away from the state of grace, but shall persevere to the end. Believers may fall into sin through neglect and temptation, whereby they grieve the Spirit, impair their graces and comforts, and bring reproach on the cause of Christ and temporal judgments on themselves; yet they shall be kept by the power of God through faith unto salvation.

Genesis 12:1-3; Exodus 19:5-8; 1 Samuel 8:4-7,19-22; Isaiah 5:1-7; Jeremiah 31:31ff.; Matthew 16:18-19; 21:28-45; 24:22,31; 25:34; Luke 1:68-79; 2:29-32; 19:41-44; 24:44-48; John 1:12-14; 3:16; 5:24; 6:44-45,65; 10:27-29; 15:16; 17:6,12,17-18; Acts 20:32; Romans 5:9-10; 8:28-39; 10:12-15; 11:5-7,26-36; 1 Corinthians 1:1-2; 15:24-28; Ephesians 1:4-23; 2:1-10; 3:1-11; Colossians 1:12-14; 2 Thessalonians 2:13-14; 2 Timothy 1:12; 2:10,19; Hebrews 11:39–12:2; James 1:12; 1 Peter 1:2-5,13; 2:4-10; 1 John 1:7-9; 2:19; 3:2.

VI. The Church

A New Testament church of the Lord Jesus Christ is an autonomous local congregation of baptized believers, associated by covenant in the faith and fellowship of the gospel; observing the two ordinances of Christ, governed by His laws, exercising the gifts, rights, and privileges invested in them by His Word, and seeking to extend the gospel to the ends of the earth. Each congregation operates under the Lordship of Christ through democratic processes. In such a congregation each member is responsible and accountable to Christ as Lord. Its scriptural officers are pastors and deacons. While both men and women are gifted for service in the church, the office of pastor is limited to men as qualified by Scripture.

The New Testament speaks also of the church as the Body of Christ which includes all of the redeemed of all the ages, believers from every tribe, and tongue, and people, and nation.

Matthew 16:15-19; 18:15-20; Acts 2:41-42,47; 5:11-14; 6:3-6; 13:1-3; 14:23,27; 15:1-30; 16:5; 20:28; Romans 1:7; 1 Corinthians 1:2; 3:16; 5:4-5; 7:17; 9:13-14; 12; Ephesians 1:22-23; 2:19-22; 3:8-11,21; 5:22-32; Philippians 1:1; Colossians 1:18; 1 Timothy 2:9-14; 3:1-15; 4:14; Hebrews 11:39-40; 1 Peter 5:1-4; Revelation 2-3; 21:2-3.

VII. Baptism and the Lord's Supper

Christian baptism is the immersion of a believer in water in the name of the Father, the Son, and the Holy Spirit. It is an act of obedience symbolizing the believer's faith in a crucified, buried, and risen Savior, the believer's death to sin, the burial of the old life, and the resurrection to walk in newness of life in Christ Jesus. It is a testimony to his faith in the final resurrection of the dead. Being a church ordinance, it is prerequisite to the privileges of church membership and to the Lord's Supper.

The Lord's Supper is a symbolic act of obedience whereby members of the church, through partaking of the bread and the fruit of the vine, memorialize the death of the Redeemer and anticipate His second coming.

Matthew 3:13-17; 26:26-30; 28:19-20; Mark 1:9-11; 14:22-26; Luke 3:21-22; 22:19-20; John 3:23; Acts 2:41-42; 8:35-39; 16:30-33; 20:7; Romans 6:3-5; 1 Corinthians 10:16,21; 11:23-29; Colossians 2:12.

VIII. The Lord's Day

The first day of the week is the Lord's Day. It is a Christian institution for regular observance. It commemorates the resurrection of Christ from the dead and should include exercises of worship and spiritual devotion, both public and private. Activities on the Lord's Day should be commensurate with the Christian's conscience under the Lordship of Jesus Christ.

Exodus 20:8-11; Matthew 12:1-12; 28:1ff.; Mark 2:27-28; 16:1-7; Luke 24:1-3,33-36; John 4:21-24; 20:1,19-28; Acts 20:7; Romans 14:5-10; I Corinthians 16:1-2; Colossians 2:16; 3:16; Revelation 1:10.

IX. The Kingdom

The Kingdom of God includes both His general sovereignty over the universe and His particular kingship over men who willfully acknowledge Him as King. Particularly the Kingdom is the realm of salvation into which men enter by trustful, childlike commitment to Jesus Christ. Christians ought to pray and to labor that the Kingdom may come and God's will be done on earth. The full consummation of the Kingdom awaits the return of Jesus Christ and the end of this age.

Genesis 1:1; Isaiah 9:6-7; Jeremiah 23:5-6; Matthew 3:2; 4:8-10,23; 12:25-28; 13:1-52; 25:31-46; 26:29; Mark 1:14-15; 9:1; Luke 4:43; 8:1; 9:2; 12:31-32; 17:20-21; 23:42; John 3:3; 18:36; Acts 1:6-7; 17:22-31; Romans 5:17; 8:19; 1 Corinthians 15:24-28; Colossians 1:13; Hebrews 11:10,16; 12:28; 1 Peter 2:4-10; 4:13; Revelation 1:6,9; 5:10; 11:15; 21-22.

X. Last Things

God, in His own time and in His own way, will bring the world to its appropriate end. According to His promise, Jesus Christ will return personally and visibly in glory to the earth; the dead will be raised; and Christ will judge all men in righteousness. The unrighteous will be consigned to Hell, the place of everlasting punishment. The righteous in their resurrected and glorified bodies will receive their reward and will dwell forever in Heaven with the Lord.

Isaiah 2:4; 11:9; Matthew 16:27; 18:8-9; 19:28; 24:27,30,36,44; 25:31-46; 26:64; Mark 8:38; 9:43-48; Luke 12:40,48; 16:19-26; 17:22-37; 21:27-28; John 14:1-3; Acts 1:11; 17:31; Romans 14:10; 1 Corinthians 4:5; 15:24-28,35-58; 2 Corinthians 5:10; Philippians 3:20-21; Colossians 1:5; 3:4; 1 Thessalonians 4:14-18; 5:1ff.; 2 Thessalonians 1:7ff.; 2; 1 Timothy 6:14; 2 Timothy 4:1,8; Titus 2:13; Hebrews 9:27-28; James 5:8; 2 Peter 3:7ff.; 1 John 2:28; 3:2; Jude 14; Revelation 1:18; 3:11; 20:1-22:13.

XI. Evangelism and Missions

It is the duty and privilege of every follower of Christ and of every church of the Lord Jesus Christ to endeavor to make disciples of all nations. The new birth of man's spirit by God's Holy Spirit means the birth of love for others. Missionary effort on the part of all rests thus upon a spiritual necessity of the regenerate life, and is expressly and repeatedly commanded in the teachings of Christ. The Lord Jesus Christ has commanded the preaching of the gospel to all nations. It is the duty of every child of God to seek constantly to win the lost to Christ by verbal witness undergirded by a Christian lifestyle, and by other methods in harmony with the gospel of Christ.

Genesis 12:1-3; Exodus 19:5-6; Isaiah 6:1-8; Matthew 9:37-38; 10:5-15; 13:18-30, 37-43; 16:19; 22:9-10; 24:14; 28:18-20; Luke 10:1-18; 24:46-53; John 14:11-12; 15:7-8,16; 17:15; 20:21; Acts 1:8; 2; 8:26-40; 10:42-48; 13:2-3; Romans 10:13-15; Ephesians 3:1-11; 1 Thessalonians 1:8; 2 Timothy 4:5; Hebrews 2:1-3; 11:39-12:2; 1 Peter 2:4-10; Revelation 22:17.

XII. Education

Christianity is the faith of enlightenment and intelligence. In Jesus Christ abide all the treasures of wisdom and knowledge. All sound learning is, therefore, a part of our Christian heritage. The new birth opens all human faculties and creates a thirst for knowledge. Moreover, the cause of education in the Kingdom of Christ is co-ordinate with the causes of missions and general benevolence, and should receive along with these the liberal support of the churches. An adequate system of Christian education is necessary to a complete spiritual program for Christ's people.

In Christian education there should be a proper balance between academic freedom and academic responsibility. Freedom in any orderly relationship of human life is always limited and never absolute. The freedom of a teacher in a Christian school, college, or seminary is limited by the pre-eminence of Jesus Christ, by the authoritative nature of the Scriptures, and by the distinct purpose for which the school exists.

Deuteronomy 4:1,5,9,14; 6:1-10; 31:12-13; Nehemiah 8:1-8; Job 28:28; Psalms 19:7ff.; 119:11; Proverbs 3:13ff.; 4:1-10; 8:1-7,11; 15:14; Ecclesiastes 7:19; Matthew 5:2; 7:24ff.; 28:19-20; Luke 2:40; 1 Corinthians 1:18-31; Ephesians 4:11-16; Philippians 4:8; Colossians 2:3,8-9; 1 Timothy 1:3-7; 2 Timothy 2:15; 3:14-17; Hebrews 5:12-6:3; James 1:5; 3:17.

XIII. Stewardship

God is the source of all blessings, temporal and spiritual; all that we have and are we owe to Him. Christians have a spiritual debt to the whole world, a holy trusteeship in the gospel, and a binding stewardship in their possessions. They are therefore under obligation to serve Him with their time, talents, and material possessions; and should recognize all these as entrusted to them to use for the glory of God and for helping others. According to the Scriptures, Christians should contribute of their means cheerfully, regularly, systematically, proportionately, and liberally for the advancement of the Redeemer's cause on earth.

Genesis 14:20; Leviticus 27:30-32; Deuteronomy 8:18; Malachi 3:8-12; Matthew 6:1-4,19-21; 19:21; 23:23; 25:14-29; Luke 12:16-21,42; 16:1-13; Acts 2:44-47; 5:1-11; 17:24-25; 20:35; Romans 6:6-22; 12:1-2; 1 Corinthians 4:1-2; 6:19-20; 12; 16:1-4; 2 Corinthians 8-9; 12:15; Philippians 4:10-19; 1 Peter 1:18-19.

XIV. Cooperation

Christ's people should, as occasion requires, organize such associations and conventions as may best secure cooperation for the great objects of the Kingdom of God. Such organizations have no authority over one another or over the churches. They are voluntary and advisory bodies designed to elicit, combine, and direct the energies of our people in the most effective manner. Members of New Testament churches should cooperate with one another in carrying forward the missionary, educational, and benevolent ministries for the extension of Christ's Kingdom. Christian unity in the New Testament sense is spiritual harmony and voluntary cooperation for common ends by various groups of Christ's people. Cooperation is desirable between the various Christian denominations, when the end to be attained is itself justified, and when such cooperation involves no violation of conscience or compromise of loyalty to Christ and His Word as revealed in the New Testament.

Exodus 17:12; 18:17ff.; Judges 7:21; Ezra 1:3-4; 2:68-69; 5:14-15; Nehemiah 4; 8:1-5; Matthew 10:5-15; 20:1-16; 22:1-10; 28:19-20; Mark 2:3; Luke 10:1ff.; Acts 1:13-14; 2:1ff.; 4:31-37; 13:2-3; 15:1-35; 1 Corinthians 1:10-17; 3:5-15; 12; 2 Corinthians 8-9; Galatians 1:6-10; Ephesians 4:1-16; Philippians 1:15-18.

XV. The Christian and the Social Order

All Christians are under obligation to seek to make the will of Christ supreme in our own lives and in human society. Means and methods used for the improvement of society and the establishment of righteousness among men can be truly and permanently helpful only when they are rooted in the regeneration of the individual by the saving grace of God in Jesus Christ. In the spirit of Christ, Christians should oppose racism, every form of greed, selfishness, and vice, and all forms of sexual immorality, including adultery, homosexuality, and pornography. We should work to provide for the orphaned, the needy, the abused, the aged, the helpless, and the sick. We should speak on behalf of the unborn and contend for the sanctity of all human life from conception to natural death. Every Christian should seek to bring industry, government, and society as a whole under the sway of the principles of righteousness, truth, and brotherly love. In order to promote these ends Christians should be ready to work with all men of good will in any good cause, always being careful to act in the spirit of love without compromising their loyalty to Christ and His truth.

Exodus 20:3-17; Leviticus 6:2-5; Deuteronomy 10:12; 27:17; Psalm 101:5; Micah 6:8; Zechariah 8:16; Matthew 5:13-16,43-48; 22:36-40; 25:35; Mark 1:29-34; 2:3ff.; 10:21; Luke 4:18-21; 10:27-37; 20:25; John 15:12; 17:15; Romans 12–14; 1 Corinthians 5:9-10; 6:1-7; 7:20-24; 10:23-11:1; Galatians 3:26-28; Ephesians 6:5-9; Colossians 3:12-17; 1 Thessalonians 3:12; Philemon; James 1:27; 2:8.

XVI. Peace and War

It is the duty of Christians to seek peace with all men on principles of righteousness. In accordance with the spirit and teachings of Christ they should do all in their power to put an end to war.

The true remedy for the war spirit is the gospel of our Lord. The supreme need of the world is the acceptance of His teachings in all the affairs of men and nations, and the practical application of His law of love. Christian people throughout the world should pray for the reign of the Prince of Peace.

Isaiah 2:4; Matthew 5:9,38-48; 6:33; 26:52; Luke 22:36,38; Romans 12:18-19; 13:1-7; 14:19; Hebrews 12:14; James 4:1-2.

XVII. Religious Liberty

God alone is Lord of the conscience, and He has left it free from the doctrines and commandments of men which are contrary to His Word or not contained in it. Church and state should be separate. The state owes to every church protection and full freedom in the pursuit of its spiritual ends. In providing for such freedom no ecclesiastical group or denomination should be favored by the state more than others. Civil government being ordained of God, it is the duty of Christians to render loyal obedience thereto in all things not contrary to the revealed will of God. The church should not resort to the civil power to carry on its work. The gospel of Christ contemplates spiritual means alone for the pursuit of its ends. The state has no right to impose penalties for religious opinions of any kind. The state has no right to impose taxes for the support of any form of religion. A free church in a free state is the Christian ideal, and this implies the right of free and unhindered access to God on the part of all men, and the right to form and propagate opinions in the sphere of religion without interference by the civil power.

Genesis 1:27; 2:7; Matthew 6:6-7, 24; 16:26; 22:21; John 8:36; Acts 4:19-20; Romans 6:1-2; 13:1-7; Galatians 5:1,13; Philippians 3:20; 1 Timothy 2:1-2; James 4:12; 1 Peter 2:12-17; 3:11-17; 4:12-19.

XVIII. The Family

God has ordained the family as the foundational institution of human society. It is composed of persons related to one another by marriage, blood, or adoption.

Marriage is the uniting of one man and one woman in covenant commitment for a lifetime. It is God's unique gift to reveal the union between Christ and His church and to provide for the man and the woman in marriage the framework for intimate companionship, the channel of sexual expression according to biblical standards, and the means for procreation of the human race.

The husband and wife are of equal worth before God, since both are created in God's image. The marriage relationship models the way God relates to His people. A husband is to love his wife as Christ loved the church. He has the God-given responsibility to provide for, to protect, and to lead his family. A wife is to submit herself graciously to the servant leadership of her husband even as the church willingly submits to the headship of Christ. She, being in the image of God as is her husband and thus equal to him, has the God-given responsibility to respect her husband and to serve as his helper in managing the household and nurturing the next generation.

Children, from the moment of conception, are a blessing and heritage from the Lord. Parents are to demonstrate to their children God's pattern for marriage. Parents are to teach their children spiritual and moral values and to lead them, through consistent lifestyle example and loving discipline, to make choices based on biblical truth. Children are to honor and obey their parents.

Genesis 1:26-28; 2:15-25; 3:1-20; Exodus 20:12; Deuteronomy 6:4-9; Joshua 24:15; 1 Samuel 1:26-28; Psalms 51:5; 78:1-8; 127; 128; 139:13-16; Proverbs 1:8; 5:15-20; 6:20-22; 12:4; 13:24; 14:1; 17:6; 18:22; 22:6,15; 23:13-14; 24:3; 29:15,17; 31:10-31; Ecclesiastes 4:9-12; 9:9; Malachi 2:14-16; Matthew 5:31-32; 18:2-5; 19:3-9; Mark 10:6-12; Romans 1:18-32; 1 Corinthians 7:1-16; Ephesians 5:21-33; 6:1-4; Colossians 3:18-21; 1 Timothy 5:8,14; 2 Timothy 1:3-5; Titus 2:3-5; Hebrews 13:4; 1 Peter 3:1-7.

The second major controversy played a major role in revising the articles of faith and policy again. The 1961 controversy was concerning a book entitled *The Message of Genesis* by Ralph Elliott. Elliott, a professor of religion at Midwestern Baptist Theological Seminary in Kansas City, Missouri, was dismissed in connection with his views on Bible interpretation. It was this controversy that led to a revision of the statement of policy and articles of faith adopted in 1925. The 1963 Southern Baptist Convention meeting in Kansas City, revised the 1925 statement. This revision became known as *The Baptist Faith and Message*. This statement of policy and articles of faith have been the official statements from 1963 to current date.

In March of 1969, a group of Baptist Educators lodged the third major controversy concerning the interpretation of the Bible in the twentieth century. A formal protest about the publicity given to a book published under Southern Baptist auspices was led by Robert Alley, a University of Richmond professor of religion. The book was *Why I Preach That the Bible is Literally True* by W.A. Criswell, the president of the Southern Baptist Convention. Professor Alley claimed that the book advocated a literalist view of the interpretation of the Bible which a group of professors did not favor.

Differences, as well as unity in Southern Baptists ranks, have been characterized in church ordinances. The ordinances are Baptism and the Lord's Supper. Baptists have agreed that Christian baptism is only for believers and that it distorts New Testament practices to apply it to unbelievers or infants. Southern Baptists have been practically unanimous that baptism should be by immersion. It has been true that some Baptists groups have baptized their converts at times by methods other than immersion. Some Southern Baptist churches have been willing to receive transfer members who have not been immersed.

Some churches in the Southern Baptist Convention admit only members of that local church to the Lord's Supper. This practice grew out of the Landmarkism movement on the American frontier. Most churches in the Convention have permitted visiting Baptists of "like faith and order" to observe this ordinance. In early Baptist history, this was known as "transient communion." About one-third of the Convention churches have practiced "open communion" and place no restrictions upon those who have desired to take the Supper.

Throughout their history, Baptists have had both open and closed communion practices. John Bunyan of *Pilgrim's Progress* advocated open communion among the Baptists in England of "like faith and order." Unity and differences in worship practices have been observed in the Southern Baptist Convention. Authentic examples of Southern Baptists worship have revealed the middle as well as the extremes of a continuum measuring worship. In the rural areas particularly in the deep South and West, informal worship with spirited gospel songs has been the norm. In the affluent city worship, stately hymns and a robed minister have been instituted.

People worship in patterns which have been comfortable and meaningful to them. The weddings, funerals and other functions have been adapted according to the norm of the particular geographic region. Just because Southern Baptist churches worship in different ways has not made them any less true and authentic Southern Baptists. Each local congregation is a complete church with full authority to determine its affairs. It is this doctrine that they have insisted upon the autonomy of each local church.

The concepts of social involvement have revealed unity and differences among Southern Baptists. The Southern Baptist Convention in 1888 ruled a temperance resolution out of order because the Convention purpose was missions and evangelism rather than the affairs of the world. In 1968 that same Convention spoke eloquently of Southern Baptists' responsibility to help solve current social and ethical problems as they adopted a "Crisis Statement" on race and the place of religion in society.

These two historical events illustrated the variety in views on social involvement. There have been some Southern Baptists who have felt that the Convention should have been mostly restricted to personal evangelism and missions. These have felt that participation in social problems has tended toward the "social gospel" and would rob Southern Baptists of their evangelistic zeal. There have been other Southern Baptists who have decided that unless they applied the Gospel to current social problems as well as to personal salvation, they were advocating only a partial gospel. The latter group has increased significantly in this century. Perhaps the largest and most responsible group have worked toward a balanced approach.

Customs among Baptists vary according to geographic regions both for adults and youths. More rhetoric has been heard against smoking in the Cotton Belt of the Deep South than among the Baptist tobacco growers of the upper South. Southern Baptists, like many other groups, inherited a strict moral code sometimes called "Puritanism." In recent years many Baptist youths and young adults have taken a new look at ethical practices their parents took for granted.

The Convention has realized that there has been unity as well as diversity in Southern Baptist life. Perhaps both have contributed in their ways to total strength in the Convention. Although Southern Baptists have been independent locally, they have discovered the value of working together. They have combined local churches into associations, and associations into state conventions, and state conventions into the Southern Baptist Convention to do together what no one church alone could have done.

WALLIE AMOS CRISWELL:
THE PERSON, THE SPEAKER, THE LEADER

CRISWELL PARADIGM

The rhetoric of speaker-leaders has always moved men. Teachers instruct, but speakers send men into action! A speaker, John Wesley, helped change England's history. That same nation was stirred toward the abolition of slavery because of the evangelistic fervor of Wilberforce. Karl Marx instructed followers regarding communism, but Lenin, the speaker-leader, fired them into action. *Mein Kampf* caught a group's attention, but through the "speaking" and leadership of Hitler, Germany was turned into a dynamic evil force.

In contemporary society the Southern Baptist Convention has emerged as a moving force in the Southland of America and W. A. Criswell was the speaker-leader. In integrating a proper balance between the influence of the personal characteristics of the speaker-leader as a person and the power of his ideas. This section of the book was fashioned to record the results obtained by the application of the descriptive analysis method. This was accomplished by answering the questions: Where did the speaking event take place and under what conditions? From the speaker's perspective what were the issues? What were the propositions advocated by the speaker? What did the speaker ask men to do?

After assessing Criswell's rhetoric before his election, representative selections were made. His perspective was revealed through the interrelation in which he viewed the issues.

THE PERSON

Rhetoricians have often declared that heredity and environment have explained much of the later speaking personality and communicative character of a speaker-leader.

The maternal ancestry revealed that Criswell's great-grandfather was a Southern Baptist preacher who went to Texas and helped organize the First Baptist Church of San Antonio. His son, Criswell's grandfather, was David Currie who was a physician who served in the Confederate Army in the Civil War. Thus, Criswell's mother came from a family with professional status.

The Story of Criswell's paternal forefathers was one of the frontiersmen. Great-grandfather John Criswell went to Texas from Knox County, Kentucky in the latter part of the 1820's. He fought through the Indian and Mexican Wars. Because of his devotion to duty in the wars, he was granted a parcel of land by General Sam Houston. Criswell's grandfather followed the typical life on the Texas prairie lands. Criswell's father, Wallie Amos Criswell, Sr., was a cowboy. He went to work on his Uncle Charles Neeley's Ranch in Greer County, Texas. In a Texas-Oklahoma boundary controversy, the Supreme Court ruled that Greer County was in Oklahoma. Old Greer County, Texas became Jackson County, Oklahoma. The land was then opened for homesteading. Criswell, Sr., filed a homestead claim on some of the land. It was there that Wallie Amos Criswell, Jr. was born December 19, 1909, at Eldorado, Oklahoma.

When Criswell was four years old, the family moved from Eldorado to a farm located in Clayton, New Mexico and Texline, Texas. He attended the grammar school at Texline where the family traded and attended church.

Mr. and Mrs. W.A. Criswell, Sr., were devout Southern Baptist church members. Although Mr. Criswell was quiet and reserved, he led the singing at church. Later he formed a band in Texline with his son at the trombone. Mrs. Criswell, the former Anna Currie, was a dynamic and outgoing church worker. She was involved in all the church activities. She aspired for her son to become a physician. The Criswells exercised a strict discipline with their children. There were four children in the family. W.A. had two older sisters and a younger brother. His parents taught young Criswell's love for the Bible:

Young Wallie's early years were hard and lacked in luxuries of life. Since there were four children in the family, Criswell stated that the family lived on "modest means." They were not "poor," they just did not have any money. As times grew harder, the father opened a barber shop in Texline to obtain income other than from the farm. As a boy, Wallie helped by doing simple chores on the farm and working in the barber shop.

In the second grade, Criswell took elocution lessons. Some famous addresses he recited were: "To the American Flag," and "What is Strength for America?" He learned early to concentrate on his school work.

Criswell's early and adolescent years were significant in religious decisions. He was converted when he was ten. Evangelist John Hicks from Dalhart, Texas came to Texline to preach a revival. The evangelist stayed in the Criswell home and talked with Wallie about making a confession of faith in Jesus Christ.

When Criswell was twelve, Evangelist Charles Whalley held a summer revival in a tent in Texline. Whalley made a special appeal for young men to dedicate their lives to the ministry. Although Criswell had felt an impression since he was six years old that he should be a preacher, it was at this revival that he made the commitment public. From that time forward every plan, purpose, and energy of his life were directed toward preparing for the ministry. As Dr. Ike Gates said, "W.A. Criswell has been preaching all his conscious life."

In the teenage years, Wallie spent the money he earned for books to have a personal library on preaching. He was not athletically inclined as a youngster. His activities at school consisted of oratory, public debating, and playing trombone in the band. Instead of focusing admiration on athletes, he directed attention to prominent religious figures such as George W. Truett of First Baptist Church Dallas and L.R. Scarborough, President of Southwestern Baptist Theological Seminary in Ft. Worth.

Fortune was cruel to the Criswell family. They moved to Amarillo, Texas in 1925 after a heart-breaking experience in dry-land farming near Texline. W.A. Criswell, Sr. worked as a barber while the four children sought an education.

While attending Amarillo High School, Criswell excelled as a debater who frequently won gold medals for oratory and played in the famed Golden Sandy band. During this time, he was a faithful member of the First Baptist Church in Amarillo where he was licensed to preach when he was seventeen years old. Experiences in Amarillo made a significant impression on Criswell. When Criswell graduated from Amarillo High School in 1927, he visited and evaluated colleges in Texas and Oklahoma. It was decided among the family that Baylor University was the college. He entered Baylor in the fall of 1927. Later he chose English as a major, and minors in philosophy, psychology, and Greek. A great love for English and American literature was enhanced by the famous Browning scholar, Dr. A.J. Armstrong.

At Baylor, Criswell was an outstanding ministerial student and an accomplished debater. He was President of Sigma Tau Delta, Ministerial Alliance, and was chosen to launch the Greater Baylor Campaign his senior year. He also found time for the Baylor band. Criswell graduated with honors from Baylor with the B.A. degree in 1931. In 1945 Baylor honored Dr. Criswell again by giving him the Doctorate of Divinity.

In the fall of 1931 W. A. Criswell entered the Southern Baptist Theological Seminary in Louisville, Kentucky. His favorite instructors were those who contributed to his appreciation of the Bible. Dr. John R. Sampey, Professor of Hebrew, assisted Criswell in the study of Old Testament. Drs. William Hersey Davis and Archibald Thomas Robertson influenced him in the study of New Testament. Dr. Jesse Burton Weatherspoon taught him techniques on Biblical preaching. While in seminary he was introduced to critical views of the Bible. An influential book on Criswell was *The Problem of the Old Testament* by James Orr. It was this book that added impetus to his continued appreciation of the Bible as the Word of God.

Criswell was awarded the Master of Theology degree in 1934. He remained in the graduate school of the seminary and studied under Drs. A.T. Robertson and W.H. Davis. During the seminary days, Criswell met Miss Betty Harris. Betty was a school teacher and played the piano where Criswell served in a student pastorate. Criswell married Miss Harris on February 14, 1935.

W.A. Criswell earned the Doctor of Philosophy degree in 1937, with a major in New Testament interpretation. His dissertation was entitled, "The John the Baptist Movement in Its Relation to the Christian Movement."

Completion of formal education did not stop Dr. Criswell's study. He has maintained diligent study of scripture approximately five hours a day. He has kept a constant pursuit of material to substantiate his conservative theological position.

The exciting story of W.A. Criswell's speaking and leadership revealed his involvements and accomplishments in his profession.

THE SPEAKER

Early Speaking Career

W.A. Criswell began speaking in churches when he was seventeen. He had student pastorates throughout his college and seminary studies. His first pastorate was at Devil's Bend near Cameron, Texas. The salary was twenty dollars per month. He conducted his first revival at Bethel Church in Coryell County, Texas. Criswell's second pastorate was at Pulltight in Coryell County. In this same county, he also preached at Pecan Grove Baptist Church and White Mound Baptist Church. He began to preach in school houses and was finally called to the First Baptist Church of Devil's Bend.

While at Southern Seminary in Louisville, Kentucky, Criswell had student pastorates in nearby villages. These part-time ministries included Mount Washington Baptist Church in Bullett County, Oakland Baptist Church and Woodburn Baptist Church in Warren County. After completion of his doctorate, Criswell was ready for his first full-time pastorate.

First Baptist Church, Chickasha

Dr. J.W. Bruner retired from his pastorate at the First Baptist Church of Chickasha, Oklahoma after a quarter of a century. Dr. B.B. McKinney recommended to that church that they call W.A. Criswell as their new pastor. Dr. Criswell accepted and began in 1937 with great zeal.

In 1939 at Chickasha W.A. and Betty Criswell welcomed their first and only child, a daughter whom they named Mabel Anne.

It was at the church in Chickasha that Dr. Criswell's ability as a bible preacher improved. He became known for his exposition of scripture.

Dr. A.N. Hall of First Baptist Church in Muskogee, Oklahoma was so impressed with young Dr. Criswell that he told his church that if anything happened to him, he wanted the church to call Criswell.

First Baptist Church, Muskogee

On Christmas day, 1940 the seventy-five-year-old Dr. A.N. Hall, pastor of the church, died. The first Sunday of the new year 1941, the pulpit committee was appointed. They phoned W.A. Criswell and invited him to become pastor of the First Baptist Church of Muskogee, Oklahoma. Dr. Criswell accepted the invitation and began his responsibilities in that church in winter 1941.

An account of the Criswell years at Muskogee was complimentary. He was described as a brilliant and concentrated pastor. The Muskogee church also had an influence on Dr. Criswell. During his five-year ministry at Muskogee, Criswell majored on Biblical preaching. Three years were especially formative and influential on expository preaching. In this church, Dr. Criswell demonstrated abilities to have learned from previous mistakes. His zeal was tempered with diplomacy and tactfulness. His tremendous leadership skills and ability to inspire the confidence of people came forth. The Muskogee period went down as a success.

First Baptist Church, Dallas

Dr. W.A. Criswell was chosen by the First Baptist Church of Dallas, Texas in an unusual way. One Sunday in 1934 in his student pastorate in Kentucky, Criswell was preaching when a prominent Baptist layman from Nashville was visiting. The visitor was John L. Hill who never forgot a speech. In 1944 after the death of First Baptist's most famed preacher, Dr. George W. Truett, the congregation consulted Hill about a successor. Hill wrote back to the church, "W.A. Criswell is the only man in all the earth for you."

For several weeks the names of celebrities were suggested as suitable successors. Only one name, however, was suggested and recommended to the church by the pulpit committee, namely W.A. Criswell.

Criswell became aware that the church did not seek someone to follow in the footsteps of their incomparable leader but rather wanted a man who could make footprints of his own. Dr. Criswell accepted the invitation and began his work in Dallas amidst a blaze of publicity. The success story of Dr. W.A. Criswell at First Baptist Church of Dallas could have sounded like a chapter out of a Texas Brag Book, but the story of his speaking and leadership was reliable. This church was big statistically, but its bigness was also expressed in a spiritual dimension. The church has grown accustomed to doing things in a big way during the half century with Criswell. For over fifty years Dr. Criswell guided a dynamic program at First Baptist which dwarfs many businesses.

Dr. Criswell has been considered one of the most excellent Bible expositors in America today. He has made use of original languages such as Greek or Hebrew in speaking. The exegesis has been clear and simple yet profound when presented. He often used church history, biographies, and philosophy as source materials.

After two years at Dallas, Criswell embarked upon a speaking journey through the Bible. On March 3, 1946, he began and completed the series on October 6, 1963.

Dr. Criswell always concluded his sermons with an evangelistic appeal. He kneels quietly with each person who has responded. He was best at introducing new members and converts.

It was informal and unhurried and proved that the church was not a city-slicker church. In the years that Criswell has spoken at First Baptist Church, Dallas there has never been a Sunday service that someone did not make a public decision.

Dr. W.A. Criswell has been outspoken on controversial issues in politics, theology, and segregation. A brief view of Criswell's mechanics of speaking was revealing. In delivery, his voice was well modulated and had good range. It was natural and forceful. He spoke without notes in an extemporaneous manner. Dr. Criswell revealed how he prepared for a speech. His pattern first involved the location of scripture. Second involved feeling the burden of the message. The third was researching the topic idea. Then the speech was planned and presented extemporaneously without notes.

A typical day spent with this famed speaker-leader was beneficial. He got up at 7:00 a.m. and had breakfast. From 8:00 to 12:30 was spent studying in the office and library in his home. After lunch, hospital visits were made from 1:30 to 2:15. At 2:30 each day Dr. Criswell went to the Y.M.C.A. for exercising. From 3:30 to 6:00 he spent time in his office at church. Then there was a dinner meeting in Dallas before he returned home to retire for the day.

Dr. Criswell has been widely sought as a speaker throughout the nation. He has spoken to seventeen of the twenty-three recognized Southern Baptist State Evangelistic Conferences. He has spoken to Ridgecrest, Glorieta, and Falls Creek Baptist conference centers almost every year since 1937. Criswell responded to invitations to speak to nearly every agency in the Convention. He toured Europe in 1947 when he attended the Baptist World Alliance in Copenhagen. In 1950 The Foreign Mission Board sent Dr. Criswell on an evangelism crusade where he spoke around the world. South America was the site for a Criswell Crusade in 1964, where he had a narrow escape from death in a jungle of Peru. In 1965 a tour of Russia caused Criswell to state that only the intervention of God could save religion in Russia. A 1968 speaking tour of Israel was successful. When Criswell returned from Africa in January 1970, he stated that the door is open for Christianity.

Objectivity demanded that the "Criswell Charisma" be seen from sympathetic and controversial perspectives. While others may criticize Criswell, he is wholeheartedly admired by his parishioners.

An interview with Texas multi-billionaire, H. L. Hunt who was a Texas oil tycoon and conservative Republican political activist, revealed admiration for Criswell:

> *I do not know of a more effective speaker-leader in religion than W.A. Criswell. I am a member of Dr. Criswell's church. He is an amazing orator, good man, fine speaker, and great organizer. W.A. Criswell really communicates to the people of Dallas and the Southern Baptist Convention. He has a tremendous faculty of knowing his subject. He is well informed. He uses no notes in speaking and has proper emphasis in delivery. Dr. Criswell speaks out for freedom and against communism. He is a moving force in the First Baptist Church and the Southern Baptist Convention. Criswell helped inspire me to write a book, WHY NOT SPEAK?*

Dr. Willis M. Tate, President of Southern Methodist University, felt it necessary to point out that Criswell is an influential local and national church leader. No other church in the United States can stand up to First Baptist of Dallas. Dr. Criswell could be the leader of anything he wanted. His choice is the Church and Southern Baptist Convention. T.A.

Patterson, Executive Secretary of the Baptist General Convention of Texas, felt that Criswell was the unifying force in and among Baptist people. John J. Hurt, Editor of the *Baptist Standard*, stated positive words about Criswell when he related that whether one liked Dr. W.A. Criswell or not, he was interesting, unique, and dogmatic in what he says. Conservative people liked that, but all people wanted Criswell because he is sincere. Dr. Robert Naylor, President of Southwestern Baptist Theological Seminary briefly described Criswell as a "phenomenal force in the Southern Baptist Convention." Franklin Paschall, Pastor of First Baptist Church of Nashville, Tennessee was impressed with the "Criswell Charisma."

Perhaps Criswell's greatest opposition came from the Association of Baptist Professors of Religion who adopted a resolution against Criswell's interpretation of the Bible in his book *Why I Preach That the Bible is Literally True*. Two of the Association's leaders have been Rev. T.C. Smith of Furman University and Rev. Robert Alley of the University of Richmond. Professor Robert Alley has been the most severe critic of Criswell's books. Alley fought for his belief when he expressed his perspective concerning Criswell's book, *Look Up, Brother*. He said it was "both sad and pathetic" and was "a pitiable display of emotionalism." Whether from friend or foe, Dr. W.A. Criswell has been described as "a cross between Billy Sunday and King Kong."

A tour of Criswell's home library on November 6, 1996, gave profound insights as to Criswell's strategy of preparing his speeches. Tim Miller gave the following account of his tour of the Criswell home library. 5901 Swiss Avenue, Dallas, Texas. Nobody knew it back in 1944 when a young pastor named W. A. Criswell first moved in here with his wife, Betty, and their young daughter, Mabel Ann, that this place would become a ground zero point: a place where every morning, without fail, Dr. W. A. Criswell had an appointment with his Lord. As a result of those meetings came some of the most powerful and influential sermons ever delivered from a Southern Baptist pulpit, but the real power behind the ministry of Dr. W. A. Criswell started right here every day.

Wouldn't you love to go inside that library to the place that is still so precious to the dear pastor and, as a young minister yourself, to hear from him firsthand the techniques that he used to generate three sermons every Sunday? Well, Dr. Criswell has generously granted us his morning to show us the library and to teach you, step-by-step, the process he used to prepare all those wonderful sermons.

[Criswell] This library is my very life as a pastor and a preacher. Next to my devotions before God, my praying, and my seeking the face and will of the Lord, the library is the foundation for all I have sought to do in my over seventy years of being a pastor and a preacher. I say to young men who are beginning their work in the ministry: if it is possible, have your library at home. The reason for that is when I get up in the morning, I come to the library; and when the evening comes, if I have any time left from the work of the end of the day, I come to the library.

I have arranged the library in this fashion. All of this section of the books have to do with commentaries. The first beginning group of books are introductory to the Old Testament, then that is followed by individual commentaries on the books of the Old Testament. Then we come to the New Testament, and we have the books that are introductory to the New Testament as such; and these volumes on the introduction of the New Testament are followed by individual books that are commentaries on the books of the New Testament.

Now in this section of the library, the lower part of it is filled with volumes that are in series on the Bible itself: the dictionaries of the Bible and all of the things that pertain to the Bible as a whole.

This section of the library is filled with general books such as the Harvard Classics, which you see them up here, and then the encyclopedias which you see here; and then down here is one of the great commentaries of the world. This one is The Pulpit Commentary, and down here on this side is The Preacher's Commentary. Then alongside of these books that are general like that, why, in that section of the library, I have historical books—the history of the church—and then right here I have doctrinal books: the great doctrines of the faith that are presented here.

Then up here in this section of the library are volumes of books composed of preachers' sermons—great preachers of the faith—and these volumes and volumes are those collections of the sermons of great preachers. Then on the shelf up there at the top and then going around into the library in the next room here, in the additional room, those books are on missions. They are missionary books. Then this section of the library, all of this section of the library, all of this section is books of sermons.

And that leads me to speak of the most advantageous and helpful of all of the discoveries I have ever made in my long life as a preacher and as a pastor, and it comes about like this: I hold in my hand a copy of a wide-margin Bible; and by the side of a text, when a book of sermons came into my hand, by the side of the text in the margin, I wrote the number of the book and, dash, the page upon which the sermon is found. And I have done that for years and years.

Any time a book of sermons came into my hand, I gave it a title, just ad seriatim. I started at the first one and then went right on through the years and the years; and in that way, when I prepared my sermons, as you will hear in just a moment, I always read what some other pastor said about the text, said about the passage. And their ideas helped me world without end; and instead of spinning the sermon out of what little I knew, I added to it the ideas and the understandings of the great preachers of the world, and I enriched my messages endlessly with this little discovery of taking any book of sermons that came into my hand and by the side of the text or by the side of the passage writing the number of the volume and the page upon which that sermon was found.

In the building of this library, they placed a wing where I could add to it; and in the providences of God, the wing is far too small, but I have to use it to the best advantage that I know how. And right here are all of the books that I have on the missionary life of the people of God; and then down here I have the books of general poetry and literature; and then in here I have the books that pertain to the history of the church and to all the things that contribute to illustration and the magnification of the ministries of the people of God.

Then in here, in here, I have my sermons and my books. I have published fifty-four books, and they are all here. Then in this last section here, I have up there the great presentation of the inspiration of the Word of God; and then all of these sections here are filled with Bibles and instructions about how to use and to study the Bible. And one of the unusual things they made for me: there is a section up here on that row and on this row of the volumes that I have published, and they all are republished under a cover that makes it all look continuous.

We're now going to follow the way I prepare a sermon—the steps I take. First of all, in preparing a message from the Bible, I look at the passage in Hebrew if it's in the Old Testament, and I look at the passage in Greek if it is in the New Testament. For example, this is my Hebrew Bible, and we begin in Genesis 1: 1: "Bereshit bara Elohim et hashamayim we'et ha'aretz. In the beginning, God created the heavens." In Hebrew, when a word ends in an "i-m" it's plural: "In the beginning, when God created the heavens," plural, "we'et and ha'aretz—the earth."

The Bible starts off saying God created, plural, the heavens—all of those vast multitudinous universes out there that we look at as stars in the sky—plural. God created all of them, and then He created our earth. So the Bible begins, and thus it is when my passage I'm expounding is in the Old Testament, I look at the original in the Hebrew; and that helps me world without end in presenting the true message of God.

Then here is my Greek New Testament; and if the passage I am expounding is in the New Testament, why, I read the passage in Greek and study it in the original language. For example, I'm holding in my hand now the Gospel of John in Greek. "En archē ēn ho Logos kai ho Logos ēn pros ton Theon kai Theos ēn ho Logos. In the beginning was the Word, and the Word was pros ton Theon—in the presence of God, face to face with God—and Theos ēn ho Logos—and God was the Word, and the Word was God." So it is as I prepare my message, why, I look at it first of all in the Hebrew or in the Greek.

Then when I get through looking at that passage in its original language, I study it in all of these commentaries that you have seen here in the library—these English commentaries. And the word that comes to my heart and to my mind as I study these commentaries on the passages, those studies bring unending wealth to my heart, to my mind; and they help me endlessly, marvelously, gloriously, as I prepare the message from the passage in the Bible.

Then after I have studied it in Greek or Hebrew and after I have studied the passage in English commentaries, then I use that marvelous, wonderful discovery that I made with the wide-margin Bible. I look at the passage in my wide-margin Bible, and I write down the numbers of the book and the pages on which the message is found. And there out of my collection of books, I take out those books of sermons, and I read what these famous and gifted pastors have written about that passage in the Bible. And it is unbelievable how many wonderful, wonderful ideas are brought to my heart and mind as I read what other preachers have said about the passage.

Then having gathered together all of the material that I can find on that passage, by that time a burning message has been born in my heart, and I sit down here at the desk and I write out from my own heart the meaning of that passage to me and the meaning that I can pray God will help me to preach it to other people.

Now, may I add one other thing to the sermon? Over here in this section of my library, I have these storages of the sermons that I have preached. They are there placed according to text starting at Genesis and going to the Revelation. Then there are other areas in which I have placed my sermons other than a text. For example, in this series that I have carefully placed in these cabinets, I will have a section, a collection, of Mother's Day sermons; then a collection of patriotic sermons delivered around July 4; then a collection of Thanksgiving sermons; then a collection of Christmas sermons; then a collection of New Year's sermons; then a collection of Easter sermons. But outside of those exceptions, all of my sermons and addresses are filed in those filing cabinets according to text.

Now let me add one other thing. On my desk, right in front of me as I study, are a few books. This is my Bible, and this book is an analytical lexicon of the Greek text. This book is the Greek text itself. This book is the dictionary of the Bible. This volume is a dictionary of the English language. This volume is a listing of all of the sermons that I have preached: first their text, then their title, and then the date that I delivered the message, and over here in this part I have the place where these messages were delivered.

Then the next thing here is my calendar, the dates that I live by; and when I have fulfilled the work of the day, I mark it out—and this is you and your coming here on this date, the eighteenth of November in 1996. Then the last volume up here before me is a concordance of the words in the Bible.

This little library book collection on a swivel, these are the books that I have at my left hand, close to my desk, that I can turn to immediately. Right here, for example, are the Bibles that I preach out of. These are the Bibles that I hold in my hand when I stand in the pulpit, and right here is that wide-margin Bible in which I have written the numbers of all of the books of sermons that are in my library. Then this volume here, these volumes here, are Ellicott's commentary on the whole Bible starting at Genesis and going through to the Revelation. Then this is the American Commentary on the Bible, and it goes through here. Then this is Gray's commentary on the Bible, and this is Jamison Fawcett and Brown's commentary on the Bible. Then I have a hymnbook here out of which our people sing.

Now right here is the text of the Old Testament in Hebrew, and this is the text of the New Testament in [Greek], and these volumes here are interlinear publications of the Bible—in English and then the Greek or the Hebrew underneath; and in this way I have right at my fingertips all the things that I need here in the Bible.

This is a volume that is most unusual: it is the Bible in twenty-six different translations. And this volume here is a beautiful publication of the Bible that is in Hebrew and Greek, and is a study Bible in English with the Hebrew and Greek underneath it. And this is a topical concordance that gives you all of the passages in the Bible according to subject. These things are just at my left hand—always present and close by to help me in my study.

In my preaching through the Bible, I have come to the Gospel of Matthew, and I am going to preach an expository sermon on the first half of Matthew 20 and the last half of Matthew 19. Now, in the preparation for that sermon, first of all I get this Greek New Testament and I read this story in Greek, and in that way I look at every nuance, every shade of meaning, and I come to a wonderful understanding of what Jesus was doing when He makes a differentiation between working for God by agreement, by what you get out of it, or working for God just for the love of the Lord and leave the reward to Him. So I look at it in my Greek New Testament.

Then, next, I get my wide-margin Bible, and I turn to the passage in my wide-margin Bible, and I take my wide-margin Bible over here where I have the number of the book, dash, and the page upon which the sermon is published. And I look through my list, and I come across the [book]. Then I have another, and I look at my books, and I come across this Bible, this book; and I take it over here to my study, and I look at the number of the page upon which the preacher has delivered a message on this passage, and I read it carefully and prayerfully. Then I take the other book and turn to the passage, and I carefully read it, and I thank God for the insight of this other preacher.

On a sheet of paper, I make notes of all of these things. All the things that I have read in my Greek New Testament, I make notes of them; and all of these things that I have read in these books that are registered in my wide-margin Bible, I make notes of all of those things. Then having put all of that together, all of these notes, page after page of them, I humbly bow my head and pray to God to give me a message that I am to deliver to those dear people. And God never fails in answering that prayer. I write down all of the things that God puts in my heart about that passage in the twentieth and nineteenth chapters of Matthew, then I make an outline of it; and I keep that outline and file it over here in this cabinet, and I stand up and I preach, and I preach according to that outline.

I make an outline on a folded piece of paper, and there are four pages to it: one page, turn it, two page, three, four. And I make a full outline of that sermon on that folded page, and when I stand up there to preach—I have a good memory—I preach down this page, then I turn it and I preach down that page, then I cross over and preach down this page, and then I turn it and I preach down the last page. And all of my sermons are prepared like that, and I deliver all of them just like that.

Now, of course, while I'm up there extemporaneously preaching, why many other things come to my heart and mind; but the great mass of the message lies in that outline that I have made on those four pages.

When I speak to preachers, and particularly young ministers, I try to tell them as fervently as I know how: when you are called to the church and stand up there in the pulpit, you make an announcement to them that you want to be left alone in the morning. Nobody calls you, nobody rings the telephone, nobody knocks at the door, nobody invite you to a committee meeting, nobody to expect you in the foyer or in the presence of the people. You tell them you want to be left alone in the morning: nobody seeks you out, call you, or interfere with your work dedicated to God in the morning.

Then tell them that you will do anything in the afternoon to further the work of the people of God: you'll go to any committee meeting, you'll make any visit, you'll do anything to help build the church. Then at night: tell them that at night you'll attend any meeting, any convocation, any group that furthers the message and ministry of the gospel; but you want to be left alone in the morning. And take that morning every morning and dedicate it to prayer, to study, to sermon preparation.

And I can tell you this: If you'll do that, when you stand up to preach the following Sunday morning, they will know that you have been with God, and the Lord will bless you and the people will be blessed by your dedication. There's not anything that could mean more to you and could mean more to the church than that you keep that morning for God.

Now I have an aside to that word. The average length of a pastorate in our Baptist denomination is hardly two years. The preacher burns out. He comes to the end of his way. But if you will do as I have outlined—keep that morning for God—you will grow and grow and grow in your pastorate; and when you come to the end of two years, you've hardly started; when you come to the end of ten years, you've hardly started; and after you've been there and pastored the church for over fifty years, you still have as many marvelous and wonderful things to preach as you did at the beginning. There's not anything that will enrich the course of a preaching ministry and a pulpit declaration of the saving grace of God as keeping that morning for the Lord and standing up there in that pulpit with a message from heaven.

Sometimes I say, "You know, a preacher paces up and down his study crying, 'O God, what shall I preach this coming Sunday? What shall I say?'" And I add, "I also pace up and down my study. Only my concern and burden is, 'Dear God, I'm going to die before I even get through this preaching of the message of Christ that I find in Holy Scripture.'"

Did you know, one time when I came here to Dallas, at the beginning of my ministry, I announced that I was going to preach through the Bible? They had never heard of anybody doing that. So the deacons gathered around me and said, "Young pastor, you're going to kill the church. Nobody is coming to the church to hear a man preach on Zechariah or Habakkuk or Nahum. I don't even know where they are in the Bible." But I did it: I started at Genesis, and I preached for eighteen years through the Bible. Where I left off Sunday morning, I started Sunday night, and I preached through to the Revelation.

I had a problem, I do admit: you couldn't get in the church house. The people so thronged to *hear those sermons on the Word of God and there wasn't room for them in our large sanctuary, and that's when I began preaching twice every Sunday morning. And many, many of those sermons have been published in the fifty-four books that have been published under my name.*

[Tim Miller] Fifty-four books over fifty years—incredible! And now it's time for you to carry on wherever the Lord leads you. Thank you, Dr. Criswell, for those long, faithful hours out of the public spotlight, pouring over those books, on your knees for God, and one incredible pulpit ministry.

THE LEADER

The leadership of Dr. W.A. Criswell was evident as he took a downtown urban church that for all practical purposes should have been dying and built it into a "successful anachronism." His leadership was not only recognized by his church and state but by the Southern Baptist Convention. Wherever he went in the Convention and the things he did have both been an extension of what he has been and done in the First Baptist Church of Dallas.

President of Southern Baptist Convention 1968

Although Dr. Criswell had been asked through the years, he would not permit his name to be nominated for Presidency of the Convention. He always declined because his first allegiance was to his local congregation. In 1968 a group consisting of Wade Freeman, Ramsey Pollard, and James Coggin went to see Dr. Criswell and encouraged him to run for the presidency at the Convention in Houston.

Then the race was on! Three men were in the race. The term "running" implied that the men were actively seeking the job. In that sense, it applied to only one of the three—Gerald Miller, pastor of Poplar Avenue Baptist Church in Memphis, Tennessee. The other two men were Owen Cooper, a Mississippi layman and Dr. W.A. Criswell, pastor of First Baptist Dallas. Cooper and Criswell were not campaigning for the office.

The mood in Houston in June 1968 of the messengers and speakers at the convention was "Come now, and let us reason together." They, like most Americans, seemed overwhelmed by the complexities of the day. In nominating Criswell for the position, James Coggin said that Criswell was the most popular and widely read pastor in the denomination.

The election results were announced. W.A. Criswell, pastor, First Baptist Church Dallas, Texas was elected president; Owen Cooper, a Yazoo City, Mississippi industrialist, first vice president; Lee Porter, pastor, First Baptist Church, Bellaire, Texas, second vice president; Porter Routh, treasurer; W. Fred Kendall, registration secretary; and Clifton J. Allen, recording secretary.

It was a general feeling that W.A. Criswell had a good prospect of going down in Southern Baptist Convention history as being one of the all-time greats among the distinguished train of leaders to fill the Convention's top position. President Criswell was already a very popular speaker; therefore, the multitude of new speaking invitations was carefully considered and only a very few accepted.

Re-election as President of the Convention 1969

The Southern Baptist Convention in New Orleans, 1969 was more interesting than was anticipated and far from routine. Perhaps the biggest item of interest was something that never happened. James Forman, the proponent of the Black Manifesto, was in the shadow of the minds of many messengers throughout the convention, but he never showed up.

While most messengers were in meetings, two dissident groups made plans for demonstrating. One of the groups was concerned members of Biblical interpretation and the other about social issues and concern. On the opening night, Dr. Criswell delivered the Presidential Address entitled "Christ in Faith and Work." He pleaded for a balanced ministry of evangelism and social responsibility in the convention.

Dr. Criswell and Dr. William C. Smith, Jr., Assistant Professor of Religion at the University of Richmond were the candidates for the presidency. Smith stated that his intention was to let the liberal wing of the convention be heard. The Baptists rejected the liberal challenge and re-elected W.A. Criswell to a second term as President. Criswell received a total of 7,482 of the 8,179 votes. Lee Porter of Bellaire, Texas was elected first vice president; Harper Shannon of Dothan, Alabama was elected second vice president. The other executive officers elected in 968 were re-elected.

Dr. Criswell affirmed that the criticism by the liberals in the convention concerning his speaking and writing prompted his desire to be re-elected. After the criticism of his books, Criswell said that he could not turn his back on the whole controversy. Adjectives used to describe the Southern Baptist Convention in New Orleans 1969 by several editorials in Baptist state papers throughout the convention ranged from "great" to "the lousiest" with all sorts of descriptive phrases in between.

Dr. W.A. Criswell—the person, the speaker, the leader, has produced both unity and controversy in the Southern Baptist Convention. Why was he elected and re-elected? The following chapters have sought to answer the question.

DR. W.A. CRISWELL SERMONS AND COMMENTARY

THE FIFTH SPARROW

Dr. W. A. Criswell
Criswell's First Sermon at First Baptist Dallas, Luke 12:16
November 19, 1944

I suppose toward the back of the auditorium you cannot see this splendid sight down here in front. Practically all the seats immediately before this pulpit are filled with young people and intermediates. It is the best sight in the world. I hope you sit there every Sunday night.

As I sit in the pulpit and look down over the congregation, I wonder who you are and what you do. That fellow with his wife, that girl over there by herself, all up and down these pews; I just wonder who you are. Well, it will take some time to know you personally, I suppose. Right now, it is like a flood; I get drowned in it all. My head swims, but by and by I hope the day will come to pass when the vast majority of the people who belong to this church, I can call them by name. "How are you, my friend Bill, Jack, John, Henry?" And if I ever get up enough nerve, "How is it with you, Elizabeth, Mary, Sarah?" and all the rest; it is lots of fun knowing people, most fun in the world. And as time goes on, I will get to associate you with different things: here's a fine-looking woman married to a sorry-looking man. I'll remember her. Here is a fine deacon and his family. Here is a fine teacher in the Sunday school. I will get to associate everybody with something. I could have only one wish against that, and that is that we could just win so many people to the Lord you would never know them all. By the time you got this far, there would be that many more new faces to know. May the Lord grant it! Why could it not be so? This vast city, teaming with thousands—of course, you are accustomed to it, but I'm not. I feel it. No wonder the Lord said "Look up." They are all around, this people to be won to the Lord. That's what we are for.

Now for the sermon: the name of it wouldn't mean much to you, it's called, "The Fifth Sparrow," or "The Christian Philosophy of Life." The words of Christ are quoted usually in several ways. Matthew will present it one way, Mark another, and Luke another. And John sometimes would see a thing one way, and again he would say the same thing just a little differently, and sometimes those differences bring out a wonderful lesson. This is the way it is in Matthew:

> *Are not two sparrows sold for a farthing?*
> *and one of them shall not fall on the ground without your Father.*
> *But the very hairs of your head are all numbered.*
> *Fear ye not therefore, ye are of more value than many sparrows."*
> > *[Matthew 10:29-31]*

Now in Luke: Are not five sparrows sold for two farthings, and not one of them is forgotten before God?

> *But even the very hairs of your head are all numbered.*
> *Fear not therefore: ye are of more value than many sparrows.*
> > *[Luke 12:6-7]*

Now look at the words over here in Matthew: "Are not two sparrows sold for a farthing" -- a penny, less than a copper cent, "two sparrows for a farthing." Now in Luke: "Are not five sparrows sold for two farthings?" Now, you look. If two sparrows cost one farthing, four sparrows could be bought for two farthings, isn't that right? If they were two a farthing, four of them would cost two farthings, but when Jesus quoted the proverb, He said, "Are not five sparrows sold for two farthings?" One farthing will buy two sparrows; two farthings will buy four sparrows and one extra, just thrown in to make it a deal. Now Jesus picked out that fifth sparrow—thrown in just extra—and said, "Not one of them," that one just thrown in for nothing, "not one of them is forgotten of God" [Luke 12:16], that fifth sparrow.

I wonder if I could make it better by taking a scene out of Jerusalem. Martha—aged Jewish mother in Israel—is a poor mother, as most aged people are poor. Every morning she made her way down the narrow, steep side streets to the place where the market man opened his shop for the poor. Dear old Martha goes to the shop as she has been doing for years and years. She inquires the price of every piece of meat in the establishment. She has always done that, and the market keeper, in patience and love, told her the price of everything. And finally, dear old Martha said, "How much are the sparrows?" And the market keeper replied, "They are two a farthing." And she untied a knot in the sash of her dress and put on the counter a coin, and the market keeper pushed forward two sparrows. The old mother busies herself on the other side of her dress and took out another piece of coin, and the old market keeper pushed across two other sparrows and then, in a question repeated so often it had arisen to the category of a proverb, "Are not five sparrows sold for two farthings?" And the market keeper smiled acquiescence and pitched in the fifth one for nothing, just to complete the trade. Martha gathers the meal together and takes it home to eat with the poor. Now Jesus had seen that all His life. Jesus had watched that from boyhood, and that little extra bird thrown in for nothing had appealed to His childish heart. When He becomes God's messenger on the earth, He said "God knew! God knew when it fell to the ground" [Matthew 10:29]. Somebody wrote a poem:

> *I am only a sparrow,*
> *A bird of low degree.*
> *My life is of little value,*
> *But the dear Lord cares for me.*
>
> *I know there are many sparrows.*
> *All over the world we are found,*
> *But our Heavenly Father knoweth*
> *If one of us falls to the ground.*

[from "A Sparrow's Song," quoted in A Christian's Secret to a Happy Life, Hannah Whitall Smith, 1875]

There are many, many things in this world that argue well as to the worthlessness of man. What is a man to the world? That is one soul among millions, yea, billions that inhabit this universe. When I read the newspapers—oh, how awful! Russia says, "We have slain eight million German soldiers." And Germany responds, "We have annihilated ten million Russian infantrymen, artillerymen and airmen." And then the world says, "Besides, Russia has lost a good fifteen million of their population." And oh! What of the Polish, the Greeks, the Slavs, and the Slovenians, and millions of others who have lost their lives in this war? What is one "fifth sparrow"?

Once in a while I think of the irony of some of our communiqués. We have invaded such-and-such an island and we have taken it with slight cost. And maybe a few days after that victory, I walk up to a door and knock, and the dear mother is bowed in grief. It was her boy who lost his life in a cheap victory—a "fifth sparrow."

All the world itself, I suppose, is so put together that a man might have reason to think that whether he lives or dies, what is it? Like a pebble on a beach, just like one other star in the sky. If one of you failed to reach home in so great a city, whose soul is sadder? Who are we in the earth, and what is our earth in its universe? When I stare into the skies, the eternal silence of the infinite terrifies me, and when they tell us of the light years and billions of light years that separate the earth from the moon, the stars, and the sun in this universe, in this great cosmic creation; and when they tell us our galaxy is one of the smallest of all, and our earth is one of the smallest planets around the sun—and could put our earth inside itself and the moon could still swing around without touching either side—when you read those astronomical figures, what is a man in the earth? What is your life, or mine?

That is the reason science ends in defeatism and despair. That is the reason infidelity is dead and cold. That is the reason that you and I have embraced the Christian philosophy of life. Jesus says that fifth sparrow, thrown in for nothing—God saw it when it fell to the ground. That lad over there who lost his life in his own blood; and that exiled Jew over there, despised by a fascist government; and those people in China and Russia were all "precious in My sight" [Psalm 116:15]. Not a one of them fell that God didn't see it; the Christian interpretation of life.

The fifth sparrow: what is it? The fifth sparrow is a little child. Why, he is that little boy that plays in your yard, and lives on your street, and you don't pay any attention to him. It is that little girl that lives down your way, and you don't pay any attention to her. Oh, how precious they are in God's sight!

You know, I wonder if I could tell you this without your thinking I am assuming too much. I was holding a meeting in Ponca City, Oklahoma, where the Conoco Oil Company has an establishment. God was there. On Tuesday night of the second week, God especially visited us in power. Many people were saved. After the service all that group were down in the front. I got in line and was shaking hands with the people, and while I was there, there was a strong, sturdy man with great big heavy hands and arms who came and looked in my face and said, "Your name is W. A." I said, "Yes." "And were you born in Eldorado?" I said, "Yes, sir." "And was your father's name Wallie?" I said, "Yes, sir." And he put his hands on my shoulders and began to cry like a baby. I was surprised! I was dumbfounded! That big man, looking into my face and just too full for words, in a moment he began to talk, "Oh, the grace of God! Oh, the glory of God!" Did you ever hear anybody shout? People, when they shout, don't say things connectedly and logically; that was the way he talked. "Oh, the grace of God! The glory of God!" He was the blacksmith in that town of Eldorado, and he was the superintendent of the Sunday school and, "You were in the Card class, and many's the day when I have beat that iron out on the anvil and that little boy, W. A. has seen the sparks fly. And I never dreamed that the little boy who stood by my anvil in the blacksmith shop—I never dreamed that God would call him to be a preacher, and the favor of God would rest on him. Tonight it is too much for me." That is not much, I know. But I tell you, the heart of that old blacksmith filled me so I can feel it yet. God has his eye on that little boy or girl; that fifth sparrow.

It is the aged, oh! the loneliest road in life for the most part. There are exceptions to it, I know, but for the most part the loneliest road in life that I know is the life of the aged. They have buried their friends; many have left them alone. They walk in sorrow, senility, age, and death. That is the reason the Book says, "Remember your father and mother." It is the first commandment with promise, "that it may be well with thee in the land that the Lord thy God giveth thee" [Exodus 20:12]. Don't forget that old, feeble, gray-headed, tottery man. Don't forget that aged mother whose children have already been buried and whose friends have already gone, and is largely forgotten; God has His eye on them. They are dear in His sight.

Who is the fifth sparrow? It is the poor. It is the poor. Listen, my brother, the church who lives tomorrow is the church that ministers to the poor today. There is no such thing as a church propagating itself in luxury. It is the poor people, the rank-and-file of the people, who tomorrow will hold the reins of this world in their hands. That is the reason God has blessed our Baptist churches. One hundred years ago, practically every Baptist church was built alongside a railroad track. It was almost a stigma to belong to a Baptist church, and it was only the poor and riffraff that belonged to the Baptist church. But those Baptist people—poor as they were, hard-working as they were—those Baptist people, please God, they were true to the Book. They held meetings. They felled the woods. They built arbors, constructed tents. They went out visiting. They won the lost. Consequently, wherever they work, they have taken the earth. So don't forget the poor. Some are poor because of mismanagement. I know from my own life that a lot of people are poor because of things over which they had no control. We were poor because the wind blew everything that we had away; when in the northwestern part of our state, the wind blew our farm away. Don't forget the poor.

"Give me that little slave boy, nobody wants him. Give him to Me," says God; and God made Booker T. Washington out of him, one of the greatest Baptists ever born. "And give Me that criminal, that outcast, and I will make Terry McAuley out of him. That poor boy living in Scotland — give him to Me, and I will make him David Livingstone, to take the light to a dark continent." The poor! The poor! And from this moment on, as God will open your hearts, I have a program to offer to this church concerning some of the people that live in Dallas; the poor—that fifth sparrow.

Who is that fifth sparrow? Could I suggest just another? That fifth sparrow is the lost. You know it is easy to spend time with you and it is pleasant. I love to come to see you and I love for you to come to see me. It is one of the happiest things of life for us to spend our time together, and oh my! What a good thing it is to have a great fellowship, and we want it that way. But listen, my brother: I will tell you what God wants us to do. He wants me to go up and down the streets of Dallas and knock on the doors of people who never think about going to church. He wants you to do the same. We could spend our lives down here loving one another and it would be easy, for you have been saved like I and have been baptized. It is easy to do it that way. He wants us to go out to see that fellow that abhors His name, and to see that family that gives their lives to iniquity. He has His eyes on them. He died for them; they are precious in His sight; that fifth sparrow, the lost! The lost!

You know, one time when I was a youngster, seventeen years old, I had just come to Baylor. I was walking along the Brazos River. I saw a little hut made out of kindling wood. It stood down there on the river where the owner didn't have to buy any property, didn't have to pay any taxes, and there was a young colored boy sitting on the steps. I walked over and looked at him. I said, "Hello, fellow." He said, "Howdy!" I said, "What are you doing here?" He said,

"Inside is an old Negro man dying, and I hated for him to die without anybody around." He was sitting here waiting for him to die, and he would go call somebody. I don't know why that thing stayed in my heart except for this; I have recalled it time and time again. And every time, with this spirit: I would give most anything if I could go back to that day when I was 17, when I was walking along the Brazos, and do you know what I would do? I would say to him, "Young fellow, if you don't mind, could I go in?" I would go in to that old fellow's house. I would look into his face, and if he were still conscious, I would say, "My friend and my brother for whom Christ died, is it all right?" If he said it was all right, I would say I wanted to pray. If he said it wasn't all right, do you know what I would do? I would do my dead level best to show him how to die, for I think he is a fifth sparrow.

> I know there are many sparrows.
> All over the world we are found,
> But our Heavenly Father knoweth
> If one of us falls to the ground.
>   [Author unknown]

Oh, what a comfort it is to me to know that my Father watches over me, and what a comfort it is to me to know that there is not one of us but for whom Christ died, whose name is in the eye of God, and He knows and He cares. Blessed be the name of our God! Blessed be His Holy name! My friend, I offer Him to you tonight; your Savior, your Friend, your Comforter, your Lover, your Redeemer, your sympathizing Savior! I offer Him to you tonight; yours for the asking, yours for the taking, the receiving. And to those who believe in the faith and in this gospel, who respond to the appeal to place their lives in this church, and who come to and for any reason, God bids you here.

COMMENTARY

The Fifth Sparrow

This was the first sermon Dr. Criswell preached at First Baptist Church, Dallas, Texas. He was warm with his first greetings to the congregation. In his colloquial way he stated, "As I stand in the pulpit and look over the congregation, I wonder who you are and what you do. That fellow with his wife, that girl over there by herself, all up and down these pews. Well, it will take some time to know you personally, I suppose. Right now, it is like a flood; I drowned in it all. My head swims, but by and by I hope the day will come to pass when the vast majority of the people who belong to this church, I can call them by name. "How are you, my friend Bill, Jack, John, Henry?" And if I ever get up enough nerve, "How is it with you, Elizabeth, Mary, Sarah?" and all the rest; it is lots of fun knowing people, most fun in the world. I will get to associate everybody with something. I could have only one wish against that, and that is that we could just win so many people to the Lord you would never know them all. By the time you got this far, there would be that many more new faces to know. May the Lord grant it! Why could it not be so? This vast city, teeming with thousands—of course, you are accustomed to it, but I'm not. I feel it. No wonder the Lord said "Look up." They are all around, this people to be won to the Lord. That's what we are here for."

The issues come out in what he called, "The Fifth Sparrow," or "The Christian Philosophy of Life." The words of Christ were usually quoted in several ways. Matthew presented it one way, Mark another, and Luke another. John sometimes would see a thing one way, and again he would say the same thing just a little differently, and sometimes those differences brought out an incredible lesson. The word said that as a man thinks, so is he. Therefore, the gospel of Jesus Christ must be presented to the people of Dallas and the whole world.

The propositions advocated by Criswell dealt with the lost souls. He simply said that there were many, many things in this world that argued well as to the worthlessness of man. What is a man to the world? That is one soul among millions, yea, billions that inhabit this universe. All the world itself, I suppose, is so put together that a man might have reason to think that whether he lives or dies, what is it? Criswell continued to ask questions. Who are we in the earth, and what is our earth in its universe? When you read those astronomical figures, what is a man in the earth? What is your life, or mine? That is the reason science ends in defeatism and despair. That is the reason infidelity is dead and cold. That is the reason that you and I have embraced the Christian philosophy of life. Jesus says that fifth sparrow, thrown in for nothing—God saw it when it fell to the ground. That lad over there who lost his life in his own blood; and that exiled Jew over there, despised by a fascist government; and those people in China and Russia were all "precious in My sight" [Psalm 116:15]. Not a one of them fell that God didn't see it; the Christian interpretation of life.

Criswell called on the congregation to take action and decide to win the lost. He put it this way, what is a man to the world? That is one soul among millions, yea, billions that inhabit this universe. The reason science ends in defeatism and despair. That is the reason infidelity is dead and cold. That is the reason that you and I have embraced the Christian philosophy of life. Jesus says that fifth sparrow, thrown in for nothing—God saw it when it fell to the ground. Who is the fifth sparrow? It is the poor. Listen, my brother, the church who lives tomorrow is the church that ministers to the poor today.

Who is that fifth sparrow? Could I suggest just another? That fifth sparrow is the lost. You know it is easy to spend time with you, and it is pleasant. I love to come to see you and I love for you to come to see me. It is one of the happiest things of life for us to spend our time together. He wants me to go up and down the streets of Dallas and knock on the doors of people who never think about going to church. He wants you to do the same. He has His eyes on them. He died for them; they are precious in His sight; that fifth sparrow, the lost!

In conclusion, Criswell asked the people to come to Christ. He stated. "I offer Him to you tonight; your Savior, your Friend, your Comforter, your Lover, your Redeemer, your sympathizing Savior! And to those who believe in the faith and in this gospel, who respond to the appeal to place their lives in this church, and who come to and for any reason, God bids you here. I will tell you what God wants us to do. He wants me to go up and down the streets of Dallas and knock on the doors of people who never think about going to church. He wants you to do the same. We could spend our lives down here loving one another and it would be easy. It is easy to do it that way. He wants us to go out to see that fellow that abhors His name, and to see that family that gives their lives to iniquity. He has His eyes on them. He died for them; they are precious in His sight; that fifth sparrow, the lost! The lost!"

THE DOWNTOWN CHURCH

Dr. W. A. Criswell
Acts 18, Janurary 3rd, 1954

For the last several years I have made a habit, fallen into the habit, I choose to do it, of preaching a sermon on the downtown church the first Sunday of each New Year. And this morning, gladly, happily, for it's in my soul, I follow that pattern. The message is on our church, located in the heart of the city of Dallas.

In our preaching through the Bible we have come to the eighteenth chapter of the Book of Acts. There is a text in this chapter that shall be a background for the message this morning, and then tonight the message will be an exposition of the passage in which the text is found. This is the word in the eighteenth chapter of the Book of Acts, the ninth and the tenth verses:

Then spake the Lord to Paul in the night by a vision, Be not afraid, but speak, and hold not thy peace:

For I am with thee, and no man shall see on thee to hurt thee: for I have much people in this city.

Acts 18:10: For I have much people in this city. Could I say first a pastoral word to our people? On the twenty-fourth day of this month, twenty-fourth of January, that would be the fourth Sunday of this month, it is our hope to have an open house all day long, and to dedicate this vast plan to the glory of Christ and to the preaching of the gospel and to the ministry of our Lord among His people. We have spent something like three and a half million dollars in preparing for this day. That glorious building there, our new activities building, that glorious building there, our parking and recreational building, and the remaking of this vast seven story of the Truett Building. All of it together has amounted to about three and a half million dollars. It will soon be complete. And on the twenty-fourth day of January, this month, we hope to have a glorious opening, a dedication, a giving of it to God, to the city, and to the Lord's people.

Now, two appeals from the heart of the pastor. First to our young people, the youth of our church: because of this vast program, we now have a debt on our church; and the reason we have that debt is for you, our young people and the youth of our church. When we first began our preparation of the plans for that building across the street, it was two stories above ground; going to be made for seven stories ultimately, but we began with two stories above the ground. Then as we began to think about the needs of our intermediates, and of our young people, and of all of our youth, we made a recommendation that was accepted by our men that we place a third story on that building, and just rough it in, not finish it at all. So it was agreed to add the third story, but not complete it, rough it in; the outside walls, put a roof on it. Then as time continued, long, the war, the steel strikes, many other things stopped us in the work, our young people's work, our intermediate work, our children's work, the whole church began to grow so tremendously until we came again before the men, our deacons, and said it will cost thousands of dollars to place the third floor, put a roof on it, when we need so desperately the fourth floor. It will have to be built. Rather than waste the thousands of dollars of finishing the building at the third floor, then starting over again, tearing off the roof, tearing off the steeple, and putting the fourth floor on it, it would be the part of wisdom in behalf of the youth of our church to go ahead, to go in debt, to build that fourth floor, and just rough it in.

So our men agree to go into debt that much more in order to place the fourth floor on that building and just rough it in. As the time went by, our people began to say, "What? Leave that unfinished? When we so desperately need the room?" There were two departments meeting in this auditorium; there were other places desperately crying for a place to grow, meet, any place. So we went again before our men and said, "Do we have enough faith in God to believe that if we finished it all, that the Lord would see us through?" The men, our deacons, brought that to you in a Sunday morning service; and you voted formally to go ahead and to complete that building upside, inside, outside, every side, up and down. That is the reason we have this debt. Young people, we did that for you, for you. And we believe that it will bear a gracious recompense in your love and your response. We believe you will form and fashion and mold here the greatest young people's program to be found anywhere in the earth.

I have one other pastoral word. May I make a plea on bended knee to our Sunday school? Today is the third of January, the first Sunday in January; next Lord's Day is the tenth; the next Lord's Day is the seventeenth; the next Lord's Day is that great high day, the twenty-fourth. On bended knee, let me make appeal to our Sunday school that by the seventeenth of this month, the third Sunday of January, that you settle down in your work. Right now, there are parts of our Sunday school that are up in the air. You don't have a place, you don't have a teacher, you haven't quite found how in this new organization and in this expanded program quite how you are to fit and to work. We can go on like that indefinitely; a year from now, two years from now, we can still be that way. On bended knee, let me plead that by the seventeenth day of this month, by the third Sunday in January, we have settled those problems. Praying to God for divine wisdom, find your place, get that classroom, seek out that teacher, and all of us together by the third Sunday of this month, Sunday week, by the seventeenth of January, Sunday School settle down, settle down, get to work. Instead of spending energy and time wondering, and hesitating, and staggering, you come down here with our educational leader, with the pastor, with your superintendent, with anybody, get the whole board of deacons together if you want to, but settle that thing. Where are you going to meet? And who's going to be your teacher? And how shall we carry on this path? Do it; your pastor begs, importunes, and pleads. You do that. If you have to quit work for a day and come down here and take half a day off or a day or a week, take it off, come down here, pray through, settle through all of those problems. Then the seventeenth day of this month, let's all be here. Then the twenty-fourth will be our great high day, we're settled, we're pulling, we're ready to go; and the Lord will give us His benedictory, rich, heavenly, rewards. I count on you doing that; I know you will. Then as we progress toward the Easter season, and our revival meeting, we shall give our time, our energies, our souls to the great work for which God hath brought us, and made us, and framed us, and fashioned us, and given us this holy and heavenly hour, all for the church of the Lord Jesus, its downtown ministry and its work.

Go to Richmond, Virginia; walk along the streets of the city of Richmond, Virginia. "Where is the First Baptist Church? I want to go to the First Baptist Church in Richmond, Virginia. I am a visitor here in the city. Where is the church?" And the policeman or the hotel man will reply, "Well, Sir, the First Baptist Church used to be right there, but now you will find it so many miles this way, and so many miles that way, and so many miles that way." Now you must go this, that and the other, and finally you'll see it way out there miles away from the downtown heart of the city.

"Thank you, Sir."

I go to the city of Kansas City, Missouri and I stop a policeman and I say, "Sir, where is the First Baptist Church? Today is the Lord's Day and I want to go to church today."

"Well," said the policeman, "Sir, the First Baptist Church used to be right there, but now you will find it so many miles this way, and so many miles that way, and so many miles that way. And you'll find it way out there somewhere miles from the downtown heart of the city." I go to the city of Memphis, Tennessee, "Sir, I'd like to go to the First Baptist Church. Where is the First Baptist Church?" And the man at the hotel, he says, "Well Sir, it used to be located right down there. But you will find it now so many miles that way, and so many miles that way, and so many miles that way."

The oldest Baptist Church in western Canada was the First Baptist Church of Winnipeg. I read a news item; the news item said, "The oldest church in western Canada, the downtown First Baptist Church of Winnipeg, has voted to disband; and they have sold their properties to the Pentecostal Holiness people." A little while later, a few months later, I read another news article; and this news item said, "The First Baptist Church, the oldest church in Winnipeg, Canada, in western Canada, it disbanded and sold its properties to the Pentecostal Holiness people. But," said this news item, "the church is no longer empty, but it is filled and it overflows every Sunday morning and every Sunday night." God bless our Pentecostal brethren. I may not believe in the second blessing only, I may believe in the third and the fourth and the fifth; and I might not be persuaded that it is wise to speak with tongues unknown in the church, I may be persuaded like Paul that it'd be better to say five words with an understanding than ten thousand words with an unknown tongue; I may not be a Pentecostal holiness; but I thank God sincerely and in my soul, I thank God that there was a people in the city of Winnipeg, Canada who had religion enough and faith enough and devotion enough to buy an abandoned downtown city property, forsaken by the First Baptist Church, and there build again a lighthouse for Jesus Christ.

We are committed, we have settled this thing, we decided: our life is here. These buildings are a vast eloquent "Amen" to that decision that was made in the days of the great pastor, Dr. Truett, and carried on in this present ministry. Our commitment is to the downtown heart of the city of Dallas; a ministry for all of the peoples of this vast metropolitan area. Now why? These things, as I shall have opportunity this morning, these things are just a few of the reaffirmations that live in our souls, we who belong to this downtown church.

We are here for an ideological reason. If I were a politician I'd say we are here for a democratic reason. If I were a sociologist I would say we're here for a social reason. If I were speaking culturally I'd say we are here for a humanitarian reason. But I like to use right now that word "ideological." You see there has been precipitated in our modern life a war that goes far beyond any battle with guns or bombs or bullets or jet planes; fundamentally, actually, really, back of this world confrontation lies a war for the hearts and the minds and the souls of men. It's a war of talk, it's a war of ideas, it is an ideological war.

Communism is not a new thing in this earth; it's about as old as humanity. It was Carl Marx and Fredrick Ingles that gave it dynamic. And in order to oppose the idea of

Communism, the idea of fascism was conceived, and you had those two tremendous forces that brought our world to its holocaust in the 1940's. And we are in that same conflict today. The fundamental drive that Communism seeks to make is always an ideological drive: they try to propagate the idea, the feelings, the emotional response, the intellectual acceptance of class distinctions, class hatreds. Communism always begins in trying to set capital against labor, the employer against the employee, the illiterate against the literate, the bourgeoisie against the proletariat, the rich against the poor. They find their foothold in any place, in any country, by driving through those bitter, hateful class distinctions. There is a tendency in society that they exploit. There is ever a tendency among humanity to fall into class groups. In a city, the rich will live somewhere; they don't live where the poor live. The poor live somewhere, they don't live where the rich live. The middle class will live somewhere, the laborer will live somewhere, the capitalist will live somewhere, and there is a tendency in all human society to pull apart. That thing is carried through in religious life and in church life. There's a rich man's church; there's a poor man's church; and there's a middle class church. And the communists have a field day in the breeding, and in the encouraging, and in the propagating of bitter class hatreds among the people. I say, there is an ideological reason for the downtown church: it has in its fold, in its fellowship, and in its membership it has the great cross section of all of the peoples of the city.

The bourgeoisie is here, that's right. The capitalist is here, that's right. The investor is here, that's right. The rich man is here; that's right. The professional man is here, that's right. The well-to-do are here, that's right. The literate and the educated are here, that's right; your PhD's and your LLD's, and your MD's, they are here, that's right. But they are not here alone. Seated by your side may be the janitor of the Baptist building across the street, or one of the kitchen help in the YMCA across that street, or one of the workmen in the building across that street. By your side may be some poor woman who works with a needle, who's a seamstress, whose hands stand between her and utter starvation; or the nurses of the community chest, we're all down here together, all of us are down here together. Our children come to the same Sunday School, we worship in the same house, we call on the name of the same Lord, we share the hymnbook, we listen to the reading of the Word, and we follow what our pastor has to say. I like it, I like it. I would not be pastor unless God sent me, made me go unto the same way that Jonah went to Ninevah; I would not be pastor of a class church. Time and time and time again was I called to be pastor of suburban churches when I was in my sixth year beyond the seminary in Louisville, Kentucky. My first six years in and Muskogee, Oklahoma, I was called, I could not tell you how many times, to the city to preach. I felt in my soul and in my heart, if I ever were anywhere I want to go to a downtown church. The problems are hard; we fight with our back to the wall by day and night. But in that church is the hub of the center of the life of our denomination. And if we lose it, someday we'll lose the entire city. I like it, I like it; the great cross section of the people of the city, everybody's church, a people's church; no snobbery, no better-than-thou, no where'd you come from, no anything but a welcome in the name of the God who loves us and the Christ who died for us all; an ideological reason why we're down here in the heart of the city.

To me, it would be unthinkable, it'd be spiritually impossible to plan a strategy for the Kingdom of Christ in the hearts of men and leave Satan's throne alone in the heart of the city of Dallas. The empire is here, and a growing one; banking, finance, insurance, marketing, merchandising. How many great vast outreaches are there in the heart of this city of Dallas? Those vast office buildings are filled with men who by day and by night are shaping the course of our empire. And down here in the heart of this city is our white way, the bright light, clubs of every kind and description, there's a dice game, and there's a joint, and there's a den, and there's a dive, all in the heart of the great city of Dallas. So we shall leave it, we shall move out where it's easy, where we can just sit down and the people come to us, while the lazy fathers and mothers just dump their children in our laps while they go off to go back to bed or to recline supinely at home. No Sir, no Sir; we'll be down here where Satan has his throne; where anybody who comes to us chooses to come. They have to get up, they have to dress, they have to get their children prepared, they have to drive miles to get down here. But we're here, we're here where the joint is, and the dive is, and the clubs are, and the great office buildings are, and the empire of the world has its throbbing heart, we're here, we're here; and we're here to stay. We're here to stay.

We're here for the stranger and the sojourner and the traveler who comes to the city of Dallas. When he goes down stairs to the desk at the Baker Hotel, or at the Adolphus Hotel, or when he drives through town and asks a policeman, "Sir, we want to go to church today. Where's the First Baptist Church?"

"Well, it's so many miles out that way, so many miles out that way, and so many miles out that way. But right here is the theatre, and right there is the nightclub, and right here is the gambling joint." No Sir, we're there where the masses of the people are; our church, our ministry, this pulpit and the preaching of the Gospel of Christ. "Sir, the First Baptist Church is right down there. Do you see that tall Republic Bank building forty stories up in the air? Just beyond the post office, and just beyond that is the glorious church. You can find it easily, easily." For the stranger and the sojourner, it's here every Sunday morning, every Sunday night, every Wednesday night, faithfully trying to preach the unsearchable riches of the gospel of the Son of God. We are here for them, for them. For what Texas means, and what America means, and what Dallas can mean to our state and to the world.

We are here for the young people who come into this city. Reason I'm doubly sensitive about that, I grew up in a little town. The little town now has a population of three hundred; when I left, two hundred and ninety-nine others left with me; used to have six hundred when I lived there. Little bitty town, grew up in a little bitty town. Don't you laugh at me as though I were a hayseed; you grew up in a little town too, or out in the country, one or the other. There are not many of you who grew up in the big city. Most of us grew up in the little country, the little town. Don't you look supercilious either brother, I know where you came from. Most of us grew up in little places.

What was the dream that I had in my heart as I grew up as a boy? When it was good, when it was bad, whether I ought to have had it, or whether I should not have had it, the dream that I had in my heart when I grew up as a boy was, "Someday, I'll get to leave this little place; I'll go away to college, I'll get educated. Then I'll go to the big city." And I wasn't any different from practically all of the young people who grow up now as then in our little places. They're not planning to stay on the farm, not many of them. Nor are they planning to stay in the little town, not many of them; practically all of our young people in their hearts are dreaming of the day when they get a job and go to the city. And they come, they come by the hundreds, they come by the thousands. They leave those little places and they come to the city; they come to Dallas. Then what? Then what?

Oh, in the heart of the city is a lighthouse; in the heart of the city is the best, finest, happiest, most golden of all the ministries that the world could ever find or see. Right over there, there's a gymnasium as big as Baylor University's; it's as big as Southern Methodist University's. We don't have as much bleacher space, we don't need it, but the gymnasium is as large. And right next to it are bowling lanes, and there's shuffle boards, and bad mitten courts, and volleyball courts, and right underneath that is a skating rink, the best one I've ever seen in my life; all of it over there. And over yonder is a craft room and an activities room; young people, for the young people that pour into this city. Somebody said to me, "Pastor, what are you going to do when you open that building over there with those bowling lanes, and that skating rink, and that gymnasium, and these craft rooms? You're going to find yourself deluged, fronted by a thousand young people. What are you going to do with them?"

I said, "Hallelujah! Let them come, I'd like to be fronted and deluged. We'll win some of them. We'll get a hold of some of them. We'll make preachers out of some of them, and deacons out of some of them, and Christians out of some of them."

Let them come, let them come. We built it for them, for them. And what about us old folks? Well, I'm not going to skate, I'm not going to do some other things up there. I'm going to bowl; I had them put the bowling alley for all of us who are old. And also, we're buying some checkers. We're all going to have a good time, all of us are. Grandad is going to have a good time. Grandma's going to have a good time. Pa and Ma, they're going to have a good time. And the children are going to have a good time. We're all going to have a good time in God's house, down here, in this beloved First Baptist Church.

And I close. We're here in behalf of the vast, uncounted, submerged, unnamed, nameless, thousands and thousands who always press into the heart of a great city. You don't know their name, you just see them passing by. I don't know their names, I just watch them and wonder who they are, how do they fare, how is it with them. Oh, the thousands and the thousands that crowd into any great city, and who crowd into ours. A ministry to them, to them, to them.

John Wesley, the friends of John Wesley, he's not buried there, they put a beautiful plaque in Westminster Abbey. And on that plaque are five of the famous sayings of John Wesley. I can't remember the middle three, but I remember the first one and the last one. The last one is this: "God buries the workman, but the work goes on." I remember that one. I remember the first one. The first one was this: "The world is my parish." He said that when the church pushed him out, didn't have any place to preach, and there wasn't a church in all England that would open its doors to John Wesley that he might preach. So John Wesley turned his back away from his church and said that sentence, "Then the world is my parish." We'd say, "The world is my field." I'm that way about the city of Dallas. The whole city is my parish. Anybody to whom we can minister, anybody whom we can help, anybody to whom we can mediate the love and the grace and the mercy of Christ Jesus our Lord in the heart of the city of Dallas, for the heart of the city of Dallas.

God bless the church on the downtown street,
That hears the city's cry
The church that throws the seed of the Word
To the masses of men that go by
The church that makes 'mid the city's roar

A place for an altar of prayer
With a heart for the rich, with a heart for the poor,
And rejoices their burden to share
The church that's moved by the call of Christ
Who wept o'er the city's need
Who sent His disciples to work for Him
Where the forces of evil breed
The church that gives and the church that lives
As seen by the Master's eye
God bless the church on the downtown street,
That answers the city's cry

[Adapted from "The City Church"; Ralph Walker]

The world is my parish, the city of Dallas is my pastorate; the Lord sanctify and hallow our efforts here for Him.

All right Billy, let's sing our song. And while we sing it, side to side, anywhere, everywhere, somebody you, this day give your heart to the Lord, give your life to Him, or come into the fellowship of this church. One somebody you, or a family you, however God shall say the word and make the appeal. While we sing our song today, would you come? Go down that stairwell, down here by me, anywhere. Find your way down here to the front, give me your hand, "Pastor, my heart I've given to God, my hand I give to you. Put my life with you in this ministry, here I come, here I am. I make it now; while we stand and while we sing."

COMMENTARY

The Downtown Church

The sermon took place at the First Baptist Church of Dallas the first Sunday of the new year. For the last several years Criswell have made a habit of preaching a sermon on the downtown church the first Sunday of each New Year. The message was on the church, located in the heart of the city of Dallas.

In preaching through the Bible Criswell revealed that they had come to the eighteenth chapter of the Book of Acts. Acts 18:10: "For I have much people in this city." Then he asked to speak a personal word to the church, "Could I say first a pastoral word to our people? On the twenty-fourth day of this month, it is our hope to have an open house all day long, and to dedicate this vast plan to the glory of Christ and to the preaching of the gospel and to the ministry of our Lord among His people. We have spent something like three and a half million dollars in preparing for this day. That glorious building there, our new activities building, that glorious building there, our parking and recreational building, and the remaking of this vast seven story Truett Building to this side of the auditorium, all of it together has amounted to about three and a half million dollars. It will soon be complete, in and out, up and down."

Dr. Criswell asked people if he could make an appeal to the church. "Now, two appeals from the heart of the pastor. First to our young people, the youth of our church: because of this vast program, we now have a debt on our church; and the reason we have that debt is for you, our young people and the youth of our church. I have one other pastoral word. May I make a plea on bended knee to our Sunday school? On bended knee, let me make appeal to our Sunday school that by the seventeenth of this month, the third Sunday of January, that you settle down in your work. Right now, there are parts of our Sunday school that are up in the air. You don't have a place, you don't have a teacher, you haven't quite found how in this new organization and in this expanded program quite how you are to fit and to work. We can go on like that indefinitely; a year from now, two years from now, we can still be that way. Instead of spending energy and time wondering, and hesitating, and staggering, you come down here with our educational leader, with the pastor, with your superintendent, with anybody, get the whole board of deacons together if you want to, but settle that thing." He revealed that people had questions such as: Where are you going to meet? And who's going to be your teacher? And how shall we carry on this path? Then he announced that the people would pray through, settle through all of those problems. He continued to proclaim, "God hath brought us, and made us, and framed us, and fashioned us, and given us this holy and heavenly hour, all for the church of the Lord Jesus, its downtown ministry and its work.

At this point in the sermon, Criswell used illustration of cities that let the downtown church move away. He stated, "Go to Richmond, Virginia; walk along the streets of the city of Richmond, Virginia. "Where is the First Baptist Church? I want to go to the First Baptist Church in Richmond, Virginia. I am a visitor here in the city. Where is the church?" And the policeman or the hotel man will reply, "Well, Sir, the First Baptist Church used to be right there, but now you will find it so many miles this way, and so many miles that way, and so many miles that way." Now you must go this, that and the other, and finally you'll see it miles away from the downtown heart of the city."

Another illustration was used, "I go to the city of Kansas City, Missouri and I stop a policeman and I say, "Sir, where is the First Baptist Church? Today is the Lord's Day and I want to go to church today." "Well," said the policeman, "Sir, the First Baptist Church used to be right there, but now you will find it so many miles this way, and so many miles that way, and so many miles that way. And you'll find it way out there somewhere miles from the downtown heart of the city."

He continued with examples as he said, "I go to the city of Memphis, Tennessee, "Sir, I'd like to go to the First Baptist Church. Where is the First Baptist Church?" And the man at the hotel, he says, "Well Sir, it used to be located right down there. But you will find it now so miles away."

Criswell then used a sadder illustration as he stated, "The oldest Baptist Church in western Canada was the First Baptist Church of Winnipeg. I read a news, "The oldest church in western Canada, the downtown First Baptist Church of Winnipeg, has voted to disband; and they have sold their properties to the Pentecostal Holiness people."

Criswell proclaimed, "We are committed, we have settled this thing, we decided: our life is here. These buildings are a vast eloquent "Amen" to that decision that was made. Our commitment is to the downtown heart of the city of Dallas; a ministry for all of the peoples of this vast metropolitan area. Now why? These things, as I shall have opportunity this morning, these things are just a few of the reaffirmations that live in our souls, we who belong to this downtown church.

At this point, he stated, "We are here for an ideological reason. If I were a politician I'd say we are here for a democratic reason. If I were a sociologist I would say we're here for a social reason. If I were speaking culturally I'd say we are here for a humanitarian reason. But I like to use right now that word "ideological." You see there has been precipitated in our modern life a war that goes far beyond any battle with guns or bombs or bullets or jet planes; fundamentally, actually, really, back of this world confrontation lies a war for the hearts and the minds and the souls of men. It's a war of talk, it's a war of ideas, it is an ideological war."

A strategic reason, a strategical reason why we're down here in the heart of the city. To me, it would be unthinkable, it'd be spiritually impossible to plan a strategy for the Kingdom of Christ in the hearts of men and leave Satan's throne alone in the heart of the city of Dallas. The empire is here, and a growing one; banking, finance, insurance, marketing, merchandising. We're here to stay.

As Criswell concluded the sermon he said, "And I close. We're here in behalf of the vast, uncounted, submerged, unnamed, nameless, thousands and thousands who always press into the heart of a great city. You don't know their names, you just see them passing by. I don't know their names, I just watch them and wonder who they are, how do they fare, how is it with them. Oh, the thousands and the thousands that crowd into any great city, and who crowd into ours. A ministry to them, to them, to them.

One somebody you, or a family you, however God shall say the word and make the appeal. While we sing our song today, would you come? Go down that stairwell, down here by me, anywhere. Find your way down here to the front, give me your hand, "Pastor, my heart I've given to God, my hand I give to you. Put my life with you in this ministry, here I come, here I am. I make it now; while we stand and while we sing."

SEGREGATION IN SOCIETY

Dr. W. A. Criswell
An Address Delivered to a Joint Session of the South Carolina Legislature
February 22, 1956

You, yourself, know how surprised I am to be here today. I have just finished speaking at the closing session of the State Evangelistic Conference of our denomination in South Carolina and I have come here without even having the opportunity to catch my breath, but it was a signal honor to come and I could do no other thing than to accept the Governor's and your gracious invitation, and if I don't address you right or begin right, why, you charge it up to gross, unadulterated, unmitigated ignorance. I just don't know how to do any better!

Now, our folks where we are, are like the folks where you are, though we're divided by the Mississippi River and by several hundreds of miles. My grandpap and my great grandpap fought in the Confederate Army – one of them on my mother's side and one of them on my father's side. And I knew them as a boy, and to this day I'll refuse to believe that any Yankee I have ever seen whipped either one of my grandpaps. I don't believe they did. I'm like that fellow who said that there was a mistake made at Appomattox Court House. It wasn't General Lee that surrendered his sword to General Grant, but it was General Grant who surrendered his sword to General Lee; and General Lee was too much of a gentleman to call the attention of the press to the mistake.

Well I am also glad not only to be a Southern but I am glad to be a Southern Baptist. You know Paul was a Southern – he was a Southern Baptist. All through those letters in the Bible he says "you all – y'all." That's in the Bible. Now, he wasn't a South Carolinian Baptist for he also said "I have learned that in whatsoever state I am therewith to be content." He wasn't a Palmettoian but he was a glorious exponent of the gospel of Christ.

Now, for just a moment – the occasion of this invitation. I came over here to preach to the State Evangelistic Conference held in the First Baptist Church in this city – a yearly convocation of the Baptist ministers of South Carolina. This is the third year that I have done that. I came on Monday when I was to begin speaking on Tuesday and I happened to be in a little group. And as I listened to the conversation of that little group, just a little informal gathering around a lunch counter, why, they began to say things like this: "Now this thing of desegregation, and this thing of integration. Now we are not to mention that, we are not to speak of that. That is a highly debatable issue, and it is not volative, and it is full of political dynamite and no mention should be said about that." And I thought: Well! Isn't it strange come to pass that a minister of the gospel of the Son of God, whose forebears and predecessors were martyrs and were burned at the stake, isn't it a strange come to pass in our day and in our generation – why the minister is cowardly to circumvent any issue such as that. Well, I just decided I'd no preparation, no plan to speak on any such thing at all. And I did. And that was the occasion of this invitation here this noon-tide. Now, for just a moment, may I say a word about that.

There are people, there are people—they are not our folks. They are not our kind. They are not our stripe. They don't belong to the same world in which we live. I mean that in many categories, lots of categories, American categories, spiritual categories, democratic categories, most every category that I am proud to belong to. There are people who are trying to force upon us a situation and a thing that is a denial of all that we believe in: the cultural life, the social background, the spiritual life in which we are really not children and to which our families belong.

Now, in saying these things we have malice toward none. We don't look down on any race or any creed or any church or any people, nor are we setting ourselves apart, as being any better than anyone else. It is just this – that one of the glories of a democratic society we can choose our friends; we can choose our companions; we can choose the mates that share with us the building of our homes. We can choose our lives. It's a free country. It's a free nation and that thing of … they don't like the word of segregation—but call it that – that thing enters all of the realms of our lives, and there is more escaping from it, if a man has the liberty of choice. For example, our daughter - - we try to rear her in a segregated life. Now, I'm not talking about just colored people. I'm talking about the whole character of her upbringing. We try to segregate her from people that are iniquitous and vile and dirty and low down. We try to throw her in certain groups. we try to pull her away from still other groups. Not that we are trying to be prudish. We are not cads. We don't feel ourselves better than anybody else. It is just the privilege of a father and mother. We have a child, one daughter, and we try to throw around her friends that will be a blessing to her and a blessing to us.

Now, that same thing happens in our homes. We have a home, but I don't go down anybody's street and say, "I'm a great commoner. All of you come into my house and into my home." Maybe I should, but I wouldn't have a home if I did. A home is a man's castle. Those four walls around him - - the word for it if you want to say it - - they're segregated in there - - my wife, my daughter, my mother-in-law, who lives with us. We have a home. We're just there in that home and we invite certain ones in there; and other we do not, not that we hate them or despite them. We just love some of them and there they are in our home. And our home is built upon that; that a man has right of choice. he can bring into that house a woman - - he can't bring just everybody - - any woman. Yes, but I don't believe in segregation. You choose and you built a home with a woman and the children and the friends you invite.

Now, the same thing is with my religion. I'm not looking for the Bishop in Dallas of the Sacred Heart Cathedral which is right over there from me – I'm not looking for that Bishop to come down the aisle at the First Baptist Church in Dallas and shake my hand and say, "Brother, we are going to desegregate. All of us Catholics are coming over here with you and we want you to come with us and we're going to do away with all these segregated church ecclesiastical lines. All of us are going to be together. Why, he's not going down that aisle and giving his life to a Baptist was of serving God. And that's not but half of it. I'm not going down to the Sacred Heart Cathedral and bow myself before what I call his images. I'm not going to do it. I don't hate that Catholic Bishop not his flock, nor his people. All I say to him is this: Your Honor and Your Grace, right over there take your people, and you take your flock, and all of them who are of your persuasion and you worship God as you feel in your heart you should, as your conscience dictates, and Bishop I'll gather my folks and I'll gather my kind, and kin, and like, and tribe and communion, and faith and congregation. We'll be here on this corner and we'll be singing and working and preaching and praising God according to the good old Southern Baptist way. And we'll get along fine and be friends—you over there swinging incense pots and bowing down and going through that litany which is the way he wants to do and I over there in my church, shouting so loud and preaching so loud you can hear me five miles away, having a great time, all of us doing what we want to do. That's America. That's freedom. That's spiritual democracy. All right, the same thing obtains with regard to our church and our colored people. I don't hate Catholics. I don't hate a colored man. I don't look down on a Catholic. I don't look down on a colored man. I don't feel that way about it. I wasn't raised, I wasn't brought up to feel that way about it. They never taught me that I as such was better than anybody else. I was just brought up like this and this is the kind of church we have.

Down there in the heart of our city of Dallas is located this great First Baptist church, a tremendous church. We don't have nine thousand members, Governor, we've got twelve thousand, and I tell you, it's growing, that is twelve now. It's a sight the way that church is growing. It's a great congregation of people. It's a wonderful congregation of people. Now, right there from our First Baptist Church right there, oh, five blocks, something like that, is the Good Street Baptist Church, colored, and they have a marvelous congregation and gifted preachers. Now right here from our First Baptist Church, a little closer is the New Hope Baptist Church, colored, a little congregation, a smaller one, but very much given unto the service and minus, oh I'd say a mile and a half, something like that, is the St. John's Baptist Church, colored. Now you haven't seen any church until you go to the St. John's Baptist Church, colored. Man, the pastor of the St. John's Baptist Church rides around in a long, sleek black Cadillac. That's more than I can do unless you come and join me and his my salary more than it is now. Why, he rides around in style with his family and when they go to church they dress beautifully, you know, with gloves. And they've got decorum and dignity. And I don't know what all they've got in that St. John's Baptist Church, colored. Brother, it's something. It's something.

Now, what I say to my brethren is this: Why under Heaven's name am I an outcast and a renegade, why am I a dirty louse, why am I un-American or undemocratic, or unspiritual or ungodly, or "unanything" else that they are trying to call me when I say, now look here, you blessed colored friends of mine, when you come down here in our church, you won't like it. Why, men, you couldn't excel in our group; you couldn't be a leader in our congregation. And my dear Mrs. Colored-Wife, you couldn't be a Sunday School teacher or a president of Women's Union here in our congregation. And these children, they'd grow up all their lives no integrated into this groups and for you to come down here with us is a violation of your privilege and your responsibilities as a family, and as a people of God. Now, this is what you do. You go right over there to that Good Street Baptist Church. You join that church or that little New Hope Baptist church or, if you've got the where whithal, join the St. John's Baptist Church. You go over there; yes sir, and if you go over there, you can be a deacon in that church, and if God calls you to be a preacher, you can be the pastor of that church. And this wonderful colored woman here, this fine Christian wife, she can be president of the Missionary Society. She can teach a fine Woman's Sunday School class. And these blessed children, they can grow up and they'll have power in the Lord. They'll express themselves within their group. They are in their social stratum, they're among their kind. They will like it and they will prosper in the Lord. And so they go there and they sing their way. I'd like to be able to sing like those colored folks sing. I just can't do it. And my folks can't do it and my choir can't do it. I tell them to sing a Negro spiritual for me, why you never heard such sorry Negro spiritual singing in your life. They can't do it. But they can go over there at that colored folks church. They've got lots of things over there at that colored folks church I wish I had. I've never seen a white preacher in my life that can preach like an honest-to-goodness, old-time, old-fashioned, colored preacher. Down in South Carolina, let me tell you that, they set my soul afire. But it is better for them to be over there in their way, in their church, with their preacher, carrying on as they like to do, and then I'm over here with my flock and my kind and we are carrying on like we want to do; and everything is *just fine. Who said it wasn't fine? I'll tell you who said it wasn't fine. It's some of those two-by scantling, good-for-nothing fellows who are trying to upset all of the things that we love as good old Southern people and as good old Southern Baptists. They are not our kind, I say. They don't know us, and I'm glad. Let them stay where they are, wherever they are, but leave us alone. We get along fine. We are not having any trouble. We are not having any trouble at all. We are just getting along the best you ever saw in your world. I have had no trouble at all, none at all.*

Now, I want to say something personal and then I am done. What is the thing that lies back of this pulling apart? Some of us are here, some of us are there, and some of us are yonder. And some of us are there and it's not just on racial lines. It's just on every kin of a line and color and complex that you can think—our people getting together. I'll just mention a few of them here. This is what lies back of it. Listen to me.

There are some things that you can be broad and liberal and open about and it doesn't matter. Who walks down Main Street? Oh, it doesn't matter who walks down Main Street. Who trades in that store? Why, it doesn't matter who trades in that store. Who is building this State House. It doesn't matter at all. These things are general. They belong to the body politic. It doesn't matter at all. But there are some things that get way down on the inside of us. And here are some of those things.

Whom are you going to marry? That's so personal. And that daughter of yours, and I can't get that out of my mind, because we've just got that one child. Whom is she going to marry? Those things are personal. All right, you listen to me. Wherever you cross over those social lines, wherever you cross over those social lines, that's going to get into your family. "Aw, preacher, they say, we're all going to be brothers and not be brothers-in-law." I have a great friend who's a federal judge in New York, and he said to me within a week, he said: "There were more than a thousand marriages last year in the state of New York between white and colored people." And I happen to know a Baptist pastor up there that has lost his church because he said, "I'll favor desegregation and all the young people being together in my church." And, lo and behold the thing happened immediately. One of his young men, white, fell in love with one of the young girls, colored, and when they had the wedding in the church, it blasted the church wide open—up there in the North, yes, sir.

Some of these things are personal. Some of them belong to the inside of your heart and your soul. They belong inside your family. Whenever you cross them over, whenever you cross them over, you're going to get into all kinds of trouble. I want my girl to be thrown with a certain kind of boy—you know what kinds I'd want. I don't want one that gambles and drinks and carouses and cusses. I'm segregating her all I can. I'm trying to out around her the friends that are like we are, of the pastor's home, and for her to marry and fall in love with a boy like that, because she's not going to fall in love with a boy she knows and goes with. And that's human nature. You're going to build your home out of the stuff that's around you. And it's a whale of a lot better for us to place our families and our young people and our children around groups like we are.

If you want this group, or that group, or that group, or that group, brother, it's a free country. If I want my group, let me have it. Let me have it. Don't force me by law, by statute, by Supreme Court decision, by any way that they can think of, don't force me to cross over in those intimate things where I don't want to go. Let me build my life. Let me have my church. Let me have my school. Let me have my friends. Let me have my home. Let me have my family. And what you give to me, give to every man in America and keep it like our glorious forefathers made it—a land of the free and the home of the brave.

COMMENTARY

Segregation in Society

Dr. Criswell was invited to speak at the annual Baptist Statewide Conference on Evangelism at Columbia, South Carolina in February 1956. The speech caused a blast of controversy when the news media stated, "Criswell said that he not only strongly favored racial segregation but that it would be best for religious groups to "stick to their own kind."

The Associated Press cited Dr. Criswell as saying, "Integration is a thing of idiocy and foolishness. Any man who says he is altogether desegregated is soft in the head."

Immediately Governor George Timmerman invited Dr. Criswell to speak at a Joint Session of the South Carolina Legislature on February 22. In assessing that speech to the Legislature, the backdrop of history revealed that 1956 was a time of national, racial unrest. In the state of South Carolina, it was made unlawful for the state or its subdivisions to employ any member of the National Association for the Advancement of Colored People. This same state provided its School Segregation Study Committee with legal status. The Legislature ordered that any state institution could be closed to anyone at anytime it desired.

Several national incidents occurred when racial integration was forced. The University of Alabama suspended its first Negro student until order could be restored. The Tennessee National Guard moved into Clinton, Tennessee as riots broke out when the town's newly integrated schools opened. The year 1956 set the format for the Little Rock riots and later passage of the 1957 Civil Rights Act.

When Dr. Criswell arrived in South Carolina, he was told that he should not mention the highly debatable issue of segregation. Although he knew that this issue was full of political dynamite, he decided that he would share his ideas about segregation. Criswell thought that the local and national issue of segregation should be discussed openly. In his speech to the Joint Session of Legislature of South Carolina, Criswell advocated several ideas on the issue of segregation.

First, segregation is natural in all areas of life in a democratic society. He said, one of the glories of a democratic society, we can choose our friends; we can choose our companions; we can choose the mates that share with us the building of our homes. We can choose our lives. It's a free country. It's a free nation and that thing of . . . They don't like the word of segregation—but call it that—that thing enters all of the realms of our lives, and there is no escaping from it if a man has the liberty of choice. He then illustrated his point further by using the home as an example of segregation. He proudly stated, "A home is a man's castle. Those four walls around him—the word for it if you want to say it—they're segregated in there—my wife, my daughter, my mother-in-law, who lives with us. We have a home. We're not against anybody else. We're just there in that home, and we invite certain ones in there; and others we do not, not that we hate them or despise them. We just love some of them and there they are in our home. And our home is built upon that; that a man has right of choice."

Second, segregation is the most workable and practical method for churches. He declared that anyone could come to his church, but not everyone would fit in. He asked, "Why under Heaven's name am I an outcast and a renegade, why am I a dirty louse, why am I un-American or undemocratic or unspiritual or ungodly, or "unanything" else that they are trying to call me when I say, now look here, you blessed colored friends of mine, you come down here in our church, you won't like. Why, men, you couldn't excel in our group; you couldn't be a leader in our congregation. And my dear Mrs. Colored-Wife, you couldn't be a Sunday School teacher or a president of our Women's Union here in our congregation. And these children, they'd grow up all their lives not integrated into this group and for you to come down here with us is a violation of your privilege and your responsibilities as a family, and as a people over there to that Good Street Baptist Church. You join that church or that little New Hope Baptist Church, or, if you've got the wherewithal, you join the St. John's Baptist Church. You go over there; yes, sir, and if you go over there, you can be a deacon in that church, and if God calls you to be a preacher, you can be the pastor of that church. And this wonderful colored woman here, this fine Christian wife, she can be president of the Missionary Society. She can teach a fine Women's Sunday School class. And these blessed children, they can grow up and they'll have power in the Lord. They'll express themselves within their group. They are in their social stratum, they're among their kind. They will like it and they will prosper in the Lord."

He then strikes against anyone who would trouble the waters by forcing integration of races in the churches. He said: It is better for them to be over there in their way, in their church, with their preacher, carrying on as they like to do, and then I'm over here with my flock and my kind, and we are carrying on like we want to do; everything is just fine. Who said it wasn't fine? I'll tell you who said it wasn't fine. It's some of those two-by scantling, good-for-nothing fellows who are trying to upset all of the things that we love as good old Southern people and as good old Southern Baptists. They are not our kind, I say. They don't know us, and I'm glad. Let them stay where they are, wherever they are, but leave us alone. We get along fine. We are not having any trouble. We are not having any trouble at all. We are just getting along the best you ever saw in your world. I have had no trouble at all, none at all."

After several arguments were presented for segregation in society, Dr. Creswell asked religious groups to "stick to their own kind" and to request, "let me have my choice in segregating my life in this society."

The speaker then gave his reasons for asking men to respond to segregation. Some of these things are personal. Some of them belong to the inside of your heart and your soul. They belong inside your family. Whenever you cross them over, you're going to get into all kinds of trouble. I want my girl to be thrown with a certain kind of a boy—you know what kind I'd want. I don't want one that gambles and drinks and carouses and cusses. I'm segregating her all I can. I'm trying to put around her the friends that are like we are, of the pastor's home, and for her to marry and fall in love with a boy like that, because she's not going to fall in love with a boy she knows and goes with. And that's human nature. You're going to build your home out of the stuff that's around you. And it's a whale of a lot better for us to place our families and our young people and our children around groups like we are.

If you want this group, or that group, or that group, or that group, brother, it's a free country. If I want my group, let me have it. Let me have it. Don't force me by law, by statute, by Supreme Court decision, by any way that they can think of, don't force me to cross over in those intimate things where I don't want to go. Let me build my life. Let me have my church. Let me have my school. Let me have my friends. Let me have my home. Let me have my family. And what you give to me, give to every man in America and keep it as our glorious forefathers made it—a land of the free and the home of the brave.

On the same day, after Criswell's speech to the Legislature, journalists contacted the most famous member of Criswell's church—Billy Graham. Evangelist Graham told the Associated Press that he and his pastor have never seen eye to eye on the race question. It was in this speech that Criswell made his most outspoken statements on segregation.

Dr. Jim Towns

THE CHURCH OF THE OPEN DOOR

Dr. W. A. Criswell
Revelation 3:7-8, June 9th, 1968

On the radio, you are sharing the services of the First Baptist Church in Dallas. This is the pastor bringing the message entitled, "The Church of the Open Door." Before I bring the word of the Lord from God's Book and the message the Lord has laid on my heart, there are two things that I would first like to mention.

The first, this has been appointed by the President of the United States as a national day of mourning. And in keeping with that appointment by the chief executive of our nation, all of us would extend to the family of Senator Kennedy our remembrance in prayer and our sympathy in the tragic loss of husband, and father, and friend. And we would take this occasion as a time of re-dedication to an ordered society, seeking in every means at our command to encourage our people and to demand of our citizen's obedience to law and respect for authority and above all, under God, a prayer that we shall come to reverence human life, which is a gift of God. And in next Sunday's sermon, I hope that I may speak of some of these things at a much deeper and lengthier and meaningful extent.

The second preliminary word concerns an exigency that has been placed upon me, for which I importune the sympathies and remembrance of our dear church. A few weeks ago, the representatives of our publication society of the Southern Baptist Convention, the Broadman Press, came to me and asked me to write a certain book. I have gathered the material for that book, and it must now be written. To show you the exigency of this hour, I have never written a book under a year, and some of them I have taken two years to write. I must write this book in three weeks. What heretofore, I have done in a year, I must do in three weeks. So you will understand if the pastor is consumed day and night and night and day in this assignment then after three weeks, why, we shall see what other fires the pastor will fall into. But right now, I'm in that one. So understand, and I will be hibernating all of the moments that I can possibly command, writing this book.

Now, to the message; in the third chapter of the Book of the Revelation, beginning at verse 7: "And to the angel of the church in Philadelphia write..." Now, verse 8: "Behold, I have set before thee an open door." This message is in no wise or in any part an exposition of the text or of the passage in God's Word in which the words are found. But it is a name for a sermon that God has sent me here at this hour to deliver. "Behold, I have set before thee an open door;" Thus, the title of the message is, "The Church of the Open Door."

One of the questions asked me again and again both in press conferences and by individual representatives of the press, and by an innumerable host of interested friends and leaders of our convention—why is it that in these years past, you have always declined the nomination to this highest place of leadership in our denomination, but now, you accept it? What has happened? Why have you changed? Why did you reject it heretofore and why do you accept it now? There are three reasons why in the years past I have declined such a nomination.

First, I never felt that it was God's will for me to do it. Nor could I quite describe all of those convictions that entered into that feeling in my soul. My classmates and men whom I have known intimately through the years have accepted such a place of responsibility. And I have loved them for it and prayed for them in it. But I never felt it was God's will for me.

The second reason; I never felt worthy to assume so tremendous an assignment. This is not false or cheap humility. I am just telling you why it is that in years past I never accepted such a proffer. I never felt worthy in my soul for such a tremendous assignment from God.

And the third reason was you, our dear church. And there were two reasons in our dear church. First, I had watched the churches of men who assumed this great far-flung mandate and their churches suffered. This church, Dr. Truett was ambassador plenipotentiary to the whole world. And the church greatly suffered. Dr. Truett was gone most of the time. And such a prospect for me and our church hurt my soul. And one of the things that I resolved when I came to be pastor of the church was that I would accept it as my chief and primary assignment. Whatever else I did, my first work under God would be this pastoral ministry. And for years, I never accepted a revival meeting. For years, I never left the church. I stayed here, every week—every Sunday. When finally, I did begin to accept revival invitations, they were never more than two. I would accept one in the spring. I would accept one in the fall. And I stayed here through the years and the years, trying to be a good shepherd for God's flock. So I refused because I did not want to hurt our church. And being gone hurts the church.

And the second thing I staggered before was this question of race. And what would be involved in our church if I were to receive an assignment such as the presidency of the Southern Baptist Convention, what it would mean to this church in the violent turmoil that has engulfed and convulsed our nation in these racial crises. I am just telling you why it is, the best I know how to say it, that in these years past, I have refused even to consider such an assignment.

Then why is it now that you have accepted it? Why? For all three of those reasons that heretofore I have refused it. First, as the days pass, and in the exigencies and fortunes and vicissitudes and turns of life, ten thousand, thousand things entered into it. I finally came to the deep conclusion and persuasion that this was something God wanted me and called me to do. My wife, Mrs. Criswell, greatly objected to it. All through these days she sought to dissuade me from it. Some of the friends who love me most and pray for me the deepest, sought to dissuade me from it. But as the days passed, and as the turns and fortunes and incidents of life would come, they increasingly pressed upon my soul the conviction that this was something God called me to do. It was God's will for me.

Second, my feeling of unworthiness; I laid before God the humblest, the most meaningful, the sincerest that I knew how and there came into my life that feeling that I had when I was a boy. In the days now so long ago, as a child and as a teenager and as a youth and as a young man, when I felt God's call to be a pastor, a preacher, in those days, now so long ago, as a child in the grammar school, I consecrated my life in preparation for that work. As I look back now in age to those childhood days, I cannot imagine such a thing could be. Yet, as sincerely and as deeply as I am now, did I then give myself in preparation for this ministry. As a child, as a teenager, as a youth, and as a young man, and I have done it all over again in these days; I have re-committed and re-consecrated my life to God.

Now, the third, what of the church? First, being gone, what of that? There is no doubt nor should we hide our faces from the fact that there will be many, many more times that I shall be away than in these days and years past. What of that and what of the church? This was a conviction that I came to about you. I believe there is also in the church such a like spirit of dedication and consecration, that we shall be more faithful to God's work than we have ever been before. We shall assume for ourselves also a contingent, component, constructive, consecrated part of this ministry. And our deacons will be more faithful now than they've ever been before. And our teachers will be more faithful. Our leaders will be more devoted. Our choir will be more faithful. Our membership will be more faithful. And our staff will be more committed than we have ever been before.

Wouldn't it be an incomparable gift to offer to God that in these next coming immediate two years we had our greatest advance? Oh, if God would just give to us! And instead of the church waning and lessening and ebbing and staggering and stumbling, that in these immediate two years that lie ahead, we should offer to God our finest achievements. And I have felt it could be done. If we would each one in his place, resolve that now, in this time and in this hour, I shall be doubly committed to my task and to my assignment.

Then what of race? The First Baptist Church and the racial tension and turmoil that we witness all around us, what of our church and race? If we had hours and hours, we could hardly, hardly enter into all that lies back of the message delivered this morning by the pastor. I have been asked countless numbers of times. How is it that there has never been an ugly, bitter, racial incident in your church? All through the length and the breadth of this land, those bitter, ugly incidents have taken place in the churches. And the churches have been torn apart and they have been decimated. And some of them have almost been destroyed by that bitter conflict and confusion.

Yet in the First Baptist Church in Dallas, there has never been even an approach to such an ugly incident. Yet, you would think that out of all of the churches of the Southern Convention, that our church would be the prime target. And you would think that of all of the pastors of the Southern Convention, that your pastor would be the first and primary target. Yet in the years and the years, and they've been many years, more than we realize now since this racial tension has been heightened in America. Yet in our church there has never been even an approach or an approximation of any ugly racial incident. Why?

And I have answered. I have never had any fear, never. There has never been any fear in my heart regarding this church and any ugly racial incident. I took it to God years ago. And I had an answer to prayer and an assurance from heaven that such an ugly incident would never come to pass, would never be seen in this congregation. And through these years, I have walked and preached unafraid. My heart has been quiet. I felt I had an answer from God. We will never have such bitterness in our church.

Then, through the years, I have watched our congregation. We have been in the years gone by, a church of Philadelphia; the Philadelphian church of the open door. And I have watched it and watched it, and prayerfully watched it through the years and the years. I have seen Japanese come down these aisles, loved and welcomed by our people. I have seen the Chinese come down these aisles, loved and welcomed by the people. I have seen the Indian, the American Indian, the Indian from India walk down these aisles, loved and welcomed by the people. I have seen Mexican families and children and young people walk down these aisles, loved and welcomed by the people. And as I watched you, and the fabric of our church, I began to see colored people walk down these aisles, loved and welcomed by the church.

What do you mean "colored people"? I mean dark people with Negro blood in them. A pressman talking to me, I asked him, "Is Adam Clayton Powell a Negro?"

"Yes," he said.

I said, "What part Negro? He looks like a white man to me?"

Coming down these aisles I have seen them. Mexican and Negro—colored people. Finally, I saw a Central American come down these aisles. He was black—loved and received by the people. And finally, I saw a Nigerian come down these aisles—loved and received by the people. Through these years, as they have continued, I have seen our church with an open heart and a compassionate spirit, welcoming into the kingdom and into the body of Christ these whose pigmentation might be different from mine and yours.

Then, a few days ago, I received a letter from a man whom I loved and admired so much; a leader of great dedication in our Convention, in our state and a loved fellow elder in this church. And out of the deepest love of his heart, he wrote me the sweetest letter. And in that letter, he said, "Pastor, I awakened in the night in South Carolina with a burden on my heart, I cannot escape. It is about you. And it is about our church. And as this presidency of the Convention is being pressed upon you, I have a burden, I am afraid designedly there will be those who will try to destroy you and destroy the church."

I, at that time—this was just a few days ago—had fully made up my mind, I would not accept such a proffer. I happened to mention it inadvertently without plan or forethought, I happened to mention that letter and my decision that I would not be pressed into such an assignment as the leadership of our Southern Baptist Churches. I happened to mention it to the finance committee that is getting ready to launch our church in a multi-million dollar building and expansion program. I happened to mention it. And I said, among other things, "On account of race, I will not respond to that appeal."

And those men, you can look at their names, they have been printed, you'll see them. Those men answered as though they had been thinking about this for a hundred years. They said, "Pastor, the time has come for us to face this now and forever."

Well, I said, "I don't want to do it now. It would be as though the pressure from others concerning the presidency of this convention had precipitated such a discussion in our church."

They said, "Pastor, the presidency of the Convention does not enter into this one way or another. Some time, somewhere, this has to be faced and now is the time to do it. We're going to do it now." So Mr. Cantrell, who was there, called a meeting of the deacons Tuesday of a week ago. And after the business of the session was done, they said, "Now, Pastor, stand up here and bare your heart." So I stood there and for an hour, I bared my soul.

What is this thing that obtains in our people and among our churches? This is what obtains. I turned my face toward the Buckner Home and the Buckner Home has in it all kinds of children—yellow, black, white, and red. And when the time came that they discussed the bringing of those children to the First Baptist Church in Dallas, as many of them are here this morning, one of the leaders came to me and said, "But Pastor, some of our children are colored, maybe we ought not to come."

I replied, "It would be unthinkable that our First Baptist Church in Dallas would refuse the Buckner Home and their ministries because you have in your love and compassionate concern a colored child. Welcome. Come." And the Buckner children have been brought these years to our dear church.

Then I turned to look at Dallas Baptist College. I went out to speak at their chapel service. And all through Dallas Baptist College, are colored young men and young woman; our Dallas Baptist College.

Then I turned to look at our Baylor School of Nursing. And in the Baylor School of Nursing are colored young women. And I walked up and down the halls of Baylor University Hospital and there, you will see all races and all colors; our hospital—seeking to minister to them all.

And when we began our retarded children's ministry, one of the sweetest in the earth, they brought down here retarded children from one of the homes in the city of Dallas. And a part of them were colored. They came to me and said, "Shall we close the door?" I said, "Close the door to these retarded children because some of them are colored? No! No!"—and they've been coming.

And as I looked through the length and breadth of our institutions, everywhere, everywhere there is that open door. And there are those hands outstretched and arms of welcome. I have said a thousand times with regard to tax money for church institutions, I have said this sentence, "You cannot separate a church from its institutions." And to give tax support to an institution owned and operated by a church is to give tax support to the church itself. And I have found myself in this congregation with our Buckner Home and our Baptist College and our nursing school and our hospital with an announced policy of one way and no announcement from our church of any way.

And finally, as I spoke to my brethren and compeers in the church, our deacons, I said, "And I bare my personal soul to you. I cannot describe and I have come to feel the weight of it and the burden of it. I cannot describe to you how I feel when I preach the gospel of the Son of God and call men to faith and to repentance, and then stand there afraid that somebody might respond who has a different pigment from mine. It is though I were living a denial of the faith, to preach and be afraid that somebody might respond."

What if there came down the aisle a Buckner child who was colored? How would I explain to that child? In ten thousand years I couldn't explain to that child. I couldn't do it. But that's not so much the point, how can I explain to God? You tell me how. You give me the words. What do I return to say to God? "This child, Lord, out here at the Buckner Home found Jesus today." What would I say?

I think of Patrick Henry who assumed the defense of the three Baptist preachers who were placed in jail for preaching the gospel of the Son of God. And in the court, the great, eloquent Patrick Henry held the indictment and waved it above his head and asked, "What does this indictment say? These men are accused of preaching the gospel of the Son of God. Great God! Great God!" And this indictment, this is the pastor who preaches the gospel of the Son of God and somebody responded, and he refused. Great God! Great God!

When the hour was done, our deacons had intended, I think, to discuss it and to speak it. But when I sat down, one of the deacons stood up immediately and said, "Every man here stand to his feet." And the deacons stood up just like that—all of them. And Chairman Cantrell called them to the front; a hundred eighty or more of them to fall on their faces and ask our deacon missionary to Nigeria, Dr. Wayne Logan to lead in the prayer.

And this is without fanfare. It is without dramatics. It is just the simple announcement that as you walk up and down the streets, as you visit the Buckner Home, as you look at those retarded children, this is just the plain, simple, unadorned announcement that the First Baptist Church in Dallas is like the Philadelphian church of the Book of the Revelation. It is a church of the open door. And when the pastor preaches, as he quotes Isaiah 55:1: "Ho, everyone that thirsteth, come ye to the water. Yea, come buy and eat without money and without price"—everyone in it. As Jesus said, in Matthew 11:28: "Come unto Me all ye that labor and are heavy-laden and I will give you rest"—anyone, everyone. As Simon Peter wrote in 2 Peter 3:9: "God wills that all should come to repentance and that none should perish." As the Book closes, in Revelation 22:17: "And the Spirit and the bride say: Come. And let him that heareth say: Come. And let him that is athirst come. And whosoever will, anybody, you, let him take the water of life freely." Come. Come. Come. And God bless us and God attend in the way as you come.

Now, we are past our time. We must sing our song of appeal. And while we sing it, a family you, a couple you, one somebody you, as the Spirit of Jesus shall press the appeal to your heart, make it now. Come now. Do it now. And bless you as you come in Jesus' name, welcome. While we stand and while we sing.

COMMENTARY

The Church of the Open Door

The first Sunday after Dr. W.A. Criswell was elected President of the Southern Baptist Convention, he made an address to the First Baptist Church of Dallas, Texas, June 9, 1968, advocating integration. In the year 1968, there were several major events which were significant in the integration controversy. Some of the events were affirmatively constructive, while some were devastating. President Johnson's National Advisory Committee on Civil Disorders revealed a polarized society. Governor Otto Kerner, head of the committee, warned that the United States could move toward two societies—one white and one black, separate and unequal. The political world witnessed some positive events for integration. The United States Senate passed a bill on open housing. Mississippi seated Robert Clark as its first Negro legislator in 74 years.

There were shocking negative events in the integration struggle. United States Civil Rights Leader, the Rev. Martin Luther King, Jr., was shot to death by a sniper in Memphis, Tennessee. Senator Robert F. Kennedy was shot in Los Angeles, California shortly after he claimed the victory in the California Democratic presidential primary. It was these conditions along with many personal reasons that Dr. Criswell spoke openly for racial integration in churches.

After being elected president of the convention, Dr. Criswell faced two issues which needed to be clarified and explained to his church. The first was why he decided to run for presidency of the convention. Second, he felt that the matter of racial integration should be treated. The two issues, presidency of the convention and racial integration, gave rise to making Criswell's perspective known publicly. He gave several propositions for each issue and idea.

First, he revealed why he refused in past days to run for presidency of the convention. He stated that he refused in days past to run for three reasons. He stated that he did not feel that it was God's will for me to accept that assignment, nor could I enter into, in a brief discussion like this, all of the reasons that lay back of that persuasion. Second, he did not feel worthy of that high place and second reason he did not allow such a nomination was because he felt unworthy of so great a responsibility. The third reason that he refused was the church. Then another reason was the thing of race, racial strife, and racial tension. From one side of this nation to the other he had seen churches torn apart by ugly, bitter racial incidents. He continued to state, "I will not allow my name to be presented nor will I serve if elected."

Dr. Criswell presented his perspective concerning the church and racial integration. He told of the battle that had been in his heart for several years concerning his stand on segregation. Criswell proclaimed that he told those deacons that as for me, my heart, my life, and my pulpit ministry he was done with the emptiness of an appeal—to say it, to preach it, and to fear that somebody of different pigment might accept it and come forward. He asked the question, "How shall I do, how shall I be, and what shall I say? For I stand up in that pulpit and preach the gospel of the Son of God and present an appeal on the basis of what He's done to save us from our sins. And stand there and plea that men whose pigment might be different from mine might accept that appeal and invitation. Preaching the Gospel of the Son of God and the grace of Jesus, what if down one of these aisles upon a day comes a little girl from the Buckner and she is black. How could I explain to that child in a thousand years that what I was preaching I didn't really mean; you go back and you go out. But only my inability to explain to that child the emptiness of my appeal and my invitation. What shall I say to God? When I return an answer to God, what shall I say? How shall I phrase the words to pronounce it? How shall I put together the sentences to say it?" In one of the most important proclamations Criswell pleaded, "Not in dramatics, not in fanfare, but in the spirit of Jesus, humbly, simply, the First Baptist Church in Dallas is now and forever a Philadelphian church of the open door. Anybody can come, anybody. And God bless him and God attend him in the way as he comes."

Criswell stated that he did not want any embarrassment to come to the church or convention because of his former stand on segregation. This stand was encouraged by one of Criswell's friends who spoke of the possibility of designed destruction, hurt, and embarrassment to our church, because of a speech he made earlier in 1956 in South Carolina before he changed his mind about segregation.

As Criswell advocated the open door policy for his church he asked men to respond. Dr. Criswell asked all men to come and be welcomed at the First Baptist Church of Dallas. He said that this is a church of the open door. Inherent in these propositions, Dr. Criswell asked his church and the convention to respond favorably to his perspective. Immediately, the Baptist state papers and mass media revealed Criswell's change. The articles carried statements such as Criswell, known as a conservative and a fundamentalist, was given a severe grilling on the racial situation by reporters after he was elected president of the Convention. Indicating that he had changed on the racial issue, Criswell said . . . following his election as SBC president. . .that all races are admitted to membership. W.A. Criswell, president of the Southern Baptist Convention—once criticized as a segregationist—condemned racism and segregation.

RELIGIOUS FREEDOM, THE CHURCH, THE STATE, AND SENATOR KENNEDY

Dr. W. A. Criswell
Delivered at First Baptist Church, Dallas, Texas, July 3, 1960

We stand in the midst of that conflict and that battle, now. Fear seems to have the pass key to whole nations. Vast changes are rapidly sweeping the world, as swirling; ocean currents sweep the seas. Misunderstandings, both national and international, seem relentless in their persistence. Wars and rumors of wars even now are casting their dark shadows across the earth. All these conditions pointedly remind us how desperately we need help above ourselves.

The right of private judgment is the crown jewel of humanity. For any person or institution to come between the soul and God is a blasphemous impertinence and a defamation of the crown rights of the Son of God. Protestants regard as an enormity any attempt to constrain men by penalty or patronage, to this or that form of religious belief. What a frightful chapter has been written, the world around, by disregard of this lofty principle of freedom of conscience and its inimitable corollary, the separation of Church and State.

Protestant's were confiscated in Connecticut. The imprisonments, persecutions of our Protestant people everywhere in old Virginia. On and on our Protestant forebears waged this unyielding battle for religious liberty. They dared to be odd, to stand alone, to refuse to conform, though it cost them suffering and even life itself. They pleaded and suffered and kept on with their protests and remonstrances and memorials until, thank God, forever their contention was won in these United States, openly and blatantly, that great principle has been publicly assured now, they won in these United States and written into our country's constitution, that church and state must be, in this land, forever separate and free. In the code of laws established by the Protestants of Rhode Island, we read for the first time since Christianity ascended the throne of the Caesars, the declaration that conscience should be free, and that men should not be punished for worshiping God in the way they were persuaded that He requires.

The Protestant contention is not for mere toleration, but for absolute liberty. There is a wide difference between toleration and liberty. Toleration implies that someone falsely claims the right to tolerate. Toleration is a concession, while liberty is a divine right. Toleration is a matter of expedience, while liberty is a matter of principle. Toleration is a gift of man, while liberty is a gift from God. It is, therefore, the consistent, insistent and persistent contention of our Protestant people, always and everywhere, that religion must be voluntary and un-coerced, and that it is not the perogative of any power to compel men to pay taxes for the support of a religious organization to which they do not belong and in which creed they do not believe. In the very nature of the case, there can be no proper union of Church and State. Jesus stated the principle in two sayings: "My Kingdom is not of this world," and "Render unto Caesar the things that are Caesar's, and unto God the things that are God's." This marked the divorcement of Church and State forever.

I speak now with special word to the Protestant people of our United States of America. While we are lamenting the loss of religious liberty in different sections of the world, it behooves us to open our eyes to insidious encroachments here in our own land. Once more, the frank declaration is here made that any trend or suggestion of the possible establishment of diplomatic relations between the United States and the Vatican would call forth an immediate and unyielding protest from uncounted millions of our American people, with them a violent issue at that time will be a violent issue again. Our doctrine of religious liberty in American is for all our men alike. The Pope is simply the honored head of the Roman Catholic Church, and the plea that his dominion over a few acres of land, called the Vatican City, gives him the status of a temporal sovereign, is essentially unreal. He has, in fact, no better title to receive governmental recognition from the United States that has the Archbishop of Canterbury, head of the Anglican Church, or the Moderator of the Presbyterian General Assembly, or the Presiding Bishop of the United Methodist Church.

The most difficult situation is created any time that you speak of the Roman Church. It is a religion, and we have an innate, congenital dislike in America to criticize another man's religion. We believe in religious freedom. The very soul has its right to join in and before God, and if a man wants to be an atheist, that is his prerogative; if he wants to be an infidel, that is his right; if he wants to become a Moslem; if he wants to be a Hindu; if he wants to be an agnostic; if he wants to be a Mormon; if he wants to be a member of the Christian Science faith; or if he wants to be a Roman Catholic; that is his choice. We have a congenital historical dislike in criticism of any man's religion and our problem lies in this: that the Roman Catholic institution hierarchy is not only a religion, but it is a political tyranny. There is not the disposition on the part of any true American or any man who loved democracy and religious liberty to attack any faith or any religion. It is only that we are faced with a political system that like an octopus covers the entire world and threatens that basic freedom and that constitutional right of Church and State for which we have died in generations past.

For example, the Vatican Ambassador is asked for on the basis that the Vatican is a political state. They say it is a sovereign government. They say it is a political entity. Then, if you say anything about them and about that, they accuse you of being a religious bigot. We are not attacking the religion nor are we attacking the institution, we are merely facing a political reality. In one instance they present themselves as religionists, then in the next instance they ask for an Ambassador to the Vatican on the basis that they are a sovereign state and a political power.

If you have ever seen the symbol of the Pope of Rome, he has two keys, one is the key of religion and the other is the key of sovereign political power and he claims to possess both of them. For example, here in America in defending nuns and priests in their religious habits and in their religious garbs, teaching in the public school systems, they say their priests and their nuns in religious garbs and religious habits have the right to teach in a public school system on the basis that they are our fellow American citizens. Fine - then they are received with the public school systems and are paid by the tax money of the American people. When the internal revenue collector seeks to have them pay taxes, income taxes, on the salaries that they receive as being public payroll and as public school-teachers—then they say, "We are not other than representatives of the Catholic Church and we pay no taxes." There are 2,055 or more nuns and priests on the public payrolls of the American people who receive salaries from the taxpayers on the basis that they are American citizens, but they pay not a dime of income tax because when it comes time to pay taxes they say: "We are the representatives of the Church." It is a hydra-headed affair, whichever head you hit, then this is the head that predominates.

They have elected for the second time a Catholic governor in the State of Ohio, and in Ohio it is the law of the land under the powers of those two Catholic governors that the Catholic nuns and sisters and priests in their garbs and in their habitats are on the public payroll as school-teachers. That is a concomitant and a corollary of this elective office when they are able to seize it. The drive for tax money to support their institutions is relentless and never, never does it withhold its pressure. They succeed tremendously in getting tax money into the support of their institutions. John McCormack, Roman Catholic from Massachusetts, who is the Democratic majority leader of the House, has been himself responsible for national legislation which has handed over to the Catholic Church more than 30 million dollars of our tax money. When you pay income taxes, a part of that income tax goes to the support of the Catholic Church in the United States of America.

The Constitution of Argentina states: "To be eligible to the office of President or Vice-President of the Nation, a person must belong to the Roman Catholic Church.

The Constitution of Paraguay states: "The President of the Republic must profess the Roman Catholic religion." The Constitution of Spain states: "To exercise the office of Chief of State or King or Regent, it shall be necessary to profess the Roman Catholic religion. In the South American nation of Columbia, during the past eight years a government dominated by the Catholic Church, 49 Protestant churches have been destroyed? 34 Protestant churches have been confiscated and 89 Protestant church leaders have been murdered.

Now, during the second World War, the American ship, Dorchester, was sunk by enemy fire. The four chaplains on the ship, two of whom were Protestants, one Jewish, and one Catholic, all gave their life preservers to four sailors and locked arm in arm and they went down with the ship, each giving his life in order that one of his fellow Americans might live. After the war, the father of one of the Protestant chaplains. Dr. Daniel A. Poling, conceived the idea of building an inter-church chapel in Philadelphia, Pennsylvania, in memory of the four chaplains.

In the fall of 1950, Dr. Poling concluded the financial campaign in which he raised money for erection of the "Chapel of the Four Chaplains" with a banquet in the Bellevue Stratford Hotel, Philadelphia. It was in inter-faith occasion, A representative of each of the three leading faiths was invited to speak on that important occasion. The Honorable Charles P. Taft, Mayor of Cincinnati, Ohio, was invited to speak for the Protestants. Senator Herbert H. Lehman was invited to speak for the Jewish faith and John Kennedy, of the United States Congress from Massachusetts, was invited - and accepted - to speak for the Catholic faith.

Dr. Poling relates how Mr. Kennedy notified him at the last minute that although he had his speech prepared, he would have to cancel his appearance due to the fact that his Eminence Denis Cardinal Dougherty had requested him not to speak at the banquet and not to appear. Dr. Poling tried to reason with John Kennedy and pointed out to him that it was a civic affair and they were meeting, not in a Protestant church, but on neutral ground in a hotel. John Kennedy replied that he understood all that, and that he had done all he could to change the Cardinal's position, but as, and I quote John Kennedy of the church, he "had no other alternative but not to come," It was too late to procure another speaker and there was no speaker representing the Catholic faith at the banquet.

Is my President of the United States to be a man who could not come into one of my services because he be contaminated by walking into the precincts of a Protestant church? And there are something like 75 million Protestant people in the United States of

America. And the president of the United States, lest he offend the priest, or lest he offend the hierarchy, could attend no religious service simply because he belonged to the Roman Catholic religion. And as a loyal son of the church, he has no alternative but not to come.

In November of 1957, Senator John Kennedy stated: "People are afraid that Catholics take orders from a higher organization. They don't, or, at least, I don't." And he continues and continues that claim.

Now, as Senator Kennedy continued in this avowal in May, of this year, 1960, the official newspaper of the Vatican L'Osservatore Romano published a special article which is labeled "authoritative binding" on all the church. It said: and I quote from the official published editorial of the Vatican paper, "The Church has full power of true jurisdiction over all the faithful and hence has the duty and the right to guide, direct and correct them on the plane of action and ideas. The church has the duty and the right to intervene even in the political field to enlighten and help conscience. A Catholic can never prescribe the teachings and directions of the church. In every section of this activities he must inspire his private and public conduct by the laws, orientation and instructions of the hierarchy."

And that was published in order that John Kennedy himself might know that despite his avowals, that he cannot be disassociated from and free from the claims of the Roman Catholic Church, the hierarchy says it is not so. Now immediately that created tremendous repercussion here in America and the following editorial comment: "U.S. Catholic officials immediately began to say that this pronouncement of the Vatican did not apply here. No, of course not, neither does the Catholic Church desire to close Protestant churches in the United States as it closes Protestant churches in Spain. But once given the power to do so without strong opposition, then what is the position? The Roman Church wins most of its victories with the weapon of time. If Kennedy wins, with strong emphasis on separation of church and state, then the door is open for another Catholic later who gives the Pope his Ambassador, the church schools state support, and finally, recognition of one church above all America.

Their religious liberty has also died in America as it has died in Spain, as it has died in Columbia, as it has died wherever the Roman Catholic hierarchy has the ability and power to shut it down and destroy it in death. In an address delivered in France, it was said: "We conceive our religion as being a personal, individual, voluntary and spiritual relationship between a man and his Creator and Savior. In our scheme of things there is no room whatsoever for coercion, or the use of physical force, in the realm of religion. For example, Gentlemen, I am a protestant and would rejoice to see men everywhere voluntarily accept the tenets of my faith, because I sincerely believe those tenets to be in harmony with the revealed truths of God; but if by the pressure of the weight of my little finger I could physically coerce every person in the world to become a protestant, I tell you frankly and truthfully, I would withhold that pressure, even of the weight of my little finger.

Religion must be free; the soul must have absolute liberty to believe or not to believe, to worship or not to worship, to say "Yes" or "No" to God, even as that soul, and that soul above shall dictate. Every true protestant in the world - and there are millions of them - would take the same stand that I take on this matter, because they believe, and I believe, that to be the clear teaching of the New Testament as to religious freedom."

COMMENTARY

Religious Freedom, the Church, the State and Senator Kennedy

In the years 1928 and 1960, Southern Baptists made a major protest against Catholics seeking the Presidency of the United State. Baptist churches throughout the nation heard speeches on historical concepts of religious liberty and church-state separation during the 1960 campaign. Most of the Baptist rhetoric charged that Roman Catholics owed complete allegiance to the Pope and that a Catholic as president would be influenced politically by the church.

On July 3, 1960, W.A. Criswell, pastor of the First Baptist Church of Dallas, Texas made an address to his local congregation entitled, "Religious Freedom, the Church, the State, and Senator Kennedy." It was evident to Southern Baptists that there was a distinct possibility that a Roman Catholic might be elected President of the United States. Several religious denominations were concerned about church-state separation.

From W.A. Criswell's viewpoint, the major issue was religious liberty. He felt so strongly about the issue and Baptist concern that he spoke openly to his church. Dr. Criswell had a multiplicity of arguments dealing with the issue of religious liberty. His propositions advocated three main ideas. First, he contended that America must have religious liberty rather than just religious toleration. He thought that The Protestant contention is not for mere toleration, but for absolute liberty. There is a wide difference between toleration and liberty. Toleration implies that someone falsely claims the right to tolerate. Toleration is a concession, while liberty is a divine right. Toleration is a matter of expediency, while liberty is a matter of principle. Toleration is a gift of man, while liberty is a fight from God.

A second idea was entailed in the characteristics and power of the Catholic Church. Concerning the characteristics of the Catholic Church, Criswell said that in one instance they present themselves as religionists, then in the next instance they ask for an Ambassador to the Vatican on the basis that they are a sovereign state and a political power. If you have ever seen the symbol of the Pope of Rome, he has two keys, one is the key of religion and the other is the key of sovereign political power and he claims to possess both of them.

He quoted from the *Vatican Observatore Romano*, the official newspaper of the Vatican, as he stated the power of the Catholic Church by saying, "The Church has full power of true jurisdiction over all the faithful and hence has the duty and the right to guide, direct and correct them on the plane of action and ideas. The church has the duty and the right to intervene even in the political field to enlighten and help conscience. A Catholic can never prescribe the teachings and directions of the church. In every section of his activities he must inspire his private and public conduct by the laws, orientation and instructions of the hierarchy."

Third Criswell believed that the political forces of the Catholic Church would overpower religious freedom. He stated, "The Roman Church wins most of its victories with the weapon of time. If Kennedy wins, with strong emphasis on separation of church and state, then the door is open for another Catholic later who gives the Pope his Ambassador, the church schools state support, and final."

Then from his viewpoint, he described the power of political system of the Roman Church as he said, "We are faced with a political system that like an octopus covers the entire world and threatens that basic freedom and that constitutional right of Church and State for which we have died in generations past." The ideas advocated by Criswell in this speech were used in the following weeks throughout the Convention to make people think about religious liberty.

Dr. Criswell boldly advocated religious liberty and the possible threat of the Catholic Church as he asked every Protestant in the nation to vote against any force that clouds the clear teaching of the New Testament as to religious freedom. He concluded, "Religion must be free; the soul must have absolute liberty to believe or not to believe, to worship or not to worship, to say "Yes" or "No" to God, even as that soul, and that soul above shall dictate. Every true protestant in the world—and there are millions of them—should take the same stand that I take on this matter, because they believe, and I believe, that to be the clear teaching of the New Testament as to religious freedom."

It was evident that Criswell was against the historical event when John Fitzgerald Kennedy was elected on November 8, 1960 to become the 35th president of the United States. At 43, Kennedy was the youngest man ever elected president and also the first Roman Catholic to win election to the presidency.

THE COUNTERFEIT CHURCH

Dr. W. A. Criswell
Revelation 13:11-18, December 9th, 1962

On the radio, you're sharing the services of the First Baptist Church in Dallas. This is the pastor bringing the 11:00 o'clock morning message entitled, Counterfeit Church, a message on counterfeit religion. In our preaching through the Bible after these many years, we have come to the Apocalypse. And in our preaching through the Revelation, now these two years, we have come to chapter 13. And last Sunday, at this hour, we spoke of the false prophet, the second beast which is described beginning at verse 11. And this morning, we are going to speak of the religion of the false prophet, which I have called the Counterfeit Church. In the Book of the Revelation, chapter 13, verse 11:

> *And I beheld another beast coming up out of the earth; and he had two horns like a lamb, but he spake like a dragon. And he exerciseth all the power of the first beast before him, and causeth the earth and them which dwell therein to worship the first beast, And he doeth great wonders, so that he maketh fire come down from heaven on the earth in the sight of men. And he deceiveth them that dwell on the earth, by the means of those miracles which he had power to do in the sight of the beast; saying to them that dwell on the earth, that they should make an image to the beast, And he had power to give life unto the image, that the image of the beast should both speak and cause that as many as would not worship the image of the beast should be killed. And he causeth all, both small and great, rich and poor, free and bond, to receive a mark in their right hand, or in their foreheads: And that no man might buy or sell, save he that had the mark, or the name, or the number of the name of the beast. Here is wisdom. Let him that hath understanding count the number of the beast: for it is the number of a man; and his number is six hundred threescore and six which is 666.*

And last Sunday, we spoke of these things. And this Sunday, we are going to speak of the religion of this false prophet. In the sixteenth chapter, in the nineteenth chapter and in the twentieth chapter of this Revelation, this second beast is called the false prophet.

The chapter begins with John standing on the sand of the sea, and out of the raging waters he sees a monster arise from the deep. That is, out of the social chaos and the social turmoil of the nations, the boiling social revolutions, the volcanic eruptions of social life, national, political life, he sees this monster rise. And that is a picture of the last political government of this earth that is headed up in an ultimate and final antichrist.

Then John saw another beast, and this one arises out of the earth. As the first one arises out of anarchy and chaos and social revolution, the raging waters of the sea of humanity, the second one arises out of the earth. That is, out of civilized, ordered, social government. And this second beast is the sovereign head of the great and ultimate and final religious system of this earth.

The Bible everywhere and especially in the Revelation, the Bible says, and all of these things are corroborated in human history, the Word of God reveals that the earth will move toward political unity. In the last days, even the ten kingdoms into which this whole earth is divided in its national life, even those ten kingdoms will give their sovereignty and their power and their might to that ultimate and final sovereign. The earth, the Bible says, moves toward one political unit. And the same Scriptures say that this earth moves toward religious unity. The development of religious life in this world will be more and more to get together – to combine, to be together – until finally, in this ultimate consummation, all of the religious systems of this world will be headed up in one beast, one monster, one false prophet.

Now, he describes this false prophet. "I beheld another beast coming up out of the earth; and he looked like a lamb. He looked like a lamb, but he spoke like a dragon" [Revelation 13:11]. He looked like a lamb; but actually, he was the mouthpiece and spokesman for the Dragon. That is the same kind of a thing as you read in LITTLE RED RIDING HOOD. That a big, bad wolf is dressed in her grandmother's garment, and he is sleeping in Grand momma's bed. But when Little Red Riding Hood looks at him, he speaks like a wolf, and he has got teeth like a wolf. And she asks him, "Where did you get those teeth? Where did you get those eyes and all of those things?" In Grand momma's garments, but he is a wolf – just like this: he looks like a lamb, looks like a lamb, but he speaks like a dragon.

Now, you cannot have government without religious devotion. That is true of even a Communist government. They make a religion out of their devotion to materialism and to blasphemy and to atheism. And without that trust and that march of religious, fanatical devotion, the system could not live. There has to be a great religious fervor that lies back of any system that obtains or that endures. So the false governmental leader must have a religion. The antichrist must have a religion, and the false prophet supplies it. And he does it through a "counterfeit church," through counterfeit religion.

Now, we are going to stop an exegesis there, and from now on I am going to speak of the counterfeit church. I am going to speak of the religion of this false prophet. There are several things that characterize the counterfeit church and its counterfeit religion. The first is that it says what the world wants to hear said. It pleases itching ears of the church, of the world, and its ministers to its desire to hear what it wants to hear.

I could not think of a better illustration of that than the story of Micaiah. When Ahab said to Jehoshaphat, "Let us go up against Ramoth-Gilead; it belongs to us; let us take it out of the hands of the Syrians," Jehoshaphat said, "Before we go, let us call the prophets together and ask them whether it is wise, whether God will bless the war or not." So Ahab gathered together four hundred of his prophets and they all said: "Go up to Ramoth-Gilead. The Lord will deliver it into your hands." But when Jehoshaphat looked at those four hundred, he said: "Is there not yet another prophet of the Lord before whom we might inquire?" And Ahab replied, "Why, yes, but I hate him. He always speaks evil of me and never good." Jehoshaphat replied, "Oh, let not the king say so. Call him."

So Ahab sent an officer of the government to Micaiah, the prophet of God, to bid him come before the king. And the officer said to Micaiah, "Micaiah, four hundred prophets are now standing before the king and they all are prophesying good. Now, Micaiah, you prophesy what will please the king. You prophesy what is good" [2 Chronicles 18:12].

And Micaiah, the man of God said, "As the Lord liveth, what God says, that will I say." And when Micaiah stood before Ahab, he said, "I saw Israel like sheep scattered on the mountains because their leader was dead."

And Ahab turned to Jehoshaphat and said, "Isn't that what I told you? I hate him. He blasphemes!" Ahab said, "Take that fellow and put him in a dungeon and feed him bread of affliction and water of affliction until I come back in peace and in triumph" [2 Chronicles 18:3-27]. So, Ahab went out to war. And then I had you read the passage. A man drew back his bow in a venture – he did not aim it – drew back his bow in a venture and let fly the arrow. But God guided that arrow and it entered the joint in the harness of Ahab, in the armor of Ahab. And *his blood flowed out by the wound. And they washed the chariot and the dogs licked up the blood according to the great saying of Elijah the prophet [2 Chronicles 18:33-34]. The point of the story is what the officer said to Micaiah, "Tell him something good," say it beautifully, say what he wants to hear said. That is counterfeit religion, the false prophet [1 Kings 22: 3-27].*

It is a rare thing that a prophet of God, a true prophet of God will ever say what the world wants to hear said. When Zedekiah, the king of Jerusalem – when Nebuchadnezzar and his Chaldean army surrounded it like a man who would hold a iron in a grasp, in a vice – when Zedekiah said to Jeremiah, "Is there a word from the Lord?" Jeremiah said, "There is. There is." And Zedekiah said, "What does God say?" And Jeremiah said, "If I tell you, you will slay me. You will put me to death." Zedekiah said, "Your life will be precious in my sight, I swear. What does God say?" And Jeremiah said, "God said this city shall be burned with fire, the Chaldeans shall take the people into captivity, your eyes will be put out and in chains you'll be carried to Babylon and die in a dungeon" [Jeremiah 38:14-23].

It is a rare thing that a man of God will deliver to the world a message the world likes to hear. When the man is suave, and sweet, and pacifying, and placating in what he says, the chances are he's that counterfeit. He's a representative of the religion of the false prophet. For the first characteristic of counterfeit religion is that it says what the world wants to hear said, not what God says.

A second characteristic of the counterfeit church, of the religion of the false prophet: it teaches what the world wants to hear taught; he believes what the world wants to believe. You know, it is a remarkable thing, the religion of the false prophet and the religion of the counterfeit church is one that looks upon all of these old doctrines as being outmoded and, "We have outlived the usefulness of the old-time faith and now we have progressed in this enlightened scientific era to where we need a new theology and a new sophistry and a new enlightenment." And it is remarkable how they purvey that and how they preach that, this counterfeit doctrine and this counterfeit religion of the counterfeit church.

They apply it first of all, to the Book itself – to the Book itself. "Why, no man in this scientific and enlightened age could believe in the miracles of the Bible. No man who lives in our day and in our generation could look with any other eye in that Book except as an antiquarian would look upon it." Way back yonder they wrote Aesop's Fables. And the man looks at Aesop's Fables and he thinks, and he has these attitudes toward Aesop's Fables. And then, way back yonder, Homer wrote his Iliad and his Odyssey, and all about those Greeks and their mythology and their legends. And so he picks up the Bible, and here is an example of those myths and of those legends. And he reads here in the Bible, as he would read about Jason and his Golden Fleece. And he empties the Bible of all of its supernatural and all of its miraculous power. And he looks upon religion as being a thing evolved like what he supposed the evolution of a whole race. "We all come from tadpoles and green scum and we gradually evolved until our arboreal ancestors quit hanging on their tails and went and walked upright. And he was a man, and behold, here we are." And that is the way they look upon religion; it was back there in those primitive Stone Ages. And then he gradually evolved until finally we have what we have today, and that to them, is the religion of the Book, and the God of the Bible. And they have with it – they have with it the same new and modern idea concerning the old-fashioned piety and the reverential awe and fear that God has taught us in the Book by which a man ought to walk humbly before the great God, his Maker. "But all of that is past and now we have new rules and we live in a new day. We have been freed from the old bondage of a morality and the piety of that old medieval and superstition and religion found in the Bible. This is a new day and we have new rules to go by."

This last week, a precious mother – the family does not belong to our church – but a dear mother came to me. Her daughter, who is but a child, her daughter is going to be an unwed mother. And so the mother, in her distress and agony said, "I took the girl, my girl, and I took the boy, and I brought them to his church and to his minister. And this man of the cloth turned to the two children and he said to the girl, "You – this is your fault; you should have protected yourself. This is not the boy's fault. He was just indulging in permissible pre-marital experience, and the reason you are in the condition you are, is because you did not protect yourself. The boy is not to blame at all."

This is a new day, this is a new theology, this is a new morality! When you empty the Book of its God and when you empty the message of the gospel of this great supernatural moral character, well he is as right as anybody else. For morality fundamentally is anchored in the character of Almighty God. When we come to the new sophistry and the new enlightenment and the new age and the new rules, why, this minister of the cloth is correct. It is her fault, she should have protected herself. For this boy was just engaging in legitimate, and permissible, and expected pre-marital experience. That is the religion of the false prophet! That is the religion of the counterfeit church! That is the religion of the Dragon.

The same attitude expressed toward the great doctrines of the faith: in this enlightened age, whose cultivated ears, whose cultural tastes, whose aesthetic nature would respond to a religion of blood – blood atonement? And they refer to it as "the religion of the slaughterhouse. This is the religion of shambles. This is the religion of the packing plant – of the butcher shop."

I have preached in churches where every hymn on the blood has been purged out. It is offensive to our aesthetic natures and it violates our cultural consciences – this religion of blood – but all through the Word of God, that story of blood atonement follows through like a scarlet thread in the Bible. And the difference between religion ultimately is this: as God said in the land of Egypt, "Sprinkle the blood on the lintels and on the door posts in the form of a cross, above and on either side, that there may be a distinction between My people and the world" [Exodus 11:7; Exodus 12:22-23].

You can classify all religion in two, in those twain: the religion of works – whether it is Mohammedanism in Africa and Indonesia, whether it is Romanism, whether it is humanism, whether it is Shinto or Buddhism – all religions that are based upon works and then that one separate and unique Gospel of the Son of God, the religion of the blood. "When I see the blood, I will pass over you" [Exodus 12:13], and "they washed their robes and made them white in the blood of the Lamb" [Revelation 7:14], and the humanist and the counterfeit hates the religion of the blood!

Their attitude is the same expressed toward the revelation of God concerning damnation and perdition and the judgment of Almighty God: Why, there is no such thing – not to the counterfeit, not to the false prophet – there's no such thing as the judgment of God. There is no such thing as the perdition and the fire of hell and eternal damnation, "For these things are superstitions; they are hangovers from a primitive and superstitious past. And we must be positive in our approach today, if you will not teach your children about sin, they will never sin. Let us be positive about it."

Isn't it a funny thing, every one of those ten commandments is a negative? "Thou shalt not," says the Lord God. You never heard anything about this new sophistry of a positive approach, "Don't ever mention sin, and there won't be sin. Don't ever teach your children about the judgment of God, and they will never fall into aberrations." God's Book says we *are born in sin and conceived in iniquity, [Psalm 51:5] and the black drop of depravity is in all of our veins. [Romans 3:23, 5:12] We are born into that kind of a judgment. But that doctrine is unacceptable to sophisticated and modern ears.*

The counterfeit church and counterfeit religion, their God is man whom they worship; and their doctrine is humanism and their paradise and Eden is the socialistic welfare state. That is the counterfeit church, that is the false prophet, and that is the counterfeit religion.

Not only does the counterfeit church say what the world wants to hear said, not only does it teach what the world wants to hear taught, but the counterfeit church and counterfeit religion, enjoys what the world enjoys. There are great cities in America where the councilmen elected are powerless and helpless before the rising tide and scourge of gambling because the Church finds its greatest lucrative source of revenue from gambling. And the city is powerless before the racketeers, and all of the dark underworld that follows, wherever gambling is regnant. And this nation of America is being plunged into the depths of alcoholism like France, because of the approval of the counterfeit church and counterfeit religion.

More and more and more, our beloved America is on a toboggan road, down and down and down. The family is destroyed by it – the homes that are broken by it, the wedding bands that are snapped by it, the children that are orphaned by it – the men's lives that are destroyed by it; the weakness of a whole nation in the aegis and in the approval and in the approbation of a counterfeit church.

This week, Dr. Fowler and I were seated side by side in a funeral home, waiting for the service to begin. While we were seated there, a big man came and stood in front of us and calling me by name, then could not speak for a moment, so filled up. Then he said, "I just wanted to thank you for the sermon last Sunday night. I listened to it on the radio and it gave me hope. It gave me hope. For you see," he said, "my son and my daughter-in-law both are alcoholics." What he was referring to was last Sunday night I spoke of a man who sat by me on an airplane in a distant state. And when I asked him where he was going – same city I was. Well, I said, "I'm going there, why are you?" He said, "I am going to hear you preach." I was going there to preach to a state evangelistic conference. "Well," I said, "that is most unusual. Why are you going down there to hear me preach?" Well, he said, "I had a series of stores, a chain of stores and a beautiful home. And I lost my stores and I lost my home in liquor, in drink. And," he said, "I lost days when I was cast out, I could not go home, I was not allowed. Lost everything." He said, "I went to a service, and I heard you preach and I gave my heart to God. And I went back, and my wife took me into her heart and home again. And now," he said, "I have more stores than I ever had before. I have a bigger chain now than I ever had." And he said, "I am a deacon in my church and I am the treasurer in my church and I am the head usher in my church, and God has blessed me." And he said, "Wherever you are in my part of the world, if I can get there, I will always go to hear you preach." That is the thing briefly that I spake of last Sunday night. And then that father said, "I just want to thank you. It gave me hope. It gave me hope for my boy and my daughter-in-law." Ah, any man in this earth who stands up and says that that is a legitimate business, to destroy homes and to destroy lives and to orphan children and to destroy the souls of men, that man is a counterfeit; I do not care who he is or what his name.

Before one of our legislative committees appointed by the legislature, listened to the discussion of a liquor bill, the bishop stood up and spoke of the liberty and the right of a man to drink. And when the bishop got through speaking his spiel before the legislative committee, a humble unnamed man stood up and he said, "My wife and I had an only son, an only child, and he fell into the terrible throes of the alcoholic. And we won, in love and in tenderness, our boy back to life again. And as our boy was ascending and God's favor was upon him, he was invited to a social gathering. And at that social gathering, a minister of the cloth stood up with a liquor glass in his hand and said, 'This is the right of any man,' and he drank and encouraged all of the others to drink. And my boy was there, and seeing a man of the cloth lead the way, he followed after. And our boy, our boy was on the toboggan road down, and our boy died of delirium tremens. And gentlemen, "the man said, "gentlemen, the man of the cloth who did that that night to our boy is the man of the cloth who has just addressed you."

When the Eighteenth Amendment was destroyed, William E. Borah of the Senate of the United States said, "God will punish America for bringing back the legalized liquor traffic." From that day until this, America has stumbled into one tragic crisis down into another. And what William E. Borah said of the nation of America in legalizing the liquor traffic, that same God Almighty that judges America is the same Lord God Almighty that shall judge the counterfeit church.

Somebody says to me, "Preacher, is there any word in the Bible about liquor?" My soul, in all of the language of the literature of the earth there was never written as scathing, as terrible a castigation as you find in the Word of God. Listen to the words of the wisest man who ever lived:

> Who hath woe? Who hath sorrow? Who hath contentions?
> Who hath babbling? Who hath wounds without cause?
> Who hath redness of eyes? They that tarry long at the wine.
> They that go to seek mixed drinks.
> Look thou not upon the wine when it is red, when it sparkles in the cup,
> At the last, it biteth like a serpent and stingeth like an adder
> [Proverbs 23:29-32].

Whoever fools with that thing, fools with death. He jeopardizes the life of his children and of other children. Don't you ever persuade yourself that when a guy is in the gutter, and he is down and out, that that is a temptation to a fine, upstanding young boy. He sees that fellow in his vomit and in his filth and in his rags and in the gutter and it is offensive to him and he passes by. Don't ever think that he is the one that destroys the boy. The man that destroys the boy is the big executive in his swivel chair, in those beautiful, beautiful offices. And he drinks, and that fine upstanding young fellow coming up, he sees the big executive and he follows after him. And that boy is destroyed. One out of every nine become problem drinkers and cannot help themselves.

And the man that leads the boy into that debauchery and into that ruin and into that damnation is accountable unto God. And the church that approves it is a derelict and a counterfeit church. This is the religion of the false prophet. He encourages to enjoy what the world enjoys. Bless you, I do not attend them, but you can go to endless social gatherings in this city, and whatever the violent, riotous, drunken debauched world is doing, there will you see the minister and there will you see the communicant – all of them enjoying alike, drunken alike, in the orgy alike. That is the counterfeit church. And that is counterfeit religion. It is impossible, it is unthinkable to the true child and the true prophet of God.

We are speaking of the false prophet who looks like a lamb; he is soft and he is sweet and he is easy. And he counsels people and he speaks of their consciences and of their souls; but he is the most dangerous monster of the two, for his heart and his leadership is of the Dragon. I speak of the last. I have spoken: the counterfeit church says what the people want to hear, saying it believes it teaches what the world wants to hear taught. It enjoys what the world enjoys. I have a last characterization that is the truth of God: it offers an institutional salvation. The counterfeit church, counterfeit religion, the false prophet; it offers an institutional salvation. That is, "You go with us and we will take you all to heaven by virtue of the fact that we are the church of God."

May I speak of it briefly? And I need an hour more here; may I speak of it briefly in two ways? They offer a national salvation by their institutional organization, the counterfeit church. The world likes to have one religion so it can dicker with it, so it can write concordats with it, so it can make treaties with it, so it can use it. It pleases the world to have "a church and a religion." Then they can do, they can assemble, and they can write, and they can discuss, and things are simplified. However, the truth of God may be, however the obedience of the Almighty may be, if they can just have a religion in a counterfeit church, why, it simplifies for the world, "There it is. There it is. You do not have to worry about what God says. You do not have to worry about what the will of the Almighty is. Here is religion and we can handle it, and use it, and dicker with it, and mold it, and plaster it, and compromise with it, and make laws concerning it, and write treaties with it; do anything we want to. Just forget about God, just forget about the will of heaven, forget about the Bible; this is religion here." And the national life is framed according to the organized expression of religion in a counterfeit church and the false prophet. I go to the last: and it offers institutional salvation to the individual heart, the counterfeit church and the counterfeit religion. You belong to mother church and mother church will take you to heaven. And outside of mother church is damnation and hell. And in that awful, awful, fearful thing they hold over the heads of their people. They live in panic and in fear at the very thought of being separated from the church, for outside of that institution there is no salvation, nothing but damnation and hell. And they live in fear and in trembling.

Oh, the awful power that lies in the minister of the cloth, among people who believe in that in his institution, in his organization, in his church is all salvation. And what he says is the rule of my life and my soul. And so he says, all of you live in adultery, all of you – all of you. You were married by Baptist minister, yet you live in adultery. You were married according to the laws of the State of Texas – you are all living in adultery. You were married by a Baptist minister, all of your children are illegitimate, all of them – all of them. They are all illegitimate, for you were married by a Baptist minister. And you have committed a mortal sin, you are in a Baptist church and listening to a Baptist minister. And that awful fear by which they govern their people makes it almost impossible to pull somebody out of it. Because to them, to leave it is to be damned. To marry outside of it is to live in adultery and to bring up your children illegitimately. You could go on for the hour and the hours; this counterfeit church, a counterfeit religion, the doctrine of the false prophet. And it pleased the world to have it so.

I must close. Like I pled with a sweet, precious, little girl last night, just building her home. Pray to God for yourself. Do not confess your sins to a man, never; confess them to God."

> He is a great High Priest who can be touched with the feeling of our infirmities;
> for in all points was He tried as we are though without sin.
> Wherefore, come boldly unto the throne of grace and find grace to help in time of need
> [Hebrews 4:15, 16],

Come for yourself, ask for yourself, pray for yourself; confess your needs to God, for yourself. And listen to the voice of the Lord who will answer by power, who will answer by word, who will answer by strength and by might and by power, who will answer from heaven. Go to God for yourself. Ask Him for yourself. Pray to Him for yourself. Look to God for yourself. "Come," says the Lord, "come." This is the true religion. This is the true church. And this is the true prophet of God.

> *And the Spirit and the Bride say, Come.*
> *And let him that heareth say, Come.*
> *And let him that is athirst come.*
> *And whosoever will, let him take the water of life freely"*
> *[Revelation 22:17]*

Come, come for yourself. Let God speak to you, heart to heart, face to face, and find life and assurance and salvation and truth in the blessedness of the name of our glorious and incomparable Redeemer. Come, come. God bids us find help from His gracious and precious hands.

We must close, and should have before. While we sing our hymn, while we sing our hymn, somebody this morning to give his heart to Jesus, come and stand by me. Somebody today to put his life with us in the fellowship of this precious congregation, come and stand by me. "Today, preacher, today, this day, I give my heart to God. I give you my hand. I give my life in trust to Jesus." Come just as you are, let God battle by your side, war down the way with you.

We have a pilgrimage remaining and we need the help and the direction, the succor, encouragement and the strength of our blessed Jesus. Come, come. "Lord, I bring myself to Thee; all the problems I have: the house in which I live, the home that I have built, the children God hath given us, the couple that we are, the one somebody that I am. Preacher, here I come. I give myself to the Lord, I make it now. I make it now." While we stand and while we sing.

COMMENTARY

Counterfeit Religion Commentary

In the nation as well as in the state of Texas, the year 1962 was tempered with events of counterfeit value. Some television quiz winners were indicted for second degree perjury. In March, a tall Texan made international news. Billie Sol Estes of Pecos, Texas and three business associates were indicted by a federal grand jury in El Paso on charges of fraud, conspiracy and interstate mailing of fraudulent mortgages. It was from events such as those that W.A. Criswell felt it necessary to speak to his church, the First Baptist Church of Dallas, Texas, concerning counterfeit values. The mood of the times in 1962 evoked Dr. Criswell to speak out on a main issue. That was the issue that false prophets advocated a religion that is counterfeit. He clarified the issue as he made his ideas evident as he said that the Bible stated, and all of these things are corroborated in human history, the Word of God reveals that the earth will move toward political unity. He continued explaining that the earth moves toward one political unit. And the same Scriptures said that this earth moves toward religious unity. The development of religious life in this world will be more and more to get together – to combine, to be together – until finally, in this ultimate consummation, all of the religious systems of this world will be headed up in one beast, one monster, one false prophet.

Now, he described this false prophet. "I beheld another beast coming up out of the earth; and he looked like a lamb. He looked like a lamb, but he spoke like a dragon." He looked like a lamb; but actually, he was the mouthpiece and spokesman for the Dragon. Then he told the analogy of the same kind of a thing as read in Little Red Riding Hood. That a big, bad wolf is dressed in her grandmother's garment, and he is sleeping in Grand momma's bed. But when Little Red Riding Hood looks at him, he speaks like a wolf, and he has got teeth like a wolf. And she asks him, "Where did you get those teeth? Where did you get those eyes and all of those things?" In Grand momma's garments, but he is a wolf – just like this: he looks like a lamb, looks like a lamb, but he speaks like a dragon. He then proclaimed that we cannot have government without religious devotion.

Dr. Criswell inferred three major ideas in relation to counterfeit religion. First counterfeit religion says what the world wants to hear said, "The first is that it says what the world wants to hear said. It pleases the itching ears of the people." He used biblical illustrations to reinforce the point. Second, counterfeit religion teaches what the world wants to hear taught,". . . .it teaches what the world wants to hear taught. The false prophet believes what the world wants to believe." He described the situation by as he said that it is a rare thing that a man of God will deliver to the world a message the world likes to hear. When the man is suave, and sweet, and pacifying, and placating in what he says, the chances are he's that counterfeit. He's a representative of the religion of the false prophet. For the first characteristic of counterfeit religion is that it says what the world wants to hear said, not what God says.

The third idea advocated in the speech was that counterfeit religion enjoys what the world wants to enjoy. He said, ". . .counterfeit religion enjoys what the world enjoys. . .men's lives are destroyed by it. . . with the approval and in the approbation of a counterfeit church!" He stated that the world like to have one religion so it can dicker with it, so it can write concordats with it, so it can make treaties with it, so it can use it. He further stated that it would please the world to have "a church and a religion." Then they could do, they can assemble, and they can write, and they can discuss, and things are simplified. However, the truth of God would be that if they can just have a religion in a counterfeit church because simplifies for the world, that there would be one religion and the national life would be framed according to the organized expression of religion in a counterfeit church and the false prophet. He started the conclusion as he stated that outside of mother church is damnation and hell.

His ideas then moved toward an old-fashioned temperance sermon as he stated, "Any man in this earth who stands up and says that that is a legitimate business to destroy homes and to destroy lives and to orphan children and to destroy the souls of men, that man is a counterfeit, I do not care who he is or what his name is." Then he asked men to take a stand.

After Criswell shared his viewpoint and documented it with the Bible, he asked men to do two things. First, he asked men to believe the Bible as the true Word of God and not listen to the world, "It is a rare thing that a prophet of God, a true prophet of God, will ever say what the world wants to hear said."

Second, Criswell asked men not to compromise with the mundane desires. He concluded by challenging them to think about their influence and the judgment of God. The man who leads the boy into that debauchery and into that ruin and into that damnation is accountable onto God and the church that approved it is a derelict and a counterfeit church. This is the religion of the false prophet who encourages to enjoy what the world enjoys. You can go to endless social gatherings in this city and whatever the violent, riotous, drunken debauched world is doing there will you see the minister and there will you see the communicant, all of them enjoying it alike, drunken alike, in the orgy alike. That is the counterfeit church and that is counterfeit religion. It is unspeakable to the true child and the true prophet of God. . . .That same God Almighty who judges America is the same Lord God Almighty that shall judge the counterfeit church. He used scripture to document the reasons for asking men to take action against the counterfeit life.

MY FAVORITE SERMON: GOD'S LAST INVITATION

Dr. W. A. Criswell
Revelation 22:17, October 4th, 1964

Turn to the last page in the Bible, Revelation chapter 22. We begin preaching and reading at verse 16. On the radio you are sharing the services of the First Baptist Church in Dallas, and this is the pastor bringing the evening message entitled "My Favorite Sermon."

Out of the thousands of sermons that I preached in the last thirty-seven years there are, I guess, a thousand of them that are my favorites. And this is one of them. It is entitled God's Last Invitation, or it is entitled "All for the Asking," or it is entitled "Revelation 22:17." That is the text, and now we read the context together. Revelation 22 beginning at verse 16 and reading to the end of the Bible, all of us out loud together:

> *I Jesus have sent Mine angel to testify unto you these things in the churches. I am the Root and the Offspring of David, and the Bright and Morning Star. And the Spirit and the bride say, Come. And let him that heareth say, Come. And let him that is athirst come. And whosoever will, let him take the water of life freely. For I testify unto every man that heareth the words of the prophecy of this book, If any man shall add unto these things, God shall add unto him the plagues that are written in this book: And if any man shall take away from the words of the book of this prophecy, God shall take away his part out of the Book of Life, and out of the holy city, and from the things which are written in this book. He which testifieth these things saith, Surely I come quickly. Amen. Even so, come, Lord Jesus! The grace of our Lord Jesus Christ be with you all. Amen.*
>
> *[Revelation 22:16-21]*

And the text, God's last invitation: And the Spirit and the bride say, Come. And let him that heareth say, Come. And let him that is athirst come. And ho thelōn, and whosoever will, let him take the water of life freely. The Spirit of God pleads with a man to come, "Come to Jesus." And the bride of Christ, His church, pleads with the man to come, come to Jesus; and let him that heareth, a passerby, a sojourner, let him repeat the glorious refrain, "Come, come to Jesus." And let him that is athirst come, come to Jesus. Our Lord said "Whosoever drinketh of the water of this life shall thirst again" [John 4:13]. If you have drunk of the water of this life and are thirsty, come, come to Jesus. Bobby Burns wrote:

> *[But] pleasures are like poppies spread,*
> *You seize the flow'r, [its] bloom is shed;*
> *Or like the snow falls in the river,*
> *A moment white – then [melts] forever;*
> *Or like the Borealis race,*
> *That flit ere you can point their place;*
> *Or like the Rainbow's lovely form*
> *Evanishing amid the storm.*
>
> *[from Robert Burns, "Tam O'Shanter"]*

Let him that is athirst come, come to Jesus. And ho thelōn, and whosoever will, let him take the water of life freely.

It is as though God had looked down from heaven on the progeny of old man Adam and said to the apostle John, "John, before the book is sealed and the revelation is forever closed, make one last and final invitation, "If a man is just willing, if he is just willing to be saved, to be a Christian, I will write his name in the Lamb's Book of Life, and I will keep him forever. Ho thelōn – write it, John. Write it, John. If a man is just willing to be saved I will save him and keep him forever, and someday he shall walk on My golden streets and live in My beautiful city, if he is just willing to be saved."

For you see, when the Lord God looked down from heaven on the children of old man Adam, he found them vile, and villainous, and wicked. The Lord had said to our first parents, "Of every tree in the garden thou mayest freely eat: but one I have reserved for Myself" [Genesis 2:16]. And they said, "No, we will not observe that interdiction," and they broke God's commandment, and they partook of that forbidden fruit, and they died [Genesis 3:6].

And the Lord God looked down from heaven, and the children of old man Adam were vile and wicked. And the Lord said, "Thus will I do to save the progeny of old man Adam." And the Lord took tables of stone, and He wrote out His Ten Commandments with His own finger [Exodus 20:1-18, 31:18]. And He handed them down to the children of old man Adam and said, "Do this and thou shalt live" [Deuteronomy 27:10]. And the children of old man Adam said, "No, we will not do this." And they broke all of God's commandments.

And the Lord God looked down from heaven on the children of old man Adam and they were vile and wicked. And the Lord said, "Thus will I do to save the progeny of old man Adam. I will send My prophets." And the prophets of the Lord Jehovah came and preached saying, "Turn ye, turn ye, for why will ye die" [Ezekiel 33:11]. And the children of old man Adam said, "No, we will not turn." And some of God's prophets they put in fiery furnaces. And some of God's prophets they put in the lion's den, and some of God's servants they sawed asunder [Hebrews 11:32-38].

And the Lord God looked down from heaven on the children of old man Adam and He said, "Thus will I do that they might be saved. I will send My messenger before My face" [Luke 7:27]. And the messenger of the great Prince of glory came and preached saying, "Repent ye; for the kingdom of heaven is at hand" [Matthew 3:1-2]. And the children of old man Adam said, "No, we will not repent." And they took God's messenger and cut off his head, and he died in his own blood [Matthew 14:8-11].

And the Lord God looked down from heaven on the villainous children of old man Adam, and He said, "But they will reverence My Son." And the Lord Jesus Christ came down from glory, and the children of old man Adam laid violent hands upon Him, dragged Him outside their city, and between the earth and the sky lifted Him up and nailed Him to a tree. And He died in shame, and in agony, and in His own blood [John 19:1-37].

And the Lord God looked down from heaven on the villainous and vile and wicked children of old man Adam. And He said, "This will I do that they might be saved. I will send them My apostles and My evangelists," and the apostles and the missionaries of the Lord came and preached, saying, "If thou shalt confess with thy mouth the Lord Jesus, and shalt believe in thine heart that He liveth, thou shalt be saved" [Romans 10:9-10]. But the children of old man Adam said, "No, we will not believe in our hearts, nor will we confess the Lord with our mouths." And they took God's apostles, and some of them they beheaded with a sword, and some of them they put on a lonely isle to die of exposure and starvation, and some of them they threw into boiling caldrons of oil, and some of them they crucified like their Lord.

And the Lord God Jehovah finally looked down from heaven on the vile and villainous and wicked children of old man Adam and said, "Thus will I do that they might be saved. John, before the Book is closed and before the revelation is sealed, you write there in My Book, *ho thelōn. If a man is just willing I will save Him.* If he won't keep My commandments, if he won't listen to My prophets, if he won't heed My messenger, and he won't turn at the voice and the call of My apostles, then write there, John, *ho thelōn.* If a man is just willing to be a Christian I will save him," said the Lord God, "I will forgive his sins, and I will write his name in the Lamb's Book of Life, and keep him forever" [Revelation 22:17].

For you see, I believe this Book is inspired word by word and syllable by syllable. I believe God's Holy Spirit wrote this one last invitation, and the Holy Spirit said to the apostle John as he wrote with his pen, "John, don't you write there *ho pisteuĀ,* 'Whosoever believeth, let him come.' Don't you write there John, *ho lambanon,* 'Whosoever receiveth, let him come. Don't you write there *ho ginoskon,* whosoever understandeth, let him come.' Don't you write there *ho phileon,* 'Whosoever loveth, let him come.' Don't you write there *ho paschon,* 'Whosoever feeleth, let him come.' But John, in that last invitation you write *ho thelōn,* 'Whosoever will, let him come, says the Lord,' and I will forgive his sins, I will wash him clean and white, I will write his name in the Book of Life, and I will save and keep him forever" [Revelation 22;17].

Now it's just like this. When I was a young fellow, starting out to preach I was holding a revival meeting under a big tabernacle, an open tabernacle in central West Texas. And on a Saturday night after I had preached the best I could and they were singing an invitation hymn and I was pleading with sinners to come to Jesus, not a soul came, not a soul moved.

So I turned to the singer and I said, "Now wait a minute." And I made a proposition. I said, "If there is anybody here in this great throng of people here tonight, if there is just somebody here that will come down this aisle and say, 'Preacher, I am willing for Jesus to save me,' and ask God to save him; if he is not saved, I'll never preach again. I'll close my Bible, I'll quit the ministry, and I'll never preach again. Now singer, heist a tune," I said, "and will anybody take me up on that proposition?"

So he started singing the invitation hymn again, and there was an old cowpoke out there on the fringes of the tabernacle who came inside and walking bow-legged with his hand extended like that came down to the front. And he said, "Preacher, I'll take you up on that proposition."

I said, "Fine. Now will all the congregation be seated?"

So they were all seated, and I said, "We are going to get down here on our knees, and we are going to ask God to save you. And you ask Him to save you, and God will save you like it says in the Book."

He said, "All right."

I said, "Now you are willing for God to save you?"

"Yes."

"And you mean it in your heart?"

"Yes," he said.

"All right," I said, "Let's kneel and ask Him." So we knelt down, and I bowed my head and I prayed, "O God, save this cowpoke and save him now." Then I said to William, "Now, Bill, you bow your head and you ask God to save you."

So he bowed his head and said the best prayer an old cowpoke could, and when he got through, I extended my hand and I said, "Bill, if God saved you, take me by the hand."

He looked at me and not too elegantly he replied. He said, "I'll swear, preacher, there ain't nothing happening to me yet. I am just like I was."

Well, I said, "Bill, we'll do it again."

"All right," he said.

So I bowed my head and I said, "O God, save this boy. Save him now." And then I said to Bill, "Now Bill, you pray." So he bowed his head and he said the second prayer the best an old cowpoke could, and when he got through I extended my hand and I said, "Bill, if God saved you take me by the hand."

He said, "Preacher, there ain't nothing happening to me. I'm just like I was."

Well, I said, "Bill, we're going to try once more."

"All right," he said.

So I bowed my head. "O Lord, You know what I have said tonight, and if I come down here and asked You to save and they weren't saved, I'd never preach again. Now Lord, save this boy and save him now." And I said, "Bill, you really ask Him."

"Oh, I will!" he said.

So he bowed his head and he prayed his third prayer. And when he got through I extended my hand, and I said, "Bill, if God saved you, take me by the hand."

He looked over at me and said, "Preacher, there ain't nothing happened to me yet. I'm just like I was."

Well, I couldn't stay there all night long. So I had the benediction and everybody went home. Well, I got in the car to go up to the ranch house where I was staying in the days of the revival. And when we all assembled in that car, they thought that was the funniest thing they ever saw in their lives, and they began to kid me about it.

They said, "Preacher, do you know what you did tonight? You said if anybody came down that aisle and asked God to save them, and was willing to be a Christian and wasn't saved, you would close your Bible and never preach again." They thought that was the funniest thing that had happened in their lives.

Well, I was about to die. I was just about to die. And when they found out I was taking it so seriously, nobody said a word. Just as silent, you could hear the flies buzzing in the milk pitcher. You could hear the grass growing, just as quiet and as silent.

So when we got up to the ranch house I dismissed myself, went into my room, shut the door, got down by the side of the bed, and I said, "Lord, this is the end for me. This is the end for me. I've just started my ministry and it's already over. This is the end for me. I don't understand, Lord. For I read in the Book where it said 'Ask, and ye shall receive; seek, and ye shall find' [Matthew 7:7] and 'Whosoever will, let him come' [Revelation 22:17]. And I don't understand, Lord. And this is the end for me."

And I went to bed, rolled and tossed all night long. Got up the next morning, the Lord's Day, dressed, and went with the family down to the tabernacle grounds. I had no idea what to do, or what to say, or where to turn.

When that car rolled up on the tabernacle grounds and stopped, I opened the door and put one foot out on the ground. And when I did, I heard a voice up the road calling to me just as loud as he could shout, "Say, preacher! Say, preacher!" And I turned to see the fellow hollering at me, and it was that bow-legged cowpoke running to me just as fast as his bowlegs would carry him. And when he got to me, he grabbed me around the neck and he said, "Say, preacher, guess what?"

And I said, "Bill, what?"

And he said, "I've been saved! I've been saved! I've been saved!"

I said, "Bill, when were you saved?"

He said, "Preacher, last night on the way home God came into my soul and I've been saved! I've been saved!"

Why, you never heard such shouting in your life. You've never heard such gladness in all the history of glory! And when we had a quorum gathered there under that tabernacle, I called them into conference. We took that boy in on his confession of faith, I had him baptized in a little pool of water by the side of the tabernacle, and let him dry out while I was preaching through the eleven o'clock Sunday morning service.

Oh, what a glory! What a glory. I don't make invitations like that anymore. I don't extend propositions like that anymore. But I'll tell you why. Because I don't have the faith now that I had when I was a seventeen-year-old boy. The world has calloused me and hardened me. But in those days, oh! the Lord seemed so near, and I just felt God would move.

Now since that time and since those years, I have been to school, and I have learned a whole lot of things. And as I have learned and studied, I have found that the gospel that I preached that night as a seventeen-year-old boy, and the invitation I extended that night as a seventeen-year-old boy, is the truest and the finest gospel according to the Word of God that a man could ever preach. And I am going to show you why, and that's the sermon tonight.

You know, there is somebody who lives on the inside of me. You don't see the real me. You just see the house made out of dust and clay and ashes. You just see the house that I live in, and I look out at you through these two windows of my eyes. But there is a me. There is a somebody me who lives on the inside of this house. I believe I could do it better by saying it like this:

There was an old man named Peas. And Peas died. And when he died, they wrote an epitaph on his tombstone, and it went like this:

> Here lies the body of old man Peas,
> Beneath the daisies and the trees.
> But Peas ain't here, only the pod,
> For Peas shelled out and gone to God.

That's what I mean. That's what I mean. On the inside of me there lives the real I. Now that I, that is the real me that lives inside of this house, is composed of three major parts. There are three great components that make up that me who lives on the inside of this house.

There is first my mind, and second my emotion, and third my will. There is my understanding, and my feeling, and my volition. Now of all of those three that make up the real me who lives on the inside of this house, where is the seed of salvation? Am I saved in my mind? Am I saved in my head? Am I saved in my understanding? Am I saved because I am smart, or erudite, or academic, or educated, or because I have a college degree? Am I saved because I have a grasp of things intellectual?

Oh, how I wish it could be done like that! Then we could just educate the world and the whole world would be saved. But in my experience I found it just the opposite. The more so-called "learned" a man is, the sometimes harder and more difficult it is to reach him for Jesus.

A good illustration lies in the most cultured and educated and intellectual of all the nations and races of people who have ever lived. We have never had a nation and we have never had a race of people who were as brilliant and as educated and as scientific as the Nazi Germans.

Nor have we ever had a people that were so merciless, and so cruel, and so diabolical! All you have to do is walk through those concentration camps at Dachau or Buchenwald and see how they used human guinea pigs for those atrocities of war. It is unthinkable, the blood that stained the hands of the Nazi Germans! And yet he was the most educated and the most cultured and the most scientific of all the nations and races that ever lived.

I am just saying, you're are not saved in your head. You're not saved in your mind. You're not saved in your understanding. You're not saved by being smart, or erudite, or learned, or academic. You're not saved because you have been to school. You're not saved in your mind.

"Well then, preacher, I know exactly where we are saved. I know exactly where the seed of salvation is. We're saved in our emotions. We're saved in our feelings. I'm saved because I feel that I am saved."

Well, I wish that were so, and most people are persuaded that it is. But, oh! Emotions are nothing but a concomitant, and a summation, and a corollary of all of the anatomical changes in our body.

When I went to school, I was taught the James Lange theory of emotions, and, "If it isn't true, you can't prove that it's not true." The James Lange theory of emotions is this: that emotion is nothing but a summation of all the anatomical changes in your body. Put them all together and that is an emotion; it is a feeling that is a physical thing. An emotion can be graphed, and your emotions can be graphed. And if you are normal your emotions rise and fall, and rise and fall, and rise and fall, and if you are normal they can be graphed.

There are certain times in the month when your emotions rise, and there are certain times of the month when they fall. And if you are normal, they rise and fall, rise and fall; all emotion does. If you are down all of the time you are afflicted with melancholia. If you are up all the time you are an idiot. But if you are normal you are up and down, and up and down, and up and down, and all emotion is like that.

Love is an emotion and it can be graphed. It rises and it falls and it rises and it falls. It goes up and down. Sometimes a man will love his wife so much he could eat her up. And the next thing he will wish he had done it. Well, that's just normal. That's just normal. All of our emotions rise and fall. They rise and fall, and they can be graphed. All emotion does. Religious emotion is no different. It rises, and you could just shout all over God's glory; and then it falls, and you are so blue and discouraged you can't hear nobody pray. That's just normal.

I heard of a testimony meeting and a dear old saint stood up, God bless her, and she says, "Pastor, sometimes my cup is full and overflowing and sometimes my cup is dry. Pray for me" and she sat down. And then a second saint stood up right behind her, and he said, "Pastor, that's not my experience at all." He said, "I was saved thirty-three years ago," and he said, "thirty-three years ago my cup was one-third full." He said, "After thirty-three years it has still stayed one-third full, and my cup is one-third full still tonight." And he sat down. And when he did, a third saint stood up right behind him and pointed to him and said, "Yes sir, and I bet thee every cent I got that your cup has got wiggle tails in it." Now that's just typical.

All emotion rises and falls. And religious emotion is no different from any other. And my brother, if you ever tie your salvation to your feelings, they will drag you to death! One day you will feel you are saved. "Man, I've got it. I am born again. I am a Christian. I'm nearer and going to glory." And the next day you will say, "You know I was mistaken. I wasn't really saved. I wasn't really regenerated. Why, I don't know the Lord. I haven't been born again." That's because feelings rise and fall.

I'm like that old Negro song, "I'm sometimes up," and I am, "and I'm sometimes down," and

I am, "but still my soul am heavenly bound." You know, a Christian is like the mercury in a thermometer. It goes up and down and up and down but always inside the thermometer. And when I am blue and discouraged, God doesn't love me any less because I am sitting under a juniper tree; He loves me more then, than at any other time because I am just not saved in my emotions and in my feelings.

You know, it's a funny thing. In the New Testament language, the Greek, and in the Old Testament language, the Hebrew, the emotions without exception were all placed in the bowels. You have sometimes in the King James Version translated "bowels of mercies." The viscera was the seat of the feelings and of the emotions. And you are not saved in your feelings. You are not saved in your emotions.

"Well then, preacher, if I am not saved in my head, in my mind, and if I am not saved in my emotions, in my feelings, then where is it that a man is saved? Where is the seat of conversion, and where does God make us new creatures, born again into the kingdom of Jesus?"

My friend, it is exactly where this holy and inspired Word says it is. A man is saved in his will. A man is saved in a choice. A man is saved in his volition. "Ho thelōn, whosoever will, let him come" [Revelation 22:17]. Let him come. Whosoever will. It's in a decision that a man makes. And when a man makes that decision for Christ, he is saved. God regenerates him.

"Well, pastor, do you mean to tell me, do you mean to tell me that a man's eternal decision, a man's eternal salvation, that a man's eternal destiny is conditioned on just one "I will?" Yes, and that is no different from all of life. All of life is just like that. It is change, it is turn, in an "I will."

I want to show you that, and take it out of the life of our Lord. Nobody could illustrate spiritual truth like our blessed Savior. Nobody could say it as our Master could. I am going to take out of the life of our Lord one of His stories. I want you to see how heaven or hell is made in that simple decision of "I will" or "I will not."

Now as you know, I grew up as a boy in far West Texas. I grew up in a line camp that one time belonged to the XIT Ranch, one of the largest ranches in the world. And as those old timers gathered in my father's shop, I would listen to them by the hour and the hour as they'd talk about the days of the XIT Ranch and all of the roundups and the things that would happen in that far high western prairie.

Now I want to take a story and tell it as Jesus would have told it had He grown up there in West Texas. The Lord said there was a Christian bossman, a Christian ranchman, and he had two sons. And upon a day, the younger of those boys came to the father and said, "Father, I'm tired of this place. I'm sick of everything around here and I'm dragging out. I'm heading west. And if there is anything coming to me, give it to me now because I am leaving home."

And the father pled with the boy, "Oh son, oh son!" But when you've lost the heart of your son, you can't keep him. So the father took the part, the portion that was coming to him, and placed it in his hands.

And say, you should have seen that boy as he headed out and dragged west. Man, he bought him the prettiest palomino pony you've ever looked upon. And he got him a silver studded saddle and a silver bridle to match. He got him hand-tooled boots and golden spurs. He got him a ten-gallon hat and headed west. And when he hit town, say, did everybody know he was there!

It wasn't that way back home. One night at the supper table the mother said to the dad, "Dad?"

And the dad said to the mother, "Mother, what's the matter, Mother?"

"Oh," she said, *"No, no, Dad, there's nothing wrong."*

"Yes," said the dad. *"What's the matter, Mother?"*

And the mother said, *"Well, Dad, if you just have to know, I was thinking about our boy."* And that evening on the veranda looking down a long, long road the big man doubled up his fist and wiped a tear out of his eye, and the mother said, *"Dad, what's the matter?"*

He said, *"There's nothing the matter. There's nothing the matter."*

She said, *"Dad, I know something's the matter. I saw you double up your fist and wipe a tear out of your eye."*

And he replied, *"Well, Mother, if you just have to know I was thinking about our boy."*

Way out there in the West, sitting on a corral fence, watching the hogs eat, sat a boy. Gone his palomino pony; gone his silver-studded saddle; gone his golden spurs. And as he sat on the corral fence watching the hogs eat, the tears made furrows through the dirt on his face as they fell down on the ground.

And as the boy sat there an old cowpoke came sauntering by and looked at him, walked over to him and said, *"Son, what's the matter?"*

"Oh," said the boy, *"there's nothing the matter. There's nothing the matter."*

"Why son, there is something the matter. Look at the furrows in the dirt on your face where the tears have been falling down. What's the matter, son? What's the matter?"

And the boy replied, *"Well sir, if you just have to know, I was thinking about home."*

The old cowpoke said, *"Son, do you have a home somewhere?"*

And the boy said, *"Yes."*

"Son, do you have a Christian father and mother somewhere?"

"Yes," said the boy.

And the old cowpoke said, *"Son, you know one time I had a Christian father and mother, and I broke their hearts. They are in heaven today. Son, I'd give my life if I could go see them. Listen, lad,"* said the old cowpoke, *"if you have a Christian father and mother and a home somewhere, son, get up and go back. Go back. Go home."*

And the old cowpoke sauntered away. And as the boy sat on the top of the corral fence, the Book says the boy replied. What did he say? *"I will. I will arise and go back to my father and home. I will"* [Luke 15:18].

And the rest of the story, don't you know? The father saw him, and the fatted calf was killed, and they began to rejoice and be merry, *"For this my boy was dead and is alive again. He was lost and is found"* [Luke 15;23-24]. And they began to be merry, and to be glad, and to thank God all because of, why? The boy, *"I will, ho thelōn."*

"Whosoever will, let him come." Let him come. Let him come.

"If he is just willing, I will save him," says the Lord. *"If he is just willing, I will write his name in the Book of Life. If he is just willing, I will save and keep him forever. If he is just willing, I will fight his battles for him. I will crown him with every victory and triumph, if he is just willing, ho thelōn. Whosoever will, let him come. Let him come"* [Revelation 22:17].

And the Lord awaits and the Lord calls. And the Lord prays. And the Lord moves. And the Lord makes appeal. All I have to do is say, *"Master, I am on the way. Here I am and here I come,"* and it's done. And it's done.

Isn't that the invitation that we sing? *"Come, every soul by sin oppressed, there is mercy with the Lord."* And while we sing it tonight, you, somebody you, make it now. Make it now. In the balcony round about, you; down one of these stairwells at the front or the back at either side, and there is time and to spare. *"Here I am, preacher. Here I come. I make it now. I will* decide for Jesus, and here I come." *The throng on this lower floor, into the aisle, and down here to the front, "Here I am, preacher. I do decide for Christ, and I am coming. God help me, and God save me, and God keep me, and God see me through. I cast my life and lot with Jesus, and here I am." Make it tonight.*

*A family coming into the fellowship of our church; how ever the Spirit of Jesus shall open the door, shall make the appeal, shall press the call to your heart, come. Come. "And the Spirit and the bride say, come. And let him that heareth say, come. And let him that is athirst come. And whosoever will, ho thelōn, and whosever will, let him take the water of life freely." Come. Come. Make it now. Make it now, while we stand and while **we sing**.*

COMMENTARY

My Favorite Sermon

In 1964 Lyndon Baines Johnson was elected President of the United States with the high record-breaking landslide vote as he campaigned for achieving "The Great Society,"

W. A. Criswell believed that the only way to have a high society was to have a Christian society. Criswell presented his ideas for a Christian society in a sermon to the First Baptist Church, Dallas Texas. He entitled it, "My Favorite Sermon." It was easy to know that the message of how to become a Christian was his favorite subject. He talked about that subject everywhere he went.

Dr. Criswell continued to proclaim that to have a Christian society there was one major issue-- How does a person become a Christian? And how does a man know that he is saved? Criswell spoke to that matter.

The question of how to become a Christian was answered by advocating three ideas:

First, a person is not saved in his head, mind or understanding. Second, a person is not saved in his emotions. Third, a man becomes a Christian by the "will."

Dr. Criswell explained this concept by making several scriptural statements. He used the Greek translation of the words to make the concepts clearer to the congregation. He stated the Holy Spirit said to the Apostle John as he wrote, "John, don't you write there *"pisteuon,"* whosoever believeth, let him come. Don't write there *"lambanon,"* whosoever receiveth, let his come. Don't you write there *"ginoskon"* whosoever understands, let him come. Don't you write there *"phileon"* whosoever loves, let him come. Don't you write there *"koscon"* whosoever feeleth, let him come. But John, in that last invitation, you write *"hopstello"* whosoever will, let his come, says the Lord and I'll give forgive his sins. I'll wash him clean and white. I'll write his name in the book of life and I'll save and keep him forever."

Criswell continued to tell his famous analogous stories from his past. He stated it's just like this. "When I was a young fellow, starting out to preach, I was holding a revival meeting under a large tabernacle, an open tabernacle in central West Texas. And on a Saturday night after I had preached the best I could and they were singing an invitation hymn, and I was pleading with sinners to come to Jesus, not a soul came, not a soul moved. So I turned to the singer, and I said, "Now wait a minute." And I made a proposition. I said, "If there is anybody here in this great throng of people here tonight, if there is just somebody here that will come down this aisle and say, 'Preacher, I am willing for Jesus to save me,' and ask God to save him; if he is not saved, I'll never preach again. I'll close my Bible, I'll quit the ministry, and I'll never preach again. Now singer, heist a tune," I said, "and will anybody take me up on that proposition?'"

When Criswell concluded his sermon on how to become a Christian, he asked the people to be willing to be saved. His final statement included these ideas: If he is just willing, I will save him, says the Lord. If he's just willing, I'll fight his battles for him. I'll crown him with every victory and triumph. If he is just willing "*hopstello*," whosoever will let him come. Criswell always concluded his sermons with some form of appeal that was similar to this statement, "The Lord awaits, and the Lord calls, and the Lord prays, and the Lord move and the Lord made an appeal. All I have to do is to say, "Master, I'm on the way Here I am, and it's done."

DRUG ADDICTION IS SPELLED D-E-A-T-H

Dr. W. A. Criswell
An Address Delivered to First Baptist Church, Dallas, Texas, March 28, 1971
and
The 92nd Congress of The United States of America, May 3, 1971

On the radio of the city of Dallas you are sharing the services of the First Baptist Church. This is the pastor bringing an address, not a sermon; an address entitled Drug Addiction is Spelled D-E-A-T-H, death. I read a Scripture as a background; the familiar and meaningful one in the twelfth chapter of the Book of Romans:

I beseech you therefore, my people, by the mercies of God, that ye present your bodies a living sacrifice, holy, acceptable unto God. And be not conformed to this world: but be ye transformed by the renewing of your mind, that ye may prove what is that good, and acceptable, and perfect, will of God.

[Romans 12:1-2]

As I begin the address, may I remind you that I cannot speak the language of the underworld? I have never been introduced to it, and when I listen to it, I am shocked beyond any way that I could describe it.

For example, behind a screen and the light beyond the screen show just the shadow of those who were standing there. And the reason for their shadowy appearance was, according to the commissioner of customs and smuggling and narcotics and dangerous drugs, these men were informers. They are men who lived in the underworld. All their lives they had lived in the underworld. And they had turned and become informers to the government. They are called fingers, and they tell these undercover agents all of those who are engaged in this illicit traffic. And their language is beyond anything I ever heard. About half of their words, I don't even know what they mean, and the other half are dirty. For example, heroin is called, and they used it a thousand times it seemed to me; heroin is called that four-lettered word for human offal and excretion. That's heroin.

It is beyond anything that I have ever seen or heard. They have a world of their own. It is down and down and down. I have never been an addict. I have never been introduced to it. Consequently, when I talk and deliver this address, it is altogether from the viewpoint of one who has been introduced to it, and I just lay before you what has been introduced to me.

First we are going to begin with definitions. And I need this. I cannot understand without it, so we shall begin with definitions. Drugs, that is any substance that has any effect upon the mind or body. Coming back Saturday from Washington I was offered liquor a half a dozen times. These airplanes are flying bars. And I said to the stewardess, "Did you know that is a powerful drug you have in your hand?"

She said, "What? This wine? It couldn't be."

It's the most powerful drug for evil that is known to humanity. Drug, any substance that has an effect upon the body or mind.

Habituation, habituation: the psychological desire to repeat the use of a drug because of emotional reasons such as escape from tensions, dulling of reality, euphoria, getting high, living in an ephemeral world. Habituation refers to the psychological need for a drug.

Addiction refers to the physical dependence upon a drug. That brings into play the word tolerance. Tolerance refers to that reaction of the body whereby the body requires a larger and larger amount of the drug to produce the same effect. Tolerance. Now, addiction also includes in it withdrawal, the symptoms of withdrawal. Withdrawal refers to when the drug is stopped. The withdrawal period is characterized by such distressing symptoms as vomiting and convulsions. And when you use the word addiction you are referring to a physical dependence upon a drug that the human body has more and more tolerance for and needs larger amounts of it to produce the same effect. And when it is stopped the user, the addict, falls into vomiting and convulsions.

Marijuana. Marijuana is an easy to grow hemp plant. It has long, narrow, jagged edged leaves growing like poorly spaced spokes on a wheel. It grows about five feet tall in this country, and here in America it is relatively weak growing here. But in old Mexico the plants are twice as strong, and in India, in the moist, warm climate of India, it is four or five times as strong. The flowering tops have a sticky resin, which produces the marijuana effect called tetrahydrocannabinol or THC. It is classified as a hallucinogen; marijuana. Hashish is the dark brown purified resin extract prepared from the dried flowers of the hemp plant, the marijuana plant. It is five times stronger than marijuana. And it is hashish that you will see that is placed in brick form and attempted to be smuggled into America.

Now these are the words the underworld use, the addicting world uses, for marijuana. It is called grass, hay, jive, mary jane, pot, tea, weed. A marijuana cigarette is called a joint, a reefer, a stick, and the stub end of it is called a roach. And they burn it down, because of the high price of it here, to that last little stick. You saw them do cigarette butts like that you'd think they were stupid and insane.

Hallucinogens: these drugs are capable of provoking changes of sensation. The resulting illusions, hallucinations and delusions may be either minimum or overwhelming, depending on the person and the dose.

LSD is the most potent of all of the hallucinogens. It comes from a fungus that spoils rye grain. A Swiss chemist, Albert Hofmann, accidentally discovered its mind-altering properties in 1943. The word psychedelic is a term invented to describe some of the effects of LSD. Now, in the underworld, LSD is called acid. And a "good trip" is someone taking LSD who has pleasant imageries and emotional feelings. But a bad trip, "a bummer", results in terrifying images and emotions of dread and horror – hallucinogens, the most potent of which is LSD.

All right, stimulants. Stimulants are drugs which increase alertness, reduce hunger and provide a feeling of well-being. The amphetamines are stimulants. They have an effect upon the central nervous system, and they are the most dangerous of the stimulants. Benzedrine, in the dark world is called bennies, beans, and cartwheels. Dexedrine is called dexiets, and methamphetamine, methedrine, is called speed, crystal, crank, meth. Now these stimulants, these amphetamines, are – down there in that underworld – called pep pills, wake ups, eye-openers, co-pilots, truck-drivers and uppers.

Now sedatives; sedatives induce sleep. In small doses they reduce tension and anxiety. The barbiturates constitute the largest group of sedatives. Down there in the underworld they are called goofballs and sleepers and downers. The tranquilizers calm and relax and diminish anxiety. Both sedatives and tranquilizers can be physically addicting.

Marijuana is not. Withdrawal effects occur when the drug is stopped. The most common mode of suicide with drugs is with these barbiturates, these sleeping pills. Depressants or barbiturates produce impaired judgment, slow reaction timing, slurring of speech, staggering, loss of balance, a quarrelsome disposition, sometimes a coma and death.

Narcotics, narcotics relieve pain and induce sleep. They are opiates. Narcotics originally came from the opium poppy, a bitter yellowish-brown drug resin prepared from the dried juice of unripe pods of a poppy plant.

Morphine, one of the active components in opium and heroin; heroin is morphine chemically altered to make it six times stronger. From the opium also comes codeine and paregoric. There are many synthetic chemicals that have morphine like effects. Heroin accounts for ninety percent of the narcotic addiction problem. In the underworld, down there, it is called "H", it is called horse, it is called junk, it is called smack. In all of the conversation I never heard it called any of that. I heard it called by that other name.

Now the session at the White House: we met in the East Wing of the White House after nine o'clock, and we stayed in that session until 7 o'clock in the evening. An aide said to me, "Ninety-eight percent of all the church members in the United States are represented here in this meeting." There were about sixty leaders. On my right sat Bishop Sasedsky, head of the National Polish Catholic Church. On my left sat the famous Rabbi Kirchner of New York City. And this good old Baptist was right in the middle.

The meeting was opened by Egil Krogh. They all called him Bud Krogh, assistant to the president for Domestic Affairs. In his introductory remarks he said, "The final answer is out of the reach of government." He introduced Attorney General John N. Mitchell. Because of his wife, Martha, I paid particular attention to his sartorial attire.

Attorney General Mitchell is an older man, but he was nattily dressed in a blue suit, in a white shirt, in a red and blue tie and a handkerchief to match. Not nearly as well dressed as I am here tonight. He impressed me. From the attorney general, the government has conducted for two years a complete drive against drug abuse. President Nixon called together the fifty governors to discuss the problem, then the radio, TV executives and now you.

Drugs make a user a slave to sensation. He asked the question, "Why not?" "This is the reason we need to confer with you, the religious leaders of the nation."

Krogh introduced John Ingersoll, the director of the Bureau of Narcotics and Dangerous Drugs. He started his speech off with a joke. He said that a visiting preacher passed the hat, and when the hat came back, he looked in it and there wasn't a thing anybody had put inside. He bowed his head for the prayer and said, "Dear Lord, I thank you that I got my hat back from this congregation." That is dedicated to Mr. Ramsour.

John Ingersoll, the director of the Bureau of Narcotics and Dangerous Drugs said, as you could know, I just take a few sentences out of the addresses they made, "The drug problem is as old as civilization. Back in 5000 BC there was a drug problem. There existed then as there is today a chemical religion with false prophets everywhere presenting its ephemeral bliss."

And were you here the Sunday before? Did you hear me talk about the ancient government of Babylon and the ancient civilization of that far-famed city? And do you remember I said a part of that religion that goes back to Babylon is translated in the Bible, "sorcery." The word is pharmakeia, pharmacy drugs, black magic. Always there has been a culture, a religion, of drugs as far back as mankind can search in archaeological records.

Krogh then introduced Miles J. Ambrose, the commissioner of the Bureau of Customs. And he spoke on smuggling. I could not believe my eyes! They had a display there half as long as this church is wide. From there to there. And I was horrified! A large percentage of that display was religious, Christian objects. They would take a cross and stuff it with heroin. Take a crucifix, a big one and in the back of it was solid heroin. Take a bronze plaque of the Lord's Supper and back of it, solid heroin. Take candles they burn in cathedrals, the inside of them, solid heroin. I couldn't believe as I looked at it. I held in my hands solid hashish. It was in the form of ancient pottery. Solid hashish; you'd never have guessed it in the earth. And the only reason the custom official became suspicious of it was because it looked like cheap pottery, like you would dig up, but they had an enormous insurance on it! Becoming suspicious they found it was solid hashish.

"The problem is compounded," said Miles Ambrose, "because there are two hundred fifty million people who come into this country every year." Our citizens go and come, go and come and others come. And there are sixty-seven million parcels that are mailed into this country every year.

There is no heroin in America; all of it has to be imported. It has to be smuggled in. Now, Dr. Laird, is there any medical use for heroin, none at all. It is solely a drug addictive smuggling operation. And yet that drug problem cost America, and that is us, that is we, it costs us eight billion dollars a year!

There was a hush. Everything stopped and somebody whispered to me, "The president is coming." He walked in. We all stood and applauded. He is personally one of the finest men you could ever meet. He is warm hearted, very open and very dedicated.

I quote from the president, I may not be supposed to, but I wrote these things down as he spoke. He said he was surprised that addiction starts at such an early age, even at twelve years of age. "We cannot approach the problem," he said, "with anger but with sorrow. We can be angry at the pusher, at the junkie, but not at the addict. We must seek after rehabilitation rather than punishment. Why does a young person," he said, "give up on the democratic system to turn to something he thinks leads to a way out but it doesn't? He has a spiritual need," that young person, the president said. "He has a spiritual need that must be filled. If there is an answer, you gentlemen have it," he said. "That young person must have something to believe in, to turn to. The worst thing that can happen to a young person is to have no faith and no belief in anything. The heart of the problem is a spiritual vacuum." That's the assize of the president of the United States.

John Broger introduced Chaplain Rowe, who had just come back from Vietnam. And as I listened to that chaplain speak, my heart was filled with indescribable sorrow. The men that are sent over there to fight for us in Vietnam are immediately introduced to the whole world of heroin and drug addiction. Now, the tragedy of the situation in Vietnam is this. For a salary of $200 a month, a soldier in Vietnam can buy the purest heroin uncut and live on it every day – on a salary of $200 a month. When the soldier comes back to the United States, it takes a minimum of $1000 a day to keep up the addictive habit he acquired in Vietnam. What happens to the soldier? He disintegrates. And the chaplain said that only in religious faith is there a hope for the return of that soldier to society. "Religious faith," he says, "is the cornerstone of rehabilitation."

I read in a book that there are practically no men who ever become addicted to heroin, who ever come back into society and take their place as once they were. The loss of human life in this drug traffic is sorrowful to make an angel weep.

Krogh introduced Dr. Bertram S. Brown of Harvard who is director of the National Institute of Mental Health. Quoting President Nixon from an early address, Dr. Brown said, "The problem has grown from one of vocal concern to one that threatens the future and well-being of America." Then still quoting the president, he said, "College is too late to face the *problem. High school is largely too late. We must meet the problem in junior high and in elementary grades! Fear and scare are not enough. They must be told and taught the reasons for refusal to indulgence."*

At the lunch hour George Romney, three times governor of Michigan and candidate for the GOP nomination for president of the United States, George Romney spoke. He is minister of Housing and Urban Development. He preached a regular sermon. That fellow is fervent. One of the things that he said, and I thought I ought to share it with you, his appraisal of the present situation in which we live. He said that "The Nixon administration inherited a greater crises than either Lincoln or Franklin Roosevelt." He said that their crises were capable of explicit definition. In the days of Lincoln it was slavery or freedom. In the days of Franklin Roosevelt it was hunger or jobs. But he said, "Today a crisis is of the spirit and defies definition." And he said, "We must have an answer that is spiritual! And the drug problem is an illustration of this spiritual vacuum that has swept over America."

Now, my words. Drug addiction is spelled D-E-A-T-H. I have a UPI story, out of the daily newspaper. Datelined; Tacoma, Washington. And I read from the UPI news story:

A railroad employee found the well-dressed body of a young man in a corner of an empty boxcar behind the Union Pacific depot. In the jagged pockets were empty pillboxes and a billfold that identified the youth. Then it goes on to tell about the boy. When the body was moved, a suicide note was found. It said:

> "Dear Dad, Dope ruined my life and took away my happiness forever. I thought I was experiencing life. I found it was death! I hope to God people taking dope find what I found in it sooner than I did. Goodbye, dad, your son.
> Love, Ricky."

You spell dope addiction D-E-A-T-H! I went to Haight-Ashbury. I was out there two or three times just looking at it. When Haight-Ashbury district in San Francisco began, it caught the attention of the world because of the idealistic flower-children who converged there. And it looked as though there was appearing on the horizon of American life a new phenomenon. Young people would travel all over the country to see it. They had vaguely heard about the drug overtone involved. But they had no introduction to it. What did Haight-Ashbury develop into? A knowledgeable writer spent many weeks with the youngsters on the streets, on their pads, and on their own. Now I am going to quote from him. This is the end of the flower children, the hippie movement. I quote from him, talking about them:

They would share their food, most of which had been panhandled on the streets. They would talk readily about free love but very little about the alarming rise of venereal disease brought on by such practices. They even wore buttons saying, "Syphilis can be fun." Gradually the ideal-ism of the streets gave way to con artists, thugs, exploiters and hardcore pushers, junkies, who made the whole community their victims. Peace and love are gone from the streets of the district today. All that remains is crime and violence and death!

Drug addiction is spelled D-E-A-T-H! Why the drug problem? And I have it summarized here so I can briefly present it. Before I do, you are not going to like it, but I am bounden and responsible to declare the truth. Why the drug problem?

Two reasons. One is found in our adult world and the other is found in our young people's world. First, the adult world. Why the drug problem? It is because of our modern drug culture *among adults. For a growing number of adults drugs are a way of life. They take pep pills to get up, tranquilizers to get down, a cocktail to start the evening. They can't talk without it, can't even carry on a conversation unless they are stimulated by some kind of a drug, like a cocktail to start the evening and a barbiturate to go to sleep. There is an estimated ten billion capsules and dangerous tablets that are produced every year in this country, no small part of which finds its way down into the underworld. The message of American advertising is cure your pains by chemicals. Adults set a powerful example – the necessary cigarette.*

I can't get it in my mind. When I came down here to look at this Institute on Basic Youth Conference, they had an intermission and all around this church house were women, women, women, girls, girls, girls out there smoking their cigarettes. They can't last through an evening without nicotine – a drug. Necessary? The necessary cigarette, the liquor before dinner, the diet pill, the sleeping pill, the tranquilizing pills, then when these same parents see their teenagers use drugs they call them thieves and criminals and degenerates! The young people merely are following in their parents and society's footsteps. If there ever lived a hypocritical culture and a hypocritical generation, it is the present culture and the present generation of American citizens.

There is not a doctor in the land but that would stand up here and say to you, and we are going to get into that in this moment now, marijuana, marijuana is no more intoxicating and no more addictive and no more with overtones of tragedy than alcohol! Let's look at this attitude toward liquor, which is liquid pot! Never, never; I was there, for example, all day long and I have listened to people discuss this I don't know how and for how long. Never, never is it proposed to attack it or oppose it as they do other drugs!

Somewhat we are getting to the place where we are willing to face nicotine and the serious, serious effects of tobacco. We are beginning to say to the advertising media, "You can't bring that stuff into our living room and parade it there before our children, for it has death in the package, as emphysema and lung cancer. You can't do that." We are facing up to the truth of tobacco, but there are no proposals to face and to outlaw liquor and alcohol! Rather, the turn of our society is in the other direction. Texas is now in the process, legally, to establish what they said they would never establish again in the history of civilization; saloons on every corner, open saloons! Texas is getting ready. For example, look at this quote. Now we are talking about marijuana and alcohol, both of them drugs. One of them liquid, the other dry. Now look at this quote. I read from Dr. Donald B. Lowry, his book entitled Drug Scene. Now listen to him: The proponents for the legalization of marijuana point out that alcohol is a dangerous drug, which is perfectly legal in our society.

That's right, isn't it? The proponents for the legalization of marijuana point out that alcohol, a dangerous drug, is perfectly legal in our society. They say that marijuana is no more dangerous than alcohol is, and that's right. There's not a doctor in the land that would stand up here and deny that. That's what the doctor is writing. The proponents for the legalization of marijuana say that marijuana is no more dangerous than alcohol is.

Now, it seems to me that what men who are red-blooded, what they ought to do is stand up and say, "Then that means as we oppose marijuana we should also oppose alcohol!" That's what you would think they would say. They don't ever say it! What do they say? "All right. Alcohol is a dangerous drug. The question is simply whether we are to add to our alcohol burden another intoxicant. In the United States there is currently a death from automobile accidents every eleven minutes and an injury every eighteen seconds. Shall we add another intoxicant, such as marijuana, and increase the number of inebriated drivers and pedestrians and attain a death rate of one every five minutes and an injury every eight seconds?"

Never is it supposed to propose that we oppose all of these drugs that have deleterious effects upon the mind. But liquor is a sacred cow. We dare not speak of it. We dare not touch it. But the proposal is made, let us fight marijuana to the death because we already have one intoxicant drug that is decimating our people, slaughtering them on the highways, breaking up our homes and families. "We already have one of them. American society and American national life cannot stand another one. Therefore, we oppose the entrance of marijuana." That is the reasoning of the educational and political and economic leadership of present day America.

We must hasten. I said there were two reasons for the drug problem. One is the hypocritical, indefensible example of these adults. As I ride these airplanes, I cannot remember when anybody else on the plane refused liquor except me. I cannot remember it. No woman, no youth, no man, no anybody! The whole world of America is sots, it drinks. It is the exception that does not. Then we turn around and look at that teenager. All right. There is an example in the adults; that's why the drug problem.

Second, in the young people there is a lack of deep spiritual dedication on the part of youth. Three things about them that lead them into drinking: one is curiosity and experimentation. The other is peer pressure. And I run across that word all the time. Peer pressure. That is, wherever the little boy is he will have a friend his own age that pushes him into it. If there is a teenager she will have a friend her age that pushes her into it. If it's a young adult, it has a friend push him into it. Peer pressure. It means a lot to a youngster, to be in, to belong.

And third, why does a young person take drugs? Curiosity. Second, peer pressure. Third, hedonistic pleasure, to have a good time in it. As Dr. Nolan Estes said to me this morning, they are taught to believe, persuaded to believe, that happiness is just a pill away. They are bored. There is nothing else to do. They will lose all of their worries, they say, and some of them are failures and this is the way out, to forget it.

Now, if the youth is experimenting, he needs to be given the facts medically, socially and legally! Drugs kill! You spell them, D-E-A-T-H! Drugs kill! And these boys and girls that are experimenting with them need to be taught those awesome and terrible facts. It kills body and soul, and you face a social problem. You face a medical problem, and you also face a legal problem.

Second, if it is peer pressure, that youngster needs the strength of the Christian community. His peers are Christians. Here is a group; belong to them. And that is why years ago, long before I ever faced any problem like this, long years ago before I ever thought of a problem like this, that is why I brought to this church and said, "By God's help, we need a program down here to call these young people out of the dens and dives and the joints and bring them here where they can have a Christian fellowship and a Christian community."

When you are out there, I don't think a young person can finally say no. They press and they push and they suggest, then finally mock and they ridicule, and most any young people will succumb! We need a Christian community where the young person can belong to it, and they are not pushers, and they are not junkies, and they are not addicts, and they are not habituates, but they love God, and they are down here where they can support one another and love one another. They can build their homes down here. They can fall in love down here. *They can marry down here. They can look forward to ever triumph in every future in unfolding years.*

All right, if it is hedonistic pleasure, if the reason the youngster uses drugs is because of the kick he gets out of it and the excitement in him, we are dealing there with a moral and a spiritual vacuum. The boy's life, the girl's life is empty, and he needs to reassess the meaning and purpose of life in Christ Jesus. As one boy said, and that was one of the most moving things I ever read in my life, as one boy said, "I was helpless, I was hooked," as they use the word. "I was hooked, but I found a Savior in the Lord, and He saved me, and He delivered me, and He sees me through." That is the road. Let's walk in it. This is the way. Let's follow it: the Jesus way, the glory road, the highway to heaven.

Are you a youngster? Make your friends down here. And when you are enticed out there, "No, no." Are you a teenager? Make your friends down here. And when it is suggested out there, "No, no." If you are an adult, put your life down here in the community of Christ. When you are invited to deny the Lord, "No." You spell drug addiction D-E-A-T-H! You spell Jesus Christ L-I-F-E!

He said, "I am come that they might have L-I-F-E and have it more abundantly, abounding, overflowing" [John 10:10]. Ah, my people, our children you, our teenagers and young people you, and our adults and parents you, let's walk in the way of the Lord, and let God give us those rich benedictory, heavenly blessings that only the riches of God could afford. In His gracious hands, how many precious gifts to bestow; and they are ours for the asking, for the having, for the taking, for the receiving.

(Conclusion at Congress) Thank you for listening. You've been listening almost an hour. God in heaven, bless to our souls and our lives, all of who are older are examples, the message of the truth of this evening.

(Conclusion at Church) We are going to sing our hymn of appeal. I am asking no commitment, not concerning this. Just as God would press its truth and its message to your heart, answer faithfully and as unto the Lord. I make no appeal, no invitation. I ask no commitment. Just as God shall speak to your heart, I do ask a commitment to Jesus, to take Him as your Savior. Would you come down here and kneel with me? "I want to give my heart to God, and I am coming tonight." Maybe to put your life in the sweet fellowship of this dear church. Would you come? A family you, a husband and wife you, just you, on the first note of that first stanza, come. Make it now. Do it tonight. Where you are seated in the balcony, on the lower floor, make the decision in your heart now. When we stand up in a moment to sing, stand up coming. Down one of these stairways, into the aisle and to kneel here with the pastor at the front, "I am coming tonight, pastor, here I am." And may God see you through and may the angels of heaven go before [you]. "I am coming. I am coming." Do it now, while we stand and while we sing.

COMMENTARY

Drugs is Spelled D-E-A-T-H

Dr. Criswell became so concerned about the misuse of drugs that he gave a Sunday morning service at First Baptist Church to address his congregation concerning the problem. Soon after this message to the church, Dr. Criswell was invited to present the same address to the 92nd Congress of the United States of America. The speech started with a disclaimer as Criswell stated, "As I begin the address, may I remind you that I cannot speak the language of the underworld? I have never been introduced to it, and when I listen to it, I am shocked beyond any way that I could describe it."

By 1971 reaction to drug use, drug abuse and the illicit traffic in the United States had progressed from mythology and hysteria to concern and awareness to search for practical solutions. There was a growing realization that the drug problem did not exist in isolation.

President Richard Nixon signed Proclamation 4080 designating Drug Abuse Prevention Week. The president stated that not so long ago it was easy enough to regard the tragedy of drug abuse as "someone else's problem." But recent years have brought that tragedy home -- often very literally to all Americans. We have learned that drug abuse refers not only to the crime-prone heroin addict that is the disease at its deadliest, with over 1,000 heroin fatalities annually in New York City. The term also refers to the suburban housewife dependent on tranquilizers and diet pills; to the student learning on amphetamines to help him cram for exams; even to preteens sniffing glue. It appeared that everyone in the audience agreed that drugs had become a problem that touches each of us. Its manifestations were many and varied, but all grow from a common root psychological and physical needs unmet through legitimate social channels -- and all feed on common ignorance of the profound harm the drug abuser did to himself and society. Substance abuse was nothing less than life and death matter for countless Americans, and for the moral fiber of this Nation. Criswell agreed that the drive to meet this threat must command from us our very best our attention, our energies, our resources and our prayers.

The paramount issue was two-fold according to Criswell. First, the public must be educated to the definitions of drugs and abuse. The second part of the issue dealt with drug addiction.

Criswell openly and boldly advocated three major propositions.
1. Drugs and drug addiction lead to a spiritual vacuum.
2. Drug addiction is spelled D - E - A - T - H.
3. The Christian way is spelled L - I - F - E.

Dr. Criswell proclaimed that, "We need a Christian community where the young person can belong to it, and they are not pushers, and they are not junkies, and they are not addicts, and they are not habituates, but they love God, and they are down here where they can support one another and love one another. They can build their homes down here. They can fall in love down here. They can marry down here. They can look forward to ever triumph in every future in unfolding years. All right, if it is hedonistic pleasure, if the reason the youngster uses drugs is because of the kick he gets out of it and the excitement in him, we are dealing there with a moral and a spiritual vacuum. The boy's life, the girl's life is empty, and he needs to reassess the meaning and purpose of life in Christ Jesus. As one boy said, and that was one of the most moving things I ever read in my life, as one boy said, "I was helpless, I was hooked," as they use the word. "I was hooked, but I found a Savior in the Lord, and He saved me, and He delivered me, and He sees me through." That is the road. Let's walk in it. This is the way. Let's follow it--the Jesus way, the glory road, the highway to heaven. Are you a youngster? Make your friends down here. And when you are enticed out there, "No, no." Are you a teenager? Make your friends down here. And when it is suggested out there, "No, no." If you are an adult, put your life down here in the community of Christ. When you are invited to deny the Lord, "No." You spell drug addiction D-E-A-T-H! You spell Jesus Christ L-I-F-E! He said, "I am come that they might have L-I-F-E and have it more abundantly, abounding, overflowing. Ah, my people, our children you, our teenagers and young people you, and our adults and parents you, let's walk in the way of the Lord, and let God give us those rich benedictory, heavenly blessings that only the riches of God could afford. In His gracious hands, how many precious gifts to bestow; and they are ours for the asking, for the having, for the taking, for the receiving."

After Criswell had presented his perspective on the serious problem, he concluded the speech by stating, "Let us love God, put Christ first, become happy, radiant Christians and set our own standards. Let's let the dope gang see how superior the "getting high on Christ" is to their "getting high on drugs." Then he asked people to walk in the way of the Lord.

THE MINISTRY OF RECONCILLIATION

Dr. W. A. Criswell
An Address to the Southern Baptist Convention, Miami Beach, Florida, May 31, 1976

I have been assigned a subject: "The Ministry of Reconciliation." The obvious scriptural text would be found in the fifth chapter of the second Corinthian letter:

> *If any man be in Christ, he is a new creation: old things are passed away; behold, all things are become new. And all things are of God, who hath reconciled us to Himself by Jesus Christ, and hath given to us the ministry of reconciliation; To wit, namely, that God was in Christ, reconciling the world unto Himself, not imputing their trespasses unto them; and hath committed unto us the ministry of reconciliation; Now then we are ambassadors for Christ, as though God did beseech you by us: we pray you in Christ's stead, be ye reconciled to God. For He hath made Him to be sin for us, Him who knew no sin; that we might be made the righteousness of God in Him.*
> *[2 Corinthians 5:17-21]*

"If any man be in Christ," not in an ameliorating organization, not in a behavioristic program, "if any man be in Christ, he is a new creation [2 Corinthians 5:17]…and there hath been given unto us the ministry of reconciliation [2 Corinthians 5:18]…we pray you therefore in Christ's stead…as though Christ did beseech you by us…be ye reconciled to God" [2 Corinthians 5:20], the ministry of reconciliation to God. If a man is reconciled to God, if a man is right with God—first, to be right with God, then he will be right with all of his fellow men in the earth.

This gospel message of redemption, and atonement, and reconciliation, is denied in this modern world. The terrific attacks, theologically and ideologically, against this message is waged on every hand; they confront us boldly, and rudely, and openly. They say, and I quote, "If you have tractors to move mountains, you don't need faith. If you have penicillin, you don't need prayer. If you have positive thinking, you don't need salvation. If you have the state, you don't need the church. If you have manuals of science, you don't need the Bible."

And if bishops do not believe in God, why should anyone else? They say, and I quote, "If there is any God in a clergyman it is because he is a welfare worker. But if clergymen are nothing other than welfare workers, why bother with clergymen? Social workers can do it better." The only good they see in a church is as a social agency. Then they add, "And if churches are nothing but social agencies, why bother with churches? Government rehabilitation programs can do it better."

The answer to such a confrontation in this modern day in which we live is found in God and in the Word of this text. The Christian message addresses itself to a far deeper and more fundamental human need; the need for change in the heart, for regeneration in the soul. It is a regenerated man who is able to create a regenerated society. An unregenerate man will never be able to build a regenerate society. Vile men build a vile society. Worldly men build a worldly society. Atheistic men will build an atheistic society. Witness the whole communist world, this Marxian—militaristic men will build a Marxist society; secular men will build a secular, materialistic society; only redeemed men will ever build a Christian society. As our Lord has avowed, the issues of life come from the heart, from the heart. It is useless to salve the pimples on the skin when the trouble is in the bloodstream, in the heart. It is futile to try to change the clothes of the outside of a man when the problem lies with the man in his soul!

O God, give us wisdom. If a man is vile in a hovel, he will be vile in a palace. If a man is a thief in poverty, he will be a thief in affluence. A dirty, lazy bum breaks into a railway freight car and steals a can of tomatoes. Dress him up, send him to Harvard, and he'll steal the entire railway system, and get away with it. All of the laws in the land will not keep a corrupt senator from his corruption, or a corrupt congressman from his corruption, or a banker or a governor from his corruption. But if the governor, and if the senator, and if the congressman is a Christian man, he has no need of the law. As Paul wrote in Romans 10:4, "For Christ is the end of the law for righteousness to all them that believe," and in the words of my text, "If any man be in Christ, he is a new creation" [2 Corinthians 5:17].

This is the heart and substance of the gospel. There are not two gospels; Dr. Pascal, there are not four or five. There is one and only one gospel. In the fifteenth chapter of the first Corinthian letter, the first three verses, Paul delineated, described minutely the gospel. "My brethren," he says:

> I make known unto you, I declare unto you, I define for you the gospel wherein you are saved. For I delivered unto you first of all that which also I received, how that Christ died for our sins according to the Scriptures.
>
> [1 Corinthians 15:1-3]

This is not a first, "I delivered unto you first of all," this is not a first in time. It is a first in importance. As there is a great and a cardinal law, so there is a great and a distinctive New Testament revelation. And it is this: the atoning, reconciling, redemptive work of Christ our Lord. No other truth stands so high. And from it, all of the other revelations of the Book pour out. In the center of the Roman forum was the golden milepost. And from it the Roman roads reached out to the ends of the civilized world. And to it the roads converged from the ends of the earth. This is the heart of the gospel of the Son of God; His atonement for our sins, His reconciliation of us to God through His suffering and His blood.

Somebody said to Charles Haddon Spurgeon, "Sir, all of your sermons sound alike." And the great London Baptist preacher replied, "That's correct. I take my text anywhere in the Bible and make a beeline to the cross." Oh, Spurgeon, Truett, Scarborough, we follow in their train. There is no pardon without atonement. There is no remission of sins without the shedding of blood [Hebrews 9:22]. There is no reconciliation without the payment of debt. Not by His holy and His beautiful life but "by His stripes we are healed." [Isaiah 53:5]. This is the distinctive, determining factor in the Christian faith and in the Christian religion. It differentiates us from all other religions it the earth.

The Christian religion is first, and above all, and primary, and fundamentally, and necessarily, and effectively a religion of redemption and reconciliation. It purports to deliver a man's soul from the power and the bondage of sin. It is not in the first place an ethic, although it is ethical. It is not in the first place a theology, though it has a theology. It is not in the first place reformation had political, and cultural, and social overtones. But it is first and above all a gospel of redemption and atonement.

The sign and the symbol of the Christian church is not a burning bush. It is not a table of stone. It is not a seven branched lampstand. It is not a halo above a submissive head. It is not even a golden crown, but it is a cross; a cross in all of its naked hideousness, as the Roman would have it; a cross in all of its philosophical irrationality, as the Greek would have it; a cross but in all of its glory and power, as Paul preached it.

> Have you been to Jesus for the cleansing power?
> Are you washed in the blood of the Lamb?

Are you fully trusting in His grace this hour?
Are you washed in the blood of the Lamb?
["Are You Washed In the Blood?" by Elisha A. Hoffman, 1878]

This is the gospel of the grace and the mercy and the atonement of the Son of God; a ministry of reconciliation.

And this is our mandate to the world. "There hath been given unto us the ministry of reconciliation," namely that God was in Christ on that cross, "reconciling the world unto Himself...and hath committed unto us the ministry of reconciliation" [2 Corinthians 5:18-19]. Any true church in this world and any true convention of churches, association of churches in this earth will set itself to the preaching of the gospel of redemption. Our Foreign Mission Board with its two thousand three hundred and beyond missionaries, working in sixty-four countries, baptizing one out of ten members—Dr. Pascal, I cannot begin to achieve that magnificent result. Our Home Mission Board with more than two thousand missionaries—these, their compatriots, working in our cities, working in our mountains, working among marginal groups, language groups, migrant groups, working through the chaplaincy, working in the department of evangelism in Cuba, in Puerto Rico, in Panama—and how desperately is that ministry needed in our homeland. Our missionary frontiers in my lifetime have changed. They used to be in Africa, in China, in the isles of the sea. But the missionary frontier today is down every village street. It crosses every college campus. It is found in every man's home.

It is like this tragic war in Vietnam. There is no line. It's fought everywhere; in the swamp, in the highlands, in the jungle, in Saigon. As I stand in our Southern Baptist Zion, in the nation around me, there are one and one-half million more unchurched in America than when we gathered in convocation this time last year in Detroit. As I stand in our Southern Baptist Zion and look northward and eastward to our great cities—oh, oh! this America around me and these vast teeming cities.

In our church a few weeks ago, there spoke an illustrious president of a divinity school from Scotland. And he said that if the erosion in the Church of Scotland the last twenty years continues for the next twenty years, Scotland will be as pagan as it was when Columba left Iona to evangelize it. When did Columba leave Iona to evangelize Scotland? In [553] AD; and the paganism that Scotland faces is the paganism of England. It is the paganism of Scandinavia. It is the paganism of the American world; it is the paganism that we face in our day and in our generation. And it is found in these great teeming cities!

The third week in July, the Home Mission Board, with our Texas Department of Evangelism, is pouring a quarter of a million dollars and hundreds and hundreds of men into an encounter crusade in Dayton, Ohio, using it as a pilot to see if God will bless it. And if God blesses it in Dayton, we shall attempt it in His grace in the other great cities of the North and of the East. And in that central encounter, they have asked me to preach in Welton Stadium, in a football field.

I said to Billy Graham, "I'm terrified. I'm affrighted. I'm paralyzed with fear—out in a stadium, nothing in front of you but the North Star and the Milky Way." And he said to me, "Well, I want you to know that I am terrified too." I said, "You?" He said, "It scares me to death. I'm frightened every time I face one of those tremendous campaigns." Well, I said, "Then what do you do?" He said, "This is what I do. I get people everywhere to pray for me. And around this world," he said, "there are people in every language under the sun who pray for these crusades."

I went back to our church. When you turn southward, there are two million people who live on the banks of the Rio Grande River from El Paso to Boca Chica, and not one percent of *them is saved. So we went to the lower Rio Grande Valley for a crusade; and they asked me to preach in that central meeting in the municipal auditorium in Harlingen. I stood in the pulpit of our church, and I told them what Billy Graham said: it paralyzed him, too. He was terrified, too. And he said, "I get people to pray for me." Now, I said, "I'm going down to the lower Rio Grande Valley. I wonder if, in this church, there will be people who will come down to the front, and fall on their faces, and humble themselves before God, and ask God to baptize us with the Holy Spirit from heaven, as we prepare and enter this encounter in the lower Rio Grande Valley?"*

They came. They are a great people. They got on their faces. They cried unto God. The next morning, I received a telephone call from Buddy Dial, a famous professional football athlete, and he said to me on the phone, "Pastor, I haven't been able to sleep. All night long I've been awake. I was there in that call, and God had said to me that I'm to go down there in that lower Rio Grande Valley, and help you in that encounter."

He took with him four other world-famed athletes, and they went from school to school, and classroom to classroom, and football stadium to football stadium. They testified to every high school student and every junior high student in the lower Rio Grande Valley. And when I stood up to preach, night after night in that municipal auditorium, you couldn't get in the place. It was jammed, it was filled; God came down.

And Dr. Rutledge, one half of those hundreds who responded were Latin Americans. There is a vacuum in their life, in their souls; they need God! We have been called of heaven to mediate that marvelous message, "Now, Lord, do it in Dayton. Do it up there." And if God will bless us there in Dayton, Ohio, in that football stadium, it may be God shall bless us in the other great cities of our North and of our East.

I turn to the golden West. I, every year, make a journey to the West. Our brethren fight against insufferable odds; my heart and prayers follow them in that work. There came to the parsonage--which is very unusual--there came to a parsonage a young woman, and knocked at the door. Her grandfather was my assistant in the church there in Dallas, and is now in glory. Her father was a preacher, and he also is in glory. And this sweet, beautiful girl married a young minister, and they felt the call to turn to the West. And out there, so desperately needing help, she had come to visit her people in Dallas and to see me—knocked at the door, and I invited her in. And she laid before me the needs of one of these cities in the Northwest, where her young husband was seeking to build a work. And then said to me piteously, "But there is nothing. There is nothing by which we can build. And we thought maybe you and this church would help." I said to her, "My dear child, our church is burdened and buried beneath an avalanche of requests, and we've tried to respond. We've tried to respond. I can no longer get my deacons to listen to another appeal. It is an avalanche, and they feel so helpless. I cannot respond. I cannot help."

She smiled graciously, and apologized for taking my time, and dismissed herself with a "Goodbye, and God bless you," and closed the front door. Our door is, the front of our house is rather a long way from the sidewalk on the street. And when she closed the door she could no longer contain her heart, and she burst into sobs. And as I stood in the house, I heard that girl cry and sob all the way the long distance down to the sidewalk and into the street.

Oh, what do you do? Where do you turn? What do you say? Is it because we are bankrupt that we cannot help? Is it because we live next to poverty and want and penury ourselves that we cannot help? There must be something in us that God must use, that thus far, we have not dedicated unto Him. And that leads me to these concluding words; I have four or five conclusions. As Paul--I tell you, an optimist is a man who thinks a guys going to quit when he says, "And finally, brethren." And that's biblical: Paul says, "Finally," and he hasn't started his epistle very well.

There are some great needs for these—for our church, for Dr. Paschall and his church, for every pastor here and his church, every association of churches—in our Southern Baptist Zions. One: we need, we need to remember that our humanity, our world, our people are inextricably bound together. We cannot escape it.

I lived in Amarillo when I was a boy; I went to school in Amarillo. I was in Amarillo when the oil boom came to the Texas Panhandle, and those tall buildings—to me they were fantastic— those tall buildings were built in the queen city of the plains. And in the middle of that oil boom something happened. On the other side of the Santa Fe railroad tracks was a little Mexican community. Nobody paid any attention to it, nobody was even sensitive to its presence. But in the middle of that oil boom, in the middle of the furious growing of Amarillo, there broke out a smallpox epidemic in that Mexican community on the other side, the wrong side of the railroad tracks. And that smallpox epidemic swept through Amarillo like a prairie fire, and the United States government came down to Amarillo and shut down that city. There was not a train allowed to enter it or to leave it. There wasn't a car, a bus, a truck, there was no person allowed to leave or to enter it. And when the United States government lifted that ban Amarillo was dead. And it took a full generation for it to recover its thrust and its march toward affluence.

I never heard of Vietnam, a swamp somewhere south of Red China; but now it seems to me that the whole earth is Vietnam. I never heard of the Viet Cong. And I'm beginning now that sorrowful journey that I knew in World War II and in the Korean War, knocking at the door of a home, "The boy has found an early grave in the jungles, or in the highlands, or in the swamps of Vietnam." I cannot disassociate myself from the families and the peoples of the world. We are one, to live or to die, whether we choose or no, God help us to remember.

A second tremendous need: we need and that note has been sounded tonight. Dr. Sullivan did it. Other of our leaders are doing it, and we need to do it: we need the spirit of missionary conquest—victory. "God is with us," Immanuel, that is His name [Matthew 1:23].

In 1908 there was held a World Mission Conference in Northfield, Massachusetts, presided over by John R. Mott and Robert E. Spear. And this great caption above that platform read like this, "The evangelization of the world in our generation." Every college campus had its aggressive student volunteer band. Such a motto like that today in our generation is unthinkable and inconceivable. Why? Because we have lost the spirit of missionary conquest! We act like a cowed and defeated band instead of the victorious Christians, who, with eleven men faced the pagan Greco-Roman world. I feel like the cry of the mystic English poet William Blake,

> *Bring me my bow of burning gold;*
> *Bring me my arrows of desire:*
> *Bring me my spear: oh clouds unfold!*
> *Bring me my chariot of fire!*
>
> *We shall not cease from battle strife,*
> *Nor shall the sword sleep in our hands*
> *Till we have built Jerusalem*
> *In this fair and pleasant land*
> *[adapted from "And Did Those Feet in Ancient Time"; W. Blake, 1808]*

That's a good place to quit, but I'm not through. We haven't got anything to do but to waste our time till we come back here in the morning. So let's just listen again.

And we need—and we need that spirit of witnessing, and praying, and giving together. If

I could, I would lead our wonderful church to subsidize the missionary outreach of this whole world. But I am one, an infinitesimal before so great a sea. Somehow we must join hands; we must combine, we must share. We must do it together; we have no other choice; we must!

In one of these visits that I made to a western city, I was walking one evening before speaking that night, and I found a little cracker box of a church house. It looked like a doll church house to me. I tried the door, and it was open; I walked inside. My hand could touch the ceiling. I could almost touch the walls from side to side; it was the smallest little doll church I ever saw. And typically, no sign on it; and I wondered, "Well what kind of a church is this?" I could have known. And I saw on the wall a large, large presentation. So I walked over to the wall and looked at it. It was a week of prayer. And there, Dr. Rutledge, were the pictures of our missionaries, and the announcement of the stated services of intercession and an offering for their support. Well, when I looked at the thing I at first thought, "How little, how small." And then, looking at those missionaries and thinking what it meant, I began to think, "How big, how great, how tall, how high, how deep, how broad, how round the whole world; this is our association of churches in the earth, great congregations, numbering a handful, great visions, so small but God is in it.

And may I add before I close, I think in our dedication, in our praying, in our commitment, in our giving, I think by the Word of God that we have a right, a right to expect that God will bless our effort. And from the days of John the Baptist, the first Baptist preacher until now, "The kingdom of heaven suffereth violence, and the violent take it by force" [Matthew 11:12]. We have a right, I think, when we dedicate ourselves to this assignment to expect that God will bless it. Dr. Rutledge, in the last century you had a great, and an eloquent, and a gifted predecessor. His name was Dr. I. T. Tichenor.

In his day, appeal was made to send missionaries to the wilderness of Texas. Oh, it was unthinkable, that wild outreach, Texas! Why, some people go from bad to worse and others from worse to Texas. Oh! A lieutenant was on maneuvers out there a week or two ago, and he wrote back and said to his wife, "Wife, if this is what we're fighting for I'm ready to quit right now," Texas!

But I. T. Tichenor, the executive secretary of the Home Mission Board, set himself to pouring money, and men, and missionaries into that wild wilderness of Texas. And today, I cannot help but say it, and today Texas is a trophy and a tribute to the vision and dedication of our Home Mission Board. I grew up long time ago in West Texas and was converted and listened to the preaching of those first missionaries. Oh, oh! I don't mean in the last century. I mean in the early 1900's. I don't want you to think I'm older than I really am, and that's enough!

And when I was a boy, one of those old pioneer preachers out there in West Texas told a story. He said that in Georgia there was a dear couple who had one boy, and they were saving up money for the education of that son. But he was prodigal, and wayward, and instead of going to school he left home, and they knew not where he went. And that couple, in a church in Georgia, heard I. T. Tichenor, the executive secretary of the Home Mission Board, make an appeal for Texas. And the couple said, "We have this money for the boy, but he's wayward and gone; we know not where he is. We shall give it for the building of a church in Texas."

And this old pioneer preacher said, "Upon a day, upon a night, there walked down the streets of a West Texas town, a wayward and a prodigal boy. He saw the lights on in a little church. He heard the singing and he remembered Georgia, and mama, and father, and home. And the boy walked in the door, and sat down in the service. And that night," the old pioneer preacher said, "that boy was saved." That's a typical story I used to hear when I was a boy, listening to those old time preachers.

Man, we'll not lose it. *The investment we make in this world, in this work, will come back to us ten thousand times as a church, as a denomination, and God shall write it over your name in glory. What a day to be alive, that God should have matched our souls with a time like this! O God, may we rise up.*

> Stir me, O stir me, Lord, I care not how,
> But stir my heart in passion for the world.
> Stir me to give, to go, but most of all to pray;
> Stir till thy blood-red banner be unfurled
> O'er lands that still in deepest darkness lie,
> O'er plains where no cross is lifted high.
>
> Stir me, o stir me, Lord! Thy heart was stirred
> By love's intensest fire, till thou didst give
> Thine only Son, Thy best beloved One,
> E'en to the dreadful cross, that I might live;
> Stir me, o stir me, Lord, that I might give myself so to Thee
> That Thou canst give Thyself again through me.
> ["Stir Me," by Mrs. Albert Head]

Bless you, Dr. Rutledge. Bless you missionary appointees. Bless us, the association of churches who comprise the bulwark of prayer, and intercession, and giving of our glorious, marching, conquering, victorious Southern Baptist Convention.

COMMENTARY

The Ministry of Reconciliation

The nature of 1976 was a year when people sought to harmonize through reconciliation. Several national and international events reflected that disposition. Representatives of sixty nations including the United States and the Soviet Union signed a United Nations Treaty which provided for the peaceful uses of outer space and banning weapons of mass destruction in space.

Martin Luther King, Jr., tried to force reconciliation as he called for a campaign of massive civil disobedience in Northern United States cities to pressure the Administration and Congress into responding to African Americans demands.

President Johnson succeeded in having a Civil Rights Act passed. He also reaffirmed the United States readiness to negotiate an end to the war in Vietnam.

Mrs. John F. Kennedy settled her dispute with William Manchester, the author, and Harper and Row, the publishers of *The Death of a President.*

Southern Baptists realized the need for propitiation. The Convention was aware of Dr. W.A. Criswell's ability to "quiet any strife among the troop." He was invited to speak at the Southern Baptist Convention on May 31, 1967, at Miami Beach, Florida.

Dr. Criswell's keen viewpoint was sought as the convention assigned him the topic, "The Ministry of Reconciliation." From his perspective, there were two major issues. The first was unity or harmony among the members of the Convention to accomplish the second issue of evangelism.

From the issues of unity and evangelization, Criswell spoke about the main ideas. First, he emphasized what Christianity can do for society. There were some people that said if you have tractors to move mountains, you don't need faith; if you have penicillin, you don't need prayer; if you have positive teachings, you don't need salvation; if you have the State, you don't need the church; if you have manuals of science, you don't need the Bible; and if bishops don't believe in God, why should anyone else? He stated that the only good some see in a church is as a social agency. They even add that if churches are no more than welfare agencies, then why bother? The Government can do it better. The answer to such a modern-day confrontation is found in God. The Christian message addresses itself to a far deeper and more fundamental human need—the need for change in the heart, for regeneration of the soul. It is a regenerated man who can create a regenerated society.

He made simultaneous application of the issues, unity, and evangelism, in his propositions. Criswell said that we need the spirit of missionary conquest. We have no other choice. After presenting the ideas entailed in evangelism and unity, Dr. Criswell urged the people to take action. Criswell re-emphasized the need for taking a decision on the issues as he said that his church in Dallas has an avalanche of requests from all over the nation to come and help establish missions. It is impossible for us to fulfill all of the requests. What do you do? Where do you turn? What do you say? Is it because we live next to poverty ourselves that we cannot help? No, there must be something in us that God can use. There must be something that we have not dedicated unto Him. There are some great needs for me, for our church, for Dr. Paschall and his church at Nashville, Tennessee for every pastor here and his church, and every association of churches in the Southern Baptist Convention.

Thus, he was asking men to meet the requests for evangelism. He asked the messengers at the 1967 Convention to dedicate themselves to the task. We have a right when we dedicate ourselves to this task to expect God to bless our efforts. The investment we make in this world, in this work, will come back to us ten thousand times. What a day to be alive that God should have matched our souls with a time like this! Oh God, may we rise!

Criswell concluded by asking the messengers to work in harmony from local to international levels. We are ever to remember the interlinking and interdependence of all humanity. We are ever to seek from God the spirit of missionary conquest. We are to share in this common endeavor of worldwide evangelism through united prayer, united witnessing and united giving. We then are to expect the marvelous blessing of God upon our dedication. In the year 1967, reconciliation played a significant role in society. W.A. Criswell's reputation for being a harmonizer in the Convention was enhanced. Because of his proven leadership, Southern Baptists re-elected him as their president in 1969. His record in the First Baptist Church of Dallas and the convention speaks for itself. W.A. Criswell spoke for himself as he gave his perspective to the annual meeting of the Executive Committee of the Southern Baptist Convention in Nashville, Tennessee, September 24, 1969.

The major issue to be faced by Southern Baptists in 1969 was that of compromising fundamental beliefs according to President Criswell. He was forceful as he advocated certain ideas. As Dr. Criswell spoke to the Executive Committee of the Southern Baptist Convention in September 1969, three propositions were supported. First, some compromises in life are necessary for compatibility of living. He said there are compromises that are a part, an inevitable and an inexorable part, of the pattern of all of life. You have those compromises daily in your own life. If you are married, you compromise many of the things that you personally might like to do . . .

Second, Baptists are beginning to have a pluralistic complexion. He stated that Baptists have an increasing pluralistic complexion in the Southern Baptist Convention. There are among us liberals and conservatives and fundamentalists. They had open communion and closed communion and alien immersionists. There are those who want greatly to emphasize the social responsibilities that as Christians we ought to assume, and there are those who would emphasize the evangelistic side and the missionary soul winning side of the Gospel.

The third idea advocated concerned doctrinal beliefs of Southern Baptists: President Criswell spoke about those who wanted to change Baptist policies and Articles of Faith. He said that the denomination was increasingly beset and beleaguered by those who want to change. He was not talking about changing in the Christian compassionate love for people—black, white, green, purple, pea green, whatever they are—He was not talking about the high sensitivity that has come to our convention about the grief and despair of humanity. He was talking about doctrinal belief and articles of faith. It was talk about being a Baptist.

He gave his view concerning religious differences and compromise. He sighed: There are no divisiveness like religious altercations and differences. They are evil. It is the over sowing of Satan, and that's my dilemma. How far am I willing to compromise? How far? "How can two walk together," said Amos, "except they be agreed?" Criswell tried to show his openness. He proclaimed that if there were something vile in those article of faith, I'd say let's call a convocation of our people and let's look at the iniquity, at the un-scriptural theme of our forefathers and let's get right with God.

After he had made the propositions evident about his dilemma of being a Southern Baptist, he asked for specific responses. As President Criswell concluded his ideas in the speech, he asked the Executive Committee to do two things and then impress these things upon the Convention.

First, do not compromise the fundamental theological beliefs of Southern Baptists. He said that he was just doing what the Apostles did. I'm just doing what the Christian martyrs did. I'm just doing what our Baptist forefathers did. I believe this about the Scriptures, and you can read it. And I believe this about God. An I believe this about the church. And I believe this about baptism and about the Lord's Supper. This is what my forefathers believed. This was what the Bible said. This is what the Bible says. And when the time comes that I cannot believe that, I ought to leave and go somewhere and join myself to people who believe what I have come to believe, but I ought not to try to change the great scriptural, apostolic commitment, that our forefathers loved, and preached, and upon which and around which they built our institutions.

Second, the President asked the committee members to support his idea that if a Baptist did not believe it, then leave it! He stated that in his humble judgment, I think we ought to take those articles of faith. This is what we believe. This is what it is to be a Baptist. Take those articles of faith—we adopted them in 1925 with Mullins. We adopted them again in 1963 under the administration of Herschel Hobbs. He continued to state; we ought to take those articles of faith and say, "This is what it is to be a Baptist. This is it." It's plain; it's written out, and it's got the scriptures, syllable by syllable and verse by verse, tells us what it is to be a Baptist. This is a Baptist seminary—this is what we believe. This is a Baptists college—this is what we believe. This is a Baptist church—this is what we believe. This is a Baptist convention—this is what we believe. This is a Baptist denomination—this is what we believe. And if you don't believe that, you are not a Baptist. You find you a place, but don't try to bore from within and destroy us. In Criswell's speaking throughout the convention, he has continued to repeat, "Believe it or leave it!"

Dr. Jim Towns

WHY I PREACH THE BIBLE IS LITERALLY TRUE

Dr. W. A. Criswell

2 Timothy 4:1-2, Criswell Bible Institute Chapel October 14th, 1980,

Now in these days, four of them, we are going to talk about four "why's" of my own preaching ministry. The first one will be Why I Preach that the Bible is Literally True; the second, Why Prayer in the Name of Jesus Means Living the Crucified Life; the third one, Why I Am a Premillennialist and not an amillennialist; and the fourth one, Why I Am a Fundamentalist and not a liberal. Those are the four "why's" of my preaching ministry. The second one has a little different turn to it because all day tomorrow, Wednesday, we are in a prayer meeting from eight o'clock in the morning until 8:15 in the evening. And the turn of the lecture tomorrow will be in the sanctuary, where all of the people who will be there with us praying. So the turn also of the message, Why Prayer in the Name of Jesus Means Living the Crucified Life.

Now today, Why I Preach that the Bible is Literally True; I wrote a book about that when I was president of the Southern Baptist Convention, and this lecture is a repercussion out of all the things that went into the background of the writing of that volume. In Acts 35, in Acts 8:35, the Book says, "And Philip began at the same Scripture, and preached unto him Jesus." And in Acts 11:13-14, the angel said to Cornelius, "Send to Joppa, and call for Simon, whose surname is Peter; who shall tell the words, whereby thou and thy house may be saved." In Psalm 119:89: "Forever, O Lord, Thy word natsab, you can translate it "settled" as it is in the King James Version, you can translate it "fixed," natsab, "fixed"; or you can translate it established, "Forever, O Lord, Thy word is fixed in heaven."

In my first and beginning pastorate out in the country, one of those farmers had a beautiful, fertile farm in the valley of the Leon River. He brought me a book, and he said, "What kind of a book is this?" Somewhere he had picked up a Spanish Bible. And I held it in my hand, and I said, "Why, this is a Bible in Spanish." He said, "I can't read Spanish. What am I going to do with it?" I thought for a moment, and I said, "Well, on your farm in a tenant house is a Mexican family, a large Mexican family," had a lot of children. I said, "You go down there and give this Book to them; and they can read it." So he went down to the tenant house on his expansive farm, and gave that Book to that Mexican family. After the passing of several weeks, when I went out to my little country church to preach, he said, he said, "You know, this family that lives on my place, those tenants, they have come to me saying, 'We have read this Book, and we have given our hearts to the Lord, and we've been saved. And it says in that Book that we ought to be baptized. And we want to be baptized.'" Now he said to me, "That posits a tremendous problem, because we don't have any Mexicans in our church. And I don't know how this is going to be." Well, the racial problems that many areas in the South experienced with Blacks, the same kind of a racial problem we have had in Texas regarding the Mexicans, same thing except over there it'd be black and over here it'd be brown.

Well, I had my first decision to make concerning that in my life. And I said to the deacon, "Well, the Book says that the Lord died for us all; and that includes them. And if they found the Lord, and they want to follow our Savior in baptism, let's accept them." So the man came with his family, and all of his kids, and I baptized the whole tribe of them.

After the passing of several months, I went out to my little country church and the deacon met me, and said, "I want to take you to visit the Mexican family, because since you've been

gone"—*I preached there every other Sunday*—" *since you were here last time their house has burned down, and I have them housed in a temporary place, quarters, on my farm. But they want me to bring you to them." Well, I said, "Fine." So I got in his car, and he drove me to a temporary housing for that Mexican family. And when we drove up, why, the father, who was the patriarch in the home, led his little flock, his wife and behind them all of those children, he led them out in a little parade to greet us as we drove up to the temporary home. And as he came out to greet us, he had a Bible, partly burned, in his hand; and held it so beautifully and so tenderly, that Bible that was partly burned. And when I stepped out of the car, why, he came up to me with that partly burned Bible, and holding it so beautifully in his hand, he said, "Pastor, the house burned down, and I rushed into its flames to rescue one thing: this Holy Word of God. And I just wanted you to see it. This Book brought us the saving life in Christ Jesus."*

Isn't that a remarkable thing? Nobody preached to him, nobody visited him about the Lord: you just didn't do that; they were Mexicans. But just because that good deacon gave the family a Bible, the whole little flock came to know Jesus as Savior. It is a remarkable repercussion in the culture and life, domestic, political, social, individual, in every area, it is a remarkable repercussion that the Bible has in the lives of people. And that's my first discussion: God's quickening Word, its marvelous power to convert.

I was preaching, as you know, both in Oklahoma and here in Dallas during World War II. And I would listen to those men as they would speak of their ship going down, or their plane shot out of the sky, and they were washed up on shores of South Pacific islands. And those men, expecting to be confronted by cannibals and Lord only knows what awaited them, they heard people singing the songs of Zion, and they saw little churches in the islands, and some of those American airmen and sailors were won to Christ by natives who were former and recently cannibals. The marvelous change I have seen in Africa, in India, in the Orient, in South America, just by the proclamation of the Word of God is miraculous in itself.

In that Second World War, I received a letter from a pilot, a captain. And in the letter he was telling me how he found Jesus as his Savior. He said, "I picked up your broadcast in my plane, high up in the sky, in Texarkana. And I listened to it until I lost it over Albuquerque, New Mexico." And he said, "Up there in the sky, listening to you preach the Word of God, I bowed my head over the controls of my bomber, and gave my heart to Jesus. I just wanted you to know." What a beautiful and precious testimony!

The universal appeal of the Bible has no end. It's a strange thing: into whatever language the Bible is translated, it seems to be at home. Whenever you translate Dante into English or some other language, you lose nine-tenths of the beauty of its poetic form. Every other translation is like that in human literature except the Bible. I remember hearing of a Hottentot who was talking to one of our American people, and he was commiserating with them: he was feeling sorry for him because he couldn't read John 3:16 in Hottentot. He said, "That's the most beautiful passage in the world." The whole Bible is just like that: whether it is for the learned or for the unlearned, for the sophisticated or the unsophisticated, for the old or the young, in whatever language it has a wonderful message, a saving, saving Word from God. And it seems to be at home wherever in the world it is preached and read.

I led the prayer at the Baptist World Alliance in London, before John Soren, who is pastor of the First Baptist Church in Rio de Janeiro for a generation, one of the noblest men of God I've ever met. John Soren preached the convention sermon, the Alliance sermon, in London. And in that message he was describing the years of his chaplaincy in World War II. The Brazilian division to which he was assigned was fighting their way up through the spine, through the Apennines, right in the middle of Italy, going northward. And when the cold of the winter came, they ceased looking for their dead because of the heavy snows that had covered them. But he said on the twenty-third of February, searching for bodies as the snow had abated, he found a Brazilian boy who had grown up in his Sunday school, in his church in Rio. Dramatically he described that boy that grew up in his Sunday school. He had fought courageously and bravely at his post, until his ammunition had run out. And the boy, being a prey for the enemy's guns, the boy was shot and killed. And he said that the blood flowing out of that boy had frozen the pages of his Bible together. And he said as he took the Bible from the frozen hands of that Sunday school boy, he looked at the place where the Bible was open: and the boy had died with his Book open at the twenty-third Psalm. As his life's blood flowed out, he was reading the twenty-third Psalm. That is the Bible. That's God's Book. And its appeal and its word of life is universal. It isn't just an Anglo, or a Brazilian, or an Indonesian; it's a Hottentot, it's an aborigine in Australia; it has an universal appeal and an universal message.

The influence of the Bible upon human life and culture is illimitable, immeasurable. In music, when you sing the glorious oratorio of Mendelssohn's Elijah, or Handel's Messiah, you're singing the text of the Bible. In literature, when you study Dante, and Milton, and Tennyson, and Carlyle, and Longfellow, and Bunyan, you are studying literature that reflects the Word of God. The basis of modern government is the law of Moses [Genesis-Deuteronomy], and the Sermon on the Mount [Matthew 5:1-7:29]. There is no limit to the vast influence of this precious Word of God.

I have just spoken of the quickening Word. The second part of the lecture concerns the Bible in the infallibility authority: its infallible authority as confirmed by Christ. Or you could say it, the infallible authority of Christ confirms the Bible as the Word of God.

These things are most familiar to us. In His temptation [Matthew 4:1-11], He answered Satan's tempting offers with, "Thus it is written," quoting Deuteronomy 8:3, Deuteronomy 6:16, and Deuteronomy 6:13; quoting the Bible. "Thy word have I hid in my heart, that I might not sin against Thee" [Psalm 119:11]. His defense against the inroads of Satan was the Word of God.

His teaching concerning the Bible was startling. Jesus would sound strange in this modern academic community of liberal, humanistic Christianity. Jesus would say, as in Matthew 5:17-18, "There is not one jot," that's the Hebrew yod, "or one tittle," that's the little horn down there on the teth, "There is not one jot or one tittle that will fail in the Word of God." His attitude toward it would be strange today in our modern academic community.

Did you ever notice the forensics of our Lord as He defended the faith and the truth of God, how He would do? For example, if you have opportunity, turn to Matthew chapter 22, and look at verse 31 and 32. The Sadducees that didn't believe in the spiritual life, in the resurrection, why, they had an old worn out story about the levirate marriage, when the man dies and doesn't have an issue, and his brother is supposed to raise up seed lest the brother's house fall into ruin [Deuteronomy 25:5-6, 7-10], and the old story of seven, had seven brothers, had that woman, and then last of all she died; and in the resurrection whose wife shall she be, for all had her? [Matthew 22:23-28]. Ha, ha, ha, ha! And they had silenced the Pharisees for generations with that same old story. Now you remember it? All right, Jesus said—now you look at this forensics, you look out how He defends the truth of God—"Ye do err not, not knowing the Scriptures, nor the power of God" [Matthew 22:29]. Now 31: "As touching the resurrection of the dead, have ye not read that which was spoken unto you by God, saying, I am the God of Abraham, the God of Isaac, the God of Jacob? God is not the God of the dead, but of the living" [Matthew 22:31-32]. He bases, Christ does, His entire doctrine of the resurrection of the dead upon the tense of a Hebrew verb. Not just the word, not just the verb, but the tense of the verb:

"I am," present tense, "the God of Abraham, Isaac, and Jacob." He is not the God of the dead, but of the living.

Can you imagine the attitude of Christ were He to be preaching today? And He takes the Bible, and not only its book, or its chapter, or its verse, or its sentence, or its syllable, but He takes the tense of the verb and bases on it a tremendous doctrine, such as the resurrection of the dead, upon the tense of the verb—the attitude of Christ toward the Word of the Lord.

We could go on and on in the life of our Savior. For preaching: they delivered to Him the scroll of the prophet Isaiah in Luke 4:14-22; and He turns the scroll to Isaiah 61:1-2, and there He preaches His message of the good news, preaching the Bible. He used the Bible for illustrations. He would talk about the queen of Sheba [Luke 11:31]. He would talk about Elijah and the widow [Luke 4:26]. He would talk about Elisha and the lepers [Luke 4:27]. He would talk about the serpent in the wilderness [John 3:14-15]. He would talk about the manna, angels' food from heaven [John 6:49, 58]. The preaching of our Lord was the Bible.

In the warnings that the Lord would deliver to the people, He used the background of a Sodom [Matthew 11:24], or a Tyre [Luke 10:13-14], or the life of Noah or of Lot [Luke 17:26-30]. And He would always, confronting His enemies, would say, "What saith the Scripture?" "Have ye not read?" "Is it not written?"

And when you turn to Luke 24—and this is Luke's account of our Lord's tremendous assignment to His disciples and to us in the earth—in verse 25, Luke 24:25, "Then He said unto them, O anoetos, O not understanding ones." When we say "fool," that has an overtone of idiocy in it. "O not knowing ones, not understanding ones, slow of heart to believe all that the prophets have spoken: Ought not Christ to have suffered these things, and enter into His glory? And beginning at Moses and all the Prophets, He expounded unto them in all the Scriptures the things concerning Himself" [Luke 24:25-27]. Now you look how He will include the whole Bible in that: look at verse 44: "And He said unto them, These are the things which I spake unto you, while I was yet with you, that all things must be fulfilled, which were written in the Law of Moses," that's the Torah, "and in the Prophets," that's the nevi'im, "and in the Psalms," that's the kethuvim, that's the Hagiographa, the Psalms, the most prominent of that kethuvim, the Hagiographa, the Writings [Luke 24:44]. Do you see what He does? It isn't that this is inspired, but this isn't. And over here we have possibly the Word of God, but this is the speculation of man. He never entered into any of those caustic, critical, tragic attitudes toward the Word of God; but expressly He spelled it out in the Torah, in the nevi'im, in the kethuvim, It's this written by the word of God. "Thus it is written, thus it behooved Christ to suffer and to rise from the dead the third day" [Luke 24:46].

Now, according to the Scriptures Christ lived; according to the Scriptures Christ died [1 Corinthians 15:3]; according to the Scriptures Christ was raised from among the dead [1 Corinthians 15:4]; and according to the Scriptures Christ will come again [Acts 1:11]. That's our Lord and His attitude toward the Holy Bible.

Out of so much that we could say, and we could just be here forever looking at these things, I want to point to you one thing: how the apostles reflected that attitude of our Lord toward the Bible. Turn to 2 Peter chapter 1. Now Simon Peter in this first chapter, beginning at verse 16, is going to describe the parousia, he calls it; the coming of the Lord: "For we have not followed," beginning at verse 16, 2 Peter 1:16:

> We have not followed cunningly devised fables, when we made known unto you the
> power and parousia, the coming of our Lord Jesus Christ, but were eyewitnesses of

His majesty. For He received from God the Father honor and glory, when there came such a voice to Him from the Excellent Glory—

[2 Peter 1:16-17]

On the Mount of Transfiguration, they heard the voice of the Father saying:

This is My beloved Son, in whom I am well pleased.
And this voice which came from heaven we heard when we were with Him in that holy Mount of Transfiguration.

[2 Peter 1:17-18; Matthew 17:5]

Now, you look at this: Simon Peter is there; he has seen that with his own eyes, he has heard that with his own ears, he has felt that in his own sensory response. It must have been an awesome experience! But after he says, "We were with Him, we saw this, we heard this, we felt this" [2 Peter 1:18], after he delineates that personal experience, now look at verse 19: "But we have a more sure word of prophecy; whereunto ye do well that ye take heed, as a light that shineth in a dark place, until the day dawn, and the day star arise in your hearts" [2 Peter 1:19]. Then he describes the infallible Word of God[2 Peter 1:20-21].

Now I can hardly get that in my head. I can hardly realize what the apostle is avowing. Having seen it, having heard it, having felt it, having been present, having experienced, he says, "But the real testimony to the deity and the parousia and the coming of our Lord is not what we have seen, for eye might mislead us; not what we've heard, our ears might deceive us; not what we have felt, because our own feelings might lead us astray: but the sure Word of God could never ever fail." I just can't imagine a testimony like that—when he was there, and shared in it himself.

Now, we're going to discuss the confirmation of the Word of God outside of the witness in the Bible. In 2 Timothy 4:1, Paul having said that the Word of God is the opneustos, it is God-breathed, it is God-inspired [2 Timothy 3:16], having said that, then on the basis of that—and it's too bad that there's a chapter heading there, because the verses ought to go together—"I charge thee therefore." "Therefore" refers to the avowal Paul has just made that all Scripture, all of it—these critics say that it is inspired in spots and they're inspired to pick out the spots—Paul says all of it is inspired, it's the opneustos, from the first syllable to the last benediction. Now, "I charge thee therefore," on the basis of the avowal of the inspiration and the infallibility of the Word of God [2 Timothy 3:16-17], "I charge you therefore before God, and the Lord Jesus Christ, who shall judge the quick and the dead at His coming and His kingdom; Preach the word!" [2 Timothy 4:1-2].

Now I want to ask you a question: can I do that, can I stand up there and preach this Book as the infallible, inerrant Word of God, and be intellectually honest? Can I? Well, let's look at it just for a moment. Preaching the Bible as the inerrant, infallible Word of God in all of its historical statements, in all of its self-disclosure of the character of deity, in the coming of our Lord, in the whole frame and paradigm and model—as I was preaching last Sunday morning, the form of sound words—can I do that and be intellectually honest? Now let me point out to you what I think is a miracle. I think it is. They have been digging there in those tells and mounds over there in those archaeological digs in the Holy Land for centuries. It isn't just something that in the last few years has been characteristic of the interest over there. For centuries they've been digging down in those areas of these past civilizations. Dr. Patterson's boy, Armor, was *over there in one of those digs, and I think Dr. Patterson himself has been over there in some of those digs. And of course, layer after layer after layer, civilization after civilization, they look at all of those artifacts that they dig up; and they find all of those cylinders, and all of those cuneiform inscriptions, and those baked tablets. And if its hermetically sealed by the sands of Egypt, you'll find it in the papyri. Well, it's just thousands and thousands and thousands of things they bring to light regarding the history of that ancient world.*

All right, the miracle: to me, this is a miracle: there has never yet been turned one spade of archaeological dirt but that confirmed the Holy Scriptures, not one. Everything they have ever discovered, everything they have ever learned, every little potsherd and tablet and inscription, hieroglyphic cuneiform, papyri, the whole gamut of it, the whole spectrum of it, for hundreds and hundreds and hundreds of years, everything they've ever discovered confirms the accuracy of the Word of God.

For example, it used to be a common thing in the critical, higher critical world, that it was impossible that Moses could have written. It says Moses wrote these things, and they scoffed at that, "Why, Moses could not have written anything. Writing wasn't invented. There was no such thing as writing back there. So that is a manifest anachronism in the Bible." Then, they began to discover those Tel el-Amarna tablets in Egypt, and all of those inscriptions they began to dig up in the Mesopotamian Valley; and today we know that writing was common thousands of years before Moses.

All right, let's take again, the Hittites. I can remember when the academic world scoffed at the Bible because the Hittites are spoken of all through the Old Testament, the Hittite. And there was no such thing as a Hittite; that was a figment of somebody's vivid imagination, the Hittite. And did you know—though I need my mouth washed out when I say it—I looked at a Life magazine, and it had the whole issue dedicated to the Hittite empire. And today, of course, we know it was a tremendous, like the great empires of the ancient past that covered the Asia Minor part of that world and most of the Levant. The Hittites, they were a great people, with a great empire. And yet I can remember when it was scoffed at.

All right, let's take Belshazzar. I don't think there ever has been anything that was a sure fire bound up thing as the critic had concerning Belshazzar. One of the reasons for that—and this is just one of the reasons—one of the reasons for that was they discovered what they called the Cylinder of Cyrus, and Cyrus had put on that cuneiform cylinder the whole dynasty of Babylon that he'd conquered. It was all written there, and all those kings written there from the start, clear down to the bottom. And there's no Belshazzar in it. And as though that were not enough, Herodotus visited Babylon, and wrote intimately of his visit to Babylon, seventy years after Babylon fell; and yet Herodotus, in writing the story of Babylon, didn't know any Belshazzar. Well, the critics had a sure fire thing there. That was just two of the many other things that they said. So they scoffed and they laughed at the idea of any such king as Belshazzar.

That is, until recently. Recently they have been digging down into those cuneiform tablets, clay baked tablets, in the ruins of Babylon, and I don't exaggerate it when I tell you, my young friends, I could write a biography about Belshazzar. I could literally do it. They have learned so much about Belshazzar: his family, his mother, his wife, his sisters, where he worshipped, what he did; his father Nabonidus had no interested in governmental affairs, and he left Babylon and lived in an oasis in the Syrian desert, and he left the kingship and the kingdom to his son Belshazzar. Man, you could go on and on what they found out about him. Never saw such mouth-stoppers in my life as these archaeological spades. It's just unbelievable—Belshazzar.

Well, let's just take one other out of a jillion of them; we could just go on forever. When I went to school, when I was in the seminary, it was the ordinary and the common thing taught, even by some of these so-called conservative professors who taught me, that John could not have been written by the sainted apostle, the dear close bosom friend of the Lord Jesus, because, they said, it would have taken two hundred fifty years for that theology to develop. While they were teaching that, in the hermetically sealed sands of Egypt, they discovered a papyrus that quotes the eighteenth chapter of John that must have been written about 95 or 98 AD! What consummate liars those people are!

That's archaeology and the Bible. There has never yet been anything discovered that contradicts any statement in the Word of God; but everything we discover affirms it and confirms it.

Now, I want in this next moment, to speak about the certainty of the text. When I open the Bible, how do I know I have in my hand what God wrote? How do I know but that the text has been amended, and changed, and added to, and taken away from until I have no idea what God wrote? Now the Lord knew all about that.

You know, it's a funny thing how an ordinary common laborer will say things that are profound. When I was a boy, I was standing by a carpenter, and his helper over there swallowed a tack. Well, I thought that was going to be terrible; he had a tack. Man alive, that'd puncture his gizzard, and puncture all the way down, and you know, that old carpenter patted me on the back, and he said, "There, there, son, don't worry. God knew we were going to swallow all kinds of tacks; so He made it so that when we swallow tacks, why, it is covered over with all of those smooth and salubrious coatings, so that when we swallow tacks it just goes right on through the elementary canal. God knew all about that," he says. Well, that's the way God is: God knew all about this thing that would arise in our day concerning the certainty of the text, the truthfulness of the text; and God made provision for that.

Now you look how He did it. One thousand five hundred years after Herodotus lived there was one manuscript of Herodotus, just one. One thousand two hundred years after Plato lived there was one manuscript of Plato. There is only one manuscript of the Annals of Tacitus, that tremendously gifted Latin historian. There's only one manuscript of the Greek Anthology. There are one or two, very few manuscripts of Sophocles, Thucydides, Euripides, Virgil, Cicero, the whole gamut of them. Now against that background you look at this: there are 4,105 ancient Greek texts of the New Testament. There are between 15,000 and 30,000 Latin versions. There are over 1,000 other early versions of the New Testament, such as Coptic, Syriac, and Aramaic. That means that we can take those thousands of manuscripts, thousands of them—I've done some of it myself in my Greek studies, back yonder years ago—take some of those thousands of manuscripts, and look at them, and compare them; and if at any place a copyist has made an emendation or a correction or a change, there it is, just look at it. You can compare it in thousands of manuscripts, to know exactly what the original was.

May I point out to you, therefore, the tremendous significance of those Dead Sea Scrolls? The latest copies we had of the Old Testament were those Masoretic texts, written somewhere around, oh, 950 to 1000 AD. That was the latest we had. So these critics say, "How do you know but that a thousand years and another thousand years and another thousand and another thousand years, in those thousands of years between the text that we have, this Masoretic text, this Bible, this Hebrew Bible that you have in your hand, and back yonder when Moses wrote it and Isaiah wrote it, how do you know but that there were a thousand changes in it?" Well, lo and behold, and amazing, and a miracle of miracles: they discovered those Dead Sea Scrolls. And if you've been to Jerusalem, they've had a shrine there; they call it "The Shrine of the Book." And that scroll of Isaiah is all the way unfolded around a cylinder in the middle of that shrine. And the marvel is this: you can read that text of Isaiah from those caves on the edge of the Dead Sea, you can read them, written about 165 or 100 BC, and compare it with the text that you have in your Hebrew Bible a thousand years later, and it is substantially the same, just the same. God saw to it that all of this was faithfully and marvelously kept and recorded.

Now, may I speak of the unity of the Book, which itself is no less miraculous. Written over a period of sixteen hundred years, by over forty different men, in different continents, languages, vocations and life, all of it is one marvelous continuing story. It's not a dead stone; it's a living organic whole. It breathes; it speaks to us. It has a great theme: it points to Jesus; it's our redemption in Christ.

I imagine many of you are aware of the fact that some time ago, New Year's Eve came on Sunday night, as it is this present year. So some of these deacons facetiously came up to me, and said, "Pastor, you're always complaining about not having any time to finish your sermon, always fussing about that clock. Sunday night, New Year's Eve, why don't you just start at seven-thirty o'clock," when we began the service in those days, "and instead of having a watch night service, why don't you just preach all the way through? Why don't you preach until past midnight? And then maybe you could finish a sermon. Why don't you do that?" Well, they said that to me in jest; to them it was a big joke, and they just laughed. I got to thinking about that. I thought, "Well, that's a marvelous idea. That's a wonderful idea." So I announced that at seven-thirty o'clock I was going to start preaching, and I was going to preach past midnight.

Were you here then? Were you here? Well, I stood up in that pulpit to start out at seven-thirty o'clock, and the house was jammed, and people were standing around the wall upstairs and downstairs. I thought as I went on hour after hour, that most of them would erode, that the congregation would gradually fade away. I want you to know, when I tried to finish—and I didn't quite make it—when I tried to finish after twelve o'clock, that throng was still there. Were you there, Charles? They were standing around the auditorium downstairs and upstairs, from 7:30 till after twelve o'clock.

"Well, pastor, what did you do for so long a period of time that kept those people listening to the message?" You already know what it was; it's been printed in a book, the summation of it. It was entitled *The Scarlet Thread through the Bible*; just one great unfolding story, page after page, after page. Now I must close because the time is already gone. I want to conclude with a word about preaching the infallible Word of God. I was in a group last night, and they were kidding me about something that I did here at the church. Dr. Truett was a marvelous preacher. Hal, did you ever hear Dr. Truett? He was our greatest Southern Baptist preacher, an incomparable man. His presence, his voice, his message, oh! he was God's man. If I were in Hollywood and choosing characters to present a story, I'd choose Dr. Truett as God. He just looked the part. Oh, he was impressive!

But Dr. Truett was a topical preacher. Weren't you here, Charles, when he was here? He never preached any other kind of a message but a topical sermon. So, after I was here one year, I made the announcement to the church that I was going to preach through the Bible; I was going to start in Genesis and go clear through to the Revelation. You never heard such lugubrious prognostications in your life! It was painful. They said, "The church will die. Who's coming to church to listen to Habakkuk? Don't even know how to pronounce the name; don't *even know where it is in the Bible. Who's coming to church to listen to all of those things that we never heard of before?" But I persevered, and I preached through the Bible for seventeen years and eight months: preaching where I left off Sunday morning, started Sunday night; where I left off Sunday night, I started Sunday morning.*

And I would listen to those people. One man would say, "When did you join the church?" He said, "Well, I joined in Isaiah. When did you join the church?" The other one would say, "Well I'm a late-comer, I joined in Philemon," or, "I joined in Jude."

The Y, as you know, is right in front of the church door. So a man came back to the clerk at the Y, and he said, "I thought you told me that was a Baptist church."

"Well, it is a Baptist church."

"No, it isn't," he said, "It's an Episcopalian church."

"Well, what makes you think it's an Episcopalian church?"

"Well," he said, "I saw the people as they came out of the church being dismissed, and each one had a prayer book in his hand." And the clerk said, "Listen, guy, you've got that wrong. They have a Bible in their hands, a Bible in their hands."

We had a real problem in the church, I do admit: and the problem was what in the earth are we going to do with these people that can't get in the house? Immediately the congregation began to grow and continued growing for all of those seventeen years and eight months. That's why we have two services, as you know, each Sunday, trying to preach to the people who wanted to listen.

So, standing on the Rock of the Word of God, our feet may tremble, but the Rock remains immutable and forever. The best way in the world to preach is a, "Thus saith the Lord God." [Amen] Oh! There is power and authority in that. Not, "Thus saith Rabbi Smell-fungus," or, "Thus saith Dr. Sounding-brass," or, "Thus saith Dr. Dry-as-dust," but, "Thus saith the Word of God." It's the way the apostles preached, Paul, and the author of the Hebrews. It's the way that the preachers of the Reformation preached, "Sola scriptura." It's the way the pioneers preached, and I listened to them when I was a little boy: they had a Bible, they had a hymnbook, and that was all; but they delivered the message, and God blessed it. And we follow in their train.

And the Lord bless us as we are faithful to that message

COMMENTARY

Why I Preach That the Bible is Literally True

Criswell explained to his church that there has never been a time in life when he was more consumed with encounter crusades, revival meetings, and other ministries of the church and beyond. He stated in an interview that there are some reasons that he would presume, that he was asked to speak on the Bible. It was to be a personal testimony from his heart. He was to tell why he preached that the Bible is literally true, not why some one else might preach that it is an aggregate of myths, legends and fairy tales.

Dr. Criswell was asked to explain why he preached that the Bible is literally true. The issue was clearly the Bible in the Christian faith. Basic to the reason Dr. Criswell preaches that the Bible is literally true have been two major propositions. First, the Bible is the Word of God and should be preached. He stated that the most important question for the religious world today is this: "Is the Bible the Word of God?" if the Bible is the Word of God we have an absolutely trustworthy guide for all the answers our souls desire to know . . . But if the Bible is not the Word of God, if it is the mere product of man's speculation, if it is not altogether trustworthy in regard to religious and eternal truth, then we are all in a trackless wilderness not knowing where to go or to turn. Criswell asserts that the Bible is the Word of God.

Second, Criswell contended that the truth in the Bible is literally true. He gave a guide to determine whether Biblical language is literal or figurative. He proclaimed that A simple rule to follow in determining what is literal and what is figurative is this: if the literal meaning of any word or expression makes good sense in its connections, it is literal. But if the literal meaning does not make good sense, it is figurative. Since the literal is the most usual signification of a word and therefore occurs much more frequently than the figurative, any term ought to be regarded as literal until there is good reason for a different understanding, and that understanding will become clear as well as we read the context and background of the passage in the Bible.

Dr. W.A. Criswell presented ideas from his perspective as to why he preached that the Bible is literally true. Dr. Criswell asked ministers to preach the Bible as the inspired, God-breathed truth. He stated that it was a remarkable repercussion in the culture and life, domestic, political, social, individual, in every area, it was a remarkable repercussion that the Bible has had in the lives of people. God's quickening Word has had a marvelous power to convert. The universal appeal of the Bible has no end. It's a strange thing: into whatever language the Bible is translated, it seems to be at home. Whenever you translate Dante into English or some other language, you lose nine-tenths of the beauty of its poetic form. Every other translation is like that in human literature except the Bible. But the real testimony to the deity and the *parousia* and the coming of our Lord is not what we have seen, for eye might mislead us; not what we've heard, our ears might deceive us; not what we have felt, because our own feelings might lead us astray: but the sure Word of God could never ever fail." I just can't imagine a testimony like that—when he was there, and shared in it himself.

After he preached the sermon, a rash of controversy was stirred up by groups in the Convention. The Association of Baptist Professors of Religion adopted a resolution in Atlanta, Georgia deploring and protesting the degree and kind of promotion given by the Southern Baptist Sunday School Board to a book which they feel denied historical-critical study of the Bible.

The 64 professors adopted the following resolution at their 42nd annual session in Atlanta on February 22, 1969:

ASSOCIATION OF BAPTIST PROFESSORS OF RELIGION 1928
Resolution:
"Whereas we, the members of the Association of Baptist Professors of Religion, are committed to the vocation of bringing young people to a knowledge of the Scriptures; and

"Whereas this vocation requires the honest and conscientious utilization of the historical-critical method of Biblical study; and

"Whereas any action by a denominational agency which gives or appears to give denominational sanction to a denial of the historical-critical approach inevitably undermines the work of Biblical teachers and alienates students from both the denomination and the Bible itself;

"Therefore be it resolved that the Association of Baptist Professors of Religion, in annual session in Atlanta, Georgia this 22nd day of February, 11969, in full recognition of the

responsibility of the Broadman Press to publish materials reflecting a variety of interpretations of the Bible, does, nonetheless, deplore and protest the nature of the promotion and publicity given to Why I Preach That the Bible is Literally True by W.A. Criswell, which clearly suggests that the position espoused in this book is the official position of the Sunday School Board of the Southern Baptist Convention.

Dr. Criswell's book got chilly reception from only a small minority in the convention. Most ministers knew that nowhere in his speaking had Criswell denied the validity of the historical-critical approach to the Bible as the professors claim. He has challenged some uses of this approach. The truth was that with an earned doctor of philosophy degree in New Testament from Southern Seminary at Louisville, Ky., and with 30 years of preaching from the Greek New Testament behind him, Criswell knew more about the historical-critical approach to the Bible than do most of the professors. His personal library of Bible study books, which he used diligently, was larger than the libraries of such books available to most of these teachers. Throughout the convention the people continue to be influenced by Criswell's speaking.

THE BAPTISM OF THE HOLY SPIRIT

Dr. W. A. Criswell
1 Corinthians 12:13, June 26th, 1983

This is the pastor bringing the message entitled "The Baptism of the Holy Spirit." The message is delivered because of the unendingness of the unscriptural response I see and hear everywhere. To summarize the unscriptural response to the truth of God: everywhere there are those that are persuaded that there is a work of grace when we are regenerated, when we are converted; something God does when we are born into the kingdom of God, born of the Spirit, born anew, born from above, anothen, born again. That is one experience of grace, a work of God. Then they avow there is a second, later work of God, an experience of grace at another time, and that is called "the baptism of the Holy Spirit." If you have not received that second work of grace, that so-called "baptism of the Holy Spirit," then you are a second-class Christian. You are down here somewhere, and those who have experienced that work of grace are up here somewhere.

That doctrine is everywhere. I run into it all the time. And in one of those strange providences that are almost inexplicable, it was furthered by great men of God like Dwight L. Moody and R. A. Torrey. His own son, Dr. Torrey's son, pled with his father to change the nomenclature he used in describing his experience, and Dr. Torrey refused to the end of his life.

In my own experience, for the years and the years, I misunderstood. I did not understand the truth of God with regard to the baptism of the Holy Spirit. One time, in these years gone by, there came two brethren here to Dallas to see me from Louisiana. They had heard me preach on the baptism of the Holy Spirit at a conference in Louisiana, and they came all the way over here to sit down with me and to teach me the Word of God. Even listening to them, I still didn't understand it.

One time, in preaching through a conference at Moody Bible Institute in Chicago, I announced my preaching on this subject, and there came to my hotel room the men who led that great Christian teaching institution. And they talked to me at length, because at that time there were excesses battling, confronting the school in this area, in this baptism, this doctrine of the baptism of the Holy Spirit.

In those long ago days, years gone by, I studied, and I studied, and I prayerfully studied, and finally came to an understanding of the truth, a clear understanding of the truth of God, the revelation of God in the Holy Scriptures, and I wrote two books on the subject: the Holy Spirit. Now coming to this hour, I felt I ought to speak concerning it. I run into it so constantly: the aberration, the misunderstanding, the misconstruction, the misinterpretation of the baptism of the Holy Spirit. Then as I struggle to combine it all and to present the quintessence of it in just one brief sermon—I was struggling with it. You need hours. As I say, I wrote two books concerning it, and how do you combine it and compress it and condense it in just a few minutes like this?

Well, I have come into the habit of studying late at night. And one night in preparation for this message and in struggling to present it in just one brief moment like this—reading the Scriptures, poring over the Word of God, preparing this message—I went to bed and went to sleep, still not knowing how, in one sermon, to present the truth of this tremendous doctrine.

And in the middle of the night, I awakened, and when I did, the entire message lay before me, from beginning to ending, every point and every discussion under every point.

I would not be so proudly spiritually egotistical as to say that an angel had presented it to me. Maybe the psychologist is right, is correct, when he says that your mind works when you are asleep as it does when you are awake, and my mind, working, arranged that whole message from beginning to end, and when I awakened, there it was. My mind had worked it through and now presents it to me. However you explain it, whether it was a gracious interposition and kindness from heaven, or whether it is psychologically conditioned that my mind was working through it even while I was asleep, the whole message was there before me.

Now the main points of it are this: the baptism of the Holy Spirit is an historical, prophetic event. Second: the baptism of the Holy Spirit is an historical, heavenly event. Third: the baptism of the Holy Spirit is an historical, ecclesiastical church event. And fourth: the baptism of the Holy Spirit is an historical, never-to-be-repeated, eternal event. And the, the conclusion: we are commanded to be filled with the Holy Spirit continuously and continually.

Now we begin. The baptism of the Holy Spirit is an historical prophetic event. It is something that God specified at a particular time, at a particular place, in one event, years and years and centuries before it came to pass. It is one historical event prophesied by the Lord God in heaven.

It is the same thing as concerning the coming of our Lord. There was a time prophesied, a specific moment when the Lord of heaven would be incarnate in human flesh. He would be born of a virgin—prophesied [Isaiah 7:14]. There was a time prophesied, one event, when our Lord would die in atoning grace for the sins of the world [Daniel 9:26]. There was a time prophesied, an event, when He would be raised from the dead [Matthew 12:40]. There is a prophesied time, an event, when the Lord will return from heaven [Acts 1:11]. It is set in heaven, prophesied, and we're waiting for that coming event.

In the same way that there is an historical prophecy, was historical prophecies, were historical prophecies concerning the birth and the atoning death and the resurrection and the return of our Lord, just so there are prophecies, historical prophecies, that point to the outpouring of the Holy Spirit of God, the baptism of the Holy Spirit of God, the pouring out of the Spirit of God upon human flesh.

Now we look at just some of those prophecies. The first one that I point to, you just read. In the second chapter of Joel:

> *It shall come to pass... that I will pour out My Spirit upon all flesh; your sons and your daughters shall prophesy, your old men dream dreams, and your young men see visions.*
>
> *[Joel 2:28]*

There is a day coming, says Joel—a prophecy when God will pour out upon this earth the Spirit of grace, the presence of the Holy Spirit of God bathed, baptized the world with the Spirit of God. In the third chapter of the First Gospel, of Matthew, in verse 11, John the Baptist preached, saying:

> *I indeed baptize you with water... but He that cometh after me, mightier than I, whose shoes I am not worthy to bear; He shall baptize you with the Holy Spirit, and with fire.*
>
> *[Matthew 3:11]*

There is a day coming, says John the Baptist, when God will pour out upon this earth—baptize this earth in the Holy Spirit. I turn the pages of the gospel, and in the seventh chapter of the Gospel of John, John explains in a parenthesis:
This spake Jesus of the Spirit, which they that believe on Him should receive; for the Holy Spirit was not yet given; because that Jesus was not yet glorified.

[John 7:39]

Isn't that a wonderful way to talk? John describes the crucifixion of Jesus as "the glorification of Jesus." What an amazing come-to-pass, that a man could look upon the execution of what had been reserved for felons and malefactors and slaves, and call that "the glorification of Christ."

Well, anyway, in the middle of Christ's ministry, in the very middle of it, the baptism of the Holy Spirit is yet to come; it is something in the future. It's a date that hasn't been arrived at: "This spake Jesus because the Holy Spirit was not yet given" [John 7:39]. I turn to the first chapter of the Book of Acts. And the Lord is speaking with His apostles, and He says:

Wait for the promise of the Father, which, saith He, you have heard of Me.
For John truly baptized with water; but ye shall be baptized with
the Holy Spirit not many days hence.

[Acts 1:4-5]

Look at this: the Lord has finished His ministry; He has died in atoning grace for our sins; He has been buried; He has been raised from among the dead [Matthew 27:32 – 28:7], and now after forty days [Acts 1:3], He is ready to ascend back to heaven from whence He came. And yet the baptism, the outpouring of the Holy Spirit, has not come—it is still in the future—but the Lord says it is coming soon. The baptism of the Spirit is not many days hence [Acts 1:5].

Then I turn to the second chapter of the Book of Acts, and in the sixteenth verse, Simon Peter says, "This is that" [Acts 2:16]—speaking of the passage, the prophecy, you just read in Joel 2:28-32. "It has come to pass." This is the specific historical event that the prophets pointed to in all of these centuries past. It has now come to pass at Pentecost.

In the tenth chapter of the Book of Acts, Simon Peter says: "This is that which was prophesied by John the Baptist" [Acts 10:37]. The great historical day has come: the baptism of the Holy Spirit, the outpouring of the Spirit of God upon human flesh [Acts 2:16-18]. Now, that's the first point: the baptism of the Holy Spirit is an historical, prophetic event, at one time, at one place, and it occurred, says Simon Peter, this day at Pentecost.

Number two: the baptism of the Holy Spirit is an historical, heavenly event. In the last chapter of the Book of Luke—Luke 24:49: "Behold," says our Lord, "I send the Promise of My Father upon you; but tarry ye in the city of Jerusalem, until you be clothed with that power from on high." That's what literally he wrote: "until the Holy Spirit clothes Himself with you, power from on high"—the Promise of My Father.

Now I turn again to the first chapter of the Book of Acts, and I see that same word again in verse 4:

And, being assembled together with them, the Lord commanded them that they should not depart from Jerusalem, but wait for the Promise of the Father.

[Acts 1:4]

The promise of the Father: the baptism of the Holy Spirit is called in these passages the fulfillment of the promise of the Father.

Now, this is what I think that means, the promise of the Father: before the foundations of the earth were laid, before God flung these planets into space, before there was matter or substance, before the creation of the world, God the Father said to the Son: "You die for the human race. You suffer in penalty for the sins of the people. You do that, and I promise You, the promise of the Father, I promise You two things." Now, I am a Calvinist, and you're going to see a little instance of it now. "I promise You," says the Lord God to His Son, "if You suffer and die on the cross, paying the penalty for the sins of the world, I promise You—one: I promise You a people. You will not die in vain. I promise You there will be those who will believe on You and trust You, and receive Your grace and forgiveness, and will love You and serve You. I promise You a people."

The Bible calls that election. There are those that are going to trust Jesus in every age and in every generation in this earth until He comes again: election.

God promises to His Son, "If You suffer and die, I promise You a people." There will be those who will respond to the announcement and the proclamation and the preaching of the gospel. "I promise You a people."

The second: "And I promise You that, because You have done this, I will pour out upon the earth the Spirit of grace and of heavenly power": the baptism of the Holy Spirit. That is the promise of the Father. It is an historical, heavenly event. God promised His Son, "You suffer and die, and I will pour out upon the flesh of the earth the Spirit of grace, and salvation, and supplication, and power; glory."

All right, number three: The baptism of the Holy Spirit is an historical, ecclesiastical event. It concerns the church. I read here in the Word of God, in the fourteenth chapter of the Book of John, our Lord says, "Ye shall know Him," this Spirit of truth, this Comforter, this alter ego, this third Person of the Trinity. "I will pray the Father. He shall give you another paraklete … for He dwelleth with you, and shall be in you," this Spirit of truth, the Holy Spirit of God: John 14:17. "He will dwell with you, and shall be in you."

Now let me expatiate on that for a moment. The Holy Spirit of God, our Lord says, is going to have a new dwelling place, a new tabernacle, a new home. It's going to be in the church, in the body of Christ. Heretofore—before Pentecost, before the outpouring, the baptism of the Holy Spirit—heretofore, the Holy Spirit had come upon differing people at differing times. Sometimes, the Scriptures say—the Holy Spirit came upon Samson at times. The Holy Spirit came upon Samuel. The Holy Spirit came upon Saul. The Holy Spirit came upon David. The Holy Spirit came upon Isaiah.

At different times, the Holy Spirit came upon different men—just the same thing as the Theophanies or the Christophanies of our Lord and Savior. The Lord was in heaven. Jesus' home was in heaven at the throne of God, but He appeared from time to time to different men. For example, He appeared to Abraham [Genesis 18:17]. He appeared to Hagar [Genesis 16:7-8]. He appeared to Jacob [Genesis 32:24]. He appeared to the elders of Israel [Numbers 11:16-17]. He appeared to Daniel [Daniel 10:5]. He appeared to Isaiah [Isaiah 6:1]. Christophanies: the appearance of our Lord while He was up there in heaven. He came down to earth and appeared to these saints from time to time, but His home was in heaven. He lived in heaven at the throne of grace.

Now, the Lord came down here to earth from heaven, and for thirty-three years He lived in human flesh. Then He returned back to heaven, when He was raised from the dead [Acts 1:9-10], and there He is now in heaven, at the right hand of the throne of God [Hebrews 12:2], awaiting that specified, prophesied, known-to-God time when He will return back to earth for His people.

The Holy Spirit is just like that. He had His home in heaven. Once in a while He would come upon a Samson or a Saul or a David, but His home was in heaven. But our Lord said, in this prophecy in the fourteenth chapter of the Gospel of John, that the day is coming when the Holy Spirit will change His central residence, will change His home from heaven to earth. And His home is going to be here, and He is going to dwell in the body of Christ, His people [1 Corinthians 6:19]. He is in the church [1 Corinthians 3:16]. That is a most wonderful thing!

A week ago, I was seated in a chair before a TV camera. They were having an interview about something, and the man who was presiding over it said to me, "I don't need to go to church. I can worship God just as well on a creek bank, fishing, as I can when I go to church." What he doesn't know is he's out there worshiping himself. That's his idea of God. That's his idea of coming into the presence of the Lord. That's his idea of the worship of God. It's his idea. It's not God's. God has commanded us "not to forsake the assembling of ourselves together" [Hebrews 10:25], and he supposes that, out there by himself, he has all of the fullness of the baptism of the Holy Spirit, out there catching a fish. Now, I'm sure in favor of catching fish. I could eat fish three times a day, but it would never occur to me that that is the substitute for the great outpouring of the Spirit of God in His church!

There is something so marvelous and wonderful about God's people being together in the church. I will praise God in the assembly. I will praise God in the church. It is a wonderful thing that happens: "I was glad when they said unto me, Let us go up [to] the house of the Lord" [Psalm 122:1]. It is a wonder and a glory to be in God's house with the Lord's people, however imperfect we may be—yet the Lord is here. He blesses our songs of praise; He blesses our instruments of music, and He hears our prayers. And we are encouraged in the faith and in the worship and work of our Lord. The Spirit of God is in His church.

Not only that, but when I am saved, when I am converted, when I am born again, the same Holy Spirit that "borns me again," that regenerates my heart, that same Spirit baptizes me into that body of Christ, the church. In 1 Corinthians 12:13: "For by one Spirit are we all baptized into one body": ebaptisthemen, from baptizo—ebaptisthemen. It's an aorist. It's an indicative. It's a passive: ebaptisthemen.

In English, we have tenses. You can't talk in English without pigeonholing what you're saying in a tense. You're talking in the present. You're talking about the future. You're talking about the past. You can't talk in English except in tenses. Every verb has a tense. It's not so in the Greek language. In the Greek language, they spoke in terms of action: what kind of action—it's pointed, it's in the past, it's in the future, it's going on right now—it's a kind of action.

Now in the verbal tenses of the Greek language, there is a whole system called aorist, "aorist tense." And an aorist tense refers to an action that happened in a point just like that and then continues thereafter. Now this is an aorist verb: ebaptisthemen. When I am saved, I am baptized by the Holy Spirit of God into the church [1 Corinthians 12:13]. And there I am forever! If I had time—and we don't have time; about the time I get started, the thing says it's time to stop. When one is baptized into the church, he's there forever. He never gets away from it. Like the prodigal son, he may go out of the hog pen, but as he sits there on the top rail, watching the hogs eat, do you know what he's thinking about? He's thinking about home. He's thinking about his father. He's thinking about his father's house [Luke 15:13-21].

No man who's ever saved ever gets away from that! He may be out there in the gutter!

He may be out there in the hog pen! But he can't forget: "I don't belong here. I'm in the wrong place. I ought to be at my Father's house. I ought to be with God's people." And he never gets away from it—never, never, ever! And, I think, according to God's promise, he'll come back someday.

That's this: when we're saved, we are baptized into the body of Christ. And we're there forever. It's a wonderful doctrine: in the 1 Corinthians, this same Corinthian letter, the sixth chapter, in the nineteenth verse, the apostle says there that "the Holy Spirit dwells in our hearts"[1 Corinthians 6:19]. And when we come to church, we bring Him with us. And that's why, when all of us are assembled together in God's presence, it's just one of the heavenliest things that mind could imagine, or that providence could arrange for: the assembly of God's people. We bring Him with us, and we're all in the body of Christ, placed there by the almightiness and the grace of God.

It's like writing our names in the Book of Life. It's something God does for us. It's the beautiful thing of being made part of God's eternal kingdom. He does it, like writing our names, I say, in the Book of Life; God does it. God does this. He adds us to the body of Christ, and we're there forever. Why, my brother, it would be unthinkable that we could look on the body and say, "I cut that hand off and then put it back on again, and then cut it off and put it back again. Or my foot: I can cut it off and then put it back on again; cut it off and put it back on again." Paul says the body of Christ is just like this: some of us are a foot, and some of us are an eye, and some of us are a hand, and some of us are an ear. We're not all foot; we're not all hand; we're not all eye. We have differing gifts and differing assignments, but it takes all of us to complete the whole body of Christ [1 Corinthians 12:12-28].

Now, when you're added, there's no such doctrine in the Bible as taking off the hand and putting it back on, or taking you out of the body of Christ and putting you back in the body of Christ. No. When God adds us to the body of the blessed Lord, we're there forever, forever: the doctrine of the security of the believer, the eternal salvation of the saints. "These," says God, "are Mine. They belong to Me!" And I repeat, some of us may be sorry, no-account, good-for-nothing representatives of the grace of God, but He is not done with us yet! We're on the way, we're on the way; we're growing in grace. It's a wonderful comfort. It's a blessed assurance. It's what we sing about, isn't that right?

Well, we've got to hasten, as I say. The fourth one: it is an historical, never-to-be-repeated, eternal event, this baptism of the Holy Spirit. Our Lord said, in John 14:16, "I will pray the Father, and He shall give you another paraklete," this One who lives with us and is in us, our Comforter, our strengthener, our encourager. "When I am gone, He will come." Now look at the Word: "That He may abide with you forever—that He may abide with you forever." This baptism of the Holy Spirit is an eternal, never-to-be-repeated event. "When He comes," says the Lord Jesus, "He will abide with you forever" [John 14:16].

Now we're going to look at how that works with us. In the second chapter of the second Thessalonians letter, Paul is writing about the end times, and the Day of the Lord, and the manifestation of what he calls the man of sin—the Antichrist, John calls him. Now in verses 6 and 7, the apostle writes:

> *You know—of course, I told you when I was there with you—what withholdeth that he might be revealed in his time. For the mystery of iniquity doth already work; only He who now letteth will let, until He be taken out of the way.*

Then shall that Wicked be revealed, whom the Lord shall consume with the spirit of His mouth, and shall destroy with the brightness of His coming.

[2 Thessalonians 2:5-8]

Now, Paul is talking about that day and that time, the end time, when the Antichrist, the man of sin, is revealed. And I think in every generation Satan has his "man of sin," his "antichrist." It will be a Hitler in one generation, as when I was a young fellow, starting out to preach. It will be a Stalin in the next generation. It will be some other character in a coming generation. But he always has his man. Satan always has his man, and the day is coming, says the apostle Paul, when, when that man of sin will be revealed. The Antichrist will be revealed. This final great ruler of the evil of the world will be revealed. But, says the apostle, he is not revealed now because there is Someone who restrains him, translated here in verse 6 "the One who withholdeth"; translated in the next verse "the One who letteth—letteth."

The word is katecho. Kata means "down," and echo means "hold." There is Someone here in this world that holds it down, that restrains, and that man of sin and that Antichrist will not be revealed until that Someone who restrains is taken out of the world. Now, who is that? As I read the Holy Scriptures, I think that One that restrains, that "holds down," that keeps this world from being drowned in a deluge and a flood tide of violence and blood and iniquity—I think the One who does that is this Pentecostal Spirit of grace that was poured out upon the earth and that dwells in the church, the body of Christ.

Now listen: there is a day coming, says our Lord and says the Holy Scriptures—and I'm going to preach on that tonight; "The Rapture of the Church," there is a day coming when the church is going to be taken out of this earth. The church is going to be "caught-up"; it's going to be "raptured," to meet our Savior in the air, to be forever with the Lord [1 Thessalonians 4:16-17]. Now, when that happens, the Holy Spirit of Pentecostal grace and power that dwells in the church will be taken up with us, because He, according to Jesus, lives in us forever [John 14:16], and when the church is raptured up, the Holy Spirit of God in Pentecostal grace goes up with us.

Now what's left behind is the Spirit of God only in His omnipresence. The Holy Spirit of God is like God, He is everywhere. He was in the creation bringing form out of chaos [Genesis 1:2]. But the Holy Spirit of God in Pentecostal grace and power is in the church, and when the church is taken up, the Holy Spirit is taken up with the body of Christ, and we have those awful days described in the Apocalypse, as it was in the days of Noah, and as it was in the days of Lot, and as it was in the days of Sodom and Gomorrah [2 Peter 2:5-8]. When the church is taken up and out, and the Holy Spirit that lives in the church is caught up back to heaven again [1 Thessalonians 4:16-17], what remains is the violence and the bloodshed and the awful he thlipse he megale—the tribulation, the great—that ends in the indescribable destruction of the battle of Armageddon[Revelation 16:16, 19:19-21].

Now I repeat the point; the baptism of the Holy Spirit [1 Corinthians 12:13], the outpouring of the Holy Spirit, is an historical, never-to-be-repeated, eternal event. The Holy Spirit abides in His people forever [John 14:16]. And when His people are caught up to meet Jesus in the air, the Holy Spirit is caught up with us, and the earth remains as it was in the days of Noah and in the days of Lot—he thlipse he megale: "the tribulation, the great." Lord, Lord, I don't want to be left behind. Now I must conclude; our time is gone.

What is this experience that we have, you and I and all of God's people? If the baptism was an historical event, one great moment in the life of the human race, the outpouring of the grace, and when we are saved we become a part of that great historical event, we are baptized into that body of Christ, then what is this that happens to us? Well, God plainly says, Ephesians 5:18: "Be not drunk with wine, wherein is excess; but be filled with the Spirit." Plerusthe, be filled with the Spirit: it's an imperative, plerusthe. It's an imperative from pleroo, which means to fill, fill up; fill. It's an imperative, plerusthe. We are commanded to be filled with the Spirit.

Will you look at it again? It is a present tense—remember what I said? In the Greek language you don't have "time tenses," you have kinds of action, and plerusthe, which we don't have any way to describe it—we don't have any nomenclature to use except what we have in our own language—but plerusthe refers to a kind of action. That is, it goes on, it goes on, it goes on continuously; it goes on continually. "Be ye filled with the Spirit," plerusthe; it is a command. It's an imperative. It's what we call "present tense," that is, in their language, it goes on and it goes on and it goes on, again and again and again, continuously. And it is "passive voice"; it is something God does through us, acts upon us.

He has a contrast here: "Be not drunk with wine, wherein is excess, but be filled with the Spirit"; passive voice, something from the outside happening to us. By contrast, he illustrates it. When a man gives himself to drunkenness, he becomes another kind of a man. You hardly recognize him. He's something else. He's given his mind to alcohol. He's given his motor reflexes to alcohol. He becomes another kind of a man!

I heard the craziest story. There was a bunch of drunks in a hotel room somewhere, and one of them said, "You know I can fly?" And he jumped out the window. Well, his friend came to see him in the hospital, and the guy in the hospital, all bunged up, said to him, "Why didn't you keep me from jumping out that window?" And his friend said, "Well, I thought you could do it!" You're somebody else when you're under the influence of alcohol. Now, he uses that by contrast.

When a man is filled with the Spirit of God—passive voice—the Lord comes in, and He takes his mind, and He takes his hand, and He takes his heart, and He takes his life, and he does things that he never dreamed for. It's a wonderful thing, and that's the way God commands us to live. We're to live in the power, and grace, and presence, and fullness of the Holy Spirit. One time God baptizes us into the body of Christ [1 Corinthians 12:13], and then He fills us again, and again, and again, and again, and that's what you read in the Bible.

In the second chapter of the Book of Acts, they were all filled with the Holy Spirit, for the Spirit was poured out [Acts 2:4]. In the fourth chapter of Acts, "And they were filled with the Holy Spirit" [Acts 4:31]. In the ninth chapter of the Book of Acts it says that Saul of Tarsus, to whom Ananias was sent—God said to him, "I have come here to open your eyes, that you can see, and that you be filled with the Holy Spirit" [Acts 9:17]. In the seventh chapter of the Book of Acts, it says, "Stephen, filled with the Holy Spirit, looked up to heaven, and saw Jesus" [Acts 7:55-56]. "And his face was as it had been the face of an angel" [Acts 6:15].

It's a wonderful thing and it's a daily experience with the people of God to be filled with the Holy Spirit. Singing in the Spirit, praying in the Spirit, studying God's Holy Word in the Spirit, worshipping in the Spirit, filled with the Spirit; it's a glorious, glorious, glorious daily experience for the child of God.

Bless your hearts, and God, fill us all to overflowing, and make our cups bigger and bigger, Lord, that God can give us more and more of Himself. Now may we stand for the prayer?

Our wonderful Lord in heaven, what a, what an incomparable blessing, providence, opportunity, privilege God hath given to us, opening the door of grace, bidding us to come in, and what a wonderful thing it is to see these whom the Holy Spirit has touched, whom God has called, answering, "Here am, Lord. Here am I." And in this moment when our people pray and we sing our hymn of appeal, a family you, a couple you, a one somebody you: "Pastor, the Lord has spoken to me, and I am on the way." If you are in the balcony, there is time and to spare. If you are on this lower floor, into one of these aisles, and down to the front: "Pastor, here I stand. I have decided for God." Bless you as you come. Angels attend you as you come. And wonderful Spirit of God, thank Thee for wooing, and convicting, and drawing, and bringing to us these whom that Lord hath called. In Thy saving and keeping name, amen. While we sing our song, a thousand times welcome, while we sing.

COMMENTARY

The Baptism of the Holy Spirit

When W.A. Criswell came to the conclusion that there have been as many interpretations of the work of the Holy Spirit as there have been theologians, he decided to present just the main points of the doctrine. Since there have been so many conflicting opinions, he wanted to try to clarify and unify thinking on the issue. He was aware of the issue. In the places where he had spoken, countless numbers of people had asked him to clarify some questions in order to understand the function of the Christian concept of the Holy Spirit.

In order to understand the function of the Holy Spirit in the Christian faith, Dr. Criswell advocated three major propositions. First, the impact of the Holy Spirit is more than just a power; He is a person. The original language clearly revealed that the Holy Spirit is a person. He contended that in the scripture the Holy Spirit is always a person, never an impersonal power.

Second, the ministry of the Holy Spirit is the work of God: He is the author of the Scriptures. The Holy Spirit is not only the author of the Scriptures; He is also the great teacher and Illuminator. The Holy Spirit convicts us of sin. He is the instrument of our regeneration. Third, the ultimate purpose of the Holy Spirit is to dwell in the man who accepts the Christian Faith and give him "abundant life." In man's "abundant life" through the Holy Spirit, he is to serve others, "The spiritual gifts are the endowments of God to make us able to do His work in the earth . . . These gifts are God's enablement for His disciples to evangelize the world." After presenting the scriptural constructs of the Holy Spirit, Dr. Criswell asked man to accept the Biblical concepts of the Holy Spirit and to live a spiritual life patterned after the life of Christ.

Dr. Criswell best explained his position when he gave a lengthy statement concerning his paradigm. He stated, "The doctrine is everywhere. I run into it all the time. And in one of those strange providences that are almost inexplicable, it was furthered by great men of God like Dwight L. Moody and R. A. Torrey. His own son, Dr. Torrey's son, pled with his father to change the nomenclature he used in describing his experience, and Dr. Torrey refused to the end of his life. In my own experience, for the years and the years, I misunderstood. I did not understand the truth of God with regard to the baptism of the Holy Spirit. One time, in these years gone by, there came two brethren here to Dallas to see me from Louisiana. They had heard me preach on the baptism of the Holy Spirit at a conference in Louisiana, and they came all the way over here to sit down with me and to teach me the Word of God. Even listening to them, I still didn't understand it. One time, in preaching through a conference at Moody Bible Institute in Chicago, I announced my preaching on this subject, and there came to my hotel room the men who led that great Christian teaching institution. And they talked to me at length, because at that time there were excesses battling, confronting the school in this area, in this baptism, this doctrine of the baptism of the Holy Spirit.

In his own words, Criswell explained his stance in the following paragraph. In those long ago days, years gone by, I studied, and I studied, and I prayerfully studied, and finally came to an understanding of the truth, a clear understanding of the truth of God, the revelation of God in the Holy Scriptures, and I wrote two books on the subject: the Holy Spirit. Now coming to this hour, I felt I ought to speak concerning it. I run into it so constantly: the aberration, the misunderstanding, the misconstruction, the misinterpretation of the baptism of the Holy Spirit. Then as I struggle to combine it all and to present the quintessence of it in just one brief sermon—I was struggling with it. You need hours. As I say, I wrote two books concerning it, and how do you combine it and compress it and condense it in just a few minutes like this?

Well, I have come into the habit of studying late at night. And one night in preparation for this message and in struggling to present it in just one brief moment like this—reading the Scriptures, poring over the Word of God, preparing this message—I went to bed and went to sleep, still not knowing how, in one sermon, to present the truth of this tremendous doctrine. And in the middle of the night, I awakened, and when I did, the entire message lay before me, from beginning to ending, every point and every discussion under every point.

I would not be so proudly spiritually egotistical as to say that an angel had presented it to me. Maybe the psychologist is right, is correct, when he says that your mind works when you are asleep as it does when you are awake, and my mind, working, arranged that whole message from beginning to end, and when I awakened, there it was. My mind had worked it through and now presents it to me. However you explain it, whether it was a gracious interposition and kindness from heaven, or whether it is psychologically conditioned that my mind was working through it even while I was asleep, the whole message was there before me."

Now the main points of it are this: the baptism of the Holy Spirit is a historical, prophetic event. Second: the baptism of the Holy Spirit is a historical, heavenly event. Third: the baptism of the Holy Spirit is a historical, ecclesiastical church event. And fourth: the baptism of the Holy Spirit is a historical, never-to-be-repeated, eternal event. And the conclusion: we are commanded to be filled with the Holy Spirit continuously and continually.

The baptism of the Holy Spirit is a historical, prophetic event. It is something that God specified at a particular time, at a particular place, in one event, years and years and centuries before it came to pass. It is one historical event prophesied by the Lord God in heaven.

It is the same thing as concerning the coming of our Lord. There was a time prophesied, a precise moment when the Lord of heaven would be incarnate in human flesh. He would be born of a virgin—prophesied [Isaiah 7:14]. There was a time prophesied, one event when our Lord would die in atoning grace for the sins of the world [Daniel 9:26]. There was a time prophesied, an event when He would be raised from the dead [Matthew 12:40]. There is a prophesied time, an event, when the Lord will return from heaven [Acts 1:11]. It is set in heaven, prophesied, and we're waiting for that coming event.

In the same way that there is a historical prophecy, was historical prophecies, were historical prophecies concerning the birth and the atoning death and the resurrection and the return of our Lord, just so there are prophecies, historical prophecies, that point to the outpouring of the Holy Spirit of God, the baptism of the Holy Spirit of God, the pouring out of the Spirit of God upon human flesh."

WHY I BECAME A PREMILLENNIALIST

Dr. W. A. Criswell

Matthew 24:29-34

First Baptist Church, Dallas, Texas, 1977

Criswell Bible Institute Chapel, November 16, 1980

Dallas Theological Seminary Chapel, March 16, 1984

I do not know of anything that appeals to me more than to accept the invitation to come and speak to you at this chapel hour. I am going to talk to you about "Why I Became a Premillennialist." It was an unusual thing. I never had a premillennial teacher in my life; so far as I know, I never saw one as I was growing up. All of my teachers, all of my mentors, all the preachers that I ever heard when I was growing up were either postmillennial; practically all of them were that or they were amillennial.

What happened to me was, over forty years ago, when I was pastor in Muskogee, Oklahoma, the under shepherd care of the church before I came here to Dallas, for some reason, and I have tried my best to ferret out why, but I can never come up with an answer, for some reason that I cannot understand, I began preaching the Bible at Muskogee, Oklahoma. Where I left off Sunday morning, I started Sunday night. Where I left off Sunday night, I began Sunday morning. And people that came to Muskogee to attend the services, who heard me preach, went away and said, "Why, that man is a premillennialist." That was the most amazing thing that I ever came across in my life. I was just preaching the Bible, that's all. And they said, "That man is a premillennialist."

I didn't quite understand the connotation of the word; I didn't know what it meant. I had heard the word, of course, many times, but I had never been introduced to it. My great teacher in Greek was Dr. A. T. Robertson. And our textbook that we studied was that big grammar, about that thick. When we came to the Revelation—we followed his syllabus through the New Testament—when we came to the Revelation, he dropped the syllabus on the podium, like that, made a resounding noise just like that, and he said, "Young gentlemen, in that syllabus you will find the separate theoretical interpretations of the Apocalypse. It will be futurist, it will be synchronistic historical, it will be continuous historical. You choose the one you like." And that was the only course that we had in the Revelation. That was the whole sum and substance of it.

That's the way I was taught. My predecessor, Dr. George W. Truett, here in the pulpit in Dallas, the greatest preacher our Southern Baptist communion has ever produced, was a postmillennialist. And he never referred to the second coming of our Lord. A funny thing, a strange thing, an unusual thing happened when the pulpit committee here, without my knowing it, when the pulpit committee here in Dallas, the First Church, was considering me, one of the executives of the convention, the association of churches in Texas, wrote to the committee and said, "In all fairness, I think you should know that the man you are considering to be your pastor is a premillennialist." Now the secretary of the committee was a layman; he was the treasurer of the Annuity Board. That's the name of our pension board in the convention. So, his boss, the executive leader over him, was Dr. Walter R. Alexander, a distinguished Philadelphian. Oh man, he was just the prince of culture and gracious courtesy! Dr. Walter Alexander was a Philadelphian. And Orville Groner, the secretary of the pulpit committee, received this letter, and took it to Dr. Alexander, and said, "Dr. Alexander, a tragedy has overwhelmed us. I don't know what this is, but one of the men in the convention has written to us saying that this man we're considering is a premillennialist." And Dr. Alexander looked at the letter, and looked at Orville Groner, and said—now this is a providence of God—he said, "Orville, thank God,

143

praise the Lord. I am a premillennialist." Orville Groner looked at him and said, "You are what?" And Dr. Alexander replied, "I am a premillennialist." And he began to talk to Orville Groner. And from then on you can imagine the force and the drive in the center of that pulpit committee that invited me to be under shepherd of the church here in Dallas.

In any event, after that I began to study what it was I was. Repeating, never introduced to it in my life, never in my life did I have anyone who spoke to me about that. So as I began to study, I learned that the primitive faith, the original faith, the pristine faith of the church was universally premillennial, all of the teaching. And I have here—and I wish we had a long time—I have here the fathers, the early Greek fathers and a few Latin fathers, the great fathers of the church, what they said; and without exception, they were dynamically, positively, wonderfully premillennial. Papias; Clement of Rome, who is doubtless referred to by Paul in Philippians 4:3; Justin Martyr; Irenaeus; Tertullian, one of the greatest Latin fathers that ever lived; Cyprian; Lactantius, who taught the son of Constantine. I have a historical summary of the primitive faith of the church by Edward Gibbon, in his incomparable The Decline and Fall of the Roman Empire. It's a magnificent summary of the patristic teaching, premillennial. And I learned that in America the founding fathers of our nation, those Puritans: Increase Mather was a devoted, vocal, verbalizing premillennialist, and his son Cotton Mather was also.

Premillennialism, I discovered, was the original faith. It is not a later doctrinal development. Amillennialism and postmillennialism—those two are bedfellows—is a later doctrinal approach to the Bible. The original one was premillennial.

Well, that's what I learned in church history. Then I began to study why it was that the church turned from premillennialism to amillennialism or postmillennialism. And the turn in the church was very apparent when you looked at its history carefully. As long as the church was persecuted, it was premillennial. When it became the state religion of the Roman Empire, it turned; and the turn was made possible because of the theological attitude of Augustine. The theology of the Roman Catholic Church is amillennial: they identify the kingdom and the Roman Catholic Church. And it had its origin in the teaching of Augustine.

He taught that the binding of Satan took place during the earthly ministry of our Lord; he spiritualized the fall of Satan. He taught that the first resurrection is the new birth of the believer; he spiritualized the resurrection. He taught that the devil is bound and expelled from the hearts of those who believe in Christ; he spiritualized the binding of Satan. He taught that the reign of the saints in their personal victory over sin and the devil is the great kingdom of our Lord; he spiritualized the coming kingdom of Jesus. He taught that the beast is this wicked world, and his image is hypocrisy; he spiritualized the Antichrist. And he taught that the millennium is this present period of the church age; we're in it now.

God help us. Can you imagine the glorious prophecies of the Old Testament? "The wolf shall dwell with the lamb, and the leopard shall lie down with the kid. . .and the lion will eat straw like an ox. . .they will not hurt nor destroy in all My holy mountain" [Isaiah 11:6-9]. That is now, according to Augustine. We're living in the millennium now. It is unthinkable! It is impossible!

Now we're going to speak of what happens to you when you turn aside from the premillennial faith and make the Bible a book of amillennial, postmillennial teaching. What you do is, you lose the biblical distinctions that makes for nothing but hermeneutical confusion, absolutely. According to Paul in 1 Corinthians 10:32, there are three divisions of all mankind: the Jew, the Gentile, and the church, made up of Jew and Gentile. Amillennialism is the tragic human interpretation that loses sight of these distinctions: it makes the Bible increasingly meaningless, and the Scriptures are finally looked upon as merely a piece of antique literature.

Now I want to show that to you. I have here in my hand a beautiful Bible with my name on it; and it is given to me by one of the affluent members of our church. It's a text book; I mean, this Bible is just the text, published by the Oxford Press, with very large print. I used to preach without any glasses, and this helped me a lot. So, I looked at the Book. And up here in Isaiah 43, it says, and these are the captions, "The church comforted with God's promises." So I looked down here in the forty-third chapter of Isaiah to read about the church comforted. And what I read is, "But now thus saith the Lord that created thee, O Jacob, and He that formed thee, O Israel, Fear not: for I have redeemed thee, I have called thee by thy name; and thou art Mine."

I turn the page and I read here "The promises of God to the church." And I look down at [Isaiah] chapter 44 to read God's promises to us in the church. And it says, "Hear, O Jacob My servant; Israel, whom I have chosen: Thus saith the Lord that made thee, and formed thee; Fear not, O Jacob, My servant; and thou Jesurun," lovely nickname for Israel, "whom I have chosen"[Isaiah 44:1-2]. I turn the pages of this unusually fine printed Bible, and I read the caption of the church: "The church's joy [Isaiah 52], the church's joy." So I expect to read down here in this chapter the church's joy; and it says, "O Jerusalem: loose thyself from the bands of thy neck...Break forth into joy, sing together, ye waste places of Jerusalem: for the Lord hath comforted His people, He hath redeemed Jerusalem" [Isaiah 52:2, 9]. I turn the page. The caption up here: "Christ's mercy toward His church." And so I read Christ's mercy toward His church [Isaiah 63], and it says, "I will make mention of the lovingkindness of the Lord toward the house of Israel...He remembered the days of old, Moses, and his people...Doubtless Thou art our Father, though Abraham be ignorant of us, and Israel acknowledges not: O Lord, our Father, our Redeemer"[Isaiah 63:7, 11, 16]. That's Christ's mercy toward His church.

And I look across the page, and it says, "The church prayeth to God. The church prayeth to God." And so I look down here for a prayer of our congregation to the Lord, and it says, "Wilt Thou refrain Thyself, O Lord? Our holy and heavenly house, where the fathers praised Thee, is burned with fire. Wilt Thou hold Thy peace, and afflict us?" [Isaiah 64:11-12]. The church prayeth to God; and the prophet here is speaking about the destruction of Jerusalem.

But this one took the cake: this ought to be enshrined in some kind of a museum. It says here, it says here, "The stability of the church. The stability of the church." That's the great caption, "The stability of the church." And it's that famous passage in Jeremiah 31: "Thus saith the Lord, as long as that sun shines in the heaven, and as long as that moon and the stars give light by night, just so long will the seed of Israel stay, stand, continue before Me as a nation, forever" [Jeremiah 31:35-36]. And yet that is the stability of the church.

Well, that's what I began to see as I started to study the Bible. The church is a musterion: it was a secret God kept in His heart. And that's not an unusual presentation in the Bible; it's over and over and over again that. It's found in Romans 11:25; it's mentioned in Romans 16:25; it's said in Ephesians 3; it's said in Ephesians 3:3; it's said in Ephesians 3:4; it's said in Ephesians 3:9; it's said in Colossians 1:26. There is a mystery that God kept in His heart, and the prophets never saw it, never [Ephesians 3:5-11]. There is no such thing as a prophecy in the Bible, in the Old Testament, concerning the church: the church is a subject of revelation, not of prophecy.

This age in which we live is a hiatus, an interpolation, an interlude between the sixty-ninth and the seventieth [weeks] of the Book of Daniel [Daniel 9:26-27]. The prophets never saw it[Ephesians 3:5]. And when you pick up the Bible and read, Israel is always Israel, the Jew is always the Jew, a Gentile is always a Gentile, and a church is always the church. And if you will preach the Bible, and let it say exactly what it says, and let it mean exactly what it purposes, you will have a marvelous introduction to the wisdom and the profundity and the depths of the riches of God in Christ Jesus, revealed to us in this Holy Word. It will fit together like a jigsaw puzzle; every piece will fall in place.

Now, not only when we turn aside from this interpretation of the Bible do we lose our hermeneutical homogeneity, but in the amillennial teaching, that God is through with Israel, that there's no future for Israel, there's no remembrance of His people in the mind of God, there's one thing to be said about it, and that is this: if God breaks His promises to the Jew, how do I know but that He will break His promise to me? Why should I think He is going to keep His promise to me, when He breaks the covenant that He made with His people Israel?

In Numbers 23:19, I read, "God is not a man, that He should lie; neither the son of man, that He should repent: hath He said, and shall He not do it? Or hath He spoken, and shall He not make it good?" If He keeps His promise to the Jew, I have every assurance He will see me through, He will keep His promise to me. And the two go together in my heart and mind. If He breaks the promise in the Old Covenant, I don't know but that He will break His promise in the New Covenant. So when I read all of those marvelous things that God hath promised to Israel, I'm assured, I'm convinced, I'm persuaded that God will do that for me.

Just look at some of the things God hath promised to Israel: "Verily I say unto you," says our Lord in Matthew 24:34, "this genea"—Peter uses another form of it, genus—"will be here till I come. He will be here, the Jew will be here till I come." Genea, genus, they all come from that same root: it means "species," it means "kind," it means "people," it means "a nation," it means "a race."

Now I want to ask you a little humble thing: in the Bible I read about Hittites, Jebusites, and Moabites, and Ammonites, and all kind of "ites." Did you ever see anybody, who ever heard of anybody, who ever heard of anybody, who ever saw anybody, who ever saw a Hittite, or an Ammonite, or a Moabite, or any of those other "ites"? Did you? You never did. They've been gone so many thousands of years that I don't know when they escaped from the books of history. But God said, "The Jew will be here, till I come" [Mark 13:30-31; Luke 21:32-33]. Man, I can introduce you to thousands of them here in Dallas.

And God said in that famous passage we looked at in Jeremiah 31, "As long as that sun shines in the sky, and as long as that moon and the stars gives light by night, just so long will the nation of Israel be a nation before Me" [Jeremiah 31:35-37]. God said that. And God said another thing: He said the land of Palestine is his forever. In Psalm 105, beginning at verse 8:

> *God hath remembered His covenant forever, the word which He commanded to a thousand generations. Which covenant He made with Abraham, and His oath unto Isaac;*
> *And confirmed the same unto Jacob for a law, and to Israel for an everlasting covenant:*
> *Saying, Unto thee will I give the land of Canaan, the lot of your inheritance.*
> *[Psalm 105:8-11]*

That's God. And the land of Canaan, the land of Palestine, the land of Israel belongs to him; it's his. God said so in an everlasting, unbreakable, enduring, eternal covenant.

And you know, there's something strange about that land and the Jew; something that just dumbfounds me and amazes me! I had just returned from Israel, and I was in Panama, where the Panama Canal is, the country of Panama. And in Panama City, I went into a silk shop to buy some silk for my wife, to bring back to her from my journey down there in South America. And I looked at the silk merchant, and I said, "You are Jewish, aren't you?" He said, "Yes." Well, I said, "In this previous journey this year, I went to Israel."

"Oh?" he said, "you have been in Israel?" I said, "Yes." Well, he said, "How is it there?" And I began to tell him the things that were developing in the recovery of the land, the nation blossoming like a rose, and all of the wonderful things that were happening in Israel. And my young men, as I talked to that man the tears flooded down his cheeks—in Panama, he'd never been to Israel. It is a phenomenon: the love in the Jew for Israel, whether he's ever been there or not. They're all like that. There is a profound enduring affection for Israel in the heart of every Jew. And to my amazement, for the most part over there he's a farmer. I never saw a Jewish farmer in my life until I went over there to Israel. They go together.

The Bible says—and I haven't time even to read the passages—he will return to Palestine to dwell forever, and he will return in unbelief [Ezekiel 36:24-28]. And the Scriptures say he will be converted; going to accept the Lord. In Zechariah chapter 12, in Romans 11, he is going to be a fellow Christian with us one of these days [Zechariah 12:10; Romans 11:25-27]. When Paul says he was born at ektroma before the time, he is referring in that beautiful word in 1 Corinthians 15:8, he is referring to the fact that someday when the Lord appears to all Israel, his people, they're all going to be saved [Romans 11:25]. But he was saved before the time, before the time.

The Lord appeared to His brethren, to James, to Jude, who write in the Bible. Why should I think it unusual the Lord should appear to His people? And they look upon Him whom they have pierced, and they will weep, and mourn, as they did in Hadad Rimmon" [Zechariah 12:10-11];and they'll be saved. It's a wonderful thing, what God purposes for His people.

Oh dear! I have here the confirmation of the word of prophecy in history. The death of postmillennialism: it's gone; you'll never see a postmillennialist. These world wars have stopped his unbelieving mouth; and you never see one. The birth of the nation of Israel; and the effective message and messenger of the man who is a Bible-believing premillennialist— there came here to Dallas two men about the same time to preach. Billy Graham came, who is a premillennialist, and a believer in the inerrancy of the Word of God. Billy Graham came here to preach. And thousands—you went out there, Cotton Bowl, and finally to the Texas Stadium, came here twice—thousands were moved to the Lord. It was a Pentecostal visitation from heaven. At the same, Paul Tillage came here to Dallas. Paul Tillage is, was, dead now— thank the Lord—Paul Tillage, Paul Tillage came to Dallas. He was the darling of the liberal neo-orthodox for years and years and years, professor at the Union Theological Seminary in New York. I talked to one of the leading elders in the Presbyterian Church where Paul Tillage spoke. And he said to me, he said, "I don't want to belittle the man, but," he said, "I listened to him every time he spoke for a solid week, and to this moment I cannot tell you a thing that he said. I have no idea what he was talking about." I'm just avowing to you that when a man is a premillennialist, he'll move more and more and more in closeness to the Word of God. When a man is an amillennialist, he'll move further, and further, and further, and further away from the Word of the Lord.

COMMENTARY

Why I Became a Premillennialist

This famous sermon took place at several locations: First Baptist Church, Dallas in 1977, Criswell Bible Institute chapel in 1980 and Dallas Theological Seminary chapel in 1984, as well as other convention meetings.

Dr. Criswell stated that ministers who listened to him started calling him a premillennialist. In his works, he gave this lengthy explanation, "I didn't quite understand the connotation of the word; I didn't know what it meant. I had heard the word, of course, many times, but I had never been introduced to it. My great teacher in Greek was Dr. A. T. Robertson.

Premillennialism, Criswell discovered, was the original faith. It is not a later doctrinal development. Amillennialism and postmillennialism—those two are bedfellows—is a later doctrinal approach to the Bible. The original one was premillennial."

From his perspective, there was a controversy concerning the theology of end times. Criswell stated that he studied each of the positions of Christ's second return to earth. As he read the Bible, he came across many things that needed to be reviewed carefully. In each of the addresses, Criswell was careful to explain the different theological positions concerning the second coming of Christ. He gave these definitions and scriptural stands:

Premillennialism is the doctrine, the interpretation of the Bible, that the earth is dark and lost, and that sin is deep and desperate, and that the world is so lost in sin that our only hope lies in the intervention of God, in the coming of Christ, and that the kingdom, the millennium, will be set up by the appearing of the Lord Himself. He can come any moment, anytime, any day, any night. That is premillennialism.

Postmillennialism is evolutionary in its background. All of us are getting better and better and better. And by the preaching of the gospel, and by the sweet influences of the Holy Spirit, we will breed out of the race the lion, and the fang, and the claw, and the tiger, and finally we all shall come into that perfect perfection of the millennial kingdom, and then Christ will come and preside over what we have done in winning the world to Christ and in doing away with sin in the human heart. That is postmillennialism.

Amillennialism, "a" is the Greek negative; it is called an alpha privative. Amillennialism means that there is no millennium at all, that whatever the Bible would speak about a future golden age in the kingdom of our Lord is altogether figure of speech. So they spiritualize it all away, and they make the Bible mean whatever the man personally would like to make it say. These are the amillennialists. These are the spiritualizers. There is to be no millennium, and everything that the Bible would say about it is just a figure of speech.

W. A. Criswell took the stance of premillennialist. This perception made him famous for his convictions. He asked the congregation to accept his interpretation as a premillennialist. People either swore by him or at him for his position. This issue is still a controversy in contemporary theology.

WHETHER WE LIVE OR DIE

Dr. W. A. Criswell
Message to the Pastors' Conference Southern Baptist Convention, Dallas, Texas
June 10th, 1985

Not in all of my life have I ever prepared an address as minutely and meticulously as I have this one tonight. I have been a pastor fifty-eight years. I began preaching at this pastor's conference at the invitation of Dr. M. E. Dodd when he founded it something like fifty years ago. And I would think more than thirty times have I spoken to this assembly of God's anointed under shepherds. But I have never, ever approached a moment like this. And the message tonight, entitled, "Whether We Live or Die," is delivered, prepared in view of the convocation of our assembled messengers beginning in the morning. The outline of the address, of the study was:

> *The Pattern of Death for a Denomination; then*
> *The Pattern of Death for an Institution; then*
> *The Pattern of Death for a Preacher, a Professor; and then finally,*
> *The Promise of Renascence, and Resurrection, and Revival.*

SO WE BEGIN: NUMBER ONE THE PATTERN OF DEATH FOR A DENOMINATION.

In the middle of the last century, a great storm arose in the Baptist denomination in Great Britain. Opposition to evangelical truths sprang from two sources. One, the publication in 1859 of Darwin's Origin of Species, which made the Genesis account of creation a myth. And second, the vast inroads of German higher criticism and rationalism that explained away the miracles of the Bible and reduced the inspired Word to merely a human book.

This fungal attack on the Scripture brought forth open and militant opposition from the mighty preacher Charles Haddon Spurgeon. He urged the Baptist Union of England to speak out against the heresy. They refused, saying Baptists believe in the priesthood of every believer, and further avowed that Baptists could believe their own way so long as they baptize by immersion. Spurgeon then published what he called "The Downgrade in the Churches."

He wrote, "Instead of submission to God's Word, higher criticism urges accommodation to human wisdom. It sets human thought above God's revelation and constitutes man the supreme judge of what ought to be true."

He wrote, "Believers in Holy Scripture are in confederacy with those who deny plenary inspiration. Those who hold evangelical doctrine are in open alliance with those who call the Genesis fall a myth."

He wrote, "A chasm is opening between the men who believe their Bibles and those who are prepared for an advance upon the Scripture. . .The house is being robbed, its very walls are being digged down, but the good people who are in bed are too fond of the warmth. . .to go downstairs to meet the burglars." "Inspiration and speculation cannot long abide side by side. . .We cannot hold the inspiration of the Word and yet reject it. We cannot hold the doctrine of the fall and yet talk of evolution of spiritual life from human nature. One or the other must go." "Compromise there can be none."

Dr. John Clifford, London pastor and president of the British Baptist Union and later the first president of the Baptist World Alliance, declared in 1888, quote, "It pains me unspeakably to see this eminent [preacher Spurgeon] rousing the energies of thousands of Christians to engage in personal wrangling and strife, instead of inspiring them to. . .herioc effort to carry the. . .Gospel to our fellow-countrymen." Sounds kind of familiar, doesn't it?

Dr. John Clifford had embraced the higher critical new theology. He believed that evangelicalism and higher criticism could be combined. Dr. Clifford presided over the Council of the Baptist Union that met in session January 18, 1888. They voted to recommend to the plenary session of the Union a vote to censure Spurgeon. Dr. John Clifford did his work well. The Baptist Union met in assembly April 23, 1888, in the City Temple of London—Dr. Joseph Parker's Congregational church, himself a critic of Spurgeon—and the recommendation of council for censure was placed before the full body. The official vote was two thousand for the motion to censure Spurgeon, and seven against.

A godly man, Henry Oakley, who was present in the Baptist Union assembly that day, wrote these words in later memory concerning the tragic meeting. Quote:

I was present at the City Temple when the motion to censure Spurgeon was moved, seconded, and carried. The City Temple was as full as it could be. I was there early but found only a standing place in the aisle at the back of the gallery. I listened to the speeches. The only one of which I have a distinct remembrance was that of Mr. Charles Williams. He quoted Tennyson in favor of a liberal theology. The moment of voting came. Only those members of the assembly were qualified to vote. When the motion of censure was put, a forest of hands went up. "Against," called the chairman, Dr. John Clifford. I did not see any hands, but history records there were seven. Before any announcement of the censure number was made by Dr. John Clifford, the vast assembly broke into tumultuous cheering, and cheering, and cheering yet. From some of the older men their pent-up hostility found vent. From many of the younger men wild resistance of "any obscurantist trammels,"—Spurgeon's preaching—as they said, broke loose. It was a strange scene. I viewed it with tears. I stood near a man I knew well. He went wild with delight at the censure. I say, it was a strange scene, that that vast assembly should so outrageously be delighted at the condemnation of the greatest, noblest, and grandest leader of their faith.

An English writer said of that downgrade controversy against Spurgeon that it quote, "entailed one of the most bitter persecutions any minister of the gospel has ever endured in this country." Spurgeon's wife Susanna said that the controversy cost him his life. He died at the age of fifty-seven. Spurgeon himself said to a friend in May, 1891, "Goodbye. You will never see me again. This tragic fight is killing me." But Spurgeon also said, "The distant future will vindicate me."

All that Mr. Spurgeon saw and said, and much more, came to pass. Baptist witness in Great Britain began to die. The Baptist Union in their minutes recognized the presence of higher criticism in their midst, but they said it would do no harm. Spurgeon answered that the future would witness a lifeless and fruitless church. As he foretold, with the accommodation of the higher critical approach to the Scriptures—which is universal among us—with the accommodation of the higher critical approach to the Scriptures, church attendance fell off, prayer meetings ceased, miracles of conversion were witnessed less and less, the number of baptisms began to decline—and for years they've been in decline with us—and the churches began to die out. The numerical graph of the British Baptists since the halcyon days of Spurgeon, their mighty champion, is down, and ever down, and for a century has been going down.

I was in India years ago when English Baptists were closing down their mission stations on the Ganges River, stations founded by William Carey. Some say the position taken by Spurgeon hurt the mission movement. My brother, if the higher critical approach to the Scriptures dominates our institutions and our denominations, there will be no missionaries to hurt! They will cease to exist!

A comment on the sad condition of Baptist churches in England is found in the latest biography of Spurgeon written by Dr. Arnold Dallimore, entitled: *C. H. SPURGEON, A NEW BIOGRAPHY*, published this last year. The comment concerning English Baptists is this, quote: "Where there is no acceptance of the Bible as inerrant; there is no true Christianity. The preaching is powerless, and what Spurgeon declared to his generation a hundred years ago is the outcome." And that statement is followed by this paragraph:

> The failure of the new theology or higher criticism, call it what we will, is forcefully brought out by E. J. Poole-Conner in his Evangelicalism in England. He tells of a conversation between the editor of an agnostic magazine and a neo-orthodox minister. The editor told the minister that despite their different vocations, they had much in common. "I don't believe the Bible," said the agnostic, "but neither do you. I don't believe the story about creation, but you don't either. I don't believe any of these things, but neither do you. I am as much of a Christian as you, and you are as much of an infidel as I.

As with the Baptists of Great Britain, whether we continue to live or ultimately die lies in our dedication to the infallible Word of God.

NUMBER TWO: THE PATTERN OF DEATH FOR AN INSTITUTION.

An institution can be like a great tree which in times past withstood the rain, and the wind, and the storm, and the lightning, but finally fell because the heart had rotted out. Insects, termites destroyed the great monarch of the woods. This is the unspeakably tragic thing that happens to many of our Christian institutions, and eventually threatens them all. They are delivered to secularism and infidelity, not because of a bitter frontal attack from without, but because of a slow, gradual permeation of the rot and curse of unbelief from within. The tragic and traumatic example of that decay is the University of Chicago.

The faithful devout Baptist people of the North set about to build, in their words, and I quote, "a great Christian university to counteract the materialism of the Middle West." God greatly, immediately blessed their effort. In May 1889, the electric news was announced to the Baptists gathered in a national meeting in Boston that Rockefeller had offered six hundred thousand dollars for the building of the Christian school if the Baptist churches would give four hundred thousand dollars. When the announcement was made, the entire assembly arose with a doxology on its lips. And Dr. Henson exclaimed, "I scarcely dare trust myself to speak. I feel like Simeon when he said, 'Now, Lord, let us now depart in peace. . .for mine eyes have seen Thy salvation'" [Luke 2:29, 30].

Appeals were sent to twelve hundred Baptist pastors in the Middle West. The second Sunday in April 1890 was made University Day. The humble, faithful loyal Baptist people in all the churches gave prayerfully and sacrificially. Their splendid school for preachers, the Baptist Theological Seminary at Morgan Park in Chicago was, under the terms of the Rockefeller gift, to be the center of the university and to become the divinity school. The university was to be built around the seminary, and all of it was to be dedicated to the evangelization of the heartland of America. It was done gloriously, victoriously. The university was built. The divinity school was opened, and they prepared preachers to win the Middle West for Christ.

Then the infiltration began. The curse, the rot, the virus, the corruption of a higher critical approach to the gospel began to work. What are the ultimate results of this almost universal higher critical teaching? Here are some of the professors who taught the preachers in that divinity school during the course of the years. Professor G. B. Smith, systematic theology, who wrote, "The spirit of democracy protests against such an idea as that God has the right to insist on a rigid plan of salvation." Professor Soares, who said, "Redemption is an absolute fancy. Revelation is self-deception. We refuse the idea that the principle business of the church is to get people converted and committed to the Christian life." And Professor G. B. Foster, Baptist teacher in the seminary, and pastor of a Unitarian Church wrote, "An intelligent man who now affirms his faith in miracles can hardly know what intellectual honesty means. The hypothesis of God has become superfluous in every science, even that of religion itself. Jesus did not transcend the limits of the purely human."

We cannot but find ourselves in sympathy with an editorial of a great Chicago newspaper which said:

> *We are struck with the hypocrisy and treachery of these attacks on Christianity. This is a free country and a free age, and men can say what they choose about religion. But this is not what we obtained these divinity professors for. Is there no place in which to assail the Bible but a divinity school? Is there no one to write infidel books except professors of Christian theology? Is a theological seminary an appropriate place for a general massacre of Christian doctrines? We are not championing either Christianity or infidelity, but only condemning infidels masquerading as men of God and Christian teachers.*

A friend of mine, a teacher, went to the University of Chicago to gain a Ph.D. in pedagogy. While there, he made the friendship of a student in the divinity school. Upon the young theologian's graduation, the budding preacher said to my teacher friend, quote, "I am in a great quandary. I have been called to the pastorate of a Presbyterian church in the Midwest, but it is one of those old-fashioned Presbyterian churches that believes the Bible. And I don't believe the Bible, and I don't know what to do." My teacher friend replied, "I can tell you exactly what you ought to do." Eagerly, the young preacher asked, "What?" And my teacher friend replied, "I think that if you don't believe the Bible, you ought to quit the ministry!"

But not only in the North have we lost our Baptist institutions such as the University of Chicago; such as Brown University; such as Crozer Theological Seminary, practically all of them. But in the South—where we live—in the South we are beginning to witness the same loss. Within these last few years, two of our senior Baptist universities in the Southern states have been removed from Baptist control. Give it another century, and the loss will be unspeakably tragic.

John Wesley at one time wrote, "I am not afraid that the people called Methodists should ever cease to exist in Europe or America. But I am afraid lest they should exist as a dead sect, having the form of religion without the power." This fear that troubled the heart of John Wesley no less troubles the hearts of believing Christians everywhere who take time to see what higher criticism can do to their institutions.

*If neo-orthodoxy were a separate movement in itself, built its own churches, launched **its** own institutions, projected its own denomination, then we could look at it as just another of the many sects that appear on the surface of history. But neo-orthodoxy in itself builds nothing. It is a parasite that grows on institutions already built.*

If these higher critical semi-Unitarians won the lost to Christ, built up the churches, sent out missionaries, ministered to the needs of the people, then we could abandon our Bibles, rest at ease in Zion, and watch the kingdom of God advance from our ivory towers. The trouble is, these self-styled superior religionists do nothing but preside over a dying church, and a dying witness, and a dying denomination.

No minister who has embraced a higher critical approach to the gospel has ever built a great church, held a mighty revival, or won a city to the Lord. They live off the labor and sacrifice of those who paid the price of devoted service before them. Their message, which they think is new and modern, is as old as the first lie, "Yea, hath God said?" [Genesis 3:1].

Let the true pastor never turn aside from his great high calling to preach the whole counsel of God, warn men of their sins and the judgment of God upon them, baptize their converts in the name of the triune Lord, and build up the congregation in the love and wisdom of Christ Jesus. If he does that he will have completed the work for which the Holy Spirit did choose him. Do not be deterred or be discouraged by what others say about you. Just keep on winning souls to Jesus!

NUMBER THREE: THE PATTERN OF DEATH FOR A PREACHER, A PULPITEER, A PROFESSOR.

There came to the Southern Seminary in 1869 a scholarly young man by the name of Crawford H. Toy. He was the first addition to the original faculty of four, and gave every promise of becoming the greatest of them all. He knew more Hebrew than his teacher, Dr. Basil Manley. Literally, he was the pride and joy of the school. He was brilliant beyond compare.

However, through studying German higher criticism and rationalism, he drifted away from the revealed truth of the Scriptures and began to teach in the seminary the pentateuchal-destructive attacks of Keunen, Wellhausen, and a host of others. It broke the hearts of President James P. Boyce and Professor John A. Broadus, but the dismissal had to come.

When Dr. Toy left, Boyce and Broadus accompanied him to the railroad station. Just before the train took him away, President Boyce placed his left arm around the shoulders of the young man, and lifting up his right hand to heaven, said, "Crawford, I would give my right arm if you were back as you were when you first came to us."

Dr. Toy went to be professor of Hebrew at Harvard University. He went into the Unitarian church and finally, never went to church at all. He was a world-famous scholar. In my library, I have Hebrew books written by Dr. Toy. He was a world-famous scholar, internationally known author, and a lovable man, but the virus of higher criticism destroyed his spiritual life and work.

This is the young man who first taught in Albemarle Female Institute in Charlottesville, Virginia, before joining the faculty of Southern Seminary. This is the young man who taught in the school attended by a most vivacious and brilliant student, Miss Lottie Moon. This is the young man with whom Lottie Moon fell in love. This is the young man to whom Lottie Moon returned from China to America to marry. This is the young man the foreign mission board of the Southern Baptist Convention in 1860 appointed a missionary to the Orient, the War Between the States preventing his going. This is the young man, Crawford H. Toy, who was idolized by the Baptist academic and religious world.

But Lottie Moon was shattered and grief-stricken by the new theology and liberal beliefs of the man she so deeply admired and so beautifully loved. She returned to China heartbroken, never to return to home in America, never to marry, and died there in the Orient, lonely in soul and pouring her very life into a ministry for her starving Chinese people.

In the current issue of Review and Expositor, the theological journal of Southern Seminary, there is an extended article on Crawford H. Toy. It is filled with lavish and extravagant praise for the Unitarian. Here are the closing sentences in the review; I quote, "So far as his critical trends developed within the ten years of his membership on the faculty, his views today would not be regarded as sufficiently revolutionary to call for drastic action. Toy's research and views were too advanced for his contemporaries." That is, if he lived and taught today, his higher-critical, destructive approach to the Word of God would be perfectly acceptable, condoned, and defended!

However much our hearts may yearn over those who are victims and carriers of modernistic fallacy, if we are to survive as a people of God we must wage a war against the disease that, more than any other, will ruin our missionary, evangelistic, and soul-winning commitment.

AND LAST: THE POSSIBILITY AND PROMISE OF RESURRECTION, RENASCENCE, REVIVAL.

If we will receive the Scriptures as of God, and be true to them as to the Holy Spirit, the Lord will use Southern Baptists to evangelize the world. Revelation 14:6 says, "And I saw an angel fly in the midst of the heaven, having the everlasting gospel to preach unto them that dwell on the earth." That angelos, having the everlasting euangelion toeuangelisai the whole world, can be Southern Baptists. We can experience in our very midst great revival, the outpouring of the saving power of the Holy Spirit upon our churches, upon our preachers, and upon our mission fields.

The way of God is always onward, forward, and upward. The Holy Spirit always announces that there is a greater day coming. The burden of the prophets and the marvelous beckoning light of biblical revelation are ever and always the same. Our mighty God is marching on. It is the message of the first page of the Bible. It is the message of the second page of the Bible. It is the message of the first book of the Bible. It is the message of the second book of the Bible. It is the message of the last page and the last book of the Bible. A glorious triumph is coming. The Lord never recedes. He necessarily advances. His creation is followed by redemption. His redemption is followed by sanctification. His sanctification is followed by glorification.

There is no formal conclusion to the Book of Acts. It is open-ended. God means for the story of Pentecostal power and revival to be prolonged after the same manner. God does not do a great thing and then an increasingly smaller thing. God does not build a portico of marble and finish the temple with decaying brick. Our greatest days are yet to come. There was a time when the Holy Spirit as a heavenly fire was a mysterious presence flashing like lightning from the skies, we knew not whence or whither; coming now upon a Moses and again upon an Elijah, sometimes appearing in the burning bush in Horeb [Exodus 3:2], sometimes falling in awesome mystery upon the altar of sacrifice of Mount Carmel [1 Kings 17:32-39], sometimes striking out in Israel's camp in destroying fury[Numbers 11:1], sometimes appearing as the Shekinah glory in the temple's Holy of Holies [2 Chronicles 7:1-3], the strange sign and symbol of Jehovah's presence and power.

Since Christ's ascension [Acts 1:9], and in the fulfillment of the prophecy of Joel 2:28-32, the Holy Spirit has been poured out upon all flesh [Acts 2:1-4, 16-33]. John 3:34 confirms that God giveth not the Spirit by measure. He is with us, within us, for us, for power, for conquest, for glory. Since Pentecost, there is no age, no century, no era, no time without the marvelous outpouring of the Holy Spirit. The soul-saving experience continues. Darkness and death and decay may reign in one place, but always light, life, and salvation will reign and vigorously abound in another.

The church at Jerusalem fell into Ebionitic legalism, but the church at Antioch experienced the greatest revival of Gentile converts the first century ever knew. When waning of piety began to empty the churches at Antioch, the churches at Ephesus and Rome and at Milan were waxing mighty in the work of the Lord. When the churches of Alexandria and Carthage were falling into empty philosophical dissertations, the churches of Gaul were winning all western continental Europe to the Lord.

While Rome was pursuing vain and sterile rituals, the churches of Ireland were baptizing the whole nation and their many tribes into the faith. While Mohammed was destroying the faith in North Africa, the Middle East, and Asia Minor, the scholars of Iona were going forth to evangelize the Northumbrians, the Scots, the Picts, the Anglo-Saxons, our ancestors.

While the pontifical court of Avignon was engrossed in seeking political power, the cities of Germany were learning the heavenly ways of the Lord Jesus. When the darkness of night and superstition were covering the churches of France, the morning stars of the Reformation were rising in England. When Italian fields were turning into useless stubble, Bohemia was alive with the converting Spirit of Christ.

When the Unitarian defection destroyed the evangelizing spirit of the congregations of New England, the pioneer preachers were advancing beyond the Alleghenies to build churches and Christian institutions in the heartland of America. And while elitism, and liberalism, and spiritual indifference are decimating the churches in the West, great revival is being experienced in Korea, in South America, and in central Africa. Why not America, and why not now?

Our own and our ultimate destiny lies in the offing—and with us, the world. Seemingly, we stand at the continental divide of history, at the very watershed of civilization. Changes of colossal nature are sweeping the world.

In years past, the French Revolution signalized a political change. The Renaissance brought intellectual change. The industrial revolution introduced economic change. The Reformation encompassed religious change. But today, we face every kind and category of change, mostly defined by the flood tides of materialism, secularism, and liberalism. In my lifetime, for the first time in world history, governments are statedly and blatantly atheistic. No ancient Greek would ever make a destiny-determining decision without first consulting the oracle at Delphi. No Roman general would go to war without first propitiating the gods. But these bow at no altar, call upon the name of no deity, and they seem to be possessing the world.

Whether we live or die lies in the imponderables of Almighty God. Will God not judge atheistic, communistic Russia? Will He not also judge secularistic, heathenistic, humanistic, materialistic America? What is the difference at the judgment bar of Christ between a God-denying Russian communist atheist and a God-denying American liberal humanist? Can God judge Sodom, and Gomorrah, and Nineveh, and Babylon, and not judge Moscow, and Peking, and San Francisco, and Dallas?

Our mission frontiers run down every street and village, through every house, home, and classroom. The whole globe today is small, compact, and shrunken. We see, hear, watch, read, follow what happens moment by moment around the world. The interdependence and the interlinking of all mankind is an actual modern fact. We all ride this planet together. Our nation is one in a dependent family of nations. Romans 14:7 avows, "For none of us lives to himself, and not one of us dieth to himself."

As Baptist churches, and as a Baptist people, we need each other. One segment of our community cannot do our work, our task, alone. Our strength lies in a common determination and a common dedication. One church can build a Sunday school, but a Sunday school *movement must be launched by an association of churches through a Sunday school board. One church can send a missionary, but a vast missionary movement must be engineered by a denomination of churches through a foreign mission board. One church can have a revival, but a revival movement must be prayed for, and prayed down, and lifted up by a community of churches through an evangelistic director.*

Years ago, I saw a pathetic picture in Life magazine. A little boy had been lost in a horizon-to-horizon Kansas wheat field, had wandered away from the house, and had lost his way in the vast sea of standing stalks. Frantically, the parents had searched for the small child to no avail. The sympathizing neighbors helped, but without success. Finally, someone suggested they join hands and comb the fields by sections. The picture I saw was the sorrowing neighbors with the family standing over the dead body of the little boy, and the cry of the father printed as the caption below: "Oh, if only we had joined hands before!"

United in prayer, preaching, witnessing, working, not around the higher-critical denial of Scripture, but around the infallible Word of God in Christ Jesus, we cannot fail. If we join hands with the blessed Savior, and deliver the message of the inerrant Word of God, God will rise to meet us.

> *And the Lord God whispered and said to me,*
> *These things shall be, these things shall be.*
> *No help shall come from the scarlet skies*
> *Till My people rise.*
> *Till My people rise, My arm is weak.*
> *I cannot speak till My people speak.*
> *When men are dumb, My voice is dumb.*
> *I cannot come till My people come.*
> *From over the flaming earth and sea,*
> *The cry of My people must come to Me.*
> *Not till their spirit break the curse*
> *May I claim My own in the universe.*
> *But if My people rise, if My people rise,*
> *I will answer them from the swarming skies.*
> *[excerpts from "God Prays: Answer, World! Angela Morgan, 1917]*

No battle was ever won by retreat, or submission, or surrender. When Alexander the Great lay dying, they asked him, "Whose is the kingdom?" And he replied, "It is for him who can take it!" It will be we, or somebody else.

> *Bring me my bow of burning gold:*
> *Bring me my arrows of desire:*
> *Bring me my spear; O clouds unfold!*
> *Bring me my chariot of fire.*
> *We shall not cease from battle strife,*
> *Nor shall the sword sleep in our hand*
> *Till we have built Jerusalem*
> *In this fair and pleasant land.*
> *God grant it! Amen.*
> *[Adapted from "Jerusalem," by William Blake]*

COMMENTARY

Whether We Live or Die

The address took place at the pastor's conference at the Southern Baptist Convention in Dallas, Texas. Criswell, as the main speaker, stated that his findings were: The Pattern of Death for a Denomination; The Pattern of Death for an Institution; The Pattern of Death for a Preacher, a Professor; and then finally, The Promise of Renascence, and Resurrection, and Revival. Criswell's stated the issues from his perspective. In many ways, the 1985 annual meeting of the Southern Baptist Convention was a watershed moment in the conservative revolution in the convention. The moderates of the convention mobilized all their resources to stop the conservative advance at the Dallas meeting.

The presidents of all six seminaries pledged their support for the moderate cause in Dallas, and Foreign Mission Board President Keith Parks wrote a letter to Southern Baptist international missionaries saying he could not support Stanley's reelection. Leading up to the annual meeting, 2,000 moderate pastors from Georgia endorsed an ad in the Atlanta Journal-Constitution urging messengers not to vote for Stanley. Conservative W.A. Criswell, the pastor of the First Baptist Church in Dallas, sent letters to 36,000 Southern Baptist pastors asking them to come, bring messengers and vote for Stanley. In the final sermon at the SBC Pastors' Conference preceding the annual meeting, Criswell rallied conservatives in what he told historian Jerry Sutton was the most important message he ever preached.

All eyes were on Dallas as the expected site of moderates' most formidable stand. It was "a point of no return." One hopeful action of the convention for Sherman and fellow moderates was the election of what became known as the Peace Committee, which would "seek to determine the sources of the controversies in our convention, and make findings and recommendations regarding these controversies."

The presidents of all six seminaries pledged their support for the moderate cause in Dallas. Leading up to the annual meeting, Criswell rallied conservatives in what he told historians was the most important message he ever preached.

All eyes were on the convention sealed conservatism for years to come. It was a point of no return as Criswell stated that would seek to determine the sources of the controversies in our convention, and make findings and recommendations regarding these controversies. The liberal and or moderate plan did not succeed. The conflict that culminated in Dallas began to percolate decades earlier as conservatives grew increasingly concerned that SBC entities had drifted from their commitment to biblical inerrancy.

Students and faculty continue to view the televising of the 1985 sermon, "Whether We Live or Die" by legendary Southern Baptist preacher W.A. Criswell during chapel services at the Baptist Theological Seminaries. When Southern Seminary viewed the famous sermon, it was announced a new academic chair in preaching in honor of W.A. Criswell, long-time pastor of First Baptist Church in Dallas, Southern Baptist statesman and two-time Southern graduate, during a chapel service in Alumni Memorial Chapel. Jack Pogue, a long-time friend of Criswell who was present for the announcement, funded the chair. After introducing him, seminary president R. Albert Mohler Jr. thanked Pogue for his generosity. President Mohler stated, "It is my great privilege to announce today, at the great generosity of this friend, the funding of the W.A. Criswell Chair of Expository Preaching," Mohler also commented about Criswell's gift of expository preaching as he said, "From the time of Charles Spurgeon to the time of W.A. Criswell, there are very few prominent preachers who are actually committed to what we would call biblical exposition."

Mohler introduced a video of Criswell's 1985 address, "Whether We Live or Die," which the seminary community viewed as part of the service. Criswell preached the message, one of his most popular sermons, at the pastors' conference held before the annual meeting of the Southern Baptist Convention (SBC) in Dallas. "There is a line that runs very straight from that day in Dallas, Texas, to this day in Louisville, Ky.," Mohler told Southern Seminary students. "We can look back at history and say, had not the convention voted as it did in the very day after Dr. Criswell preached that sermon, we would not be sitting in this chapel today. It would be a very different world and a very different institution." In the sermon, preached during one of the most intense times of controversy over the inerrancy of the Bible in SBC life, Criswell outlined how acquiescence to liberal theology leads to the death of denominations and institutions. As examples, he pointed to Charles Haddon Spurgeon's defense of the Bible in the "Downgrade Controversy" among English Baptists in the late 1800s and the University of Chicago's fall into liberalism after its founding as an Orthodox school to train ministers.

Criswell illustrated the influence of liberalism within the Southern Baptist Convention with the story of Professor Crawford H. Toy's dismissal from Southern Seminary in 1879, due to his acceptance of German higher criticism. He pointed to the seminary's subsequent acceptance of Toy's theology, citing a 1985 issue of Southern Seminary's at-the-time academic journal, Review, and Expositor. The issue — published shortly before Criswell's address — included an article describing Toy's beliefs, which Criswell cited as "perfectly acceptable, condoned, and defended," were Toy to teach at the seminary then.

Later at the 1985 Convention, Southern Baptist messengers elected Charles Stanley, pastor of First Baptist Church in Atlanta, Ga., as president of the convention. Stanley's presidency continued a line of conservative presidents and helped secure the success of the conservative movement, known as the "Conservative Resurgence."

Concerning the context of Criswell's sermon, Mohler said the legendary preacher and former SBC president delivered the sermon under "conditions of maximum warfare." The 1985 Southern Baptist Convention annual meeting, Mohler said, was one of the great turning points in the SBC."

The presidents of all six seminaries pledged their support for the moderate cause in Dallas, and Foreign Mission Board President Keith Parks wrote a letter to Southern Baptist international missionaries saying he could not support Stanley's reelection. Leading up to the annual meeting, 2,000 moderate pastors from Georgia endorsed an ad in the Atlanta Journal-Constitution urging messengers not to vote for Stanley. Conservative W.A. Criswell, the pastor of the First Baptist Church in Dallas, sent letters to 36,000 Southern Baptist pastors asking them to come, bring messengers and vote for Stanley. In the final sermon at the SBC Pastors' Conference preceding the annual meeting, Criswell rallied conservatives in what he told historian Jerry Sutton was the most important message he ever preached.

THE OLD-TIME RELIGION

Dr. W. A. Criswell
Acts 8:8, February 3rd, 1998

[Dr. Homer Lindsay, Jr.] And down through the years, Dr. Criswell always took time to write me a little note, encourage me, and I am so thankful that we are able to have him tonight. My dear dad is in glory with Jesus, and as I saw Dr. Criswell come in and sit down my heart just sort of gripped, and it was just like my dad being here. And this is a very, very precious night for me, and I believe it's going to be a precious night for all of us. [applause]

[Dr. W.A Criswell] *All right. All right. Thank you. Bless you, son, you dear boy. Oh dear! Thank you. Thank you. Oh dear! Thank you. Thank you. I have never been more intimidated in all of my life than I have been tonight. Our church, the First Baptist in Dallas, is supposed to be the largest of our Southern Baptist congregations, but it is nothing like this. Our church looks like a little mission compared to this great congregation.*

I loved Dr. Lindsay, this boy's father. I have preached many times in the old church—held a revival meeting there. I look upon this boy as one of my own, and I am so grateful to God that he has been carrying on and out the marvelous ministry of his father and his sainted mother [applause].

Dr. Vines has been an untold help in continuing that glorious ministry of Dr. Lindsay. So he wrote me a note, and he said, "Some time ago I heard you preach a sermon on 'This I Know,' and I thought you might preach it when you come to our conference in February." Well, I took it to heart, and I thought and prayed, but the more I did, the more that subject of "The Old-Time Religion" came into my soul. This coming year I will be ninety years of age, ninety years of age [applause]. And as I thought through the wonderful fellowship of these godly men and the attendance from all over America, I thought I would just go back through those years and speak of "The Old-Time Religion."

And our background text will be in the eighth chapter of the Book of Acts that describes the ministry of Philip, who left Jerusalem and went down to Samaria and preached the Gospel unto them. "And with one accord they gave heed to what Philip had to say . . . and there was great joy in that city." Great joy in that city: The Old-Time Religion.

When I was growing up, I could buy a hamburger for a nickel. When I was growing up, I could buy a lavish dinner for twenty-five cents. When I was growing up, I could buy a big sack of popcorn for five cents. When I was growing up, I never paid more than one dollar for a tie. When I was growing up, I never paid more than nineteen dollars for a suit. When I was growing up, I never paid more than five dollars for a pair of shoes. As I began my ministry as a pastor and a preacher when I was seventeen, I bought a Chevrolet car, a new Chevrolet, and I paid three hundred dollars for it. When I bought a gallon of gasoline, I paid nine cents.

And the whole world out there before me was so different from what it is now. I was grown before I ever saw anybody divorced. I never saw the front door of a house locked. I never knew what it was to think of an athletic contest on the Lord's day, on Sunday. If I were asked, "On what day of the week would you suppose the Super Bowl game will be played?" I would say, "It will be played on Sunday." It's a different world in which we live now.

And as I go back into those days, and I think of the church, I never saw a church that didn't have a pot-bellied stove. And on this side of the river, the fire would be kindled with wood. Way out there in the Northwest where I was fetched up, it was a fire made with coal. And when you went to church, all of the men, it seemed to me, chewed tobacco. And when they were about to drown in ambeer, they would go to the stove, lift up the lid, and put out the fire.

A pastor of real thought bought some cuspidors and after a while took them out. And one of those ambeer specialists went to the pastor and said, "I miss the cuspidors." And he replied, "That's why we have taken 'em out, because you missed them."

Every one of those churches had a conference on Saturday afternoon once a month. And always, as you have in your church, there is somebody there who is in the kickative case and in the disapproving mood. So one of the men stood up in the conference and said, "I make a motion we buy a chandelier." And that kickative member stood up and said, "I'm agin' it. For one thing, we don't have anybody to play it. For another thing, I don't want to think of buying something the name of which I can't spell, and what this church needs is more light!"

Another fellow stood up and said, "I make a motion we build a fence around the cemetery." And that kickative member stood up and turned to him and said, "Do you know anybody on the outside that wants in, and do you know anybody on the inside that can get out? Then why build a fence around the cemetery?"

The services in that old-time church were everlastingly interesting and moving. They were filled with people who shouted. In the little town in which I was fetched up—three hundred citizens—when the Methodists would have a revival meeting, I have seen them pour out of the church and shout all over the little town. Can you imagine a Methodist church like that today? And when I preached as a boy, world without end did members stand up and shout the praises of God.

I was invited to hold a meeting in a county seat town, and when I got through preaching that morning, the pastor stood up to receive those who had responded. And as he stood up, down the aisle came a fine-looking woman. She was the wife of a leading citizen of the county. She came forward and stood before two young men on the front row. She put her hand on top of one of the boys and said, "Today I prayed God would give me one of my boys." She put her hand on the other boy and said, "But God has been better to me than my prayers. He has given me both of my boys." And up and down the aisle and across and back again, she began to shout the praises of God, "Oh, glory to God! The Lord has given me both of my boys. Praise His name forever!" That's the kind of religion I grew up in as a boy.

In the passing of the years, for example, in our church in Dallas, at the end of the ministry of Dr. Truett, a woman in the congregation began to shout. His brother-in-law, Dr. Oscar Marchman, ran over to her and was escorting her out. And Dr. Truett raised his hand and said, "There, there, Oscar, leave her alone. She's just happy in the Lord." O God, what a day, what a day!

I am reminded of a young fellow that happened to attend a liturgical church, and the preacher way up there in the pulpit said something good about Jesus, and he said, "Amen!" And the preacher lost his place. As the time continued, he said something else good about Jesus, and that young fellow said, "Praise the Lord!" And that time he really forgot his whole message.

So the usher came to him and patted him on the shoulder and said, "Shut up! Don't you see you're bothering our preacher?"

And he replied, "But I am just praising the Lord."

And the usher said, "But you can't praise the Lord here."

And the young fellow replied, "But I got religion!"

And the usher said, "Well, you did not get it here. Shut up!" Shut up—oh dear! Oh dear! How the days have changed in the years and the years of my life.

So way back yonder, the preacher came from our county-seat town to hold revival in our little village, and he stayed in our home. Every night mother would give him a glass of fresh-churned buttermilk. And as he sat, he would talk to me about Jesus. Upon a weekday of the revival, I asked mother, "Mother, could I be dismissed from school and attend the service?"

"Oh yes," she said.

So I went to the church, the little white crackerbox of a church house. And I happened to be seated back of my sainted mother. When the invitation was given, she turned to me and was crying with many tears, and said to me, "Son, today would you give your heart to the Lord Jesus? Would you take Him as your Savior?"

I said, "Oh, mother, yes."

And with many tears I stepped into the aisle—could hardly see the preacher for crying. Upon my confession of faith, I was baptized and became a member of our blessed Baptist communion.

As I said, when I was about seventeen years of age, I began to preach and to pastor my little country church. It was named Pulltight, and it didn't have a church house. They met in a schoolhouse. But they had a campground and a tabernacle. And on the fourth Friday before July, when the crops were laid by, the people from the ends of the earth came there to attend that tabernacle revival and the camp on the ground. We had a prayer meeting before the service. The women met in the tabernacle, and the men met in a grove, a grove prayer meeting.

I never, in all of my life, heard such testimonies as those men gave in that grove prayer meeting. One would say, "I was plowing with a pair of mules, and the Lord sent a fireball from heaven and struck me to the ground. And how long I lay there I don't remember, but when I came to." Then he described how the mules looked, how the plow looked, how the field looked, all the things that had come into his heart.

Again one of the men stood up and in his testimony spoke of an angel God sent from heaven to tell him the way of salvation. And sweet people, I came to the conclusion that I was not saved. I had never seen a ball of fire. I had never seen an angel who instructed me in the way of the Lord. And you won't believe this. For a long, long, long time, I would prepare my sermons to be delivered to the little congregation, then I would cry to God, "O God, help me! Please God, send a sign from heaven, an angel or a ball of fire, that I may know that I am converted, that I've been saved, my name in the book of life."

And a miracle happened. God looked down from glory and saw me in my agony, and I had an experience I could hardly ever describe. I dreamed that the saints of God were marching in, and I assayed to join their number. And when I got to the pearly gates, the Lord stopped me and said, "By what prerogative do you enter My beautiful city and walk on My golden streets?"

And I said to Him, "Dear God, I know I'm saved. I know I'm saved. I saw a ball of fire fall down from heaven and strike me to the land.

And Satan there laughed, "Hah, hah, hah, hah! He saw a ball of fire fall from heaven. I sent that ball of fire just to deceive him, just to fool him." And he drags me down to perdition and damnation and hell. What could I say? What could I say?

Or the great throng is marching into the New Jerusalem, and I assay to join their number and the Lord stops me, and He says, "By what prerogative, by what right, do you enter My beautiful city and walk on My golden streets?"

And I reply, "O God, I've been saved. I know I've been saved. I saw an angel from heaven come down to instruct me in the way of life."

And Satan, standing there, laughs, "Hah, hah, hah! He saw an angel. I transformed myself into an angel of light just to deceive him." And he seizes me and drags me down to perdition and damnation and hell. What could I say?

Then God spoke to me. When I assay to enter that beautiful city, and the Lord asks me, "By what prerogative and by what right do you pass through My pearly gates and walk on My golden streets?" and I say to him, "Lord, when I was about ten years of age, my sainted mother, with many tears, asked me to take You as my Savior. And Lord Jesus, that day I gave my heart to Thee. And Lord Jesus, I'm just depending upon You to keep Your Word that You'll never leave me or forsake me." [applause] O God!

And I dare Satan to lie or to scoff. Sweet people, my salvation is not a matter between me and him. My salvation is a matter between me and Jesus, and He will never let me down. [applause]

Ah! Sing with me:

It's the old-time religion.
It's the old-time religion.
It's the old time religion,
And it's good enough for me.

May I take, before I am seated, may I take one more leaf out of my life? When I was growing up, I never saw or heard a preacher who doubted that Holy Word, [applause] never in my life, never in my life, never ever.

So, as time went on, I was introduced to another world. Here is a little description of it. There were two mischievous boys who got a hold of the preacher's Bible and glued some of the pages together. And the preacher stood up to deliver his sermon, and he read his text, "And in those days, Noah took unto himself a wife." And he turned what he thought was one page and continued to read, "And she was . . . fifteen cubits broad," [applause] "thirty-five cubits long, made out of gopher wood, and daubed on the inside with pitch." [applause]

He held up the Book and said, "My brothers and sisters, that's the first time I've ever read that in the Word of God, but if the Word of God says it, I believe it!" [applause] Amen … amen, amen. "Just goes to show," he said, "we are wonderfully and fearfully made."

So I grew up believing every word of this Book is inspired, inerrant, and infallible. Amen. Amen.

So a young fellow in Dad's barbershop—my father was an uneducated cowpoke, never went to school, learned to read and was an avid reader. But when the barbed-wire fence was invented, a great mass of those cowboys lost their jobs, and that included my father. So he learned to cut hair, and he cut those cowboys' hair. And on a line camp of the X.I.T. Ranch, "Ten in Texas," ten big counties up there in the Northwest, in a line camp, he had a little shop. And on Saturday afternoon I would sit down in that shop and listen to the stories of those cowboys.

You know, it's a funny thing to me. Out of all, all, all of the westerns that you see on television, I have never yet seen one that followed a beautiful Christian story, and I heard them world without end. And here's one of them.

A young cowpoke came back from the range to get a fresh mount. He came to the corral. He picked out a horse. He put a rope around its neck. He bridled it, he saddled it, he mounted it, and he rode out from the pen. But the pony had not been wholly broken, and it began to buck and to pitch and to sidestep. And you never threw—you never threw a real cowboy. He might fall for some other reason, but you'd never pitch him off of a mount. And what happened that day, as the pony began to pitch and to sidestep, the horse lost its footing and fell back over on the cowboy and crushed him. The pony got up and ran away, but the cowboy was hurt internally and bleeding at his mouth.

Jake, the cook in the camp, had watched what had happened. And he ran over there to the lad, and tenderly picked him up, brought him into the camp, and put him on a cot. But what could a cook do for a boy that was crushed internally, and blood pouring from his mouth?

And as the boy's life ebbed away, he said to the cook, "Jake, you know that big black Book that the boss man is always readin' to us. Jake, get that Book and bring it to me." Jake went to the chuck wagon and dug around through the personal effects of the boss man and found the Bible, brought it to the lad. And the boy said, "Jake, can you find John 3:16?" [Someone shouts, "The Word of God!"] Amen. And Jake went through the Bible and found the Gospel of John, went through John, chapter 3, went down the verses to 16. And the boy said, "Jake, read that verse to me.

And the cook read John 3:16: "For God so loved the world, that He gave His only begotten Son, that whosoever believeth in Him should not perish, but have everlasting life."

And the boy said, "Jake, take that Bible and put it on my chest just so. Now, Jake, take my finger and put it on that verse. And when the boss man comes in the evening, you tell him that I died with my finger on John 3:16."

One glad smile of pleasure
O'er the cowboy's face was spread.
One dark convulsive shadow,
And the tall young lad was dead.
Far from his home and family
They laid him down to rest
With a saddle for a pillow
And that Bible on his chest.

I have announced from the pulpit that when I die, I want them to take my Bible and put it on my chest. And when the people pass by to see me for the last time, I want them to see me with a Bible in my hand. O God, O God [applause], O God, O God, O God! Sing it with me:

Give me that old-time religion.
Give me that old-time religion.
Give me that old-time religion.
It's good enough for me.

It was good for Paul and Silas.
It was good for Paul and Silas.
It was good for Paul and Silas,
And it's good enough for me.

It will do when I am dying.
It will do when I am dying.
It will do when I am dying,
And it's good enough for me.

It will take us all to heaven.
It will take us all to heaven.
It will take us all to heaven,
And it's good enough for me.

Sweet people, would you stand and sing it one more time. And this time raise your hand to heaven. Sing it now:

Give me that old-time religion.
Give me that old-time religion.
Give me that old-time religion.
It's good enough for me.

It will take us all to heaven.
It will take us all to heaven.
It will take us all to heaven.
It's good enough for me.

Give me that old-time religion.
Give me that old-time religion.
Give me that old-time religion.
It's good enough for me.

Precious, I'll see you here, there, or in the air. I'll meet you at the feet of our precious Jesus before the throne of God. Amen, and God keep you. You may be seated. [applause]. Amen. Amen. [applause]

COMMENTARY

The Old Time Religion

W.A. Criswell, pastor emeritus of First Baptist Church in Dallas preached to a full auditorium at Southwestern Baptist Theological Seminary in February 1998. Criswell retold story after story of memories, all interwoven with the thread of old-time religion. He started the sermon as he stated, the subject is "The Old-Time Religion" came into my soul. This coming year I will be ninety years of age, ninety years of age. He stated that he had been a pastor for 70 years, and beyond 85 years a child of faith. The old-time religion was a delight to his soul beyond verbalization. Criswell told of the last revival service he held as pastor of First Baptist, Dallas.

Criswell recounted stories of his first quarter-time church at the start of his ministry, where the congregation heard their circuit-riding expositor only one Sunday a month in a school. He spoke at open tabernacles on the campgrounds. He told of his conversion and call to the pastorate as a young boy in revival meetings filled with emotions and feeling and tears. Criswell also noted old-time religion's absolute belief in the inspiration, infallibility and authority of the Bible. He stated that many of our young people go away to infidel, secular, agnostic institutions of higher learning. They returned asking, 'You believe in that book? I've learned it's full of Aesop's fables, myths and all kinds of things that are man-made and man-thought. Then he exposed the fallacies of reasoning that the highly educated tend to use when dealing with faith. Criswell concluded by proclaiming that kind of old-time religion still good enough for me.

Criswell enjoyed telling old western stories from his past by making this statement. "May I take one more leaf out of my life? When I was growing up, I never saw or heard a preacher who doubted that Holy Word. He told another of his favorite stories. He stated that as time went on, he was introduced to another world. There were two mischievous boys who got a hold of the preacher's Bible and glued some of the pages together. And the preacher stood up to deliver his sermon, and he read his text, "And in those days, Noah took unto himself a wife." And he turned what he thought was one page and continued to read, "And she was . . . fifteen cubits broad," "thirty-five cubits long, made out of gopher wood, and daubed on the inside with pitch." He held up the Book and said, "My brothers and sisters, that's the first time I've ever read that in the Word of God, but if the Word of God says it, I believe it!" "Just goes to show," he said, "we are wonderfully and fearfully made." So I grew up believing every word of this Book is inspired, inerrant, and infallible.

Dr. Criswell announced from the pulpit that when he died, he wanted them to take his Bible and put it on his chest. And when the people pass by to see me for the last time, he wanted them to see me with a Bible in my hand. His wishes were granted.

CHRIST IS COMING BACK

Dr. W. A. Criswell's last sermon, as Pastor Emeritus, at FBC Dallas
John 14:3, April 1st, 2001,

Our Lord is coming back. This is His word in John chapter 14:3: "If I go, I will come again." "If I go, I will come again." This is the very fabric of the New Testament. Unless He comes back visibly, bodily, all is inevitably and indubitably lost. There are three words in the New Testament that describe the ultimate end of the world and the presence of our living Lord. The three words are: atonement, advocacy, and advent.

On the cross He bore our sins; this is the word "atonement." In heaven He intercedes for us; He is our Advocate. And He will complete the work and change our bodies like unto His own at His coming: this is His advent. We speak first of the atonement of our Lord.

In all of my years, I have never seen a drawn picture of Jesus as He actually died for us and promised to return for us. Any picture I have ever seen of the Lord, He always has about Him a loincloth. He was never dressed like that. Our Lord died naked: He had no clothing whatsoever. And His death was one of mutilation and tragic, tragic separation from us.

Our Lord died, I say, naked. He had no clothing whatsoever. He died without anything to separate Him from us. He died in mutilation. I suppose there was never a body that was so abused as the body of Jesus our Lord, paying the price for our sins. His head was crushed; He was crowned with thorns. And His face was mutilated as the people struck Him, and accused Him of every vile and evil thing [Matthew 27:27-50; Mark 15:15-37]. And His body was mutilated. As you know, a soldier without any reverence at all, a soldier standing by thrust into His heart and into the interior of His body an iron sword [John 19:34]. And He was crucified. And not only nailed with His hands and His feet to the cross, but His inward life was poured out; and blood and water poured out of His body as He was nailed there to the cross.

Sweet people, if I can speak of this without appearing so inane—our Lord died a criminal's death. His body was mutilated with every stroke that the harsh Roman army could apply. He was there nailed to the tree, and had no way or thought of defense.

Could I say, without being crude and abrupt, our Lord was there nailed to the cross, and had no way of defense. He suffered and died because of me [1 Corinthians 15:3]. He had the burden of all the sins of this world cast upon Him [2 Corinthians 5:21]. And let me be crude enough to describe His death. Every time I have seen a picture of the death of our Lord, He is always up there somewhere. He is raised up high. And over here on one side will be one of the tragic men who's a thief, and in every way a violator of what is right; that's on one side, is one of those men. On the other side is another one of those men, only this one is unrepentant. He is vile and vicious, and even in death he blasphemes the name of the Lord. And every picture I have ever seen of the death, the crucifixion of Jesus, is like that: He is raised up high, He is up here, and over here on one side is one of those men who is being crucified for his wrong and evil, and on this side is the other one who dies in blasphemy and in cursing [Luke 23:39-40]. Every picture I have ever seen of our Lord is like that, way up there.

Actually, the death of Jesus was just the opposite. Jesus died right there, right in front of me. And those evil men could speak to one another just right there to right there. And our Lord could reply right there, right there. I could touch Him. And when He bled, my hands could feel the cross. That's the way Jesus died, right there, right in front of you, where He could talk to you, and you could talk to Him. And those two thieves could speak to one another from here to there, and there to there. But I have never seen, in all of my long life, I have never seen a picture of the death of our Lord as He actually died.

O God! how I feel when I think of the atonement of Jesus! That's what He did for me. He took my sins and bore them on the cross [1 Peter 2:24]. That is God's atonement. And I must never forget it. I must kneel in His presence, as you all did a moment ago. And I must confess my wrong, and my trepidation, and my sins, and I must ask God to forgive me. I must come to the Lord on my face and on my knees, and with a broken heart. That is the atonement [1 John 1:9].

And that will be followed by His advocacy of me in heaven. He will complete the work of intercession and change, and my body awaits for that great and ultimate and final triumph: He is coming at His advent [Acts 1:11]. And when He comes, He is bringing me with Him. I am not coming alone; I am coming by the side of my Savior [1 Thessalonians 4:14; Revelation 19:14]. And He will present me to you, and to the world—the advent of our Lord. And He is coming for our advocacy [1 Corinthians 15:55-57]; to speak of our victory over sin, and over death, and over the grave.

Whenever we take the Lord's Supper, we witness to His death and His abounding remembrance of us. "Ye do show His death till He come," when we have the Lord's Supper, in 1 Corinthians [11:26]. O God, how we bow in Thy presence!

In our text, our Lord said, "If I go, I will come again" [John 14:3]. The certainty of His coming is one of the avowals of the intrepid, indefensible Word of God. Heavenly messengers proclaimed it in Acts 1:9-11: Jesus, while talking to His disciples, was received into heaven. And as the disciples looked upon Him lovingly, two witnesses came and stood by their side, and said, "This same Jesus shall come in like manner as ye have seen Him go. This same Jesus"—not someone else, not something else, but the same Lord Jesus who suffered and died for our sins. It is that Lord who is coming back again.

Following Christ's life from Bethlehem, His manger to the cross, are these ascension heights. He, who after His life here in the earth, had eaten and drunk in their presence [Luke 24:41-43; John 21:12-15]; it is that Jesus who is coming again [Acts 1:11]. He will be here one of these days. I can hardly realize it! When we have the Lord's Supper, He will be one who will partake of it. And when we sing our songs of loving remembrance, He will be one who will be singing with us. It will be the same Lord Jesus who lived here in this earth, who died here in that incomparably sad and tragic way. It will be that same Jesus who will be in our midst and will take the Lord's Supper with us [Revelation 19:6-9]. I can hardly believe that it will be the same Jesus who went away, who is coming back again. O God!

He went in a cloud; "They shall see the Son of Man coming in a cloud," Luke 21:27. "So shall come again the Lord Jesus, as ye have seen Him go" [Acts 1:11]. As the disciples looked and the Lord rose from the earth, and a cloud received Him out of their sight [Acts 1:9], it will be like that when Jesus comes. He will come in one of those wonderful clouds: visible to the whole world. And we shall welcome Him lovingly, tenderly.

The parables teach that. Not only by personal promise and angelic messenger, but His coming back again is a central truth in the teaching of the parables. The Savior likened His return to a nobleman's boy. And the nobleman received the lad with loving kindness [Luke 15:21-24, 32]. That's going to be the way we receive our Lord: with loving kindness, thanking Him for dying for us, thanking Him for interceding for us; for He is right now up there in glory, naming my name and yours [Hebrews 7:25], and getting ready to come back to receive us to Himself. O, what a day that will be, when the Lord shall come and bring with Him our glorious reward! [Isaiah 40:10].

I repeat the text: our Lord said, "If I go, I will come again." This is the rapture of the church. "If I will go, I will come again, and receive you unto Myself" [John 14:3]. Yes, Christ will come back for us. For the Lord Himself shall descend from heaven with a shout of the victory, and to be forever with us [1 Thessalonians 4:16-17].

There will be no more separation. There will be no more death. There will be no more graves. There will be no more crying and weeping. We'll all be together. I'll be with you, and have the rest of eternity to talk about our victory in Christ; and you'll be with me, and we'll have an eternity to enjoy together. This event is called the rapture of the church. Paul says, "We shall not all sleep; but we shall all be changed in a moment, in the twinkling of an eye" [1 Corinthians 15:51-52]. It will be like this: "There shall be two in the field; one shall be taken, and the other left. Two women shall be grinding at the mill"—I often wonder at that, not two men, two women—"Two women shall be grinding at the mill; the one shall be taken, and the other left" [Matthew 24:40-41]. That is the rapture of the church. Getting ready for Him, looking forward to His return, happy in Jesus, glad to be here with you today, and even gladder when our Lord comes and sits in our midst. At the sight of so much glory, no wonder one of our Christian men wrote:

Oh, joy! Oh, delight! should we go without dying,
No sickness, no sadness, no dread and no crying.
Caught up through the clouds with our Lord into glory,
When Jesus receives His own.

O Lord Jesus, how long, how long
Ere we shout the glad song,
Christ returneth! Hallelujah!
Hallelujah! Amen.
    ["Christ Returneth"; H. L. Turner]

We have that to look forward to. And with what joy and gladness shall we wait for His return. Remember my text: He said, "If I go, I will come back" [John 14:3]

Yes, when the Savior comes, the saints who have died will be raised from out the grave; and at the same time, living Christians will be caught up in their bodies, glorified [1 Thessalonians 4:14-17], made like Christ's body. This is the promise, and I read it: "We know that when He shall appear, we shall be like Him; for we shall see Him as He is" [1 John 3:2]. God's faithful word: I'll be like Jesus. O God, could it be? Could it be?

"Our citizenship is in heaven; from whence also we look for the Savior, the Lord Jesus: who shall change our weak body, that it may be fashioned like unto His glorious body" [Philippians 3:20-21. Someday I'll have a body like my Lord's. I can hardly realize such a thing. O God, not to be weak anymore, not to be sick anymore, not to wait for the coming of death anymore, but waiting for Jesus. And when He comes, I'll be like Him, and you will be like Him, and we all shall be like Him and shall rejoice in the presence and the blessing and the goodness of God. "When Christ, who is our life, shall appear, then shall also we appear with Him in God's glory" [Colossians 3:4].

I shall be like Him, I shall be like Him,
When in His beauty and glory, I shall arise.
I shall be like Him, wondrously like Him,
Jesus, the Savior divine.
    ["I Shall Be Like Him"; W. A. Spencer]

Oh, what a marvelous, marvelous day we awaits in this body of death, when we shall have our new body, and our new home, and our present Lord!

"The great multitude, which no man could number, of every kindred and tribe and tongue," mentioned in Revelation the seventh chapter [verse 9], will be with us; and we'll all be together. O God! When the Antichrist shall be put to death [Revelation 19:20], and we shall be with our Lord, sharing the glorious reign of Christ on earth with His saints for a thousand years [Revelation 20:6], and when the Son of Man shall come in His glory, and all the holy angels with Him, then shall He sit upon the throne of His glory [Matthew 25:31]; and we shall share that wonderful, triumphant moment with Him. When the Lord shall come, when the Lord shall come, we shall be like Him, all thrilled with the light, and the presence, and the glory of God.

And when we have been there ten thousand years,
Bright shining as the sun.
We'll have no less days to sing God's praise
Than when we have first begun.
        ["Amazing Grace"; John Newton]

"And the Spirit and the bride say, Come, come, come. And let him that is athirst come. And let him that is hungry come. And whosoever will, let him take the water of life freely" [Revelation 22:17]. "He which testifieth these things saith, Surely I come quickly. Amen. Even so, come, blessed Lord Jesus" [Revelation 22: 20].

If I know my heart, I am ready. Any day, any hour, any moment, Lord; You said You could come at any time [Mark 13:32]. If that time is now, I'm ready, Lord. If it is tonight, I'm ready. If it's in the morning, I'm ready. Anytime You arrive, Lord, I'm ready. What a privilege to kneel in Thy presence and to kiss Thy hand, and to tell You with what joy and gladness I receive Your presence. O God, can I cease speaking? Won't die, won't be sick unto death, won't know any of the trials of that separation; but all that remains will be to welcome my Lord, and to rejoice in His coming, and to be there with you, and to thank God that we have the privilege of being together at the return of Jesus. "If I go away," He says, "I will come again" [John 14:3].

God bless you, love you in the faith, and look forward to the day of our separation when I die, or when one of you dies, and we go to meet with our blessed Lord in the wonderful world that is yet to come. God be good to you, sweet and dear people, and give you every continuing victory.

COMMENTARY

Christ is Coming Back

This sermon was the last time Dr. Criswell would preach at the First Baptist Church of Dallas, Texas. It is believed that he was aware of the condition of his physical body. He knew it was only a short time before he would be absent from the body and present with the Lord.

The issue of the sermon was preparing for death. Criswell stated that in all of his years, he had never seen a drawn picture of Jesus as He died for us and promised to return for us. He recounted that every picture he had ever seen of the Lord, He always has about Him a loincloth. He continued the description of the Lord dying naked because had no clothing whatsoever. He described Jesus' death as one of mutilation and tragic, tragic separation from us. Criswell continued saying that Lord died a criminal's death and His body was mutilated with every stroke that the harsh Roman army could apply.

169

Criswell did not desire to be crude enough to describe His death. He stated that on one side was one of the tragic men who was a thief, and in every way, a violator of what was right and on the other a vile and vicious man who blasphemed the name of the Lord. Those two thieves spoke to one another from here to there. He completed the work of intercession.

He stated several times during the sermon that the greatest proposition in the world was what the Lord said, "If I go, I will come again." Then Criswell boldly proclaimed that Jesus' coming back again is a central truth in the teaching of the parables. Then Criswell repeated the text: our Lord said, "If I go, I will come again." This is the rapture of the church. "If I will go, I will come again, and receive you unto Myself." Yes, Christ will come back for us. For the Lord, Himself shall descend from heaven with a shout of the victory, and to be forever with us.

There will be no more separation. There will be no more death. There will be no more graves. There will be no more crying and weeping. We'll all be together. I'll be with you, and have the rest of eternity to talk about our victory in Christ; you'll be with me, and we'll have an eternity to enjoy together. This event is called the Rapture of the church. Paul says, "We shall not all sleep; but we shall all be changed in a moment, in the twinkling of an eye" [1 Corinthians 15:51-52]. quoting the text that our Lord said, "If I go, I will come again and receive you unto Myself." With weeping eyes, Dr. Criswell made a proclamation that there will be no more separation, no more death, no more graves, no more crying, and weeping. We'll all be together. Then with a gleam in his eyes, he whispered, that believers will have the rest of eternity to talk about our victory in Christ and you'll be with me, and we'll have an eternity to enjoy together. This event is called the Rapture of the church. Paul says, "We shall not all sleep; but we shall all be changed in a moment, in the twinkling of an eye. That is the rapture of the church. Getting ready for Him, looking forward to His return, happy in Jesus, glad to be here with you today, and even gladder when our Lord comes and sits in our midst.

Criswell asked the audience to be ready for the day that they will die. We have that to look forward to. And with what joy and gladness shall we wait for His return. Then with a strong voice, he proclaimed, my citizenship is in heaven; from whence the Lord Jesus shall change our weak body, that it may be fashioned like unto His glorious body."

Dr. W. A. Criswell concluded the sermon by saying, "If I know my heart, I am ready. Any day, any hour, any moment, Lord; You said You could come at any time. If that time is now, I'm ready, Lord. If it is tonight, I'm ready. If it's in the morning, I'm ready. Anytime You arrive, Lord, I'm ready. God bless you, love you in the faith, and look forward to the day of our separation when I die, or when one of you dies, and we go to meet with our blessed Lord in the wonderful world that is yet to come. God be good to you, sweet and dear people, and give you every continuing victory."

RETROSPECTIVE

In society organizations emerge, and leaders rise. It is through rhetoric and public address that organizations and leaders become a moving force! In contemporary society, the Southern Baptist Convention has emerged, and W.A. Criswell was the President.

When W.A. Criswell was a small boy, he slugged another child who tried to insult him by calling him a "little Bible reader." As pastor of the 12,000 member First Baptist Church of Dallas, Texas, and President of the 11.5 million Southern Baptists Convention, he was a fighter and a Bible reader until his death. The goal of this book was to discover whether W.A. Criswell was elected President of the Southern Baptist Convention to perpetuate the status quo of the system or to institute changes as shown by a pre and post election descriptive rhetorical analysis of convention policy, perspective, and public address of Criswell.

It is significant to focus on the perspective and rhetoric of a man because he is a dynamic center. The leader has to keep the convention going. The convention is the system. The study was empirical research in rhetoric and public address rather than a theological inquiry.

The justification for a study of this nature was revealed in the following:

1. It was an attempt to move toward research in "real life" behavior.

2. It was designed to test public address as an analytical tool of social condition.

3. The Southern Baptist Convention is the largest religious Protestant denomination.

4. The Southern Baptist Convention is a moving force in the Southland of America.

5. It is through perspective and public address that the relationship of leader to the organization is apparent.

6. That which Criswell did as the leader advanced or retarded the Southern Baptist Convention.

7. Criswell was the leader-speaker of the largest Baptist Church in the world.

8. Criswell had more books in print than any other living Protestant minister.

9. Criswell was the only existing Protestant minister to do an exhaustive expository analysis of every chapter in the Bible and present it to a church for an application.

10. Criswell was a speaker-leader known around the world.

The term "perspective" has been adopted to denote the speaker leaders perception of his office and toward the issues facing the convention. The term "issue" was employed to connote the matters of concern by Criswell and the convention. By the term "proposition" was meant the ideas advocated by Criswell.

The following methodology was employed. First, there was an examination in the form of a historical resume of the impetus and development of the organization. Such data as tracing the significant developments and beliefs of the Baptists were compiled and described. The focus of this analysis was to provide a historical perspective for convention policy and Articles of Faith.

The second procedural step was an examination of the speaker-leader of the organization. The biographical analysis presented selected data regarding foundations for why this speaker-leader maintained his particular position on the issue involved. In addition to these data on life foundations, data was also gathered concerning his personality and professional positions.

The third step was an examination of selected rhetoric from 1956 to 2001 which included pre and post-election speeches and books. For each event, there was a re-creation of the developments in the society that evoked the particular rhetorical situation. This gave rise to several questions which had to be answered:

1. Where did the speaking event take place and under what conditions?

2. From the speaker's perspective, what were the issues?

3. What were the propositions advocated by the speaker?

4. What did the speaker ask men to do?

In answering these questions, the last step was to describe the perspective and propositions of the speaker-leader and to compare this information with statements of convention policy and articles of faith to determine whether Criswell was elected to perpetuate the status quo of the system or to institute changes.

The Organization

The Christian faith has been a controversial topic since the creation of man. Before the time of Christ, men looked forward to His birth. Since biblical days men have looked backward to Christ to find meaning in the faith.

The organization called Baptists trace their concepts concerning faith to religious groups which emerged before and during the Renaissance and Reformation. These religious groups have been referred to as the left-wing of Protestantism. National churches were characteristic of the right-wing of Protestantism.

Nonconformists called Waldensians broke step with the national churches. This group became congregational in policy and highly evangelical.

The Anabaptists were descendants of the Waldenses and the direct ancestors of present day Baptists. Anabaptist was a name given to denote "those who baptize again" or "rebaptize." They objected to infant baptism; therefore, they rebaptized the adults who were once baptized as children.

As the group became more evangelical in following the teachings of the New Testament, they became known as Baptists. Early Baptist leaders were John Smyth, Thomas Helwys, and John Murton.

Baptist Churches of three kinds arose in England. The first were General Baptist Churches believing in a general atonement. Particular Baptists followed the limited atonement ideas of John Calvin. The Immersion Baptists broke from Particular Baptists and wrote their Confession of Faith in 1644. This confession was known as the *London Confession of 1644*. It was adopted by seven Baptist Churches in that city and was the first statement of faith and policy ever made by a group of Baptist Churches.

In the early part of the seventeenth-century religious leaders became interested in escaping persecution and going to the New World. The leaders in the early Baptist movement in America were Roger Williams, John Clarke, and William Screven.

Between 1725 and 1750, and continuing for many years, the Great Awakening swept America. This movement in history was characterized by significant and prolonged religious revivals. Baptists were not as intimately involved at first in the Great Awakening as some other groups but shared in the results.

The Baptist work spread down the eastern seaboard and westward. Baptists were instrumental in the early national days of America in helping develop religious liberty.

Perhaps the separation of Northern and Southern Baptists would have become inevitable with the outbreak of the Civil War, but it preceded that conflict.

In 1810 Baptists left foreign missions largely up to other churches. The Congregational, Presbyterian, and Dutch Reform Churches formed the American Board of Commissioners for Foreign Missions.

On May 18, 1814, the General Convention of the Baptist Denomination was organized. At that meeting in Philadelphia, eleven states were represented by thirty-three delegates who attended this first denominational meeting of American Baptists. This meeting became known as the Triennial Convention.

The General Convention dealt only with foreign missions. The North wanted to spend energies on foreign missions, and the South was concerned with missions at home. In April 1812 the American Baptist Home Mission Society was formed.

The Board of the Baptist State Convention of New Hampshire adopted the *New Hampshire Declaration of Faith in 1833*. This was the most famous statement of faith and policy for nearly one hundred years among Baptists both North and South.

It was evident that within thirty years of the organization of the General Convention, at least three major divisive issues emerged causing the separation between Northern and Southern Baptists:

1. The Northern Baptists wanted separately organized conventions for each phase of work. The Baptists in the South desired to have only one organized convention with agencies to accomplish the goals.

2. Baptists in the South charged that the Home Mission Society was neglecting the mission fields in the Southland.

3. The explosion that produced separation came when the Foreign Mission Society refused to appoint a slave-holder as a missionary.

The Baptists in the South assembled to form their group. The Constitution adopted on May 10, 1845, created the Southern Baptist Convention. A Charter was enacted by the state of Georgia. As the Convention was formed, *The New Hampshire Declaration of Faith* was adopted as articles of faith and policy. The Southern Baptist Convention was organized for the purpose of eliciting combining and directing the work of the whole denomination. The Convention conducted denominational work through various boards. Each board was elected periodically by the general body and directly responsible for it. This principle has safeguarded the autonomy of the local churches and the independence of the associations and state conventions.

As the need has arisen, Southern Baptists have carried on their work through agencies in promoting denominational interests. Boards, committees, institutions, and commissions have served as agencies in the Convention.

In 1925 the Southern Baptist Convention revised the *New Hampshire Declaration of Faith* with some deletions, changes in wording and ten additional articles with a separate section on science and religion. This was prompted by the evolutionary controversy which was raging at the time. The revision became known as *A Statement of the Baptist Faith and Message*.

The 1963 Southern Baptist Convention meeting in Kansas City, revised the 1925 statement. This revision became known as *The Baptist Faith and Message*. This statement of policy and Articles of Faith has been the official statement from 1963 to the current date. Distinctive Southern Baptist beliefs and practices were revealed:

1. The authority and sufficiency of the Bible.

2. The responsibility and competency of the individual to deal directly with God.

3. Salvation as God's gift of divine grace received by man through repentance and faith.

4. A regenerated church membership.

5. Each church as an independent, self-governing body of immersed believers, the members possessing equal rights and privileges.

6. The ordinances as symbols and reminders.

7. Baptism, by immersion, of believers only.

8. Religious liberty for all.

9. The separation of church and state.

The Convention realized that there was unity as well as diversity in Southern Baptist life. Perhaps both have contributed in their ways to strength in the Convention. Although Southern Baptists have been independent locally, they combined local churches into associations, and associations into state conventions, and state conventions into the Southern Baptist Convention to do together what no one church alone could have done.

The Speaker-Leader: W.A. Criswell

Wallie Amos Criswell, Jr. was born December 19, 1909 at Eldorado, Oklahoma. When he was four years old, the family moved from Eldorado to a farm located in Clayton, New Mexico, and Texline, Texas. He attended public school in Texline.

Dr. Criswell's adolescence was a time of relative personal security, increased socialization, and evident happiness, but not of immunity from the realities of the world. When he was ten, he was converted and started preaching at seventeen. The family moved to Amarillo, Texas, where Criswell graduated from high school.

The pattern of Criswell's behavior in childhood, adolescence and young adulthood suggests that he was goal oriented. He derived personal satisfaction from doing a job well. He held student pastorates during his college and seminary studies. Criswell graduated with honors from Baylor University with the B.A. degree in 1931. He was awarded the Master of Theology degree in 1934 and earned the Doctor of Philosophy degree in 1937 from Southern Baptist Theological Seminary. In 1945 Baylor honored him again by giving him the Doctorate of Divinity.

The story of W.A. Criswell's speaking and leadership revealed his involvement and accomplishments in his profession. He served as pastor of First Baptist, Chickasha, Oklahoma from 1937-1941. He then moved to the First Baptist Church, Muskogee, Oklahoma, and in 1944 went to the First Baptist Church of Dallas, Texas.

The success story of Dr. W.A. Criswell at First Baptist Church of Dallas could have sounded like a chapter out of a Texas Brag Book, but the story of his speaking and leadership was reliable. This church was big statistically, but its bigness was also expressed in a spiritual dimension. The church grew accustomed to doing things in a big way during the quarter century with Criswell. Membership more than doubled to 15,000; the budget has increased from 377,151 to almost 3,000,000 dollars in 1970 and more than 6,000 average Sunday School attendance each Sunday. For over fifty five years Dr. Criswell guided a dynamic program at First Baptist which dwarfs many businesses.

The church employs 125 full-time staff members. Buildings cover five downtown Dallas city blocks. Included in the buildings are thirty floors or sixteen acres of educational space, two parking garages, gymnasium, bowling alley and skating rink. In addition to the main auditorium, the church has a small auditorium seating seven hundred and a chapel for two hundred. Criswell's church has been called a "successful anachronism."

Dr. W.A. Criswell was outspoken on controversial issues in politics, theology, and segregation. Almost six decades of speaking, leading, and writing has put him on "the top of the heap."

Dr. Criswell was widely sought as a speaker throughout the nation. He has spoken to seventeen of the twenty-three recognized Southern Baptist State Evangelistic Conferences. He spoke to Ridgecrest, Glorieta, and Falls Creek Baptist assemblies almost every year since 1937. Criswell has responded to invitations to speak to nearly every agency in the Convention. He toured Europe in 1947 when he attended the Baptist World Alliance in Copenhagen. In 1950 the Foreign Mission Board sent Dr. Criswell on an evangelism crusade where he spoke around the world. South America was the site for a Criswell Crusade in 1964, where he had a narrow escape from death in a jungle of Peru. In 1965 a tour of Russia caused Criswell to state that only the intervention of God could save religion in Russia. A 1968 speaking tour of Israel was successful. When Criswell returned from Africa in January 1970, he stated that the door is open for Christianity.

The leadership of Dr. W.A. Criswell has been evident as he took a downtown urban church that for all practical purposes should have been dying and built it into a successful institution. His leadership was not only been recognized by his church and state but by the Southern Baptist Convention. Wherever he went in the Convention as well as the things he did were both an extension of what he was at the First Baptist Church of Dallas.

Criswell was a trustee of Baylor University and Baylor Hospital, a past president of the Sunday School Board, director of the Baptist Standard and served on the Executive Board of the Texas Convention.

Dr. Criswell was elected President of the Southern Baptist Convention in 1968 and re-elected in 1969. He produced both unity and controversy in the Convention.

Rhetorical Propositions Before Election

Through all of W.A. Criswell's rhetoric, before he was elected President of the Southern Baptist Convention, several issues and proposals emerged:

FIRST, THE BIBLE AND THE HOLY SPIRIT.
1. The Bible is the inspired word of God and is relevant for today's world.
2. The Holy Spirit is more than just power; He is a person.
3. The ministry of the Holy Spirit is the work of God.

SECOND, EVANGELISM.
1. Tell the world the meaning and message of "the people called Baptists."
2. The ways of the world produce a counterfeit religion.
3. Christianity provides regenerated men who can create a regenerated society.

THIRD, DISSENSION-UNITY IN THE CONVENTION.
1. Work in unity and rise above weaknesses.
2. The Southern Baptist Convention must join hands, combine, share, do the job together.
3. Dissension is non-Christian.

FOURTH, RACIAL ISSUES.
1. Segregation is natural in all areas of life in a democratic society.
2. Segregation is the most workable and practical method for churches.

FIFTH, SOCIAL CONCERN AND RESPONSIBILITY.
1. Evangelize first then help meet sociological needs.
2. Let every man prosper within his segment of society.

SIXTH, RELIGIOUS LIBERTY.
1. America must have religious liberty rather than just religious toleration.
2. The political forces of the Catholic Church would overpower religious freedom.
3. Methods and approaches for imparting the faith should be progressive.

Rhetorical Propositions After Election

The rhetorical propositions of W.A. Criswell after he was elected President of the Southern Baptist dealt with the same issues as before he was elected.

FIRST, THE BIBLE.
1. The Bible is the word of God and should be preached.
2. The truth in the Bible is literally true.
3. Criswell does not object to the historical-critical method of Bible study, but he does object to some of the inferences made.

SECOND, EVANGELISM.
1. Faith is believing. The action of faith is evangelism.
2. After "believing" comes "doing."
3. Evangelize from local to international levels.

THIRD, DISSENSION-UNITY IN THE CONVENTION.

1. There is a tendency for man to lose sight of command and bog down in disunion.
2. Christendom has divided.
3. Baptists face a crisis, there must be unity in the ranks of Southern Baptists.
4. Baptists are beginning to have a pluralistic complexion.
5. Believe it or leave it!

FOURTH, RACIAL ISSUE.

1. There was a battle in Criswell's heart concerning the racial issue.
2. To separate by coercion the body of Christ on the basis of skin pigmentation in unthinkable, un-Christian, and unacceptable to God.
3. The First Baptist Church of Dallas is a church of the open door.
4. The Southern Baptist Convention is making progress in integrating.

FIFTH, SOCIAL CONCERN AND RESPONSIBILITY.

1. The Christian has a responsibility in social betterment for all men.
2. There should be a balance between evangelism and social actions.
3. Christ had something to say about a cup of cold water, seeking the lost sheep, knocking at the door, and honoring a despised Samaritan.

SIXTH, METHODS AND APPROACHES FOR CONVENTION LIFE.

1. Christian leadership must be relevant.
2. Methods and approaches of imparting the Christian faith must be updated.
3. The message must be anchored to the Book, geared to the times!
4. Whatever they discover tomorrow that will help us mediate the truth and mind of God that is in Jesus Christ, we are ready for that too.

Similarities and Differences Between Propositions Before and After Election

Through all of W.A. Criswell's rhetoric, six major issues always merged: the Bible, evangelism, dissension-unity, racial, social concern, and methods and approaches for Convention life.

He remained remarkably consistent on the first three issues. In every rhetorical effort made by Dr. Criswell, he always stated his perspective on the Bible, evangelism, and unity in the churches and Convention. His rhetorical propositions on these issues have remained consistent before and after being elected President of the Southern Baptist Convention.

With the first issue, the Bible, Dr. Criswell remained constant in advocating that the Scriptures are the inspired Word of God. He has upheld that the Bible is workable and practical in the lives of contemporary men.

The issue of evangelism is an obsession with the speaker-leader of the Southern Baptist Convention. Criswell has been consistent in pursuing the conviction that evangelism is the tool for imparting the Christian faith. He practiced the belief that the Christian is commanded to evangelize from the local level to international.

A third major issue which Criswell has remained constant in advocating is that of dissension—unity in the churches and the Convention. He upheld the idea that when there is "feuding, fussing, and fighting' the effectiveness of the Christian faith is impaired. He sought to bring unity.

Furthermore, two issues (the fourth and fifth repesctively) revealed significant differences in the perspective and rhetorical propositions of W.A. Criswell before and after he was elected President of the Convention. They were the racial issue and social concern. Dr. Criswell made a complete about-face on the racial issue. Before his election, it was known by the Convention that W.A. Criswell was a segregationist. The most ardent statement of segregation came in a speech that Dr. Criswell made in South Carolina in 1956. Then after he was elected President in 1968, Criswell made a famous address to the First Baptist Church of Dallas advocating racial integration in society and churches.

Social concern and responsibility were another issues that revealed a change in propositions. Before election, it was evident that Criswell had a limited degree of social concern. Social responsibility was always overshadowed by evangelism in his ideas before the election. After the election, he advocated and upheld a proper balance between evangelism and social concern.

A sixth issue, methods, and approaches of imparting the Christian faith, was always inescapable in his rhetorical propositions. Dr. Criswell always been relatively progressive in methods and procedures. He defended the concept that the Christian faith should be anchored to the Book, geared to the times! After he had been elected President of the Convention, more people became aware of the progressiveness of his methods and approaches.

Finally, Dr. Criswell remained constant in his belief for religious liberty and conservative theology before and after being elected to the highest position in the Convention.

Rhetorical Propositions Compared to Convention Policy

An assessment of the evolving of the Articles of Faith from the *London Confession of 1644* through *The New Hampshire Declaration of Faith* to the current *Baptist Faith and Message* revealed the same Biblical, doctrinal statements of the Baptist perspective of the Christian faith. The revisions were made to update the language and grammatical style. Through the revisions, some articles were added to clarify the Baptist and finally Southern Baptist viewpoint of the scriptural basis for a document of their denominational belief. The Southern Baptist concept of *The Baptist Faith and Message* adopted in 1963 remained consistent with the Biblical doctrine in earlier statements.

The analysis revealed no notable differences between Criswell's rhetorical propositions and policy of the Southern Baptist Convention. After comparing Criswell's rhetorical propositions to convention policy, a significant question must be considered. Were there any ideas or concepts in convention policy that were avoided by Dr. Criswell or which were not consistent with his rhetorical propositions? An Assessment of convention policy revealed no ideas or concepts that were avoided by Criswell or which were not consistent with his rhetorical propositions.

The Office of President of the Southern Baptist Convention

The leadership role of the President is very real. It is a charismatic phenomenon. Since the office does not depend on administrative powers from convention policy, it is significantly dependent on rhetoric and public address for the power of influence. This comes through public pronouncements in spoken and written form, activities in the convention, and his lifestyle perspective.

The Convention President is the only person elected directly by the Convention who is a member of the Executive Committee and all boards. He is the only person, therefore, who can provide a broad leadership over the overall program and who is responsible directly to the Convention itself.

The position of the current President of the Southern Baptist Convention has been greatly influenced by contemporary communication techniques and transportation facilities. He has been the charismatic leader of the Convention. Although he has not proposed to speak as the "voice" of the Convention, his statements have been given considerable weight by Baptists and by the secular world. From this context of charismatic leadership came a significant question, was W. A. Criswell elected to perpetuate the status quo or institute changes in the Convention?

Conclusion and Summary of the Legend
The following conclusions seemed warranted by evidence discovered:

1. The office of President of the Southern Baptist Convention is more than just an honor conferred upon an admired member of the Convention. It is a leadership position that is a charismatic phenomenon of power through rhetoric and public address. This comes through public pronouncements in oral and written form, leadership in the Convention, and generally the "life-style perspective" of the President. Therefore, public address is an analytical tool of social conditions. It is through perspective and public address that the relationship of leader to organization is apparent.

2. Dr. W.A. Criswell was elected President of the Southern Baptist Convention basically to perpetuate the status quo of convention policy and conservative theology. The majority of the Convention was conservative in theological beliefs and social practices. The Convention voted for Criswell because of his reputation and they thought he would maintain the status quo of the system. W.A. Criswell was not unaware of his influence and of the respect of the convention. He knew the conservative status quo of the Convention. Criswell made a political move by waiting until after he was elected to make a statement for integration. In this respect Criswell led the Convention from segregation to integration. He knew that he would be elected to perpetuate the status quo of conservative theology and evangelism. If Criswell had openly disturbed the waters by making a statement for integration before June, 1978, he might not have been elected.

A significant question arises; was this change concerning segregation a philosophic or pragmatic decision? The impetus was philosophical but the force was pragmatic. He could have taken another ten years to think through the issue, but pragmatically, time would not permit that! When Criswell was elected President of the Convention, he acted immediately to save First Baptist Church in Dallas from any embarrassment about his former stand on segregation. He was elected June 5, and gave the "Church of the Open Door" address June 9, 1968. Criswell was regarded as a segregationist before election. Since he reversed this position, his influence and leadership has been much more effective than would have been a man who had always been for integration. No one in the Convention anticipated his reversal on the segregation

179

issue. The liberals who opposed Criswell before he was elected the first time were surprised.

3. In some ways, Dr. Criswell was elected President to institute changes in the methods and approaches of the Southern Baptist Convention. The Convention knew that he was progressive in methods. Criswell had not advocated any changes in the Constitution, Bylaws, or Articles of Faith, but he led in instituting new methods and approaches in making the Christian faith relevant. He did not produce many methods to be implemented. He advocated what should be done, then leaves the specific helpful hints on how to do it up to specialists. Criswell then served as the motivating force of the Convention. Through the forcefulness and enthusiasm of his charismatic leadership, Criswell helped Southern Baptists to be anchored to the Book, geared to the times! The liberals in the Convention were falling into the same old trap into which the fundamentalists fell. They demand that a rhetorician use certain words and phrases in terminology to satisfy them. They demanded a certain interpretation. The Southern Baptist Convention cannot progress in that manner. It must allow for variations among members of the Convention and at the same time there must be some basic things of common unity in belief:

    A. The Bible as divine revelation.
    B. The Lordship of Christ.

4. The hard-core conservatives were responsible for electing Criswell. Although the hard-core conservatives were responsible for electing Criswell, the mild conservatives and liberals may have been happier about his administration than the hard-core. Criswell has maintained the status quo in theology but led in instituting changes in integration and social responsibility.

5. The Southern Baptist Convention is making progress. There has been a lot of confusion concerning the ministry of the church and the responsibility of individual Christians in regard to political, social, and economic involvement. A popular sport has been that of berating the evangelical wing of Christendom as though it had no social conscience, and as though it advocated Christian non-involvement in problems in a secular society. The Baptist view has been that the Church as a Church has no mandate to get involved in socio-political matters, but it is the duty of individual Christians to do so. Southern Baptists have felt that evangelism was first and foremost. If people are not committed to Christ then they are not going to do much in ethics and social concern. It was good for the Convention that Dr. Criswell was concerned with social responsibility. There is a social awareness today among Southern Baptists as never before! In concept and commitment there is a balance that is very healthy. Whatever criticisms are hurled at Southern Baptists, they have plenty of proof that churches who go all social responsibility and forget evangelism decrease in number unless they merge with other congregations.

6. Dr. W.A. Criswell had a distinct colloquial style in an affluent society. He had a style of "folksy anecdotes" which communicated in the southland of America.

Summary

The leadership of W.A. Criswell in the First Baptist Church and the Southern Baptist Convention has been dynamic in the direction of polarization and unity. He involved the Convention in issues of evangelism and social responsibility.

Criswell gave an emphasis on doctrinal integrity. Contemporary society is in an age of theological confusion. People do not know what they believe, not to speak of knowing why they believe. The "now generation" wants to know what is behind a certain belief.

There is a "hair of difference" between a conceited man and a humble man. The conceited man says, "See what I have done!" A humble man says, "I recognize that I had a part in leading, but I acknowledge the Source of my strength in the accomplishments." Wallie Amos Criswell was –a speaker, a leader—a humble man.

Criswell's honors are too lengthy to list. He was president of the Southern Baptist convention, has written over 50 books, has spoken in Baptist meetings all over the world and counted several presidents of the United States in his Sunday morning audiences. But ask him what will be his enduring legacy, what he will be remembered for, and he unhesitatingly said the college which bears his name.

On January 11, 2002, Dr. W. A. Criswell died at the age of 92. The following was his obituary in the Dallas Morning News:

DALLAS, Jan. 12— The Rev. W. A. Criswell, a leader of the conservative movement now in control of the Southern Baptists and former pastor of the First Baptist Church of Dallas, one of the denomination's first megachurches, died on Thursday in Dallas. He was 92. He was the former head of the Southern Baptist Convention and was pastor of First Baptist, the nation's largest Southern Baptist congregation, from 1944 until 1991, becoming pastor emeritus in 1994. The author of "Why I Preach That the Bible Is Literally True" and 53 other books, Mr. Criswell was a target of both denomination liberals and conservatives during his two terms as convention president in 1968-70. He openly clashed with liberal theologians over the issue of Biblical inerrancy, inviting them to "get out" of the convention. "He's done more to change the face of Christianity around the world for our generation than anyone else," said the Rev. Mac Brunson, now pastor of First Baptist here. "He turned an entire denomination back from liberalism to a conservative stance on God." Mr. Criswell helped First Baptist to grow from 5,000 members and an annual budget of $150,000 in 1944 to nearly 26,000 members and a budget of more than $11 million. The church also has a small college, private school and homeless shelter. "I never dreamed what God would do in this church," he said in a 1984 interview. The evangelist Billy Graham has considered Mr. Criswell his pastor since the early 1950's, when Mr. Criswell persuaded him to join First Baptist. "His preaching was electric in its power," Mr. Graham said. "His counsel and love to me meant more than he ever knew." Mr. Graham admired Mr. Criswell's knowledge of the Bible, his extensive home library and his ardent defense of the faith was unsurpassed, said a Graham spokesman, A. Larry Ross. Mr. Criswell's performance at the pulpit was a fiery exhibition, a roller coaster of whispers, bellows and shouts, tempered by the occasional joke. He refused to move First Baptist from its downtown location to the suburbs, believing he could better serve Dallas from the city's heart. Born on Dec. 19, 1909, Wallie Amos Criswell grew up in Texline, a tiny Panhandle farming community. His father eked out a living as a barber. Although his mother led her children in devotions and often sang hymns to them, Mr. Criswell said he encouraged him to become a doctor. But Mr. Criswell once said: "Ever since I can remember, I've been preparing to be a preacher. I have never deviated from that."

As a freshman at Baylor University, Mr. Criswell preached in a Waco jail and on street corners. A straight-A English major, he worked as pastor of a county congregation to put himself through college. He earned his doctorate in theology and held two pastorates before First Baptist called in 1944. Mr. Criswell quickly rose to prominence within the Southern Baptist Convention, earning a reputation as a skilled orator. A scholar in both Hebrew and Greek, he spent 18 years preaching through every verse of the Bible. Over two decades, Mr. Criswell's Bible-based views prevailed in the 15.6-million-member denomination, which is based in Nashville. The conservative leadership passed a resolution against the ordination of women in 1984, supported a boycott of The Walt Disney Company in 1997 and called in 1998 for women to "submit graciously" to their husbands' leadership. "Somebody said that Dr. Criswell preached the crusade and the younger generation carried it out, and I suppose there's a lot of truth in that," said Paige Patterson, president of Southeastern Baptist Theological Seminary in Wake Forest, N.C. Mr. Criswell once told the South Carolina Legislature that integration was "idiocy," but he announced after his election to the convention presidency in 1968 that he was renouncing segregation, a practice that was then common in Southern churches and elsewhere. Mr. Criswell later drew criticism when he suggested that Baptist leaders could open a dialogue with the National Council of Churches, which Southern Baptists considered too liberal in its religious and political outlook. Moderate Baptists who regret the path that staunch conservatives have taken with Mr. Criswell's influence say they still respected his devotion and focus on Scripture. "I obviously have a different perspective of what it means to be a Baptist," said David Currie, Mr. Criswell's cousin and executive director of the moderate Texas Baptists Committed. "In terms of where the Southern Baptist Convention is now, it's tragic." But Mr. Currie called Mr. Criswell a "great pastor" who made "significant contributions to Baptist faith." Mr. Criswell mostly eschewed politics. But in 1976, while President Gerald Ford was seated in his congregation, Mr. Criswell endorsed him for re-election over Jimmy Carter, a Southern Baptist who was Mr. Ford's opponent. In 1982, Mr. Criswell arranged for the Prime Minister Menachem Begin of Israel to come to First Baptist, but Mr. Begin canceled the visit when his wife died.

Mr. Criswell's salary was never disclosed publicly, but he lived in a large house on the city's historic Swiss Avenue. "I'm an affluent preacher," Mr. Criswell reflected in an interview. "I often wonder how it would be if I didn't have these things. I like the life I live. I like the car, the house, the place in the community. I like the prestige. I like the people I go with. "Sometimes I wonder if I am as worldly as the materialistic people in this city." Mr. Criswell is survived by his wife, Betty; a daughter, Mabel Ann; and two grandsons. (1)

End of Criswell Era

In 2006 the headline following the death of Dr. W.A. Criswell's wife, Betty Criswell, of the Texas Baptist Standard read, "Criswell era ends at Dallas First Baptist." The article stated:

> DALLAS—An era ended at First Baptist Church of Dallas Aug. 2. Betty Criswell, the widow of legendary Pastor W.A. Criswell, died at Baylor University Medical Center of Dallas of respiratory illness at age 93.
>
> Mrs. Criswell stood beside her husband through his early pastorates in rural Oklahoma and nearly a half-century of ministry at the downtown Dallas church. She also taught a popular and influential Sunday school class at First Baptist Church that was broadcast regionally on the radio for close to 30 years. She taught the class—attended by up to 300 people—for the last time July 9.
>
> "She devoted herself to Dr. Criswell's gospel ministry during his life, and after his death continued to preserve his legacy through First Baptist Church and the Criswell College," a statement posted on the church's website said.
>
> "'Mrs. C' was a blessing and a beacon to all who knew her, as well as the many thousands who listened from her radio audience. We mourn her loss as a church family and staff and celebrate her home going to see her Savior face to face, whom she has so wonderfully served."
>
> Evangelist Billy Graham—a non-resident member of First Baptist Church in Dallas—issued a statement from his home in Charlotte, N.C.: "We join in rejoicing that Betty Criswell has joined her husband in heaven at the feet of the Lord Jesus Christ, whom she has served for so long. Her tremendous ministry will be greatly missed at First Baptist Church of Dallas."
>
> Mrs. Criswell born in Louisville, Ky. She graduated from Western Kentucky University.
>
> She was preceded in death by both her husband and their daughter, Mable Ann Criswell, in 2002. She is survived by two grandsons and their families.
>
> (1) Dallas Morning News January 12, 2002, p.1.

[Author's Personal Note]

The last time I spoke with Dr. W. A. Criswell, I asked him what were his greatest words of wisdom. Without hesitation, he stated that I should tell everyone that:

There are three great components that make up the soul living inside of my body. There is first my mind, and second my emotion, and third my will which is my volitional choice decision making will. All of those three that make up the real "me." Where does salvation happen? Am I saved in my mind? Am I saved in my head? Am I saved in my understanding? Am I saved in my emotions? Am I saved because I am smart, or erudite, or academic, or educated, or because I have a college degree? Am I saved because I have a grasp of things intellectual? Oh, how I wish it could be done like that! Then we could just educate the world and the whole world would be saved. But in my experience I found it just the opposite. The more so-called "learned" a man is, sometimes the harder and more difficult it is to reach him for Jesus. I am just saying, you're not saved in your head. You're not saved in your mind. You're not saved in your understanding. You're not saved in your emotions. You're not saved by being smart, or erudite, or learned, or academic.

When I went to school, I was taught the James Lange theory of emotions that states that emotion is nothing but a summation of all the anatomical changes in your body. Put them all together and that is an emotion; it is a feeling, it is a physical thing. If you are normal, your emotions rise and fall, and rise and fall, and if you are normal they can be graphed. Religious emotion is no different from any other. If you ever tie your salvation to your feelings, they will drag you to death! One day you will feel you are saved. The next day you will say, "You know I was mistaken. I wasn't really saved. I don't feel like I know the Lord." That's because feelings rise and fall. A Christian is like the mercury in a thermometer. It goes up and down and up and down but always inside the thermometer. And when I am blue and discouraged, God doesn't love me any less because I am sitting under a juniper tree; He loves me more than at any other time because I am just not saved in my emotions and in my feelings. If I am not saved in my head, in my mind, and if I am not saved in my emotions, in my feelings, then where is it that a man is saved? A man is saved in his will. A man is saved by making a choice. A man is saved in his volition choice. "*Whosoever* will, let him come."

When a man makes that decision for Christ, he is saved. God regenerates him. A man's eternal salvation, his eternal destiny is conditioned on just one "I will." Yes, and that is no different from all of life. Daily change and eternal destiny are based one choosing to choose to believe and say, "I will choose Jesus as Savior and Lord." Then salvation is settled. Oh, how I wish everyone would make the choice to ask Jesus to be their savior and lord. W. A. Criswell's legacy has been burnt deeply into the brand of Texas and Baptist churches around the nation and the world. It is a legacy that not ride quietly into the sunset.

W. A. Criswell has indeed left a legacy. He became a master wordsmith in syllable and sentence by studying, traveling and Divine inspiration. He was a master communicator delivering the message of Jesus Christ. His legacy lives on in his audio-video-print libraries. His legacy lives on by all who have heard his words. His legacy is simple but rich. Dr. W. A. Criswell touched lives with scripture.

Jim Towns

W.A. CRISWELL TIMELINE

1909___Born in Eldorado, Okla., to W.A. and Anna Currie Criswell.

1927___Graduated from high school in Amarillo and headed for Baylor University, where he began serving a series of small Texas churches as pastor.

1931___Graduated from Baylor University with major in English.

1934___Earned master of theology degree from Southern Baptist Theological Seminary in Louisville, Ky.

1935___Married Bessie Marie Harris, a schoolteacher in his Kentucky congregation.

1937___Earned doctor of philosophy degree from Southern Seminary.

1937___Called as pastor of First Baptist Church of Chickasha, Okla.

1939___Daughter Mabel Ann born in Chickasha.

1941___Called as pastor of First Baptist Church of Muskogee, Okla.

1944___Called to succeed George W. Truett as pastor of First Baptist Church of Dallas. Criswell recalled 3,000 people were present that day at the church, which boasted a membership of 7,000 and a budget of $200,000. "When I knelt to pray, that massive throng burst into tears," he recalled more than 50 years later. "That memory is the most precious moment of the glorious ministry that the Lord gave us in the years that followed."

1946___ Began preaching through the Bible, word by word, a project that lasted 17 years.

1956___ Received national attention for saying integrationists are "a bunch of infidels, dying from the neck up."

1960___Preached against the election of John F. Kennedy, warning a Catholic would be too influenced by the Vatican. He later changed his views, inspired in part, he said, by Kennedy's fairness.

1968___Declared First Baptist Church open to people of all races in a sermon.

1968___Elected president of the Southern Baptist Convention, serving two one-year terms.

1969___Published his book "*Why I Believe the Bible is Literally True*," which is credited with energizing the conservative movement that eventually would change the course of the SBC.

1971___Criswell Bible Institute, now known as Criswell College, was founded in Dallas to train ministers in conservative biblical theology.

1972___Led First Baptist to open a church school, now known as First Baptist Academy.

1973___Affirmed the Supreme Court's Roe vs. Wade decision permitting abortion. Religious News Service quoted Criswell as saying, "I have always felt that it was only after a child was born and had life separate from the mother that it became an individual person, and it always has, therefore, seemed to me that what is best for the mother and for the future should be allowed." Criswell later changed his position on abortion, becoming a staunch opponent of the procedure.

1976____ Endorsed Gerald Ford's presidential bid in an address on the front steps of First Baptist Church, shunning fellow Southern Baptist Jimmy Carter.

1976____Saw a vision for a Christian radio station serving the Dallas market, leading to formation of KCBI radio.

1979____Published the Criswell Study Bible.

1979____ Nominated Adrian Rogers for SBC president during the annual meeting in Houston, formally launching the conservative movement to change the convention's leadership.

1980____By the 1970s and '80s, Criswell led First Baptist Church to worldwide recognition at the largest and wealthiest Southern Baptist congregation in the world. The church rolls boasted 26,000 members, and the congregation owned five blocks of downtown Dallas real estate.

1982____Offered to buy the financially troubled Dallas Baptist College for $6.5 million, citing hopes he could develop it into "a Wheaton College of the South." The board of trustees declined his offer.

1983____Delivers a check for $1 million to the Baptist General Convention of Texas, making good on a pledge by the church to give the record-setting amount to the Cooperative Program budget of the state and national conventions. "God, give us more dreamers like W.A. Criswell," said BGCT Executive Director James Landes.

1984____In an interview with the Baptist Standard, Criswell defended the emerging conservative movement in the SBC, saying he "hardly recognizes" his seminary alma mater. "What these men are doing is trying to keep our denomination conservative, that's all. And when these liberals say, 'But I am a conservative,' we have to redefine our terms and get some other nomenclature for us, because they are not conservative."

1984____Delivered the benediction over President Ronald Reagan as Reagan accepted the Republican Party's re-nomination in Dallas.

1984____In a nationally televised newscast, he explained, "I believe this notion of the separation of church and state was the figment of some infidel's imagination."

1985____Members of First Baptist gave a record $1.85 million offering on Criswell's 41st anniversary at the church. It was believed at the time to be the largest one-day cash offering ever taken by a church.

1986____In a sermon at First Baptist's School of the Prophets, he declared that "a laity-led, layman-led, deacon-led church will be a weak church anywhere in God's earth. The pastor is the ruler of the church."

1986____Told the First Baptist congregation of his desire to call a co-pastor to work alongside him and prevent any "hiatus" should he become incapacitated. This launched years of speculation and auditioning for the coveted role of Criswell's successor.

1988____Speaking at the SBC Pastor's Conference in the heat of battle between convention moderates and conservatives, he explained that moderates are the same as liberals: "A skunk by any other name still stinks."

1991___Named senior pastor of First Baptist Church, as the congregation called Joel Gregory as Criswell's successor.

1992___Gregory abruptly resigned as pastor of First Baptist, later explaining he had not been allowed full authority as pastor due to Criswell's continuing influence.

1994___Celebrated 50 years as pastor of First Baptist Church with a week of festivities.

1998___A bout with colon cancer sent the 88-year-old to bed for five months, but he rallied and spoke from the pulpit at First Baptist on the 54th anniversary of his first sermon there.

2002___Criswell succumbed, dying as his friend of 30 years read to him from the Bible.

2006___Mrs. Criswell died. This ended the Criswell era.

REFERENCES

Books

Adams, Richard N., and Preiss, Jack J., eds. *Human Organization Research.* Homewood, Ill.: Dorsey Press, Inc., 1960.

Armitage, Thomas. *A History of Baptists.* New York: Bryan, Taylor, and Co., 1887.

Armstrong, O.K., and Armstrong, Marjorie Moore. *The Indomitable Baptists.* Garden City, N.Y.: Doubleday and Company, Inc., 1967.

Backus, Isaac. *A History of New England with Particular Reference to the Denomination of Christians Called Baptists.* Edited by David Weston. Vol. II. Newton, Mass.: Backus Historical Society, 1871.

Baird, A. Craig. *American Public Addresses 1740-1952.* New York: McGraw-Hill Book Company, Inc., 1956.

Baker, Robert A. *A Baptist Source Book.* Nashville: Broadman Press, 1966.

_____. *A Summary of Christian History.* Nashville: Broadman Press, 1959.

_____. *Relations Between Northern and Southern Baptists.* Fort Worth: Seminary Press, 1948.

Barnes, William Wright. *The Southern Baptists Convention 1845-1953.* Nashville: Broadman Press, 1954.

Bates, Ernest Southerland. *American Faith.* New York: W.W. Norton and Co., 1940.

Benedict, David. *A General History of the Baptist Denomination in America and Other Parts of the World.* New York: Lewis Colby and Co., 1848.

Carroll, J.M. *A History of Texas Baptists.* Edited by J.B. Cranfill. Dallas: Baptist Standard Publishing Co., 1923.

Criswell, W.A. *Did Man Just Happen?* Grand Rapids: Zondervan Publishing House, 1957.

_____. *Expository Sermons on Revelation.* 5 vols. Grand Rapids: Zondervan Publishing House, 1962-1966.

_____. *Expository Sermons on the Book of Daniel.* Grand Rapids: Zondervan Publishing House, 1968.

_____. *Expository Notes on the Gospel of Matthew.* Grand Rapids: Zondervan Publishing House, 1961.

_____. *Five Great Affirmations of the Bible.* Grand Rapids: Zondervan Publishing House, 1959.

_____. *Five Great Questions of the Bible.* Grand Rapids: Zondervan Publishing House, 1958.

_____. *In Defense of the Faith.* Grand Rapids: Zondervan Publishing House, 1967.

_____. *Joining the Church.* Dallas: First Baptist Church Printing, 1964.

_____. *Look Up, Brother.* Nashville: Broadman Press, 1970.

_____. *Our Home In Heaven.* Grand Rapids: Zondervan Publishing House, 1964.

_____. *Preaching at the Palace.* Grand Rapids: Zondervan Publishing House, 1969.

_____. *The Bible for Today's World.* Grand Rapids: Zondervan Publishing House, 1965.

_____. *The Gospel According to Moses.* Grand Rapids: Zondervan Publishing House, 1960.

_____. *The Holy Spirit in Today's World.* Grand Rapids: Zondervan Publishing House, 1966.

_____. *These Issues We Must Face.* Grand Rapids: Zondervan Publishing House, 1953.

_____. *Why I Preach That the Bible is Literally True.* Nashville: Broadman Press, 1969.

Crouch, Austin. *How Southern Baptists Do Their Work.* Nashville: Broadman Press, 1951.

Duncan, Pope A. *Our Baptist Story.* Nashville: Convention Press, 1958.

Estep, William R. *Baptists and Christian Unity.* Nashville: Broadman Press, 1966.

Ford, W. Herschel. *Old-Time Religion.* Grand Rapids: Zondervan Publishing House, 1968.

Friedmann, Robert. *Mennonite Piety through the Centuries.* Goshen, Ind.: The Mennonite Historical Society, 1949.

Garrett, James Leo, Jr. *Baptist Church Discipline.* Nashville: Broadman Press, 1962.

Gaustad, Edwin Scott. *The Great Awakening in New England.* New York: Harper And Brothers, 1957.

Hobbs, Herschel H. *Fundamentals of Our Faith.* Nashville: Broadman Press, 1960.

_____. *What Baptists Believe.* Nashville: Broadman Press, 1964.

Hunt, H. L. *Why Not Speak?* Dallas: H. L. Hunt Press, 1964.

Lumpkin, William L. *Baptist Foundations in the South.* Nashville: Broadman Press, 1961.

May, Lynn E., Jr. *Baptists.* Nashville: Private Printing, 1967.

McBeth, Leon. *The First Baptist Church of Dallas.* Grand Rapids: Zondervan Publishing House, 1968.

Newman, A.H. *A History of the Baptist Churches in the United States.* Vol. II. New York: Charles Scribner's Sons, 1907.

Orchard, G.H. *A History of the Baptists in England.* Edited by J.R. Graves. Nashville: Southwestern Publishing House, 1861.

Oxnam, G. Bromley. *The Church and Contemporary Change.* New York: The MacMillan Company, 1950.

Pendleton, J.M. *Baptist Church Manual.* Nashville: Convention Press, 1961.

Porter, J.W. *The World's Debt to Baptists.* Louisville: Baptist Book Concern, 1914.

Riley, B.F. *The Baptists in the Building of the Nation.* Louisville: Baptists Book Concern, 1922.

Stokes, Anson Phelps. *Church and State in the United States.* 3 vols. New York: Harper and Brothers, 1950.

Straus, Oscar S. *Roger Williams: The Pioneer of Religious Liberty.* New York: D. Appleton-Century Co., 1936.

Sweet, William Warren. *American Culture and Religion: Six Essays.* Dallas: Southern Methodist University Press, 1951.

_____. *Makers of Christianity.* New York: Henry Holt and Company, 1951.

_____. *Religion in Colonial America.* New York: Charles Scribner's Sons, 1942.

_____. *Religion on the American Frontier—The Baptists.* Chicago: University Of Chicago Press, 1931.

_____. *Revivalism in America.* New York: Charles Scribner's Sons, 1945.

_____. *The Story of Religion in America.* New York: Harper and Brothers, 1930.

Taylor, Adam. *History of the English General Baptists.* London: T. Bore, 1818.

Torbet, Robert G. *A History of the Baptists.* Philadelphia: The Judson Press, 1950.

Towns, James E. *The Social Conscience of W. A. Criswell.* Dallas, Crescendo Press, 1977.

Troeltsch, Ernst. *The Social Teachings of the Christian Churches.* 2 vols. New York: Harper and Brothers, 1960.

Vedder, Henry C. *A History of the Baptists in the Middle States.* Philadelphia: American Baptists Publication Society, 1898.

_____. *A Short History of the Baptists.* Philadelphia: American Baptist Publication Society, 1907.

Articles

"Baptists Face Issues—In Living Color." *Christianity Today*, XIII (June 6, 1969), 41.

"Baptists: Where God's Business Is Big Business." *Time*, November 8, 1968, p. 79.

"Billy Graham Says He Agrees With Criswell on Liberalism." *Baptist New Mexican*, LVIII (January 3, 1970), 6.

Bonham, Tal D. "Fifteen Minutes with Dr. W.A. Criswell Molded My Study Habits." *Sermon Builder*, (July, 1969).

Bray, Austin, and Smith, Charles. "The Story of First Baptist Church, Dallas." *First Baptist Reminder*, (August 31, 1956), 4.

Clark, Carl A. "What Do Southern Baptists Believe?" *Baptist Standard*, LXXVIII (April 6, 1966), 24.

Craig, Coleman. "Wallie Amos Criswell." *The Baptist Review*, XVI (November, 1961), 3.

"Criswell Answers Critics in New Book." *Baptist Standard*, LXXXII (January 21, 1970), 10.

"Criswell Challenges First, Dallas to Reach All Races." *The Illinois Baptist*, LXI (June 19, 1968), 1.

"Criswell Condemns Racism." *The Baptist Messenger* (July 18, 1968), 4.

"Criswell: 'How long can we hold together?'" *The Illinois Baptist*, LXIII (October 1, 1969), 1.

"Criswell Please for Unity." *The Illinois Baptist*, XLVIII (September 25, 1968), 1.

Croft, Albert J. "Functions of Rhetorical Criticism." *The Quarterly Journal of Speech*, XLII (October, 1956), 289.

Dawson, Joseph M. "Baptists in the Founding of the Nation." *Encyclopedia of Southern Baptists*. Edited by Norman Wade Cox, 1958, p. 145.

Eggler, Bruce W. "Non-Progress Report on Southern Baptists: That Old-Time Religion." *The New Republic* (October 1, 1969), 15-17.

"Is Dr. W.A. Criswell Misunderstood?" *Biblical Record*, CXXXIV (June 15, 1968), 20.

"It Took Courage to Say What W.A. Criswell Said." *Biblical Recorder* (September 28, 1968), 3.

McBeth, Leon. "Do Baptists Deserve a History?" *Home Missions*, XLI (January, 1970), 13-17.

_____. "Who Are the Southern Baptists?" *The Illinois Baptist*, LXII (May 14, 1969) 3.

Morrison, Charles Clayton. "Open Letter to Senator Kennedy." *Christianity Today*, (September 112, 1960).

Newton, Jim. "Sentiment Favors Criswell's Book." *The Illinois Baptist*, LXII (April 23, 1969), 1.

"Our Baptist Beliefs." *The Baptist Messenger*, LVIII (August 4, 1968), 2-15.

"SBC Executive Committee Hears Plea for Unity from Criswell." *Capital Baptist*, XIV (October 3, 1968), 1.

"Southern Baptists and the Bible." *Christianity Today*, XIII (April 25, 1969), 34.

"Southern Baptists and the Bible Controversy." *Christian News*, II (April 21, 1969), 1.

"Southern Baptists Avert Showdown." *Christianity Today*, XIII (July 4, 1969), 33.

Storer, J. W. "Southern Baptist Convention, The." *Encyclopedia of Southern Baptists.*Edited by Norman Wade Cox, 1958, p. 1244-1262.

"W.A. Criswell Answers Critics in Latest Book." *The Baptist Messenger*, LIX (January 22, 1970), 4.

"W.A. Criswell is New President." *Baptist Standard*, LXXX (June 12, 1968), 6-7.

"W.A. Criswell—Man of the Hour." *Baptist Standard*, LXXX (July 24, 1968), 7.

"Will the Religious Issue Stop Kennedy in '60?" *United States News and World Report*, XLVII (September 7, 1959), 42-43.

Reports

Annuals of the Southern Baptist Convention. Nashville: Southern Baptist Convention Printing, 1967, 1968, 1969.

Unpublished Material

Bryson, Harold T. "The Expository Preaching of W.A. Criswell in His Sermons on The Revelation." Unpublished Master's Thesis. New Orleans Baptist Theological Seminary, 1963.

DuCasse, Robert W. "A History of the First Baptist Church, Dallas, Texas." Unpublished Master's Thesis, Dallas Theological Seminary, 1964.

Towns, James E. "The Rhetoric and Leadership of W.A. Criswell as President of the Southern Baptist Convention: A Descriptive Analysis through Perspective and Public Address." Unpublished Ph.D. dissertation, Department of Communication, Southern Ilinois University, 1970.

Speeches

Coggin, James E. "Nomination Address for W.A. Criswell." Southern Baptist Convention, Houston, Texas, June 5, 1968.

Interviews

Personal Interview with W.A. Criswell, Pastor of First Baptist Church of Dallas, Texas, and President of the Southern Baptist Convention. January 4, 7, 9, 10, 11, 22, 23, 24, 25, 1970.

Personal Interview with H.L. Hunt, President, H.L. Hunt Industries, Active Baptist Layman, Dallas, Texas. January 11, 1970.

Personal Interview with Leon McBeth, Professor of Church History, Southwestern Baptist Theological Seminary, Fort Worth, Texas. January 26, 1970.

Public Documents

Charter of the Southern Baptist Convention.
Constitution of the Southern Baptist Convention.
London Confession of 1644.
New Hampshire Declaration of Faith.
The Baptist Faith and Message.
United States Constitution, Amendment 1.

Encyclopedia

Cathcart, William, ed. *Baptist Encyclopaedia.* Philadelphia: Louis H. Everts, 1883.

Cox, Norman Wade, ed. *Encyclopedia of Southern Baptists.* Nashville: Broadman Press, 1958.

"Criswell, W.A." Who's Who in the South and Southwest. IX. Chicago: Marquis Publishing Company, 1965.

Appendix One

London Baptist Confession of 1644

A CONFESSION OF FAITH of seven congregations or churches of Christ in London, which are commonly, but unjustly, called Anabaptists; published for the vindication of the truth and information of the ignorant; likewise for the taking off those aspersions which are frequently, both in pulpit and print, unjustly cast upon them. Printed in London, Anno 1646.

But this I confesse unto thee, that after the way which they call heresie so worship I the God of my Fathers, beleeving all things that are written in the Law and the Prophets, and have hope towards God, which they themselves also allow, that there shall be a resurrection of the dead both of the just and unjust. - Acts xxiv. 14, 15.

For we cannot but speak the things that we have seen and heard. - Acts iv. 20. If I have spoken evill, bear witnesse of the evill; but if well, why smitest thou me? - John xviii. 23. Blessed are yee when men revile you, and say all manner of evil against you falsly for my sake. Rejoice, etc. - Matth. v.11, 12. & xix. 29.

I.

That God as He is in Himself, cannot be comprehended of any but himself, (1) dwelling in that inaccessible light, that no eye can attain unto, whom never man saw, nor can see; that there is but (2) one God, one Christ, one Spirit, one Faith, one Baptism; (3) one rule of holiness and obedience for all Saints, at all times, in all places to be observed.

1) 1 Tim. 6:16
2) 1 Tim. 2:5; Eph. 4:4-6; 1 Cor. 12: 4-6,13; John 14
3) 1 Tim. 6:3,13,14; Gal. 1:8-9; 2 Tim. 3:15

II.

That God is (1) of Himself, that is, neither from another, nor of another, nor by another, nor for another: (2) But is a Spirit, who as his being is of Himself, so He gives (3) being, moving, and preservation to all other things, being in Himself eternal, most holy, every way infinite in (4) greatness, wisdom, power, justice, goodness, truth, etc. In this Godhead, there is the Father, the Son, and the Spirit; being every on of them one and the same God; and therefore not divided, but distinguished one from another by their several properties; the (5) Father being from Himself, the (6) Son of the Father from everlasting, the (7) Holy Spirit proceeding from the Father and the Son.

1) Isa. 43:11; 46:9
2) John 4:24
3) Exod. 3:14
4) Rom. 11:36; Acts 17:28
5) 1 Cor. 8:6
6) Prov. 8:22-23
7) John 15:16; Gal. 4:6

III.

That God has (1) decreed in Himself from everlasting touching all things, effectually to work and dispose them (2) according to the counsel of His own will, to the glory of His name; in which decree appears His wisdom, constancy, truth, and faithfulness; (3) Wisdom is that whereby He contrives all things; (4) Constancy is that whereby the decree of God remains always immutable; (5) Truth is that whereby He declares that alone which He has decreed, and though His sayings may seem to sound sometimes another thing, yet the sense of them does always agree with the decree; (6) Faithfulness is that whereby He effects that He has decreed, as He has decreed. And touching His creature man, (7) God had in Christ before the foundation of the world, according to the good pleasure of His will, foreordained some men to eternal life through Jesus Christ, to the praise and glory of His grace, (8) leaving the rest in their sin to their just condemnation, to the praise of His justice.

1) Isa. 46:10
2) Eph. 1:11
3) Col. 2:3

4) Num. 23:19-20
5) Jer. 10:10; Rom. 3:4
6) Isa. 44:10
7) Eph. 1:3-7; 2 Tim. 1:9; Acts 13:48; Rom. 8:29-30
8) Jude 4,6; Rom. 9:11-13; Prov. 16:4

IV.

(1) In the beginning God made all things very good, created man after His own (2) image and likeness, filling him with all perfection of all natural excellency and uprightness, free from all sin. (3) But long he abode not in this honor, but by the (4) subtlety of the Serpent, which Satan used as his instrument, himself with his angels having sinned before and not (5) kept their first estate, but left their own habitation; first (6) Eve, then Adam being seduced did wittingly and willingly fall into disobedience and transgression of the Commandment of their great Creator, for the which death came upon all, and reigned over all, so that all since the Fall are conceived in sin, and brought forth in iniquity, and so by nature children of wrath, and servants of sin, subjects of (7) death, and all other calamities due to sin in this world and for ever, being considered in the state of nature, without relation to Christ.

1) Gen. 1; Col. 1:16; Heb. 11:3; Isa. 45:12
2) Gen. 1:26; 1 Cor. 15:45-46; Ecc. 7:31
3) Psa. 49:20
4) Gen. 3:1, 4, 5; 2 Cor. 11:3
5) 2 Peter 2:4; Jude 6; John 8:44
6) Gen. 3:1, 2, 6; 1 Tim. 2:14; Ecc. 7:31; Gal. 3:32
7) Rom. 5:12, 18, 19; 6:23; Eph. 2:3

V.

All mankind being thus fallen, and become altogether dead in sins and trespasses, and subject to the eternal wrath of the great God by transgression; yet the elect, which God has (1) loved with an everlasting love, are (2) redeemed, quickened, and saved, not by themselves, neither by their own works, lest any man should boast himself, but wholly and only by God of (3) His free grace and mercy through Jesus Christ, who of God is made unto us wisdom, righteousness, sanctification and redemption, that as it is written he that rejoices, let him rejoice in the Lord.

1) Jer. 31:2
2) Gen 3:15; Eph. 1:3, 7; 2:4, 9; 1 Thes. 5:9; Acts 13:38
3) 1 Cor.5:21; Jer. 9:23, 24

VI.

(1) This therefore is life eternal, to know the only true God, and whom He has sent Jesus Christ. (2) And on the contrary, the Lord will render vengeance in flaming fire to them that know not God, and obey not the Gospel of our Lord Jesus Christ.

1) John 17:3; Heb. 5:9; Jer. 23:5, 6
2) 2 Thes. 1:8; John 3:36

VII.

The rule of this knowledge, faith, and obedience, concerning the worship and service of God, and all other Christian duties, is not mans inventions, opinions, devices, laws, constitutions, or traditions unwritten whatsoever, but only the word of God contained in the Canonical Scriptures.

John 5:39; 2 Tim. 3:15-17; Col. 21:18, 23; Mat. 15:9

VIII.

In this written Word God has plainly revealed whatsoever He has thought needful for us to know, believe, and acknowledge, touching the nature and office of Christ, in whom all the promises are Yea and Amen to the praise of God.

Acts 3:22, 23; Heb. 1:1, 2; 2 Tim 3:15-17; 2 Cor. 1:20

IX.

Touching the Lord Jesus, of whom (1) Moses and the Prophets wrote, and whom the Apostles preached, is the (2) Son of God the Father, the brightness of His glory, the ingrave form of His being, God with Him and with His Holy Spirit, by whom He made the world, by whom He upholds and governs all the works He has made, who also (3) when the fullness of time was come was, was made man of a (4) woman, of the Tribe of (5) Judah, of the seed of Abraham and David, to wit, of Mary that blessed Virgin, by the Holy Spirit coming upon her, and the power of the most High overshadowing her, and was also in (6) all things like unto us, sin only excepted.

1) Gen. 3:15; 22:18; 49:10; Dan. 7:13; 9:24-26
2) Prov. 8:23; John 1:1-3; Col. 1:1, 15-17
3) Gal. 4:4
4) Heb. 7:14; Rev. 5:5 with Gen. 49:9-10
5) Rom. 1:3; 9:5; Mat. 1:16; Luke 3:23, 26; Heb. 2:16
6) Isa.53:3-5; Phil. 2:8

X.

Touching His office, (1) Jesus Christ only is made the Mediator of the New Covenant, even the everlasting covenant of grace between God and man, to(2) be perfectly and fully the Prophet, Priest and King of the Church of God for evermore.

1) 2 Tim. 2:15; Heb. 9:15; John 14:6
2) Heb. 1:2; 3:1, 2; 7:24; Acts 5:31

XI.

Unto this office He was fore-ordained from everlasting, by the (1) authority of the Father, and in respect of His manhood, from the womb called and separated, and (2) anointed also most fully and abundantly with all gifts necessary, God having without measure poured the Spirit upon Him.

1) Prov. 8:23; Isa. 42:6; 49:1,5
2) Isa. 11:2-5; 61:1-3 with Luke 4:17, 22; John1:14,16; 3:34

XII.

In this call the Scripture hold forth two special things considerable; first, the call to the office; secondly the office its self. First, that (1) none takes this honor but he that is called of God, as was Aaron, so also Christ, it being an action especially of God the Father, whereby a special covenant being made, He ordains His Son to this office: which Covenant is, that (2) Christ should be made a sacrifice for sin, that He shall see His seed, and prolong His days, and the pleasure of the Lord shall prosper in His hand; which calling therefore contains in it self (3) choosing, (4) for-ordaining, (5) sending. choosing respects the end, foreordaining the means, sending the execution it self, (6) all of mere grace, without any condition fore-seen wither in men, on in Christ Himself.

1) Heb. 5:4-6
2) Isa. 53:10
3) Isa. 42:13
4)1 Peter 1:20
5) John 3:17; 9:27; 10:36
6) John 8:32

XIII.

So that this office to be Mediator, that is, to be Prophet, Priest, and King of the Church of God, is so proper to Christ, as neither in the whole, not in any part thereof, it can be transferred from Him to any other.
1 Tim. 2:15; Heb. 7:24; Dan. 5:14; Acts 4:12; Luke 1:23; John 14:6

XIV.

This office it self to which Christ was called, is three fold, of (1) a Prophet, of (2) Priest, and of (3) King: this number and order of offices is showed; first by men's necessities grievously laboring (4) under ignorance, by reason whereof they stand in infinite necessity of the Prophetical office of Christ to relieve them. Secondly, (5) alienation from God, wherein they stand in need of the Priestly office to reconcile them.

Thirdly, our (6) utter disability to return to Him, by which they stand in need of the power of Christ in His Kingly office to assist and govern them.

    1) Deut. 18:15 with Acts 3:22-23

    2) Psal. 110:3; Heb. 3:1; 4:14-15; 5:6

    3) Psal. 2:6

    4) Acts 26:18; Col. 1:3

    5) Col. 1:21; Eph. 2:12

    6) Song of Sol. 1:3; John 6:44

XV.

Touching the Prophesy of Christ, it is that whereby He has (1) perfectly revealed the whole will of God out of the bosom of the Father, that is needful for His servants to know, believe, and obey; and therefore is called not only a Prophet and a (2) Doctor, and the (3) Apostle of our profession, and the (4) Angel of the Covenant; but also the very (5) wisdom of God, and the (6) treasures of wisdom and understanding.

    1) John 1:18; 12:49-50; 15; 17:8; Deut. 18:15

    2) Mat. 23:10

    3) Heb. 3:1

    4) Mal. 3:1

    5) 1 Cor. 1:24

    6) Col. 2:3

XVI.

That He might be such a Prophet as thereby to every way complete, it was necessary that He should be (1) God, and withall also that He should be man; for unless He had been God, He could have never perfectly understood the will of God, (2) neither had He have been able to reveal it throughout all ages; and unless He had been man, He could not fitly have unfolded it in His (3) own person to man.

    1) John 1:18; 3:13

    2) 1 Cor. 2:11, 16

    3) Acts 3:22 with Deut. 18:15; Heb. 1:1

XVII.

Touching His Priesthood, Christ (1) being consecrated, has appeared once to put away sin by the offering and sacrifice of Himself, and to this end has fully performed and suffered all those things by which God, through the blood of that His Cross in an acceptable sacrifice, might reconcile His elect only; (2) and having broken down the partition wall, and therewith finished and removed all the rites, shadows, and ceremonies, is now entered within the vail, into the Holy of Holiest, that is, to the very Heavens, and presence of God, where He forever lives and sits at the right hand of Majesty, appearing before the face of His Father to make intercession for such as come to the Throne of Grace by that new and living way; and not that only, but (3) makes His people a spiritual House, an holy Priesthood, to offer up spiritual sacrifice acceptable to God through Him; neither does the Father accept, or Christ offer to the Father any other worship or worshipers.

    1) John 17:19; Heb. 5:7-9; 9:26; Rom. 5:19; Eph. 5:12; Col. 1:20

    2) Eph. 2:14-16; Rom. 8:34

    3) 1 Peter 2:5; John 4:23, 24

XVIII.

This Priesthood was not legal, or temporary, but according to the order (1) of Melchisecdec (2) not by a carnal commandment, but by the power of endless life; (3) not by an order that is weak and lame, but stable and perfect, not for a (4) time, but forever, admitting no successor, but perpetual and proper to Christ, and of Him that ever lives. Christ Himself was the Priest, Sacrifice and Alter: He was (5) Priest, according to both natures, He was a sacrifice most properly according to His human nature: (6) where in Scripture it is wont to be attributed to His body, to His blood; yet the chief force whereby this sacrifice was made effectual, did depend upon His (7) divine nature, namely, that the Son of God did offer Himself for us: He was the alter properly according to His divine nature, it belonging to the (8) Alter to sacrifice that which is offered upon it, and so it ought to be of greater dignity then the Sacrifice itself.

    1) Heb. 7:17

    2) Heb. 7:16

3) Heb. 7:18-21
4) Heb. 7:24-25
5) Heb. 5:6
6) Heb. 10:10; 1 Peter 1:18-19; Col. 1:20-21; Isa. 53: 10; Mat. 20:28
7) Acts 20:28; Rom. 8:3
8) Heb. 9:14; 13:10, 12, 15; Mat. 23:17; John 17:19

XIX.

Touching His Kingdom,(1) Christ being risen from the dead, ascended into Heaven, sat on the right hand of God the Father, having all power in Heaven and earth, given unto Him, He does spiritually govern His Church, exercising His power(2) over all angels and men, good and bad, to the preservation and salvation of the elect, to the over-ruling and destruction of His enemies, which are reprobates,(3) communicating and applying the benefits, virtue, and fruit of His Prophecy and Priesthood to His elect, namely, to the subduing and taking away of their sins, to their justification and adoption of Sons, regeneration, sanctification, preservation and strengthening in all their conflicts against Satan, the World, the Flesh, and the temptations of them, continually dwelling in, governing and keeping their hearts in faith and filial fear by His Spirit, which having(4) given it, He never takes it away from them, but by it still begets and nourishes in them faith, repentance, love, joy, hope, and all heavenly light in the soul unto immortality, notwithstanding through our own unbelief, and the temptations of Satan, the sensible sight of this light and love be clouded and overwhelmed for the time.(5) And on the contrary, ruling in the world over His enemies, Satan, and all the vessels of wrath, limiting, using, restraining them by His mighty power, as seems good in His divine wisdom and justice to the execution of His determinate counsel, delivering them up to a reprobate mind, to be kept through their own deserts, in darkness and sensuality unto judgment.

1) 1 Cor. 15:4; 1 Peter 3:21-22; Mat. 28:18-20; Luke 24:51; Acts 1:11; 5:30-31; John 19:36; Rom. 14:17
2) Mark 1:27; Heb. 1:14; John 16:7,15
3) John 5:26-27; Rom. 5:5-7; 14:17; Gal. 5:22,23; John 1:4,13
4) John 13:1; 10:28-29; 14:16-17; Rom. 11:29; Psal. 51:10-11; Job 33:29-30; 2 Cor. 12:7, 9
5) Job 1, 2; Rom. 1:21; 2:4-6; 9:17-18; 2 Peter 2

XX.

This Kingdom shall be then fully perfected when He shall the second time come in glory to reign among His saints, and to be admired of all them which do believe, when He shall put down all rule and authority under His feet, that the glory of the Father may be full and perfectly manifested in His Son, and the glory of the Father and the Son in all His members.

1 Cor. 15:24,28; Heb. 9:28; 2 Thes. 1:9, 10; 1 Thes. 4:15-17; John 17:21,26

XXI.

That Christ Jesus by His death did bring fourth salvation and reconciliation only for the(1) elect, which were those which(2) God the Father gave Him; and that the Gospel which is to be preached to all men as the ground of faith, is, that(3) Jesus is the Christ, the Son of the ever blessed God, filled with the perfection of all heavenly and spiritual excellencies, and that salvation is only and alone to be had through the believing in His name.

1) John 15:13; Rom. 8:32-34; 5:11; 3:25
2) Job 17:2 with 6:37
3) Mat. 16:16; Luke 2:26; John 6:9; 7:3; 20:31; 1 John 5:11

XXII.

That faith is the(1) gift of God wrought in the hearts of the elect by the Spirit of God, whereby they come to see, know, and believe the truth of the(2) Scriptures, and not only so, but the excellency of them above all other writing and things in the world, as they hold forth the glory of God in His attributes, the excellency of Christ in His nature and offices, and the power of the fullness of the Spirit in His workings and operations; and thereupon are enabled to cast the weight of their souls upon this truth thus believed.

1) Eph. 2:8; John 6:29; 4:10; Phil. 1:29; Gal. 5:22
2) John 17:17; Heb. 4:11-12; John 6:63

XXIII.

Those that have this precious faith wrought in them by the Spirit, can never finally nor totally fall away; and though many storms and floods do arise and beat against them, yet they shall never be able to take them off that foundation and rock which by faith they are fastened upon, but shall be kept by the power of God to salvation, where they shall enjoy their purchased possession, they being formerly engraven upon the palms of God's hands.

Mat. 7:24, 25; John 13:1; 1 Peter 1:4-6; Isa. 49:13-16

XXIV.

That faith is ordinarily (1) begot by the preaching of the Gospel, or word of Christ, without respect to (2) any power or capacity in the creature, but it is wholly (3) passive, being dead in sins and trespasses, does believe, and is converted by no less power, (4) then that which raised Christ from the dead.

1) Rom. 10:17; 1 Cor. 1:21
2) Rom. 9:16
3) Rom. 2:1, 2; Ezek. 16:6; Rom 3:12
4) Rom. 1:16; Eph. 1:19; Col 2:12

XXV.

That the tenders of the Gospel to the conversion of sinners, (1) is absolutely free, no way requiring, as absolutely necessary, any qualifications, preparations, terrors of the Law, or preceding ministry of the Law, but only and alone the naked soul, as a (2) sinner and ungodly to receive Christ, as Christ, as crucified, dead, and buried, and risen again, being made (3) a Prince and a Savior for such sinners.

1) John 3:14, 15; 1:12; Isa. 55:1; John 7:37
2) 1 Tim. 1:15; Rom. 4:5; 5:8
3) Acts 5:30-31; 2:36; 1 Cor. 1:22-24

XXVI.

That the same power that converts to faith in Christ, the same power carries on the (1) soul still through all duties, temptations, conflicts, sufferings, and continually whatever a Christian is, he is by (2) grace, and by a constant renewed (3) operation from God, without which he cannot perform any duty to God, or undergo any temptations from Satan, the world, or men.

1) 1 Peter 1:5; 2 Cor. 12:9
2) 1 Cor. 15:10
3) Phil. 2:12, 13; John 15:5; Gal. 2:19-20

XXVII.

That God the Father, and Son, and Spirit, is one with (1) all believers, in their (2) fullness, in (3) relations, (4) as head and members, (5) as house and inhabitants, as (6) husband and wife, one with Him, as (7) light and love, and one with Him in His inheritance, and in all His (8) glory; and that all believers by virtue of this union and oneness with God, are the adopted sons of God, and heirs of Christ, co-heirs and joint heirs with Him of the inheritance of all the promises of this life, and that which is to come.

1) 1 Thes. 1:1; John 14:10, 20; 17:21
2) Col. 2:9, 10; 1:19; John 1:17
3) John 20:17; Heb. 2:11
4) Col. 1:18; Eph. 5:30
5) Eph. 2:22; 1Cor. 3:16-17
6) Isa. 16:5; 2 Cor. 11:3
7) Gal. 3:26
8) John 17:24

XXVIII.

That those which have union with Christ, are justified from all their sins, past, (1) present, and to come, by the blood of Christ; which justification we conceive to be a gracious and free (2) acquittance of a guilty, sinful creature, from all sin by God, through the satisfaction that Christ has made by His death; and this applied in the manifestation of it through faith.

1) John 1:7; Heb 10:14; 9:26; 2 Cor. 5:19; Rom. 3:23
2) Acts 13:38, 39; Rom. 5:1; 3:25, 30

XXIX.

That all believers are a holy and (1) sanctified people, and that sanctification is a spiritual grace of the (2) New Covenant, and effect of the (3) love of God, manifested to the soul, whereby the believer is in (4) truth and reality separated, both in soul and body, from all sin and dead works, through the (5) blood of the everlasting Covenant, whereby he also presents after a heavenly and evangelical perfection, in obedience to all the commands, (6) which Christ as Head and King in this New Covenant has prescribed to him.

1) 1 Cor. 1:1; 1 Peter 2:9
2) Eph. 1:4
3) 1 John 4:16
4) Eph. 4:24
5) Phil. 3:15
6) Mat. 28:20

XXX.

All believers through the knowledge of(1) that justification of life given by the Father, and brought forth by the blood of Christ, have this as their great privilege of that New(2) Covenant, peace with God, and reconciliation, whereby they that were afar off, were brought nigh by(3) that blood, and have (as the Scripture speaks) peace(4) passing all understanding, yes, joy in God, through our Lord Jesus Christ, by(5) whom we have received the Atonement.

1) 2 Cor. 5:19
2) Isa. 54:10; 26:12
3) Eph. 2:13-14
4) Phil. 4:7
5) Rom. 5:10-11

XXXI.

That all believers in the time of this life, are in a continual warfare, combat, and opposition against sin, self, the world, and the Devil, and liable to all manner of afflictions, tribulations, and persecutions, and so shall continue until Christ comes in His Kingdom, being predestined and appointed there unto; and whatsoever the saints, any of them do possess or enjoy of God in this life, is only by faith.

Eph. 6:10-13; 2 Cor. 10:3; Rev. 2:9, 10

XXXII.

That the only strength by which the saints are enabled to encounter with all opposition, and to overcome all afflictions, temptations, persecutions, and trials, is only by Jesus Christ, who is the Captain of their salvation, being made perfect through sufferings, who has engaged His strength to assist them in all their afflictions, and to uphold them under all their temptations, and to preserve them by His power to His everlasting Kingdom.

John 16:33; Heb. 2:9, 10; John 15:5

XXXIII.

That Christ has here on earth a spiritual Kingdom, which is the Church, which He has purchased and redeemed to Himself, as a particular inheritance: which Church, as it is visible to us, is a company of visible(1) saints,(2) called and separated from the world, by the Word and the(3) Spirit of God, to the visible profession of the faith of the Gospel, being baptized into the faith, and joined to the Lord, and each other, by mutual agreement, in the practical enjoyment of the(4) ordinances, commanded by Christ their head and King.

1) 1 Cor. 1:1; Eph. 1:1
2) Rom. 1:1; Acts 26:18; 1 Thes. 1:9; 2 Cor. 6:17; Rev. 18:18
3) Acts 2:37 with Acts 10:37
4) Rom. 10:10; Acts 2:42; 20:21; Mat. 18:19, 20; 1 Peter 2:5

XXXIV.

To this Church He has(1) made His promises, and given the signs of His Covenant, presence, love, blessing, and protection: here are the fountains and springs of His heavenly grace continually flowing forth;(2) thither ought all men to come, of all estates, that acknowledge Him to be their Prophet, Priest, and King, to be enrolled amongst His household servants, to under His heavenly conduct and government, to lead their lives in His walled sheepfold, and watered garden, to have communion here with the saints, that they may be made to be partakers of their inheritance in the Kingdom of God.

1) Mat. 28:18-20; 2 Cor. 6:18

2) Isa. 8:16; 1 Tim. 3:15; 4:16; 6:3, 5; Acts 2:41,47; Song of Sol. 4:12; Gal. 6:10; Eph. 2:19

XXXV.

And all His servants are called thither, to present their bodies and souls, and to bring their gifts God has given them; so being come, they are here by Himself bestowed in their several order, peculiar place, due use, being fitly compact and knit together, according to the effectual working of every part, to the edification of itself in love.

1 Cor. 12:6, 7, 12, 18; Rom. 12:4-6; 1 Peter 4:10;Eph. 4:16; Col. 2:5, 6, 19; 1 Cor. 12:12ff

XXXVI.

That being thus joined, every Church has(1) power given them from Christ for their better well-being, to choose to themselves fitting persons into the office of(2) Pastors, Teachers, Elders, Deacons, being qualified according to the Word, as those which Christ has appointed in His Testament, for the feeding, governing, serving, and building up of His Church, and that none other have to power to impose them, either these or any other.

1) Acts 1:2; 6:3; 15:22, 25; 1 Cor. 16:3

2) Rom. 12:7, 8; 16:1; 1 Cor. 12:8, 28; 1 Tim. 3 chapt.; Heb. 13:7; 1 Peter 5:1-3

XXXVII.

That the Ministers aforesaid, lawfully called by the Church, where they are to administer, ought to continue is their calling, according to God's ordinance, and carefully to feed the flock of Christ committed to them, nor for filthy lucre, but of a ready mind.

Heb. 5:4; Acts 4:23; 1 Tim. 4:14; John 10:3, 4; Acts 20:28; Rom. 12:7, 8; Heb. 13:7, 17

XXXVIII.

That the due maintenance of the officers aforesaid, should be the free and voluntary communication of the Church, that according to Christ's ordinance, they that preach the Gospel, should live on the Gospel and not by constraint to be compelled from the people by a forced law.

1 Cor. 9:7,14; Gal. 6:6; 1 Thes. 5:13; 1 Tim. 5:17-18; Phil. 4:15-16

XXXIX.

That Baptism is an ordinance of the New Testament, given by Christ, to be dispensed only upon persons professing faith, or that are Disciples, or taught, who upon a profession of faith, ought to be baptized (Added later: "...and after to partake of the Lord's Supper.")

Acts 2:37, 38; 8:36-38; 18:8

XL.

The way and manner of the(1) dispensing of this ordinance the Scripture holds out to be dipping or plunging the whole body under water: it being a sign, must answer the thing signified, which are these: first, the(2) washing the whole soul in the blood of Christ; secondly, that interest the saints have in(3) death, burial, and resurrection (of Christ) ; thirdly, together with a(4) confirmation of out faith, that as certainly as the body is buried under water, and rises again, so certainly shall the bodies of the saints by raised by the power of Christ, in the day of the resurrection, to reign with Christ.

1) Mat. 3:16; John 3:23; Acts 8:38

2) Rev. 1:5; 7:14; Heb. 10:22

3) Rom. 6:3-5

4) 1 Cor. 15:28, 29

XLI.

The persons designed by Christ, to dispense this ordinance, the Scriptures hold forth to a preaching Disciple, it being no where tied to a particular church, officer, or person extraordinarily sent, the commission enjoining the administration, being given to them under no other consideration, but as considered Disciples.

Isa. 8:16; Mat. 28:16-19; John 4:1-2; Acts 20:7; Mat. 26:26

XLII.

Christ has likewise given power to His whole church to receive in and cast out, by way of Excommunication, any member; and this power is given to every particular congregation, and not one particular person, either member or officer, but the whole.

Acts 2:47; Rom. 16:2; Mat. 18:17; 1 Cor. 5:4; 2 Cor. 2:6-8

XLIII.

And every particular member of each Church how excellent, great, or learned soever, ought to be subject to this censor and judgment of Christ; and the church ought with great care and tenderness, with due advise to proceed against her members.

Mat. 18:16-18; Acts 11:2. 3; 1 Tim. 5:19-21

XLIV.

And as Christ for the(1) keeping of this church in holy and orderly communion, places some special men over the church, who by their office are to govern, oversee, visit, watch; so likewise for the better keeping thereof in all places, by the members, He has given(2) authority, and laid duty upon all, to watch over one another.

1) Acts. 20:27, 28; Heb. 13:17, 24; Mat. 24:25; 1 Thes. 5:14
2) Mark 13:34, 37; Gal. 6:1; 1 Thes. 5:11; Jude 3, 20; Heb. 10:34-35; 12:15.

XLV.

That also such to whom God has given gifts, being tried in the church, may and ought by the appointment of the congregation, to prophesy, according to the proportion of faith, and so teach publicly the Word of God, for the edification, exhortation, and comfort of the Church.

1 Cor. 14 chapter; Rom. 12:6; 1 Peter 4:10-11; 1 Cor. 12:7; 1 Thes. 5:17-19

XLVI.

Thus being rightly gathered, established, and still proceeding in Christian communion, and obedience of the Gospel of Christ, none ought to separate for faults and corruptions, which may, and as long as the church consists of men subject to failings, will fall out and arise amongst them, even in true constituted churches, until they have in due order sought redress thereof.

Rev. 2, 3 chapters; Acts 15:12; 1 Cor. 1:10; Eph. 2:16; 3:15-16; Heb. 10:25; Jude 15; Mat. 18:17; 1 Cor. 5:4, 5

XLVII.

And although the particular congregation be distinct and several bodies, every one a compact and knit city in itself; yet are they all to walk by one and the same Rule, and by all means convenient to have the counsel and help one of another in all needful affairs of the church, as members of one body in the common faith under Christ their only Head.

1 Cor. 4:17; 14:33, 36; 16:1; Mat. 28:20; 1 Tim.3:15; 6:13-14; Rev. 22:18-19; Col. 2:6, 19; 4:16

XLVIII.

That a civil magistrate is an ordinance of God set up by God for the punishment of evil doers, and for the praise of them that do well; and that all lawful things commanded by them, subjection ought to be given by us in the Lord: and that we are to make supplication and prayer for Kings, and all that are in authority, that under them we may live a peaceable and quiet life in all godliness and honesty.

Rom. 13:1-4; 1 Peter 2:13, 14; 1 Tim. 2:2

XLIX.

The supreme Magistrate of this Kingdom we believe to be the King and Parliament freely chosen by the Kingdom, and that in all those civil laws which have been acted by them, or for the present is or shall by ordained, we are bound to yield subjection and obedience unto in the Lord, as conceiving our selves bound to defend both the persons of those chosen, and all civil laws made by them, with our persons, liberties, and estates, with all that is called ours, although we should suffer never so much from them in not actively submitting to some ecclesiastical laws, which might be conceived by them to be their duties to establish which we for the present could not see, nor our consciences could submit unto; yet are we bound to yield our persons to their pleasures.

L.

And if God should provide such a mercy for us, as to incline the magistrates hearts so far to tender our consciences, as that we might be protected by them from wrong, injury, oppression and molestation, which long we formerly have groaned under by the tyranny and oppression of the Prelatical Hierarchy, which God through mercy has made this present King and Parliament wonderful honorable; as an instrument is His hand, to throw down; and we thereby have had some breathing time, we shall, we hope, look at it as a mercy beyond our expectation, and conceive ourselves further engaged for ever to bless God for it.

1 Tim. 1:2-4; Psal. 126:1; Acts 9:31

LI.

But if God with hold the magistrates allowance and furtherance herein;(1) yet we must not withstanding proceed together in Christian communion, not daring to give place to suspend our practice, but to walk in obedience to Christ in the profession and holding forth this faith before mentioned, even in the midst of all trails and afflictions, not accounting out goods, lands, wives, husbands, children, fathers, mothers, brethren, sisters, yea, and our own lives dear unto us, so we may finish our course with joy: remembering always we ought to(2) obey God rather then men, and grounding upon the commandment, commission, and promise of our Lord and Master Jesus Christ, who as He has power in heaven and earth, so also has promised, if we keep His commandments which He has given us, to be with us to the end of the world: and when we have finished our course, and kept the faith, to give us the crown of righteousness, which is laid up for all that love His appearing, and to whom we must give an account of all our actions, no man being able to discharge us of the same.

1) Acts 2:40,41; 4:19; 5:28,29,41; 20:23; 1 Thes. 3:3; Phil. 1:27-29; Dan. 3:16,17; 6:7, 10, 22, 23.

2) Matth. 28:18-20; 1 Tim. 6:13-15; Rom. 12:1.8; 1 Cor. 14:37; 2 Tim. 4:7,8; Rev. 2:10; Gal 2:4,5

LII.

And likewise unto all men is to be given whatsoever is their due; tributes, customs, and all such lawful duties, ought willingly to be by us paid and performed, our lands, goods, and bodies, to submit to the magistrate in the Lord, and the magistrate every way to be acknowledged, reverenced, and obeyed, according to godliness; not because of wrath only but for conscience sake. And finally, all men so to be esteemed and regarded, as is due and appropriate for their place, age, estate, and condition.

Rom. 13:5-7; Mat. 22:21; Titus 3; 1 Peter 3:13; 5:5; Eph. 5:21, 22; 6:1, 9

LII [sic].

And thus we desire to give God that which is God's, and unto Ceasor that which is Ceasor's, and unto all men that which belongs unto them, endeavoring ourselves to have always a clear conscience void of offense towards God, and towards man. And if they take this that we have said, to be heresy, then do we with the Apostle freely confess, that after the way which they call heresy, worship we the God of our Fathers, believing all things which are written in the Law and in the Prophets and Apostles, desiring from our souls to disclaim all heresies and opinions which are not after Christ, and to be steadfast, unmovable, always abounding in the work of the Lord, as knowing our labor shall not be in vain in the Lord.

Mat. 22:21; Acts 24:14-16; John 5:28; 2 Cor. 4:17; 1 Tim. 6:3-5; 1 Cor. 15:58, 59

Conclusion

Thus we desire to give unto Christ that which is His, and unto all lawful Authority that which is their due, and to owe nothing to any many but love, to live quietly and peaceably, at is becometh saints, endeavoring in all things to keep a good conscience, and to do unto every man (of what judgment soever) as we would they should do unto us, that as our practice is, so it may prove us to a conscionable, quiet, and harmless people, (no ways dangerous or troublesome to human Society) and to labor and work with our hands, that we may not be chargeable to any, but to give to him that needeth both friends and enemies, accounting it more excellent to give than to receive. Also we confess that we know but in part, and that we are ignorant of many things which we desire and seek to know: and if any do show us that friendly part to show us from the Word of God that we see not, we shall have cause to be thankful to God and them. But if any man shall impose upon us anything that we see not to be commanded by out Lord Jesus Christ, we should in His strength, rather embrace all reproaches and tortures of men, to be stript of all outward comforts, and if it were possible, to die a thousand deaths, rather than to do anything against the least tittle of the truth of God, or against the light of our own consciences. And if any shall call what we have said heresy, then do we with the Apostle acknowledge, that after the way they call heresy, worship we the God of our Fathers, disclaiming all heresy (rightly so called) because they are against Christ, and to be steadfast and immovable, always abounding in obedience to Christ, as knowing our labor shall not be in vain in the Lord.

1 Corinthians 1:24
Not that we have dominion over your faith, but
are helpers of your joy: for by faith we stand.

Psalm 74:21, 22
Arise, O God, plead mine own cause. Remember how the foolish man blasphemeth Thee daily. O let not the oppressed return ashamed, but let the poor and needy praise Thy name.
Come, Lord Jesus, come quickly.

Appendix Two

The New Hampshire Baptist Confession. A. D. 1833.

[This Confession was drawn up by the Rev. John Newton Brown, D.D., of New Hampshire (b.1803, d.1868), about 1833, and has been adopted by the New Hampshire Convention, and widely accepted by Baptists, especially in the Northern and Western States, as a clear and concise statement of their faith, in harmony with the doctrines of older confessions, but expressed in milder form. The text is taken from the Baptist Church Manual, published by the American Baptist Publication Society, Philadelphia.]

Declaration of Faith.

I. OF THE SCRIPTURES. We believe that the Holy Bible was written by men inspired, and is a perfect treasure of heavenly instruction; that it has God for its author, salvation for its end, and truth, without any mixture of error, for its matter; that it reveals the principles by which God will judge us; and therefore is, and shall remain to the end of the world, the true centre of Christian union, and the supreme standard by which all human conduct, creeds, and opinions should be tried.

II. OF THE TRUE GOD. We believe that there is one, and only one, living and true God, an infinite, intelligent Spirit, whose name is JEHOVA, thy Maker and Supreme Ruler of heaven and earth; inexpressibly glorious in holiness; [and] worthy of all possible honor, confidence, and love; revealed under the personal and relative distinction of the Father, the Son, and the Holy Spirit; equal in every divine perfection, and executing distinct but harmonious offices in the great work of redemption.

III. OF THE FALL OF MAN. We believe that man was created in a state of holiness, under the law of his Maker; but by voluntary transgression fell from that holy and happy state; in consequence of which all mankind are now sinners, not by constraint but choice; being by nature utterly void of that holiness required by the law of God, wholly given to the gratification of the world, of Satan, and of their own sinful passions, therefore under just condemnation to eternal ruin, without defense or excuse.

IV. OF THE WAY OF SALVATION. We believe that the salvation of sinners is wholly of grace; through the Mediatorial offices of the Son of God, who by the appointment of the Father, freely took upon him our nature, yet without sin; honored the divine law by his personal obedience, and made atonement for our sins by his death; being risen from the dead he is now enthroned in heaven; and uniting in his wonderful person the tenderest sympathies with divine perfections, he is every way qualified to be a suitable, a compassionate, and an all sufficient Saviour.

V. OF JUSTIFICATION. We believe that the great Gospel blessing which Christ of his fullness bestows on such as belief in Him, is Justification; that Justification; That Justification consists in the pardon of sin, and the promise of eternal life, on principles of righteousness; that it is bestowed not in any consideration of any works of righteousness which we have done, but solely through His own redemption and righteousness, by virtue of which faith his perfect righteousness is freely imputed to us of God; that it brings us into a state of most blessed peace and favor with God, and secures every other blessing needful for time and eternity.

VI. OF THE FREENESS OF SALVATION. We believe that the blessings of salvation are made free to all by the Gospel; that it is the immediate duty of all to accept them by a cordial, penitent, and obedient faith; and that nothing prevents the salvation of the greatest sinner on earth except his own inherent depravity and voluntary refusal to submit to the Lord Jesus Christ, whihc refusal will subject him to an aggravated condemnation.

VII. OF GRACE IN REGENERATION. We believe that in order to be saved, we must be regenerated or born again; that regeneration consists in giving a holy disposition to the mind; and is effected in a manner above our comprehension or calculation, by the power of the Holy Spirit, in connection with divine truth, so as to secure our voluntary obedience to the Gospel; and that its proper evidence is found in the holy fruit which we bring forth to the glory of God.

VIII. OF REPENTANCE AND FAITH. We believe that repentance and Faith are sacred duties, and also inseparable graces, wrought in our souls by the regenerating Spirit of God; whereby being deeply convinced of our guilt, danger, and helplessness, and of the way of salvation by Christ, we turn to God with unfeigned contrition, confession, and supplication for mercy; at the same time heartily receiving the Lord Jesus Christ as our Prophet, Priest, and King, and relying on him alone as the only and all sufficient Saviour.

IX. OF GOD'S PURPOSE OF GRACE. We believe that Election is the gracious purpose of God, according to which he graciously regenerates, sanctifies, and saves sinners; that being perfectly consistent with the free agency of man, it comprehends all the mean sin connection with the end; that it is a most glorious display of God's sovereign goodness, being infinitely free, wise, holy, and unchangeable; that it utterly excludes boasting, and promotes humility, love, prayer, praise, trust in God, and active imitation of his free mercy; that it encourages the use of means in the highest degree; that it may be ascertained by its effects in all who truly believe the gospel; that it is the foundation of Christian assurance; and that to ascertain it with regard to ourselves demands and deserves the utmost diligence.

X. OF SANCTIFICATION. We believe that Sanctification is the process by which, according to the will of God, we are made partakers of his holiness; that it is a progressive work; that it is begun in regeneration; and that it is carried on in the hearts of believers by the presence and power of the Holy Spirit, the Sealer and Comforter, in the continual use of the appointed means -- especially the Word of God, self-examination, self-denial, watchfulness, and prayer.

XI. OF THE PERSEVERANCE OF SAINTS. We believe that such only are real believers as endure unto the end; [2119] that their persevering attachment to Christ is the grand mark which distinguishes them from superficial professors; that a special Providence watches over their welfare; and they are kept by the power of God through faith unto salvation.

XII. OF THE HARMONY OF THE LAW AND THE GOSPEL. We believe that the Law of God is the eternal and unchangeable rule of his moral government; that it is holy, just, and good; and that the inability which the Scriptures ascribe to fallen men to fulfill its precepts arises entirely from their love of sin; to deliver them from winch, and to restore them through a Mediator to unfeigned obedience to the holy Law, is one great end of the Gospel, and of the means of grace connected with the establishment of the visible Church.

XIII. OF A GOSPEL CHURCH. We believe that a visible Church of Christ is a congregation of baptized believers, [2127] associated by covenant in the faith and fellowship of the gospel; [2128] observing the ordinances of Christ; [2129] governed by his laws, [2130] and exercising the gifts, rights, and privileges invested in them by his Word; [2131] that its only scriptural officers are Bishops, or Pastors, and Deacons, [2132] whose qualifications, claims, and duties are defined in the Epistles to Timothy and Titus.

XIV. OF BAPTISM AND THE LORD'S SUPPER. We believe that Christian Baptism is the immersion in water of a believer, into the name of the Father, and Son, and Holy Ghost; to show forth, in a solemn and beautiful emblem, our faith in the crucified, buried, and risen Saviour, with its effect in our death to sin and resurrection to a new life; that it is prerequisite to the privileges of a Church relation; and to the Lord's Supper, in which the members of the Church, by the sacred use of bread and wine, are to commemorate together the dying love of Christ; proceeded always by solemn self-examination.

XV. OF THE CHRISTIAN SABBATH. We believe that the first day of the week is the Lord's Day, or Christian Sabbath; and is to be kept sacred to religious purposes, by abstaining from all secular labor and sinful recreations; by the devout observance of all the means of grace, both private and public; and by preparation for that rest that remaineth for the people of God.

XVI. OF CIVIL GOVERNMENT. We believe that civil government is of divine appointment, for the interests and good order of human society; and that magistrates are to be prayed for, conscientiously honored and obeyed; except only in things opposed to the will of our Lord Jesus Christ, who is the only Lord of the conscience, and the Prince of the kings of the earth.

XVII. OF THE RIGHTEOUS AND THE WICKED. [We believe] that there is a radical and essential difference between the righteous and the wicked; that such only as through faith are justified in the name of the Lord Jesus, and sanctified by the Spirit of our God, are truly righteous in his esteem; while all such as continue in impenitence and unbelief are in his sight wicked, and under the curse; and this distinction holds among men both in and after death. We believe that the end of the world is approaching; that at the last day Christ will descend from heaven, and raise the dead from the grave to final retribution; that a solemn separation will then take place; that the wicked will be adjudged to endless punishment, and the righteous to endless joy; and that this judgment will fix forever the final state of men in heaven or hell, on principles of righteousness.

Appendix Three

1963 Baptist Faith and Message
of the Southern Baptist Convention
May 9, 1963

REPORT OF COMMITTEE ON BAPTIST FAITH AND MESSAGE

The 1962 session of the Southern Baptist Convention, meeting in San Francisco, California, adopted the following motion.

"Since the report of the Committee on Statement of Baptist Faith and Message was adopted in 1925, there have been various statements from time to time which have been made, but no overall statement which might be helpful at this time as suggested in Section 2 of that report, or introductory statement which might be used as an interpretation of the 1925 Statement.

"We recommend, therefore, that the president of this Convention be requested to call a meeting of the men now serving as presidents of the various state Conventions that would qualify as a member of the Southern Baptist Convention committee under Bylaw 18 to present to the Convention in Kansas City some similar statement which shall serve as information to the churches, and which may serve as guidelines to the various agencies of the Southern Baptist Convention. It is understood that any group or individuals may approach this committee to be of service. The expenses of this committee shall be borne by the Convention Operating Budget."

Your committee thus constituted begs leave to present its report as follows:

Throughout its work your committee has been conscious of the contribution made by the statement of "The Baptist Faith And Message" adopted by the Southern Baptist Convention in 1925. It quotes with approval its affirmation that "Christianity is supernatural in its origin and history. We repudiate every theory of religion which denies the supernatural elements in our faith."

Furthermore, it concurs in the introductory "statement of the historic Baptist conception of the nature and function of confessions of faith in our religious and denominational life." It is, therefore, quoted in full as part of this report to the Convention.

(1) That they constitute a consensus of opinion of some Baptist body, large or small, for the general instruction and guidance of our own people and others concerning those articles of the Christian faith which are most surely held among us. They are not intended to add anything to the simple conditions of salvation revealed in the New Testament, viz., repentance towards God and faith in Jesus Christ as Saviour and Lord.

(2) That we do not regard them as complete statements of our faith, having any quality of finality or infallibility. As in the past so in the future Baptists should hold themselves free to revise their statements of faith as may seem to them wise and expedient at any time.

(3) That any group of Baptists, large or small have the inherent right to draw up for themselves and publish to the world a confession of their faith whenever they may think it advisable to do so.

(4) That the sole authority for faith and practice among Baptists is the Scriptures of the Old and New Testaments. Confessions are only guides in interpretation, having no authority over the conscience.

(5) That they are statements of religious convictions, drawn from the Scriptures, and are not to be used to hamper freedom of thought or investigation in other realms of life."

The 1925 Statement recommended "the New Hampshire Confession of Faith, revised at certain points, and with some additional articles growing out of certain needs ..." Your present committee has adopted the same pattern. It has sought to build upon the structure of the 1925 Statement, keeping in mind the "certain needs" of our generation. At times it has reproduced sections of the Statement without change. In other instances it has substituted words for clarity or added sentences for emphasis. At certain points it has combined articles, with minor changes in wording, to endeavor to relate certain doctrines to each other. In still others e.g., "God" and "Salvation" it has sought to bring together certain truths contained throughout the 1925 Statement in order to relate them more clearly and concisely. In no case has it sought to delete from or to add to the basic contents of the 1925 Statement.

Baptists are a people who profess a living faith. This faith is rooted and grounded in Jesus Christ who is "the same yesterday, and to-day, and forever." Therefore, the sole authority for faith and practice among Baptists is Jesus Christ whose will is revealed in the Holy Scriptures.

A living faith must experience a growing understanding of truth and must be continually interpreted and related to the needs of each new generation. Throughout their history Baptist bodies, both large and small, have issued statements of faith which comprise a consensus of their beliefs. Such statements have never been regarded as complete, infallible statements of faith, nor as official creeds carrying mandatory authority. Thus this generation of Southern Baptists is in historic succession of intent and purpose as it endeavors to state for its time and theological climate those articles of the Christian faith which are most surely held among us.

Baptists emphasize the soul's competency before God, freedom in religion, and the priesthood of the believer. However, this emphasis should not be interpreted to mean that there is an absence of certain definite doctrines that Baptists believe, cherish, and with which they have been and are now closely identified.

It is the purpose of this statement of faith and message to set forth certain teachings which we believe.

Herschel H. Hobbs, Chairman Howard M. Reaves Ed. J. Packwood C.Z. Holland W.B. Timberlake C.V. Koons Malcolm B. Knight Dick H. Hail, Jr. Charles R. Walker Walter R. Davis Garth Pybas V.C. Kruschwitz Luther B. Hall Robert Woodward Douglas Hudgins Paul Weber, Jr. R.A. Long Nane Starnes C. Hoge Hockensmith Hugh R. Bumpas David G. Anderson E. Warren Rust James H. Landes R.P. Downey

I. THE SCRIPTURES

The Holy Bible was written by men divinely inspired and is the record of Gods revelation of Himself to man. It is a perfect treasure of divine instruction. It has God for its author, salvation for its end, and truth, without any mixture of error, for its matter. It reveals the principles by which God judges us; and therefore is, and will remain to the end of the world, the true center of Christian union, and the supreme standard by which all human conduct, creeds, and religious opinions should be tried. The criterion by which the Bible is to be interpreted is Jesus Christ.

> Ex 24:4; De 4:1-2; 17:19; Jos 8:34
> Psa 19:7-10; 119:11, 89, 105, 140
> Isa 34:16; 40:8; Jer 15:16; 36:1-32
> Mat 5:17-18; 22:29; Lu 21:33; 24:44-46
> Joh 5:39; 16:13-15; 17:17; Ac 2:16; 17:11
> Rom 15:4; 16:25-26; 2Ti 3:15-17
> Heb 1:1-2; 4:12; 1Pe 1:25; 2Pe 1:19-21

II. GOD

There is one and only one living and true God. He is an intelligent, spiritual, and personal Being, the Creator, Redeemer, Preserver, and Ruler of the universe. God is infinite in holiness and all other perfections. To Him we owe the highest love, reverence, and obedience.

The eternal God reveals Himself to us as Father, Son, and Holy Spirit, with distinct personal attributes, but without division of nature, essence, or being.

A. God the Father

God as Father reigns with providential care over His universe, His creatures, and the flow of the stream of human history according to the purposes of His grace. He is all powerful, all loving, and all wise. God is Father in truth to those who become children of God through faith in Jesus Christ. He is fatherly in His attitude toward all men.

> Gen 1:1; 2:7; Ex 3:14; 6:2-3; 15:11; 20:1

Lev 22:2; De 6:4; 32:6; 1Ch 29:10; Psa 19:1-3
Isa 43:3, 15; 64:8; Jer 10:10; 17:13
Mat 6:9; 7:11; 23:9; 28:19; Mark 1:9-11
John 4:24; 5:26; 14:6-13; 17:1-8; Acts 1:7
Rom 8:14-15; 1Co 8:6; Gal 4:6; Eph 4:6
Col 1:15; 1Ti 1:17; Heb 11:6; 12:9; 1Pe 1:17; 1Jo 5:7

B. God the Son

Christ is the eternal Son of God. In His incarnation as Jesus Christ he was conceived of the Holy Spirit and born of the virgin Mary. Jesus perfectly revealed and did the will of God, taking upon Himself the demands and necessities of human nature and identifying Himself completely with mankind yet without sin. He honored the divine law by His personal obedience, and in His death on the cross He made provision for the redemption of men from sin. He was raised from the dead with a glorified body and appeared to His disciples as the person who was with them before His crucifixion. He ascended into heaven and is now exalted at the right hand of God where He is the One Mediator, partaking of the nature of God and of man, and in whose Person is effected the reconciliation between God and man. He will return in power and glory to judge the world and to consummate His redemptive mission. He now dwells in all believers as the living and ever present Lord.

Gen 18:1; Psalm 2:7; 110:1; Isa 7:14; 53:1-12
Mat 1:18-23; 3:17; 8:29; 11:27; 14:33; 16:16, 27
Mat 17:5; 27; 28:1-6, 19; Mark 1:1; 3:11
Luke 1:35; 4:41; 22:70; 24:46
John 1:1-18, 29; 10:30, 38; 11:25-27; 12:44-50
John 14:7-11, 16:15-16, 28; 17:1-5, 21-22; 20:1-20, 28
Acts 1:9; 2:22-24; 7:55-56; 9:4-5, 20
Rom 1; 3-4; 3:23-26; 5:6-21; 8:1-3, 34; 10:4
1Co 1:30; 2:2; 8:6; 15:1-8, 24-28; 2Co 5:19-21
Gal 4:4-5; Eph 1:20; 3:11; 4:7-10; Php 2:5-11
Col 1:13-22; 2:9; 1Th 4:14-18; 1Ti 2:5-6; 3:16
Tit 2:13-14; Heb 1:1-3; 4:14-15; 7:14-28
Heb 9:12-15, 24-28; 12:2; 13:8; 1Pe 2:21-25; 3:22
1Jo 1:7-9; 3:2; 4:14- 15; 5:9; 2Jo 7-9
Rev 1:13-16; 5:9-14; 12:10-11; 13:8; 19:16

C. God the Holy Spirit

The Holy Spirit is the Spirit of God. He inspired holy men of old to write the Scriptures. Through illumination He enables men to understand truth. He exalts Christ. He convicts of sin, of righteousness and of judgment. He calls men to the Saviour, and effects regeneration. He cultivates Christian character, comforts believers, and bestows the spiritual gifts" by which they serve God through His church. He seals the believer unto the day of final redemption. His presence in the Christian is the assurance of God to bring the believer into the fulness of the stature of Christ. He enlightens and empowers the believer and the church in worship, evangelism, and service.

Gen 1:2; Jud 14:6; Job 26:13; Psa 51:11; 139:7
Isa 61:1-3; Joel 2:28-32
Mat 1:18; 3:16; 4:1; 12:28-32; 28:19; Mk 1:10, 12
Luke 1:35; 4:1, 18-19; 11:13; 12:12; 24:49
John 4:24; 14:16-17, 26; 15:26; 16:7-14
Acts 1:8; 2:1-4, 38; 4:31; 5:3; 6:3; 7:55; 8:17, 39 Acts 10:44; 13:2; 15:28; 16:6; 19:1-6
Rom 8:9-11, 14-16, 26-27; 1Co 2:10-14; 3:16; 12:3-11
Gal 4:6; Eph 1:13-14; 4:30; 5:18; 1Th 5:19

1Ti 3:16; 4:1; 2Ti 1:14; 3:16; Heb 9:8, 14
2Pe 1:21; 1Jo 4:13; 5:6-7; Rev 1:10; 22:17

III. MAN

Man was created by the special act of God, in His own image, and is the crowning work of His creation. In the beginning man was innocent of sin and was endowed by his Creator with freedom of choice. By his free choice man sinned against God and brought sin into the human race. Through the temptation of Satan man transgressed the command of God, and fell from his original innocence; whereby his posterity inherit a nature and an environment inclined toward sin, and as soon as they are capable of moral action become transgressors and are under condemnation. Only the grace of God can bring man into His holy fellowship and enable man to fulfill the creative purpose of God. The sacredness of human personality is evident in that God created man in His own image, and in that Christ died for man; therefore, every man possesses dignity and is worthy of respect and Christian love.

Gen 1:26-30; 2:5, 7, 18-22; 3; 9:6
Psa 1:1-6; 8:3-6; 32:1-5; 51:5; Isa 6:5; Jer 17:5
Matt 16:26; Acts 17:26-31
Rom 1:19-32; 3:10-18, 23; 5:6, 12, 19; 6:6
Rom 7:14-25; 8:14-18, 29; 1Co 1:21-31; 15:19, 21-22
Eph 2:1-22; Col 1:21-22; 3:9-11

IV. SALVATION

Salvation involves the redemption of the whole man, and is offered freely to all who accept Jesus Christ as Lord and Saviour, who by His own blood obtained eternal redemption for the believer. In its broadest sense salvation includes regeneration, sanctification, and glorification.

A. Regeneration, or the new birth, is a work of God's grace whereby believers become new creatures in Christ Jesus. It is a change of heart wrought by the Holy Spirit through conviction of sin, to which the sinner responds in repentance toward God and faith in the Lord Jesus Christ. Repentance and faith are inseparable experiences of grace. Repentance is a genuine turning from sin toward God. Faith is the acceptance of Jesus Christ and commitment of the entire personality to Him as Lord and Saviour. Justification is Gods gracious and full acquittal upon principles of His righteousness of all sinners who repent and believe in Christ. Justification brings the believer into a relationship of peace and favor with God.

B. Sanctification is the experience, beginning in regeneration, by which the believer is set apart to Gods purposes, and is enabled to progress toward moral and spiritual perfection through the presence and power of the Holy Spirit dwelling in him. Growth in grace should continue throughout the regenerate person's life.

C. Glorification is the culmination of salvation and is the final blessed and abiding state of the redeemed.

Gen 3:15; Ex 3:14-17; 6:2-8
Mat 1:21; 4:17; 16:21-26; 27:22-28:6
Luke 1:68-69; 2:28-32
John 1:11-14, 29; 3:3-21, 36; 5:24; 10:9, 28-29
John 15:1-16; 17:17; Acts 2:21; 4:12; 15:11; 16:30-31
Acts 17:30-31; 20:32; Rom 1:16-18; 2:4; 3:23-25; 4:3
Rom 5:8-10; 6:1-23; 8:1-18; 29-39; 10:9-10, 13
Rom 13:11-14; 1Cor 1:18, 30; 6:19-20; 15:10
2Co 5:17-20; Gal 2:20; 3:13; 5:22-25; 6:15
Eph 1:7; 2:8-22; 4:11-16; Php 2:12-13; Col 1:9-22; 3:1
1Th 5:23-24; 2Tim 1:12; Titus 2:11-14

Heb 2:1-3; 5:8-9; 9:24-28; 11:1-12:8, 14
James 2:14-26; 1Pe 1:2-23; 1Jo 1:6-2:11
Rev 3:20; 21:1-22:5

V. GOD'S PURPOSE OF GRACE

Election is the gracious purpose of God, according to which He regenerates, sanctifies, and glorifies sinners. It is consistent with the free agency of man, and comprehends all the means in connection with the end. It is a glorious display of Gods sovereign goodness, and is infinitely wise, holy, and unchangeable. It excludes boasting and promotes humility.

All true believers endure to the end. Those whom God has accepted in Christ, and sanctified by His Spirit, will never fall away from the state of grace, but shall persevere to the end. Believers may fall into sin through neglect and temptation, whereby they grieve the Spirit, impair their graces and comforts, bring reproach on the cause of Christ, and temporal judgments on themselves, yet they shall be kept by the power of God through faith unto salvation.

Gen 12:1-3; Ex 19:5-8; 1Sa 8:4-7, 19-22
Isa 5:1-7; Jer 31:31
Mat 16:18-19; 21:28-45; 24:22, 31; 25:34
Luke 1:68-79; 2:29-32; 19:41-44; 24:44-48
John 1:12-14; 3:16; 5:24; 6:44-45, 65; 10:27-29
John 15:16; 17:6, 12, 17-18; Acts 20:32
Rom 5:9-10; 8:28-39; 10:12-15; 11:5-7, 26-36
1Co 1:1-2; 15:24-28; Eph 1:4-23; 2:1-10; 3:1-11
Col 1:12-14; 2Th 2:13-14; 2Ti 1:12; 2:10, 19
Heb 11:39-12:2; 1Pe 1:2-5, 13; 2:4-10
1Jo 1:7-9; 2:19; 3:2

VI. THE CHURCH

A New Testament church of the Lord Jesus Christ is a local body of baptized believers who are associated by covenant in the faith and fellowship of the gospel, observing the two ordinances of Christ, committed to His teachings, exercising the gifts, rights, and privileges invested in them by His Word, and seeking to extend the gospel to the ends of the earth.

This church is an autonomous body, operating through democratic processes under the Lordship of Jesus Christ. In such a congregation members are equally responsible. Its Scriptural officers are pastors and deacons.

The New Testament speaks also of the church as the body of Christ which includes all of the redeemed of all the ages.

Mat 16:15-19; 18:15-20
Acts 2:41-42, 47; 5:11-14; 6:3-6; 13:1-3; 14:23, 27
Acts 15:1-30; 16:5; 20:28; Rom 1:7
1Co 1:2; 3:16; 5:4-5; 7:17; 9:13-14; 12
Eph 1:22-23; 2:19-22; 3:8-11, 21; 5:22-32
Php 1:1; Col 1:18; 1Ti 3:1-15; 4:14

VII. BAPTISM AND THE LORD'S SUPPER

Christian baptism is the immersion of a believer in water in the name of the Father, the Son, and the Holy Spirit. It is an act of obedience symbolizing the believers faith in a crucified, buried, and risen Saviour, the believers death to sin, the burial of the old life, and the resurrection to walk in newness of life in Christ Jesus. It is a testimony to his faith in the final resurrection of the dead. Being a church ordinance, it is prerequisite to the privileges of church membership and to the Lords Supper.

The Lord's Supper is a symbolic act of obedience whereby members of the church, through partaking of the bread and the fruit of the vine, memorialize the death of the Redeemer and anticipate His second coming.

> Mat 3:13-17; 26:26-30; 28:19-20; Mk 1:9-11; 14:22-26
> Luke 3:21-22; 22:19-20; John 3:23
> Acts 2:41-42; 8:35-39; 16:30-33; 20:7
> Rom 6:3-5; 1Co 10:16, 21; 11:23-29; Col 2:12

VIII. THE LORD'S DAY

The first day of the week is the Lords Day. It is a Christian institution for regular observance. It commemorates the resurrection of Christ from the dead and should be employed in exercises of worship and spiritual devotion, both public and private, and by refraining from worldly amusements, and resting from secular employments, work of necessity and mercy only being excepted.

> Ex 20:8-11; Mat 12:1-12; 28:1; Mk 2:27-28; 16:1-7
> Luke 24:1-3, 33-36; John 4:21-24; 20:1, 19-28
> Acts 20:7; 1Co 16:1-2; Col 2:16; 3:16; Rev 1:10

IX. THE KINGDOM

The Kingdom of God includes both His general sovereignty over the universe and His particular kingship over men who willfully acknowledge Him as King. Particularly the Kingdom is the realm of salvation into which men enter by trustful, childlike commitment to Jesus Christ. Christians ought to pray and to labor that the Kingdom may come and Gods will be done on earth. The full consummation of the Kingdom awaits the return of Jesus Christ and the end of this age.

> Gen 1:1; Isa 9:6-7; Jer 23:5-6
> Mat 3:2; 4:8-10, 23; 12:25-28; 13:1-52; 25:31-46; 26:29
> Mk 1:14-15; 9:1; Luke 4:43; 8:1; 9:2; 12:31-32
> Luke 17:20-21; 23:42; John 3:3; 18:36
> Acts 1:6-7; 17:22-31; Rom 5:17; 8:19
> 1Co 15:24-28; Col 1:13; Heb 11:10, 16; 12:28
> 1Pe 2:4-10; 4:13; Rev 1:6, 9; 5:10; 11:15; 21-22

X. LAST THINGS

God, in His own time and in His own way, will bring the world to its appropriate end. According to His promise, Jesus Christ will return personally and visibly in glory to the earth; the dead will be raised; and Christ will judge all men in righteousness. The unrighteous will be consigned to Hell, the place of everlasting punishment. The righteous in their resurrected and glorified bodies will receive their reward and will dwell forever in Heaven with the Lord.

> Isa 2:4; 11:9; Mat 16:27; 18:8-9
> Mat 19:28; 24:27, 30, 36, 44; 25:31-46; 26:64
> Mark 8:38; 9:43-48; Luke 12:40, 48; 16:19-26
> Luke 17:22-37; 21:27-28; John 14:1-3
> Acts 1:11; 17:31; Rom 14:10; 1Co 4:5
> 1Co 15:24-28, 35-58; 2Co 5:10; Php 3:20-21
> Col 1:5; 3:4; 1Th 4:14-18; 5:1; 2Th 1:7; 2:1-17
> 1Ti 6:14; 2Ti 4:1, 8; Tit 2:13; Heb 9:27-28
> James 5:8; 2Pe 3:7; 1Jo 2:28; 3:2
> Jude 14; Rev 1:18; 3:11; 20:1-22:13

XI. EVANGELISM AND MISSIONS

It is the duty and privilege of every follower of Christ and of every church of the Lord Jesus Christ to endeavor to make disciples of all nations. The new birth of mans spirit by Gods Holy Spirit means the birth of love for others. Missionary effort on the part of all rests thus upon a spiritual necessity of the regenerate life, and is expressly and repeatedly commanded in the teachings of Christ. It is the duty of every child of God to seek constantly to win the lost to Christ by personal effort and by all other methods in harmony with the gospel of Christ.

Gen 12:1-3; Ex 19:5-6; Isa 6:1-8
Mat 9:37-38; 10:5-15; 13:18-30, 37-43; 16:19
Mat 22:9-10; 24:14; 28:18-20; Luke 10:1-18; 24:46-53
John 14:11-12; 15:7-8, 16; 17:15; 20:21
Acts 1:8; 2; 8:26-40; 10:42-48; 13:2-3
Rom 10:13-15; Eph 3:1-11; 1Th 1:8; 2Ti 4:5
Heb 2:1-3; 11:39-12:2; 1Pe 2:4-10; Rev 22:17

XII. EDUCATION

The cause of education in the Kingdom of Christ is co-ordinate with the causes of missions and general benevolence, and should receive along with these the liberal support of the churches. An adequate system of Christian schools is necessary to a complete spiritual program for Christs people.

In Christian education there should be a proper balance between academic freedom and academic responsibility. Freedom in any orderly relationship of human life is always limited and never absolute. The freedom of a teacher in a Christian school, college, or seminary is limited by the pre-eminence of Jesus Christ, by the authoritative nature of the Scriptures, and by the distinct purpose for which the school exists.

De 4:1,5,9,14; 6:1-10; 31:12-13; Neh 8:1-8; Job 28:28
Psa 19:7; 119:11; Pro 3:13; 4:1-10; 8:1-7, 11; 15:14
Ecc 7:19; Mat 5:2; 7:24; 28:19-20; Luke 2:40
1Co 1:18-31; Eph 4:11-16; Php 4:8; Col 2:3, 8-9
1Ti 1:3-7; 2Ti 2:15; 3:14-17; Heb 5:12-6:3
James 1:5; 3:17

XIII. STEWARDSHIP

God is the source of all blessings, temporal and spiritual; all that we have and are we owe to Him. Christians have a spiritual debtor to the whole world, a holy trusteeship in the gospel, and a binding stewardship in their possessions. They are therefore under obligation to serve Him with their time, talents, and material possessions; and should recognize all these as entrusted to them to use for the glory of God and for helping others. According to the Scriptures, Christians should contribute of their means cheerfully, regularly, systematically, proportionately, and liberally for the advancement of the Redeemers cause on earth.

Gen 14:20; Lev 27:30-32; De 8:18; Mal 3:8-12
Mat 6:1-4, 19-21; 19:21; 23:23; 25:14-29
Luke 12:16-21, 42; 16:1-13; Acts 2:44-47
Acts 5:1-11; 17:24-25; 20:35; Ro 6:6-22; 12:1-2
1Co 4:1-2; 6:19-20; 12; 16:1-4; 2Co 8-9; 12:15
Php 4:10-19; 1Pe 1:18-19

XIV. COOPERATION

Christs people should, as occasion requires, organize such associations and conventions as may best secure cooperation for the great objects of the Kingdom of God. Such organizations have no authority over one another or over the churches. They are voluntary and advisory bodies designed to elicit, combine; and direct the energies of our people in the most effective manner. Members of New Testament churches should cooperate with one another in carrying forward the missionary, educational, and benevolent ministries for the extension of Christs Kingdom. Christian unity in the New Testament sense is spiritual harmony and voluntary cooperation for common ends by various groups of Christs people. Cooperation is desirable between the various Christian denominations, when the end to be attained is itself justified, and when such cooperation involves no violation of conscience or compromise of loyalty to Christ and His Word as revealed in the New Testament.

> Ex 17:12; 18:17; Jud 7:21; Ezr 1:3-4; 2:68-69; 5:14-15
> Ne 4; 8:1-5; Mat 10:5-15; 20:1-16; 22:1-10; 28:19-20
> Mk 2:3; Luke 10:1; Acts 1:13-14; 2:1; 4:31-37; 13:2-3
> Acts 15:1-35; 1Co 1:10-17; 3:5-15; 12; 2Co 8:1-9:15
> Gal 1:6-10; Eph 4:1-16; Php 1:15-18

XV. THE CHRISTIAN AND THE SOCIAL ORDER

Every Christian is under obligation to seek to make the will of Christ supreme in his own life and in human society. Means and methods used for the improvement of society and the establishment of righteousness among men can be truly and permanently helpful only when they are rooted in the regeneration of the individual by the saving grace of God in Christ Jesus. The Christian should oppose in the spirit of Christ every form of greed, selfishness, and vice. He should work to provide for the orphaned, the needy, the aged, the helpless, and the sick. Every Christian should seek to bring industry, government, and society as a whole under the sway of the principles of righteousness, truth, and brotherly love. In order to promote these ends Christians should be ready to work with all men of good will in any good cause, always being careful to act in the spirit of love without compromising their loyalty to Christ and His truth.

> Ex 20:3-17; Lev 6:2-5; De 10:12; 27:17
> Psalm 101:5; Mic 6:8; Zech 8:16
> Mat 5:13-16, 43-48; 22:36-40; 25:35
> Mk 1:29-34, 2:3; 10:21; Luke 4:18-21; 10:27-37; 20:25
> John 15:12; 17:15; Rom 12-14; 1Co 5:9-10; 6:1-7
> 1Co 7:20-24; 10:23-11:1; Gal 3:26-28; Eph 6:5-9
> Col 3:12-17; 1Th 3:12; Phm 1:1-25; Jas 1:27; 2:8

XVI. PEACE AND WAR

It is the duty of Christians to seek peace with all men on principles of righteousness. In accordance with the spirit and teachings of Christ they should do all in their power to put an end to war.

The true remedy for the war spirit is the gospel of our Lord. The supreme need of the world is the acceptance of His teachings in all the affairs of men and nations, and the practical application of His law of love.

> Isa 2:4; Mat 5:9, 38-48; 6:33; 26:52; Luke 22:36,38
> Rom 12:18-19; 13:1-7; 14:19; Heb 12:14; Jas 4:1-2

XVII. RELIGIOUS LIBERTY

God alone is Lord of the conscience, and He has left it free from the doctrines and commandments of men which are contrary to His Word or not contained in it. Church and state should be separate. The state owes to every church protection and full freedom in the pursuit of its spiritual ends. In providing for such freedom no ecclesiastical group or denomination should be favored by the state more than others. Civil government being ordained of God; it is the duty of Christians to render loyal obedience thereto in all things not contrary to the revealed will of God. The church should not resort to the civil power to carry on its work. The gospel of Christ contemplates spiritual means alone for the pursuit of its ends. The state has no right to impose penalties for religious opinions of any kind. The state has no right to impose taxes for the support of any form of religion. A free church in a free state is the Christian ideal, and this implies the right of free and unhindered access to God on the part of all men, and the right to form and propagate opinions in the sphere of religion without interference by the civil power.

Gen 1:27; 2:7; Mat 6:6-7, 24; 16:26; 22:21
John 8:36; Acts 4:19-20; Rom 6:1-2; 13:1-7
Gal 5:1, 13; Php 3:20; 1Ti 2:1-2; Jas 4:12
1Pe 2:12-17; 3:11-17; 4:12-19

XVIII. THE FAMILY (Added in 1998)

God has ordained the family as the foundational institution of human society. It is composed of persons related to one another by marriage, blood or adoption.

Marriage is the uniting of one man and one woman in covenant commitment for a lifetime. It is Gods unique gift to reveal the union between Christ and His church, and to provide for the man and the woman in marriage the framework for intimate companionship, the channel for sexual expression according to biblical standards, and the means for procreation of the human race.

The husband and wife are of equal worth before God, since both are created in Gods image. The marriage relationship models the way God relates to His people. A husband is to love his wife as Christ loved the church. He has the God-given responsibility to provide for, to protect, and to lead his family. A wife is to submit herself graciously to the servant leadership of her husband even as the church willingly submits to the headship of Christ. She, being in the image of God as is her husband and thus equal to him, has the God-given responsibility to respect her husband and to serve as his helper in managing the household and nurturing the next generation.

Children, from the moment of conception, are a blessing and heritage from the Lord. Parents are to demonstrate to their children Gods pattern for marriage. Parents are to teach their children spiritual and moral values and to lead them, through consistent lifestyle example and loving discipline, to make choices based on biblical truth. Children are to honor and obey their parents.

Ge 1:26-28; 2:18-25; 3:1-20; Ex 20:12; De 6:4-9; Jos 24:15
1Sa 1:26-28; Ps 78:1-8; 127:1-4; 128:1-6; 139:13-16
Pro 1:8; 5:15-20; 6:20-22; 12:4; 13:24
Pro 14:1; 17:6; 18:22; 22:6,15
Pro 23:13-14; 24:3; 29:15,17; 31:10-31
Ec 4:9-12; 9:9; Mal 2:14-16
Mt 5:31-32; 18:2-5; 19:3-9
Mr 10:6-12; Ro 1:18-32; 1Co 7:1-16
Eph 5:21-33; 6:1-4; Col 3:18-21; 1Ti 5:14; 2Ti 1:3-5
Tit 2:3-5; Heb 13:4; 1Pe 3:1-7

Appendix Four

CHARTER OF THE SOUTHERN BAPTIST CONVENTION

An ACT to incorporate the Southern Baptist Convention.

Be it enacted by the Senate and House of Representatives of the State of Georgia, in General Assembly met, and it is hereby enacted by the authority of the same. That from and after the passing of this act, That William B. Johnson, Wilson Lumpkin, James B. Taylor, A. Docrey, R. B. C. Howell and others, their associates and successors, be and they are hereby incorporated and made a body politic by the name and style of the Southern Baptist Convention, with authority to receive, hold, possess, retain, and dispose of property, either real or personal, to sue and be sued, and to make all bylaws, rules, and regulations necessary to the transaction of their business, not inconsistent with the laws of this State or of the United States – said corporation being created for the purpose of eliciting, combining, and directing the energies of the Baptist denomination of Christians, for the propagation of the gospel, any law, usage, or custom to the contrary not withstanding.

[Signed:]

Charles J. Jenkins
Speaker of The House of Representatives

Absalom H. Chappell
President of the Senate

Approved, December 27th, 1845
Geo. W. Crawford
Governor

Appendix Five

CONSTITUTION of the SOUTHERN BAPTIST CONVENTION

The messengers from missionary societies, churches, and other religious bodies of the Baptist denomination in various parts of the United States met in Augusta, Georgia, May 8, 1845, for the purpose of carrying into effect the benevolent intention of our constituents by organizing a plan for eliciting, combining, and directing the energies of the denomination for the propagation of the gospel and adopted rules and fundamental principles which, as amended from time to time, are as follows:

Article I. The Name: The name of this body is the "Southern Baptist Convention."

Article II. Purpose: It is the purpose of the Convention to provide a general organization for Baptists in the United States and its territories for the promotion of Christian missions at home and abroad and any other objects such as Christian education, benevolent enterprises, and social services which it may deem proper and advisable for the furtherance of the Kingdom of God.

Article III. Composition: The Convention shall consist of messengers who are members of Baptist churches in cooperation with the Convention. The following subparagraphs describe the Convention's current standards and method of determining the maximum number of messengers the Convention will recognize from each cooperating church to attend the Convention's annual meeting.

1. The Convention will only deem a church to be in friendly cooperation with the Convention, and sympathetic with its purposes and work (i.e., a "cooperating" church as that term is used in the Convention's governing documents) which:

    (1) Has a faith and practice which closely identifies with the Convention's adopted statement of faith. (By way of example, churches which act to affirm, approve, or endorse homosexual behavior would be deemed not to be in cooperation with the Convention.)

    (2) Has formally approved its intention to cooperate with the Southern Baptist Convention. (By way of example, the regular filing of the annual report requested by the Convention would be one indication of such cooperation.)

    (3) Has made undesignated, financial contribution(s) through the Cooperative Program, and/or through the Convention's Executive Committee for Convention causes, and/or to any Convention entity during the fiscal year preceding.

2. Under the terms above, the Convention will recognize to participate in its annual meeting two (2) messengers from each cooperating church, and such additional messengers as are permitted below.

3. The Convention will recognize additional messengers from a cooperating church under one of the options described below. Whichever method allows the church the greater number of messengers shall apply:

    (1) One additional messenger for each full percent of the church's undesignated receipts which the church contributed during the fiscal year preceding through the Cooperative Program, and/or through the Convention's Executive Committee for Convention causes, and/or to any Convention entity; or

    (2) One additional messenger for each $6,000 which the church contributed during the fiscal year preceding through the Cooperative Program, and/or through the Convention's Executive Committee for Convention causes, and/or to any Convention entity.

4. The messengers shall be appointed and certified by their church to the Convention, but the Convention will not recognize more than twelve (12) from any cooperating church.

5. Each messenger shall be a member of the church by which he or she is appointed.

6. If a church experiences a natural disaster or calamitous event and, as a result, the church is not qualified to appoint as many messengers as the church could appoint for the Convention's annual meeting immediately before the event, the church's pastor or an authorized church representative may, for no more than the three (3) annual meetings after the event, certify the facts to the registration secretary and obtain the same number of messengers it could have certified for the Convention's annual meeting immediately before the event.

Article IV. Authority: While independent and sovereign in its own sphere, the Convention does not claim and will never attempt to exercise any authority over any other Baptist body, whether church, auxiliary organizations, associations, or convention.

Article V. Officers:

1. The officers of the Convention shall be a president, a first and a second vice president, a recording secretary, a registration secretary, and a treasurer.

2. The officers shall be elected annually and shall hold office until their successors are elected and qualified. The term of office for the president is limited to two (2) years, and a president shall not be eligible for re-election until as much as one (1) year has elapsed from the time a successor is named. The first vice president shall be voted upon and elected after the election of the president has taken place; and the second vice president shall be voted upon and elected after the election of the first vice president has taken place.

3. The president shall be a member of the several boards and of the Executive Committee.

4. The treasurer of the Executive Committee shall be the treasurer of the Convention.

5. In case of death or disability of the president, the vice presidents shall automatically succeed to the office of president in the order of their election.

Article VI. The Boards, Institutions, and Commissions – Their Constitution and Powers:

1. The general boards of the Convention shall be composed as follows, unless otherwise provided in their charters.

    (1) Twelve (12) members chosen from the city or vicinity of the state in which the board is located, but not more than three (3) local members elected from the same church.

    (2) One (1) member chosen from each cooperating state; and one (1) additional member from each state having two hundred and fifty thousand (250,000) members, and another additional member for each additional two hundred and fifty thousand (250,000) members in such state.

    (3) The members shall be divided into four (4) groups as nearly equal as possible, and one (1) group shall be elected each year to serve four (4) years. Board members having served two (2) full terms of four (4) years shall not be eligible for re-election until as much as two (2) years have elapsed. This shall also apply to the Executive Committee.

2. The trustees of institutions and directors shall be composed as follows:

    (1) The trustees or directors shall be elected in keeping with the requirements of the charter of the entity as printed in the 1948 Book of Reports or subsequently amended with the prior approval of the Convention.

(2) If the composition of the trustees or directors is not determined by charter requirements, the body of trustees or directors shall be composed of one (1) member chosen from each cooperating state and eight (8) local members from the city or vicinity in which the entity is located, but not more than two (2) local members shall be chosen from the same church.

(3) Unless it is contrary to the charter requirements of the entity, the trustees or directors shall be divided into four (4) groups as nearly equal as possible and one (1) group shall be elected each year to serve four (4) years. Members having served two (2) full terms of four

(4) years shall not be eligible for re-election until as much as two (2) years have elapsed after one has served two (2) full terms. (4) Regardless of charter provisions, no trustee or director shall be eligible for re-election until as much as two (2) years have elapsed after the trustee or director has served two (2) full terms.

3. Terms of Service: No trustee of a board, institution, or commission, or a member of the Executive Committee shall be eligible to serve for more than two consecutive terms. A trustee or member of the Executive Committee who has served more than half a term shall be considered to have served a full term.

4. The governing groups of the entities may elect executive, administrative, finance, investment, and other committees if desired.

5. Each entity shall elect a president, a recording secretary, a treasurer, and such other officers as may be required. The president may be named as treasurer.

6. The compensation of its officers and employees shall be fixed by each entity, but no salaried employee or officer shall be a member of the directors of the entity.

7. Each entity is authorized to adopt its own bylaws.

8. Fifty percent of the members of the governing group shall constitute a quorum of the entity directors for transaction of any business

Article VII. Duties of Officers of Boards, Institutions, and Commissions: All officers shall be subject to the control and direction of their directors in matters pertaining to the work and obligations of the board, institution, or commission. They shall perform such duties as commonly appertain to such officers.

1. The executive head of each board, institution, and commission shall be responsible to the directors for all the work of the entity and shall carry on the work as the directors may direct.

2. The recording secretary of each entity shall keep a record of all meetings of directors, if not otherwise provided for, and shall keep the records in fireproof safes, vaults, or files.

3. The treasurer of each entity shall follow approved methods of accounting, keep the books, receipt for all monies and securities, deposit all funds with a depository or depositories approved by the directors, and render full statements as required to the directors or to the Convention. The treasurer shall not pay out money except as the directors may order and direct.

Article VIII. Church Membership: Officers of the Convention, all officers and members of all boards, trustees of institutions, directors, all committee members, and all missionaries of the Convention appointed by its boards shall be members of Baptist churches cooperating with this Convention.

Article IX. Missionaries' Qualifications: All missionaries appointed by the Convention's boards must, previous to their appointment, furnish evidence of piety, zeal for the Master's kingdom, conviction of truth as held by Baptists, and talents for missionary service.

Article X. Distribution of Funds: The Convention shall have the right to designate only undesignated funds, the right of contributors to the work of the Convention to designate the objects to which their contributions shall be applied being fully recognized.

Article XI. Meetings:

1. The Convention shall hold its meetings annually at such time and place as it may choose.

2. The president may call special meetings with the concurrence of the other officers of the Convention and of the Executive Committee.

3. The Executive Committee may change the time and place of meeting if the entertaining city withdraws its invitation or is unable to fulfill its commitments.

4. The Convention officers, the Executive Committee, and the executive heads of the Convention's boards and institutions acting in a body may, in case of grave emergency, cancel a regular meeting or change the place of meeting.

Article XII. As to Conflict with State Laws: All incorporated entities of the Convention shall be required to comply with the letter and spirit of this Constitution, the Bylaws, and the Business and Financial Plan insofar as they are not in conflict with the statute law of the state in which an entity is incorporated, and nothing herein contained shall be construed to require any such incorporated entity to act and carry on its affairs in conflict with the law of the state of its incorporation. In case any action of any entity of the Convention is found to be a violation of the law of the state of its incorporation, said action shall be reported by that entity to the Convention for appropriate action.

Article XIII. Definition of a State: The District of Columbia shall be regarded as a state for the purpose of this Constitution, the Bylaws, and all actions of the Convention.

Article XIV. Amendments: Any alterations may be made in these Articles at any annual meeting of the Convention by a vote of two-thirds of the messengers present and voting at the time the vote is taken, provided that an amendment shall be so approved by two (2) consecutive annual meetings of the Convention.

CPSIA information can be obtained
at www.ICGtesting.com
Printed in the USA
FSOW04n1519260917
39062FS